# INTERPRETATION IN TEACHING

*Other books by I. A. Richards*

PRACTICAL CRITICISM

THE PRINCIPLES OF LITERARY CRITICISM

MENCIUS ON THE MIND

THE PHILOSOPHY OF RHETORIC

BASIC ENGLISH AND ITS USES

HOW TO READ A PAGE

COLERIDGE ON IMAGINATION

BASIC IN TEACHING: EAST & WEST

THE REPUBLIC OF PLATO: A VERSION

IN SIMPLIFIED ENGLISH

INTERNAL COLLOQUIES

POETRIES AND SCIENCES

TOMORROW MORNING, FAUSTUS!
*with C. K. Ogden and James Wood*

THE FOUNDATIONS OF AESTHETICS
*with C. K. Ogden*

THE MEANING OF MEANING

# INTERPRETATION IN TEACHING

BY *I. A. Richards,* C. H.

FELLOW OF MAGDALENE COLLEGE,
CAMBRIDGE

NEW YORK
HUMANITIES PRESS

*First published in* 1938
*Second edition* 1973
*Published in the United States of America*
*by Humanities Press, Inc.*
*450 Park Avenue South*
*New York, N.Y.* 10016
*Copyright I. A. Richards* 1938, 1973

ISBN 0 391 00282 1

*Printed in Great Britain*

# Preface

These pages came into being under the kindly stimulus of the General Education Board, as a Statement on the Application of Theory of Interpretation to General Education; my thanks are due to the Board for permission to publish them. They were written for teachers and concern the layman only in the degree to which he recognizes that in the matter of the conduct of our native language we are all our own pupils.

The argument from time to time looks forward to the general achievement—in a perhaps not very distant future—of levels of intelligence in interpretation higher than those yet reached. Failure to attain such levels here does not put that prospect in doubt. It may be called a dream of impossibilities—more hopelessly beyond human powers than even our present verbal and mathematical skills must have seemed to the earliest users of language had *they* speculated about the future; but it is always absurd to set limits to intelligence.

Those who sigh or fret at such optimism will find plenty in this book to confirm them in a low estimate of our current linguistic ability. Part of its bulk comes from the documentation I have included. Every candid teacher knows already the main fact that it illustrates: the majority of his pupils at the end of all their schooling understand remarkably little of what they hear or read. But to reflect profitably on the modes and the causes of these failures we need detailed examples rather than principles.

The most general principles and upshot I have summarized in the Introduction and the various Landing Stages which punctuate the course of the argument. These might be glanced through first to give a perspective which may be lost in the detailed treatment. The analytic contents may also assist and I have gathered into an Appendix some further examples of the class-room exercises through which the aims and attitudes recommended would have to be translated into teaching procedure.

The weighty and all but overwhelming objection which every reader will feel is that many of the topics suggested are 'right over the heads,' far beyond the reach, of any probable students. When Mr A. D. Sheffield was addressing an audience of working men, a voice exclaimed, 'Say, Prof! Your sentences skid off our domes!' I am aware enough, I believe, of this objection. It is the prime difficulty of the whole undertaking that the thoughts we most need are those that are hardest to elicit. But this does not invalidate the choice of topics. A certain kind of thought about language, if instigated early, is our surest remedy for the cruel waste of effort (for teacher and pupil alike) our present courses entail. But only certain kinds of thought about language are fruitful, and I have tried to separate them from other kinds which have been, and still are, a hindrance to everyone rather than a help.

Once the desired modes of reflection upon language are distinguished, the best methods of inducing them will be developed less by conjecture than through class-room experience. The initial difficulty is to make a theory of interpretation sufficiently explicit for experience of its applications to begin to accumulate. Trial sieves out what is practicable from the rest—which passes into the teacher's theoretical reserve. But without a well-developed theoretical reserve, some of the most important points are likely to be mishandled—as, I think, my selection of *experimental material* (pp. 26, 27 and 79) shows. With an improvement in the theoretical reserve, much in it that at first seems to be impracticable as teaching theme may go over adapted into the lesson. My main argument indeed is that it is the pupil's theoretical weakness which halts him. He must amend it by exercise under guidance. We cannot give him better ideas, he must grow them; but the better *our* ideas about interpretation are, the more we may help him.

The whole subject requires to be simplified, but we cannot simplify any confused subject without a preliminary treatment which seems at first to make it more complex. That is only a first stage. The result, if the work were properly done, would be to make safe simplifications much easier. We are mainly suffering from premature false simplifications.

No excuse is needed for treating the conduct of the mind in interpretation as a philosophical subject, or, if we distrust that word, as a subject that requires us to attend critically to its methods and assumptions. I take the doctrine of 'usage' and the theory of metaphor as examples of inquiries which will yield nothing profitable unless they are so treated. *Then,* they replace, it seems to me, many of the more traditional philosophic questions which, while they were neglected, have been labour in vain.

Reviewers of *The Philosophy of Rhetoric* have complained variously. Since this is a more detailed development of the same positions, I may perhaps summarize these objections. Most of them concern the stabilities of words. I have been accused of making meaning in each case unique. But, for me, meanings arise only through recurrences and what is unique would be ineffable. For the same critic, I deny the principle of contradiction by saying that if a passage means one thing it can at the same time mean other incompatible things, or, as Freud puts it, a symbol may be overdetermined. But the principle of contradiction has to do with *logical* relations between meanings, not with the *psychological* concomitance of contradictory meanings. For the same writer, I deny that words may refer to constant things. But my point was that there are many types of constancy and many types of things and that these ought to be distinguished. Again, I am supposed, by one critic, both to harbour a dislike for traditional reason and to be 'determined to begin only with the verifiable facts and to draw from them only such inferences as can be checked against other facts.' But that seems no bad description of the traditional process of reason.

In general it is not easy to make the scale, or mesh, which is being used in the inquiry clear to the reader. Confusion naturally ensues if what is seen through a lens is mistaken for the naked eye appearance, and the degree of magnification attempted in these analyses varies. This parallel is defective and we know less about the laws connecting interpretations than about the laws of optics. But charges of perversity must arise unless the influence of the general purposes governing the work are taken into account. We can use lenses in studying vision without recommending that everything be seen through a microscope all the time. Such misunderstandings are to be expected in this subject. Some further remarks on this point will be found at the opening of Chapter XVI.

But one set of complaints has a specific source—a misapprehension of the 'special and technical sense' I gave to the word *context* in my account of meaning. ' "A word means the missing part of its context": this remark,' writes Mr Sackville West in *The Spectator*, 'is easy to misunderstand; but it is worth understanding aright, and Mr Richards sees that we do so.' Unhappily, I did not equally succeed with other readers. By them the technical sense of *context* was identified with that of *literary context*, and then the whole theorem becomes nonsense. A note on these two senses in this prominent place may help to prevent some confusion. For further explanations I must refer to *The Meaning of Meaning*.

(1) A word, like any other sign, gets whatever meaning it has through belonging to a recurrent group of events, which may be called its context. Thus a word's context, *in this sense*, is a certain recurrent pattern of *past* groups of events, and to say that its meaning depends upon its context would be to point to the process by which it has acquired its meaning.

(2) In another, though a connected, sense, a word's context is *the words which surround it in the utterance*, and the other *contemporaneous* signs which govern its interpretation.

Both senses of 'context' need to be kept in mind if we are to consider carefully how interpretations succeed or fail. For clarity we may distinguish the second sort of context by calling it the *setting*. It is evident that a change in the setting may change the context (in the first sense) in which a word is taken. We never, in fact, interpret single signs in isolation. (The etymological hint given by *inter* is very relevant here.) We always take a sign as being *in some setting*, actual or supplied, as part of an interconnected sign-field (normally, with verbal signs, a sentence and an occasion). Thus, insufficient attention to the accompanying sign-field (the setting and occasion) which controls the context (recurrent groups of events in the past) is a frequent cause of mistaken understanding. But equally, no care, however great, in observing the setting will secure good interpretation if past experience has not provided the required originative context. Here comes in the stress which teachers are so often forced to put upon the need for 'actual experience' in the individual's past history if verbal representations are to be understood. The stressing is justified if it does not overlook the indirect ways in which words can analyze features of experience and recompound them into wholes which may never have occurred in the reader's history. It is these *features of experience,* not specific integral experiences as distinct moments of being, which enter into contexts with words. If words—to be understood—must reinstate such integral experiences, the services of language to us would be far less than they are. A crude view here would obviously deprive literature of some of its greatest values.

The interactions of what I am calling the contexts and settings are as intricate and incessant as life itself. Thus a general exposition of them would be inherently a difficult matter. Sign-fields (or settings), by recurring, generate contexts (under certain conditions of interest structure); and which contexts are operative (how the signs are read) is determined later by the new settings. Thus the contexts which control meanings are always fluctuating with changes in the setting: the teacher's aim is to help them to become as orderly, as supple, and as serviceable as possible.

Such an account makes us expect the widest variability in the senses of our words, and is the theoretical ground for objecting to over-simplified doctrines of usage. It does not deny, however, the part played by convention in language, nor the stabilities, of various orders, which come from the uniformities of contexts. It only attempts the beginning of an explanation of these constancies. Nor does it overlook the importance of the distinction between words as *symbols* and sounds, or marks, as *signs.* A symbol is a higher level co-ordinating unit by which we are enabled to take any one of a class of perhaps very different sounds or marks as being, for interpretative purposes, the same symbol. To describe words as signs is a way of reminding ourselves of the mode by which they acquire and maintain their meanings and a useful warning against simplemindedness.

Finally, as to the limitation of this study to the interpretation of *language.* I would urge that there is no such separation between verbal and non-verbal intelligence, rightly conceived, as is sometimes suggested. There are trivial ways of studying language which have no connection with life, and these we need to clear out of our schools. But a deeper and more thorough study of our use of words is at every point a study of our ways of living. It touches all the modes of interpretative activity—in technique, and in social inter-course—upon which civilization depends. It touches them, more-over, at the most malleable points, at the most convenient points, where most may be expected from an effort to clarify and assist them.

Peking, June, 1937.                                    I. A. R.

# Analytic Contents

Rhetoric, Grammar and Logic, the first three Liberal Arts, need to be restored, 3. They must not be separated, 3. They are the study of the difficulties of fair interpretation, which recur, and are only mastered by being recognized, 4. Language is the incomparable means of considering how we are thinking and so of improving our thinking, 5. But mere practice with language is insufficient. Reflection upon it is necessary, 6. The danger is that we put Rules and Theory in the place of understanding, 9. This happens today with Psychology and has happened in the past with Rhetoric, Grammar, Logic, Prosody, Philology and Phonetics, 9-11. Our aim throughout is improved interpretation, not discourse upon interpreting, 11.

Rhetoric is 'the art by which discourse is adapted to its end,' 12. The varied ends of discourse (the language functions) are the main study, but are best approached indirectly after the student has, through examples, realized what he is already doing about them, 12-15. The examples concern the figures of speech—similes, metaphors, analogies, comparisons,—which, when interrogated, become exercises in Logic, the critical examination of likenesses and unlikenesses, the study of our sortings and their manipulation, 15-16. A reflective awareness of how we are sorting, and why, is the aim of Logic, which is prevented from taking its proper place in education mainly by misunderstandings and historical accidents, which have separated it unduly from the general study of Language, 16. Grammar—the study of the co-operations of words with one another in their contexts—equally loses its power to help when separated, 16. To restore it we need to disentangle the utterly diverse inquiries that go by that name, thus removing the tyranny of uncomprehended rules and replacing blind correctness by insight, 16-18. This can be done by developing further the skills by which we have already learnt to speak a native language, and by avoiding techniques thought appropriate to learning a foreign language, 18.

## PART ONE: RHETORIC

A first experiment offered to a Cambridge audience of some 200 was a passage of florid rant from *Elmer Gantry* together with a hostile note upon it by Mr. Biaggini (author of *English in Australia*). The audience were invited to discuss both; the conditions of the experiment described, 23-25. The question, 'Was Mr. Biaggini's comment fair?' led to discussion both of the varied functions of language and of problems about metaphor, 28. The scribble that presented this has to be read with caution, 29. But, so has philosophy, 30.

Had Elmer Gantry's sermon any 'simple sense'? 30; and what should we mean by 'simple sense'? Various commentators opposed it to myth and emotive utterance, 31; took it as literal reading, 32; or as Dictionary Sense, 32; or supposed that words can warm us, like a stove, without saying anything, 33; or work evocatively like a picture, 34. But the same problem arises with representation in art, 34; and men's mental pictures are discrepant, 35. Why look for the sense? 36. Mediating references to 'imagination'; and 'seeing eye to eye with the author,' 37. The evidence of hand-writing, 38. The music of words and amorous inanities, 38. Confusion of 'the sense' with 'the letter,' 39. The ambiguities of 'say,' 40. Complex sense and 'boiling everything down,' 41. An able analysis, 42. All-justifying sincerity, 42. Anti-logic, 43. Mr. Biaggini too mild, 44. An extreme case of misreading, 45.

The process of abstracting, 47. The theory of metaphor is an attempt to take critical account of skills we already possess, 47. Its difficulty not a matter of shortage of technical terms, but of our universal and inevitable use of metaphor in thinking, 48. Contexts and settings, 48. Thought is itself metaphoric, 49. The excessive multiplicity of the machinery for describing intellectual processes, 50. Whence disputes between users of alternative logical languages, 50. The wrong question has no right answer, 51.

The criticism of comparisons is a normal task which arises every hour, 52. What is the difference between saying, 'Love is a rainbow' and, 'A

The doctrines introduced in the protocols are not to be taken too seriously, 130. Is metaphor in its own nature untranslatable? 131. Untranslatable through close accuracy of resemblance; Hulme's statement, 131. But resemblance between what? 132. Not necessarily between tenor and vehicle, since disparity action must not be overlooked, 133. The special dangers of half-technicalized terms, 133. The ambiguity of 'express'; its unrestricted use, 135. Any translation expresses only part of the original meaning, 135. The uses of partial translations, 136. The main ambiguity of 'metaphor' is supported by all the ambiguities of 'meaning' and its synonyms, 136. 'Metaphor' as vehicle only and as tenor + vehicle, 137. A diagrammatic representation of the shift, 137. A table of the main normal confusions, 138. What is the whole of an analogy? 139. The compression in metaphor, 140. Adventitious variety values, 140. Individuality doctrine, 141. A muddle about personal positive emotional attitudes and exposition, 142. The use of 'logical' and its partial equivalents, 143. The opportunity, 144.

Different writers called different things 'definite' and meant different things by the word, 145. To plot the shifts of this landmark is helpful with many confusions, 146. Our use of 'definite' is not simple, but plays with likenesses, differences and implications, 147. A first main division of its senses separates definite 'things' from definite representations, 147. Three senses in which things may be definite, 147-8. The Second Group contains senses in which some representation, idea, expression or desire of or for something may be definite, 148. Important not to state these in terms of correspondence, 149. If we do, truth-troubles are incurred, 149. The familiarity of the problem in specific forms, 150. A reformulation in terms of two thoughts, 150. 'This is red' is more definite than 'this is coloured,' 150. This sense has reference to other representations that might be made instead, 151. Ideas cannot be too definite, statements can, 152. 'Definite' as explicit, detailed, 152. As unambiguous, 153. Ambiguities that words will not clear up but familiarity can, 154. Multiplicity of meaning distinguished from ambiguity, 154. 'Definite' as clear, evident, 154. 'Definite' as decided, confident, 155. Can an attitude be more or less definite in itself? 156. 'Definite' as highly organized, 156. 'Defi-

## PART TWO: GRAMMAR

# Retrospect

This book, coming back now into print after thirty years, has constantly seemed to me, of all my writings, the most worth *while*. It takes a longish time to read and asks for more than a little patience from its reader. But I have felt that it can repay. Re-reading it now, almost as another person, I find it teaching me things I willingly relearn.

Among them, that the tasks it set itself are no less urgent than they were. Better diagnosis of the causes of our manifold defects in comprehension, more efficient design in forfendings and remedies: work toward these is certainly no less needed than before. The undertaking is doubtless far larger than that now remote author could suppose, though he wrote so large a book as a sketch of how it should be attempted. But the huge scale of the enterprise, granted the need, should not be discouraging—in these days, when nothing seems too great for man to tackle. As to the need, that is established, I believe, by the protocols on which the book labours—these being the freely-written comments by more than ordinarily favoured students, on matters of central significance to every would-be capable reader. Some chapters may at times seem over-loaded with excerpts from their scribblings and with my comments. But not if it is recognized that this is the beginning of what should be a vast collective *clinical* study of the aberrations of average intelligence, and in duty bound to adduce its evidence as much as, say, any psycho-analyst's case-book. It is an extensive piece of natural history, collecting, arranging, displaying and hazarding observations upon its selected specimens. If the observations are mistaken they are there to be corrected—the aim being just to develop better judgment as to central matters upon which the health of thought depends.

Apart from the commentary, the specimens still offer an opportunity—not so easily found elsewhere—to note and compare diverse opinions on selected and identified points, some hitting the mark, some wide astray.

Almost the only parallel opportunity I know of is *Practical Criticism*. I have often wondered why that display of people's judgments of poems should have met with an eager, if often aghast or hilarious welcome, but *Interpretation in Teaching*, though offering a deeper examination of concerns nearer everyman's essential capacities, was comparatively little studied. Perhaps its title and approach handed it over to a more professionalized company, better organized for self-defence. How significant it is that the word 'Teaching' should stir in so many the feelings it does!

Why there is such a shrinking from attempts to amend our intellectual ways is a question that should have had its own chapter. Some conjectures will be found to have been ventured, especially around the interludes or *Landing Stages*—a device I borrowed from *The Friend,* since Coleridge's hopes there were freshly before me in this attempt to put his life-long aim upon a rather more scientific footing. A growing avoidance of what seem evidently the more pressing, if more difficult, tasks, a selection of more alluring though easily postponed engagements, a concern with *belles lettres* rather than with what is *necessary* if rewarding interests are to survive: these I take to be symptoms of the corruption that has been spreading so widely since the two world wars. Man's destructive capacities—physical and spiritual—have so far exceeded his restorative powers, though already these could remake him, if he would. The very people who should most be helping have lost heart. They squat in the gutter, broken-spirited, aimless, strumming rhythms of despair, though they could well be building up the morale and the insight needed for the instauration of a renewed world.

Of the circumstances under which this book was written I have said something in the interview included in the celebration volume edited by Reuben Brower (Oxford University Press). As Brower well remarks there, this was the grand hinge on which I swung away from literary into educative pursuits and ceased to write books that were surprisingly successful in

favour of others, not at all astonishingly, the reverse. Actually
the experience of reading the protocols for these two books,
*Practical Criticism* and *Interpretation in Teaching*, intently enough
to choose my comments, had been decisive. Ordinary examining
is seldom so searching. I found I had at least to try to do something about the general condition of incompetence I had
uncovered. I felt (and still feel) it to be too threatening to the
human prospect to be left uncured. Looking again at the
resultant book with this much of hindsight, I can see how
ambitious it was, superbity itself, not only in its aim, but in the
cool way it handled the current Cambridge (and other) philosophic fashions. It took the oldest and hardiest perennial doctrines,
from theories of Truth down, and made them over into mental
tools to be used when they could serve and changed when
they did not—undaunted by the troubles such a new style of
verbal behaviour might stir in the reader. How thinking
could be encouraged, how intelligence is most often stultified,
by what exercises it might be restored to freedom and power:
these were its prime concerns. I can still feel enough of the
fervour of those nights and days to see why it so seldom
asked itself whether it would be understood. In general, it
dealt as directly as did Aristotle with the prime themes of
self-instruction and the rectification of the mind. Its watchword
it borrowed from C. S. Peirce: 'Logic is the ethics of thinking—
in the sense in which ethics is the bringing to bear of self-
control for the purpose of realising our desires.'

As to how most easily to see the book as a whole my recommendation is: from Preface and Introduction skip to the First
Landing Stage (p. 74) with the three preceding pages on
Motivation. Thence to the Second and Third Landing Stages.
Then run through the Analytic Contents glancing into the
text as required. Turn then to the last pages of Chapter Twenty-
three and the Final Landing Stage. Those following this
prescription will be well placed to decide whether to read the
book or not. If you elect to do so, include the 'classroom
exercises' at the end.

A word as to its relation to my later writings. They have
almost all been in their various ways, attempts, more or less
conscious, to benefit from the positions occupied here or to

support or extend them. The latest, my *Poetries: Their Media and Ends,* (Mouton, 1973) relies on them. My forthcoming *Beyond* (Harcourt Brace Jovanavich) stems from the Tenor-Vehicle opposition (in an expanded interpretation) and from the Logical Machinery Chapters. It returns to the greatest works of literature with freedoms learnt through a classroom exercise (pp. 407–15) on

Why do we believe that $2 + 2 = 4$?

*Harvard, 1972*                                             I.A.R.

# INTRODUCTION

# Introduction

*The teaching they gave to their pupils was ready but rough. For they used to suppose that they trained people by imparting to them not the art but its products, as though anyone professing that he would impart a form of knowledge to obviate pain in the feet, were then not to teach a man the art of shoemaking, or the sources whence he can acquire anything of the kind, but were to present him with several pairs of shoes of all sorts: for he has helped him to meet his need, but has not imparted to him any art.* ARISTOTLE, *De Sophisticis Elenchis*

Less by design than from the nature, history and life of its subject, this treatise has grown into three parts which correspond roughly to ancient provinces of thought. Rhetoric, Grammar and Logic—the first three liberal Arts, the three ways to intelligence and a command of the mind that met in the Trivium, meet here again. And though each is for us today cumbered with much deadfall and much obsolete technical tackle which we must shift from the path, neither the general problem nor the plan of attack can be new. To orientate, to equip, to prepare, to encourage, to provoke, a mental traveller to advance by his own energies in whatever region may be his to explore; to make him think for himself *and* make him able to do so sanely and successfully, has always been the aim of a civilizing education. How to hand back the gains of the more experienced to the less experienced in the least hampering and most available form is the general problem. And, since language must be the medium, the three traditional modes of the study of language keep or renew their importance. They meet and mingle incessantly; they cannot, as we shall see in detail, be separated without frustration, and separation has historically been the most frequent cause of failure. But still, Rhetoric, Grammar and Logic, if we set aside their repulsive terminologies and associations, are the headings under

3

which to arrange what the student we hope to help needs most to study.

The prime obstacle in general education is a feeling of helplessness before the unintelligible. Every problem is new to the mind which first meets it and it is baffling until he can recognize in it something which he has met and dealt with already. The all important difference between the mind which can clear itself by thought and the mind which remains bewildered and can proceed only by burying the difficulty in a formula—retained, at best, by mere rote memory—is in this power to recognize the new problem as, in part, an old conquest. Language, with its inexhaustible duplications (which here are duplicities), ceaselessly presents to us the old as though it were new, familiar ideas in novel disguises, understood distinctions as fresh opportunities for confusion, already assimilated combinations as unforeseeable conjunctions. The teacher meets with all this whenever he reads anything which stretches his intelligence; the pupil meets with it all the time, and if he is being well taught he should be expecting it and enjoying the sense of increasing power that his progressive mastery of it can afford. For this growth in power is, fundamentally, the vitalizing incentive with which education builds.

The beginner, in studying the most elementary matters, is doing nothing which is (or should be) *for him* any simpler than what we are doing when we try to follow a new and difficult author. And we can only help him in a fashion parallel to that in which we ourselves would wish to be helped or to help ourselves: that is, not by supplying the 'right answer' to the difficulty (with some unexamined criterion of 'right answers') but by making clearer what the difficulty itself was, so that when we meet it again we shall not have to 'remember the answer' but shall see what it must be from our understanding of the question. A learner at all stages learns—for serious purposes—only in so far as he is a thinker, and the difficulties of thinking are never new. We overcome them—in elementary mechanics, and in the Theory of Relativity, in learning to read words of one syllable and in reading *Ulysses,* alike—by taking account of them, by seeing what we are doing and setting aside other things which we should not be trying to do there. We solve them finally by discovering how much more simple the task was than we had hitherto supposed.

As language, in its multiplicity of modes, and our always incomplete mastery of them, is the source of most of our preventable stultifications, so the study of how language works and fails is our great opportunity.

With reason did Coleridge dilate upon 'the advantages which language alone, at least which language with incomparably greater ease and certainty than any other means, presents to the instructor of impressing modes of intellectual energy so constantly, so imperceptibly . . . as to secure in due time the formation of a second nature.' Well did he urge his generation 'to value earnestly and with a practical seriousness a means, already prepared for us by nature and society, of teaching the young mind to think well and wisely by the same unremembered process and with the same never forgotten results, as those by which it is taught to speak and converse.' (*Biographia Literaria*, II, p. 117.) We cannot think, as Coleridge thought, about language, without recognizing that he is not overstating its powers. How to use them, how to develop the instructive possibilities of this universal switchboard, how, by investigating them, to improve, at the same time, our command of all the interconnections of thought, non-verbal as well as verbal, is our problem. We are better placed for this than Coleridge's contemporaries were, because we have come to see still more clearly how central the fact of language is.

The unintelligibility of a problem may sometimes be due to lack of special experience, but most often it is due to the language in which the problem comes to us—or to our lack of experience with such language, or with the ways of language as such. As Sayce said, in his *Introduction to the Science of Language*, p. 337, 'If we are suddenly brought into contact with experts in a subject we have not studied, or dip into a book on an unfamiliar branch of knowledge, we seem to be listening to the meaningless sounds of a foreign tongue. The words used may not be technical words; but familiar words and expressions will bear senses and suggest ideas to those who use them which they will not bear to us.' From this situation there are two escapes. Acquaintance with the special topic, and, which is more widely useful, a general readiness to expect words to change their senses with their contexts, together with an aptitude for divining their probable meanings even in unfamiliar fields. And this last, which involves intelligence in its highest form, comes only from reflection upon our experience with language in fields with which we are already familiar.

To suppose that this necessary experience can be gained by mere practice with language, without reflective study of it, is an error which recurrently dominates education. Every great persistent error is perhaps a mode of escape from worse errors, and here, doubtless, a bitter lesson, from the futility of those studies in grammar and logic which used to be inflicted upon the helpless pupil, is behind the widespread current opinion that it is better just to make the pupil read and write as much as possible rather than to waste his time so. Better no studies at all of the theory of language than these. It may be so. I am not sure, though, that the results obtained by even the dreariest early 19th Century drillings in parsing and the syllogism did not compare favourably with current output. But the comparison is not fair. There were, for one thing, fewer pupils. Setting this aside, however, we can see that these now obsolete forms of language study, if they sometimes did some incidental good, flagrantly violated the first principle of education—the principle of intelligibility which I have begun by stressing.

We may recall how even a Milton complained that the Universities presented to 'unlearned novices, at their first coming, the most intellective abstracts of Logic and Metaphysics.'

In place of insight into language they put subservience to rules—to rules which could not appear to the learner as anything but inexplicable arbitrary impositions from without. The Rules of Grammar and of Logic and of Good Usage were nothing but Orders, Commands laid down to be obeyed, utterly mysterious and incomprehensible both as to their origin and their justification. As such they were an outrage to every mind which realized—as every mind, however young, realizes when it is awake—that it must be its own keeper.

'It is not only possible, but necessary,'' wrote Charles Hoole, in his *New Discovery of the Old Art of Teaching School,* with a flash of insight he never managed to put into effect, 'to make children understand their tasks, from their very first entrance into learning; seeing that they must everyone bear his own burden, and not rely upon their fellows altogether.'

It is no part of these proposals that anything at all resembling the traditional Grammar or Logic should be reintroduced into education. Nothing in the theory of the uses of language should be admitted which cannot, as it is admitted, be made satisfyingly intelligible. I hope to show however that it is possible, even under this restriction, to include much more of the supposedly recondite parts of the subject than most modern educationists have imagined.

These problems: as to why we may say one thing but not another, why one word or phrase is 'right' and another 'wrong,' why one 'reason' is fitter than another, have an absorbing interest, even for very young minds, an interest which none of the usual methods for damping it quite succeed in extinguishing. Granted that the Logic, Grammar and Rhetoric of the Manuals can go near to putting it out and can frighten all but the most obstinate intelligences from free speculation on these matters (and most others) for the rest of their lives, this is not the fault of the problems but of the fashion in which inquiry into them is discouraged. The speculative interest—which is thought at work on its own most urgent needs— is often far stronger in the pupil than in the teacher, who cannot afford to be too patently out of his depth. But thought in this figure is just swimming. I shall have much more than enough to say in what follows about the gross evasions of the most interesting issues in the theory of the use of language which make up so large a part of current Manuals of Composition and Rhetoric and of more ambitious discussions of Prose Style. The disconnected dogmas and mystifying assumptions with which they parry questions which every alert mind *feels*—if it does not formulate them—create self-distrust, as well as dishonesty, in the pupil; whence the stupidity, whether it shows itself in mere inertia or in self-assertive and confident parroting, which drives the teacher to distraction or to a reconsideration of his technique.

There can be no pretence, of course, that how language works can be fully explained. And there is much to be said for insisting early that in this as in everything else we have to start from as well as work towards the unintelligible. Evidently we cannot understand our foundations in anything; nor can we fly outside the Universe. We must accept our fundamental facts as unexplained, and we never reach a view which does not generate new questions.

'In wonder, said Aristotle, does philosophy begin; and in astoundment, said Plato, does it culminate.' For philosophy it does no harm here to substitute 'thought.' Thought about language keeps these limits constantly present to us; and there is nothing paralyzing about that kind of unintelligibility. An aeroplane must have a base as well as a ceiling. What is paralyzing is the frequent occurrence in our minds of unsuspected pockets of another kind of unintelligibility. Our thought is riddled with unnecessary vacancies where problems, which we could and should have thought through, have been encased, unexplored, in a phrase. Thereafter, since argument is very largely, and rightly, an exchanging and substitution of phrases, all kinds of confusion and distortion are made possible, and, as my protocols will show, they do not fail to occur.

These blank and treacherous pockets of incomprehension must occur in proportion as we leave important and life-bringing questions unconsidered, or seal them with a fraudulently conclusive 'answer.' And the most important and most generally vitalizing of all questions are those which concern language. They are needed, not only for this particular problem or that, but for the reasonable conduct and discipline of all thinking. All instruction through words is, of course, a process of answering such questions more or less indirectly. Whether we are talking *about* words and their meanings or merely *with* them, we are finding our way through an endless series of alternatives between meanings. We may choose so quickly that the other possibilities never come into clear consciousness, but it is a disastrous error of over-simplification to suppose that we are not choosing, or that there are no alternatives balancing against one another in our interpretation. Fast or slow, thought, in this sense, is questioning. We may, and usually do, restrict the term 'question' to the slower cases where the choice would be undecided without a supporting rally of further considerations. But whether the process is swift or leisurely, implicit and summary or explicit and discursive, our interpretation is never a mere taking up of an isolated self-complete and single meaning. For the meaning is itself a process of growth and the outcome of a balance between possibilities of being.

This, however, is a doctrine to be discussed in detail and with examples. I shall be doing so, at intervals, throughout. Here the point is comparatively simple, that the ordinary answering of such merely local questions about language as all use of language entails, is not enough. By answering, say, sixty specific problems in the use of language that happen to be parallel, we shall not have made it easier to answer a sixty-first parallel problem *unless* the respects in which the problems are parallel have been reflected upon. Unless, that is, we have replaced the specific problems by a general problem. But the general problem must not merely replace them in space and time; it must genuinely represent, embody, offer them again, it must be a natural outgrowth and development from them. In understanding it we must know that we are understanding them also and see how we are doing this. Here, as we all recognize with sorrow, is the difficulty; and near it opens the gate to that Paradise of Teachers which notoriously so much resembles the Paradise of Fools. So easy is it to put general views in the place of particular perceptions— without the one having, necessarily, any effective connection whatever with the other. How *to generalize,* as opposed to how to learn general formulas, how to pass from a momentary triumph over a particular language-problem back to a perception of the problem *in itself* rather than of its answer, and so to achieve the power to recognize and meet (though *not* necessarily to classify) the problem again when it rises in a new instance, that is our problem here—and, I insist, not a whit more difficult essentially than the schoolboy's task in seeing what sort of a sum he has been set and how he is to tackle it.

The way to the generalizing power, or better, to the general insight that we seek, does not lie through classification or a listing of uniformities. This is another grand traditional error. Catalogues of predicaments and arguments, of typical fallacies with representative examples, tables of grammatical constructions with their appropriate breaches, classifications of tropes and modes and genres —these may have done some good; but time and effort have shown often enough that they will not give us what we want. They look like the fumbling first steps of young sciences: what we want is the further development of what is already an advanced art, the art of intellectual discernment. For this reason—and here I am probably turning my blows from dead donkeys to a live enough lion—educational psychology is not what we want. That, too, is still a toddling infant science and our ordinary tact and skill and common sense are far in advance of the utmost reach of its present purview. I would not (and could not if I would) discourage the labours of those who are enquiring methodically, in the psychological laboratories, into the learning process, into memorization, the conditions of retention and undistorted recall, into I.Q.s and other factors, and transferences of ability; into typology, needs, motivation and the rest. May they succeed beyond all expectations—but would they even *then* have found out anything which for practical purposes (as apart from theoretical interest) would add to our present powers? I wish I could hope so. What I have seen of this work makes me think that it will yield increasingly exact but *increasingly abstract* statements of laws with whose general form we are already sufficiently acquainted to be able to use them in practice, though we need not necessarily be able to state them. That these refinements will have much direct bearing upon teaching I doubt. Refinements in the Theory of Gravitation make no difference whatever to the way we throw stones. The sort of psychological laws we use in teaching are like the physical laws we use in playing baseball; if we knew them more precisely we still would not use the refinements. The complexity of the conditions would make the attempt unprofitable. *Theoretically,* on the other hand, it may happen—I believe it is happening—that exact experiment and abstract reflection, in that branch of biology which we call psychology and in its other branches, may make immense changes in our whole *conception* of education. The changed conception may well change our aim but we should still try to attain that aim by ways that we know about already—that we know about, at least, when we wake up to ask ourselves what we are doing.

To put this, possibly ungracious, point briefly: Our errors in teaching technique can be corrected more easily, and more safely, I believe, from our own awareness of how we ourselves learn and think, than from the recommendations of educational psychology, which at present only confirm some parts of common knowledge. And where, as with some work on intelligence-testing, psychology offers to correct this vaguer common knowledge, difficult and unsettled matters of interpretation enter. The psychology and the common knowledge may not be judging the same things. There is therefore danger in attempting to make practical immediate use of psychological findings,—a danger that was illustrated in the days when the mental testers laid simple uncritical stress upon the speed with which tasks could be performed, as though problems could be identified merely through their formulation in a supposed standard context.

I have touched here upon educational psychology for three reasons. To explain why in what follows I shall be attempting no direct applications from it. Secondly, because it has recently had an increasing place in the training and studies of teachers, and I believe that they could learn whatever they learn from it that will be useful to them *as teachers* much more easily without it, and their time is badly needed for other studies and *for reflection*. Thirdly, because the replacement of insight into the learning process by a rote acquaintance with the jargon of the subject and its typical formulations is such an excellent example of the disease of abstractionism with which the whole undertaking is perennially afflicted. I know no sadder or more disheartening reading than some of the educational theory which leans upon psychology—unless perhaps the dreary pages of those masters of Rhetoric who thought themselves perfectly acquainted with the subject when they had learnt only to name some of its tools.

The direction then in which an enhancement of general intelligence and understanding must be sought is not in any introduction of 'intellective abstracts,' whether of Educational Psychology or of Rhetoric or of Logic or of Grammar, or of any other section of Pedagogy, into teaching. The history of the subject shows how great the danger of such blundering is. We may compare the odd fashion in which Prosody, Philology, and Phonetics, for example, followed Grammar in climbing from the humble handmaid station they originally held. They came to rival, and sometimes to dominate, the literature in the enjoyment of which they were to assist. Back to their combs (or, if they are haughty, out among the sciences) with them all! And so too with the study of interpretation if it pretends to set itself up as a rival to the general practice of understanding and distracts the student from his work—which is to interpret, not to discourse on interpretation.

So, in what follows, I beg that the theoretical expatiations on interpretation, its assumptions, its conditions and its risks, be not confused with the practical exercises designed to improve students in their performance. I shall be analyzing and attempting to diagnose hundreds of representative misinterpretations; but I do not propose that such anatomizings should be imposed in teaching,— though they should be induced in our pupils' minds. If they were imposed in instruction, that fact would confess that the right plan had not been found. Our aim, to take the obvious examples, is not to produce Logicians, or Grammarians, but sound thinkers and clear writers, a different thing altogether.

But subject to this caution—which is appallingly easy to forget— a training in Rhetoric, Grammar and Logic, *as Arts* not as sciences, a training which is at present almost entirely lacking in the curriculum, is what is most needed. It may especially take the place of much of the unchecked perusal (see p. 218) and undirected scribbling in which time is now spent. To expect those to write who have developed no power either to read or to think is both foolish and cruel. It is, at best, only encouraging a malady to which we are all too prone. To quote an unpublished note that Coleridge wrote in the margin of an essay by Southey, 'The Pen is the tongue of a systematic dream—a Somniloquist. The sunshine comparative power, the distinct contra-distinguishing judgment of Realities as other than Thoughts is suspended!—During this state of continuous, not single-mindedness, but *one-side*-mindedness, writing is a manual somnambulism—the somnial magic superinduced on, without suspending, the active powers of the mind.' But the business of a teacher is to awaken, to bring 'the sunshine comparative power' out of its clouds of dream, to stir his pupil into distinguishing between thought and fancy, into caring seriously whether he understands what he reads and says or not. We have to help him to know when he has understood and when he has not, and to prepare him, when he has not, to face and defeat the unintelligible with his own awakened intelligence.

I will briefly sketch the contents of the main divisions of my subject, with some of their interrelations, adding some defensive indications of how I shall *not* be treating them.

Rhetoric I take to be 'the art by which discourse is adapted to its end.' This makes it very inclusive. What should be among its topics may be seen from the contents of George Campbell's *The Philosophy of Rhetoric* (1823), a book which deserves more attention than it is likely ever again to receive. After a chapter on 'The Relation which Eloquence bears to Logic and Grammar,' he goes on to 'The different sources of Evidence,' dividing them into *'Intuitive Evidence*— Mathematical axioms, Consciousness and Common Sense'—and *'Deductive Evidence'*—subdivided elaborately into scientific and moral, and treating of no less matters than 'the nature and origin of experience,' 'Analogy,' and 'Calculations of Chances.' Soon after comes a chapter, 'Of the Consideration which the Speaker ought to have of the Hearers as Men in general'—which should favour mercy. Later come 'Of Perspicuity' and 'The Obscure,'—'from using the same word in different senses,' 'from too artificial a structure of the Sentence,' 'from Technical Terms;' 'The Double Meaning'—'Equivocation,' 'Ambiguity;' 'The Unintelligible'—'from Confusion of Thought,' 'from Affectation of Excellence,' and 'from Want of Meaning.' Then a chapter with the fine title, 'What is the cause that nonsense so often escapes being detected, both by the writer and by the reader?' This he treats with a dissertation on 'The Nature and Power of Signs' which leads him on to 'The extensive Usefulness of Perspicuity.'

Campbell does not fulfil this programme, which indeed almost comprises all we need to know; but he does lift the subject into a light in which its central position in education can be fairly seen. Later Manuals by trying to dodge the difficulties (which are its value) have degraded it.

The most *general* task of the Art would be to distinguish the different sorts of ends, or aims, for which we use language, to teach how to pursue them separately and how to reconcile their diverse claims when, as is usual, the use of language is mixed. That our uses of language can be divided under several different main heads, no one will doubt; though just which divisions are the most illuminating and convenient in teaching may be a puzzling matter. This is that question of 'the classification of the Language Functions' which makes a brief and unsatisfactory appearance among the preliminaries of many works on general linguistic.

How many things does language do? It is possible to make a very baffling tangle (Stern, for example, in his valuable *Meaning and Change of Meaning,* does so) out of the different answers: that it records or *communicates* thought, *expresses* mental processes, *symbolizes* states of affairs, *promotes* human co-operation, and so on. 'The interrelations of the functions are not known in detail,' observes Stern, p. 21. They *cannot,* of course, be known, until the functions themselves have been more clearly determined and distinguished. Which we take to be fundamental and how we arrange the others, are not matters to be settled until we have decided *why* we are distinguishing them, for what purposes. This first language problem, like a hundred later ones, is apt to be stated in a way which from the start prevents any progress. Language has infinite uses, and which main categories we introduce to facilitate study of these infinite uses, depends upon the proposed scope and aim of our study. The psychologist, the jurist, the social historian, the logician, the lexicographer, the semanticist tracing the history of sense changes, the critic, and the pedagogue will use different principles of classification. The apple grower establishes *grades* among his fruit for marketing purposes which are of no significance whatever to the plant physiologist.

For our purposes the last thing we wish to do (literally the last thing) is to introduce a classification to be taught and relied on. To introduce one too early would interfere with one of the most healthy exercises that the student can indulge in. As we shall see, it is easy to offer him passages in a way which will force him to work out for himself some of the implications of the perception that a plain neutral statement of fact is in some way different from an appeal to passion. To start out, *in teaching,* from a division between, say,

(1) pure scientific impersonal or neutral statement, and

(2) emotive utterance which expresses and evokes states of feeling, is a good way of helping him to encyst, and so to dodge or hide from himself, just the very things whose differences and connections he should be puzzling over. I mention this here as another example of the danger, throughout the subject, of supposing that instruction in linguistic theory (whether Rhetorical, Logical or Grammatical) can replace insight into, self-discovery of and thus understanding of, the matters with which it is concerned. (If I insist too often upon this, the fault will be readily forgiven me by those who realize what a new world that would be in which there was no need especially to remind ourselves of this failing!)

The general task of Rhetoric is to give, not by dogmatic formula but *by exercise in comparisons,* an insight into the different modes of speech and their exchanges and disguises. The chief divisions of these general fields for comparison may be: statement, full and explicit, or condensed (by abstraction, ambiguity or implication, the hint, the aposiopesis); statement literal or direct, and indirect (by metaphor, simile, comparison, parallel etc.); suasion, open (from appeal to cajolery) or concealed (either as mere statement or as mere ornament) and so on.

But we should do little good by explaining this, even with examples. All our pupils know it already. What they do not know is how to distinguish and meet the varying modes of language *in practice.* The theory of the divisions is only useful when it comes in later to aid them in noticing explicitly what they are already doing—for good or ill.

The more special problems of Rhetoric have to do with the Figures of Speech—about which current theory is oddly out of date, and our practice most deceiving. Experiments with figures easily awaken a raging curiosity which, if it is suitably fed and not choked with formulas, can cut deep and spread wide. Well led, it should be able to fertilize almost any topic, redeeming it from the status of desert to be crossed to that of region to be cultivated.

Some figures of speech can be translated into relatively non-figurative language with ease, others only with difficulty and some perhaps not at all. Such translation exercises (if used with discretion; they can be paralyzing) are an invaluable device for redirecting attention to what is being said and how it is being understood. They lead naturally and insensibly into Logic. I might equally say that Logic, for our purposes, is just a more thorough inquiry into these translations. For example, if we try to say what is said in one metaphor by means of another metaphor (e.g. try replacing the water-figure at the end of the last paragraph by a fire or light-figure) we find ourselves really studying in the most practical and immediate way the process of *abstraction* itself. And to ask whether or not a parallel, e.g.

> Meaning is an arrow which reaches its mark when least encumbered with feathers

really supports the view it is introduced to state, or whether it weakens it unnecessarily, is a better exercise in argument than any that formal instruction in the syllogism provides. (See Appendix.) Generalization is systematic *abbreviated* parallelling, and choice among similes or metaphors is chiefly a matter of rapid recognition of likes and discrimination between unlikes. Mathematics and the sciences, so often praised, and rightly, for the training in Logic they provide, are the leisurely, analyzed, explicitly recorded, developments of the very same processes that, well or ill, operate in the main mode of metaphor.

For all thought is sorting, and we can think of nothing without taking it as of a sort. Logic is the Art or discipline of managing our sortings and it is of little use to study it only in an abstract science, if we have no command over the play of metaphor where logic should most intimately steer our thought. The logic required is of course subtler than that needed in a prepared abstract science, but if this is our peril it is at the same time our hope of remedy. Sentimental folk who 'like to think' that the figures of speech (being 'imaginative,' sometimes) are beyond the reach of logic, may consider again what they are saying. They have probably some view of logic which makes it less than 'the ethics of thinking,'[1] a principle of order upon which all good life, including all imaginative life, depends.

Rhetoric, then, leads naturally into Logic. But where does Grammar come in? Being, for *our* purposes, nothing but *the study of the co-operation of words with one another in their contexts,* it comes in everywhere. But Grammar is notoriously the subject in which it is hardest to remember what we are studying, in which a focus upon detail most blurs the background and the formation of opinion most occults the very assumptions which set the local problem. Nowhere more than in Grammar are utterly diverse inquiries likely to be mistaken for one another, and the right task be abandoned for others which are irrelevant though identical in their verbal formulation. These are reasons for despair of Grammar, as an educational discipline, if we do not recognize and deal with them in teaching. Recognized frankly and entered into carefully, they are, for this very reason, an irreplaceable opportunity for promoting insight, by natural development, into the key secrets of the use of language. The resentment, too, which all good minds feel against the futilities, unintelligible dogmas, and arbitrary rulings of so much traditional grammatical teaching is a useful handle.

A good way to arouse a lively interest in Grammar is to begin

[1] C. S. Peirce. 'Logic is the ethics of thinking in the sense that ethics is the bringing to bear of self-control for the purpose of realising our desires.' This may seem a catch-phrase unless we see how deeply Peirce, the founder of pragmatism and, at the same time, one of the main inspirers of modern, antipragmatist, formal Logic, meant his phrase to be taken.

with specimens of the outrages of past grammarians, inviting and guiding some attempts to explain how such absurdities could ever have come about. What were they trying to do and what did they think they were doing? From this we may pass to a separation of the different kinds of inquiries which may masquerade as Grammar by using a common apparatus of questions; and thence to an understanding of the control of the setting upon interpretation. These are not difficult steps, though in an abstract exposition they would seem an intolerably confusing and recondite affair. So an anatomical description apart from suitable sections and preparations to consult will seem beyond the wit of man to follow.

With suitable examples by which to display these divergent interests and their contexts in operation, we can exploit a natural skill in interpretation that is as common as the developed capacity for sustained meditation in abstract terms is rare. More perhaps with Grammar than even with any other branch of teaching, we have to distinguish between ability to see the point in the actual (which is all that we wish to develop) and ability to describe it in the abstract—a gift hitherto of no great service even to professional grammarians.

These, of course, are sentiments that all, including the worst culprits in the history of Grammar, would applaud. 'Don't bother the boys with the reasons! Give them *the rules,* with examples, and make them learn them and apply them!'—that is the recipe they would derive from them and *that* is the plausible program against which I most wish to protest. For it exploits a perilous equivocation in the sense of *Rules* (with *Law, Order, and its other partial synonyms*) which goes right through every branch of language study; and will be found, in fact, dominating the most fundamental issues in biology. It may seem a far cry from the elementary teaching of Grammar to the problem of the constitutive laws of development of an organism (and the free-will, determinism, vitalism, mechanism, cross-purposed controversy); but when we learn anything we are quite obviously exemplifying biologic laws. How we suppose we learn, then (and thus how we propose to teach), is not independent of our theories, or assumptions, as to the process of growth and the laws of development. And though there is learning which may be regarded as a mere yielding to repetitive pressure from without, a mere moulding by an external law, which comes to us as a dark rule, still the learning that is fruitful—in such a matter as the development of the most highly organized of man's activities, the control of his thought through language—is better treated as growth from within; and *that* feels, as we make it, like insight. It feels not like an alien dark compulsion but like an enlightening discovery of our own making. The only *rules* in intellectual discipline that a teacher may willingly make use of are records of the pupil's own helpful self-determinations.

These, which are today the commonplaces of pedagogy in other subjects, are, for reasons upon which it is very profitable to speculate, still usually ignored in language study. We still here attempt to impose the forms upon the matter instead of encouraging the matter to develop for itself its appropriate forms. And the 'matter' is here just that activity of self-discovering thought, which of all activities least deserves to be so distrustfully and disdainfully treated.

For, as a prime guiding principle, we have to remember that here, as in all teaching but more so, all that we can do is to provide opportunities for an extension and refinement of skills which are inexplicably, unimaginably and all-but-triumphantly, successful already. In the Confucian *Chung Yung* the clue to the self-completing growth of the mind is given in the aphorism:

> In hewing an axe handle, in hewing an axe handle, the model for it is in our hand. (XIII, 2—See *Practical Criticism,* p. 284.)

So here in this instance of language-study, the pupil, however stupid and inert he may seem, has already somehow learnt to talk, which is much more than we could teach him to do if he did not do it for himself! He comes to us with these uncanny powers already highly developed, and we have only, if we can, to help him to develop them a little further.

That, at present, we so often do no more than put unnecessary obstacles in his way is explained largely by our own unhappy histories. They are mostly the obstacles we encountered ourselves and did not really overcome as often as we may later suppose. But it would be painful to dwell upon this. A contributory cause is the influence, on the study of the native language, of procedures that should belong only to the quite different business of learning a foreign language. We do not enough realize what an artificial operation the grafting of a foreign language on a mind by systematic teaching is. Historically, Grammar has very largely developed as an aid in this violent grafting process. As such its schematizations are of no *direct* service in increasing our command over our own language.

# *Part One:* RHETORIC

*The end or scope of philosophy is, that we may make use
to our benefit of effects formerly seen; or that, by the application of bodies to one another, we may produce the
like effects of those we conceive in our mind, as far forth
as matter, strength and industry will permit, for the com-
modity of human life. For the inward glory and triumph
of mind that a man may have for the mastery of some
difficult and doubtful matter, or for the discovery of some
hidden truth, is not worth so much pains as the study of
Philosophy requires; nor need any man care much to
teach another what he knows himself, if he think that
will be the only benefit of his labour. The end of knowledge is power; and the use of theorems (which, among
geometricians, serve for the finding out of properties) is
for the construction of problems; and, lastly, the scope of
all speculation is the performance of some action, or thing
to be done.*

THOMAS HOBBES, *The Elements of Philosophy*

# *Chapter One:* Simple Sense

> *The light got from the opposite arguings of men of parts,*
> *showing the different sides of things, and their various*
> *aspects and probabilities, would be quite lost, if everyone*
> *were obliged to say after the speaker.*     LOCKE

The comments with which I am illustrating this discussion were
supplied by the audience at my course of Lectures at Cambridge in
1935. The title of the course was *Practical Criticism, Prose,* and
some 200 on an average attended. I have no means of knowing just
what subjects they were officially reading, or what their standing
was in the University. Perhaps half of them were reading for the
English Tripos; but there must have been as many who were working in other subjects. Men preponderated to a degree which surprised me. At some lectures there were four men for every woman.
I suspect that had the subject been poetry this would have been
otherwise.

No pressure from supervisors or any expectation that the course
would be academically useful brought them. The lectures occurred
at 9.0 a.m. in the uncomfortable Lent Term three times a week.
For some weeks the numbers increased and then with the turn of
the Term there was a not unexpected drop. This corresponded
roughly with my passage from Grammar to Logic, but may have
meant no more than that they tired. A contributing cause must have
been that I grew tired too. The mass of protocols supplied was at
times overwhelming.

I see no reason to doubt that this audience represented—favourably—the general level of ability among those reading for Honours
at the University. I shall not be concerned here, save incidentally,
with the disturbing reflections which this assumption may give rise
to in connection with some of the protocols I shall cite. But this
moral may be drawn without fear: that if such a direct attack as
was here attempted were *even in a slight degree* a remedy for the

23

intellectual habits it revealed, room can well be made for it in any curriculum. These habits must make worthless a vast amount of the industry lavished on all subjects which presuppose at least a moderate reading ability. I shall offer evidence, in plenty, that passages of ordinary everyday prose of no unusual difficulty whatever, needing no special information or training or any experience which is not commonly assumed to be inevitable, were wildly and inexplicably misread, not by a few stray souls from India who may have been in the audience, but by so many seemingly qualified persons that we can assume no one to be exempt from such aberrations.

The conditions, of course, under which the protocols were written need to be carefully considered. I issued the passages upon which comments were invited at the beginning of the hour, after a few, usually very few, remarks indicating the sort of discussion I hoped for. The time allowed varied from 20 minutes to as much sometimes as 45 minutes. So far as possible the examination mood was discouraged. The writers were anonymous, free to write or not as they pleased, no marks were to be awarded and as much informality as so large a crowd permitted was maintained. I could observe from my desk a little quiet whispered consultation and collaboration here and there, and could follow the general progress of the work. There was no frenzied scribbling against time and no strain beyond the normal tension of meditation. Not until a large majority seemed to have satisfied themselves that they had said what they found to say did I apply a closure and take up again my share of what was felt, I believe, to be a co-operative inquiry.

This absence of hurry and of the task-slave's mood should be stressed. It very much affects what may be inferred from the protocols. In general it would be absurd, and we should be showing ourselves stupidly blind to the complexities of the situation, if we concluded from stray sentences in a protocol, which seem to have nothing whatever to do with anything that can legitimately be taken to be in the passage commented upon, that the writer had really been as erratic in his reading as his sentences suggest. People called upon in a hurry to say something, must not rashly be supposed to have really meant what they said. Only when we are so fortunate as to have been able to think before we speak or write are we strictly chargeable with what we say. And it would be ridiculous, and a waste of everyone's time, to consider closely, as a product of erratic thinking, what is merely a train of word-works going off at random against a background of blank obfuscation. But here time for reflection, for re-reading, and for correction was afforded, and, to the best of my observation, was used by almost all for this purpose.

As the basis for the first experiment I chose two passages from Mr Biaggini's *English in Australia*, pp. 45-7 and 59-60, an admirable book in general and a highly relevant document in this inquiry. I had and have some hesitation in using this passage here. It is a page at which Mr Biaggini's passionate concern for standards of judgment has, I believe, betrayed him, and as such it may give a misleading impression of his work as a whole. But, as a slip of the kind that every teacher and every critic must expect to make, I felt that its educative possibilities were too great to be forgone, and I hope that he will forgive me for lending it such accidental prominence.

## EXERCISE ONE

Read the following and comment on the second passage as a criticism of the first.

'Love! Love! Love! How beauteous the very word! Not carnal love but the divine presence. What is Love? It is the rainbow that stands out, in all its glorious many-coloured hues, illuminating and making glad again the dark clouds of life. It is the morning and the evening star, that in glad refulgence, there on the awed horizon, call Nature's hearts to an uplifted rejoicing in God's marvellous firmament! Round about the cradle of the babe, sleeping so quietly while o'er him hangs in almost agonized adoration his loving mother, shines the miracle of Love, and at the last sad end comforting the hearts that bear its immortal permanence, round even the quiet tomb, shines Love.

'Oh, do you not sometimes hear, stealing o'er the plains at dawn, coming as it were from some far distant secret place, a sound of melody? When listening to Holy Music do you not seem sometimes to catch the distant rustle of the wings of cherubim? And what is music, lovely, lovely music, what is fair melody? Ah, music, 'tis the voice of Love! Ah, 'tis the magician that makes right royal kings out of plain folks like us! 'Tis the perfume of the wondrous flower, 'tis the strength of the athlete, strong and mighty to endure 'mid the heat and dust of the valorous conquest. Ah, Love, Love, Love! Without it we are less than beasts; with it, earth is heaven and we are as the gods!'

To save students from being bamboozled by specious writers, I make it a point to tell them to examine the simple sense of what is stated in a passage, as those of them without original sensibility and a sense of logic live in a world as full of pitfalls as Christian himself did; and how easily they are deceived is apparent from the evidence.

Those that applied the instruction here would have discovered some remarkable things. Love, for example, is no less than five incompatible things—a rainbow, the morning star, the evening star, a miracle which shines around the cradle of the babe, and something which shines round the quiet tomb. Music is equally remarkable, although it is only four in one—the voice of love, a magician who makes humble people kings, the perfume of the flower, and the strength of the athlete. Worse nonsense than this is difficult to conceive; it is much as if one argued that a motor-car was a bag of potatoes, a hollyhock, a flying cloud, and the sound of the sea. I should apologize, perhaps, for treating inanity so seriously, but my chief purpose in this book is to demonstrate rather than to express unsupported opinion; and, if we are to know how the masses (rich and poor) think, we have to realize that a statement to the effect that love and music are both several incompatible things is what, to many, and perhaps the majority of people, passes for a satisfactory statement.

The first two paragraphs are a passage from *Elmer Gantry* in which Mr Sinclair Lewis is caricaturing Gantry's florid appeal and unscrupulous emotionality. Then comes Mr Biaggini's comment on it, written in the heat of his discovery that Gantry, set as a test in discrimination, was still capable of winning the allegiance of his pupils.

For my purposes the main reasons for choosing these two passages to open the course were as follows. They would, I hoped, without any prompting, raise the general question of the kinds of ends in discourse (the divisions of the language functions) in a wide and searching fashion; and show what current opinion is upon this, and what current assumptions can do with it. Secondly, they would do the same with a wide variety of prejudices and commonplaces about metaphor. Thirdly, a problem in critical justice—even for the worst criminals—was offered which might, I thought, suggest both the difficulty of, and the need for, dispassionate reflection and perhaps serve later as a convenient reminder. Fourthly, I followed a theory that the best way to set our minds to work on critical questions is to give them *a passage and a comment upon it together*—not a mere bare specimen of writing by itself. This is the natural, the conversational, cue for discussion. It is a more complex cue—which does not mean that it will be harder to interpret—and it is more provoking. These advantages have long been recognized in the questions set in examinations such as the English Tripos, which do not ask a 'plain question' but offer some critic's opinion for application and comment. By so doing we overcome, in part, that blank negative feeling of limitless freedom, with no obvious starting points, which is the source of so many vagaries. We can also sometimes enlist the aid of that hunter's impulse which is such a dangerous drive, as a rule, in criticism, and yet by supplying an outlet prevent it from wrecking, as it too often does, the whole undertaking.

As to the two principal aims—the exhibition in practice of current notions about the *language functions* and about *metaphor*—the protocols do, I believe, show us, as clearly as we can expect, what happens. But I shall begin with the problem in justice—Was Mr Biaggini's comment fair?—since this is where most of the protocol-writers began. Their wrestlings with further problems were usually attempts to find the reasons for their decision. As we shall see, points

about the varied uses of language and points about metaphor were
not easily separated. Indeed to awaken a power of distinguishing
between these two different though connected sets of questions,
and thus to prevent, as far as we can, confusion between them, is a
simple and definite aim that the teacher may set himself.

In putting together these selections from the protocols, the first
evident danger I have to guard against (and the teacher equally who
makes, on a smaller scale, a parallel display in class) is that they may
create merely a vast blurred dim impression of confusion, a formless
hubbub of conflicting voices. The derivative, and worse, danger is
that in attempting to arrange my exhibits in distinct divisions, I
shall impose more order than my evidence will support. To note
both risks may help a little: to remember them always would be
the only remedy.

If we stand back, for still a moment, to consider yet again what
it is that we are trying to examine, compare and understand, that
may help too. These scraps of scribble are no more than faint and
imperfect indications—distant and distorted rumours—of the fleeting processes of interpretation we are trying to study. They are
never to be read *by the letter* (another of the tired pedogogue's
besetting sins); they do not tell their own story; they are mere clues
for us to place and interpret in *our* turn. What they indicate are
phases, moments, slices or sections—abstractly [1] registered and perpetuated for our inspection—of processes which were on their way
before the pen walked on the paper, processes which went on in
semi-independence while it walked and afterwards. We have to
remember, unless we are to forget all that we have to teach, that
what the writer meant is not to be simply equated with what he
*wrote*. We shall find the variety of the views suggested very great
and we have to decide continually whether we are dealing with different views or merely with different ways of uttering similar views.
As we ponder our choices here we are reflecting *pari passu* upon

[1] It may be of assistance to consider the case of anatomy, which is in some ways
parallel. The biologist is concerned with the life of the whole organism, that is, with
a process in space-time. Anatomical specimens give him at best spatial configurations
of moments in the process. Thus, though, in one pair of uses of those confusing
terms, a pickled specimen may seem a highly *concrete* object in comparison with the
creature's way of living; it is, in a more reflective sense, an *abstraction* from the
concrete object of biological study. Similarly a recorded opinion is an abstraction
from the process of thinking which we have to study.

two topics—the variety of the ways of thought and the variety of the modes in which any one of them may be expressed. We have to hit a balance in our apportionment between these two sources of literal diversity.

The same set of difficulties would come up for anyone writing, say, a critical history of Scholasticism. Just where did Aquinas and Scotus differ in view and where only in phraseology? Our problems with the protocols are both easier and harder. Easier because the level or quality of the thought we are studying is more familiar to us. Harder because the thought is vaguer and less disciplined in itself. The comparison of the protocol scribbles with the most arduous pages of philosophy may at first sight seem absurd, but not after closer examination. Thought is not a prerogative of great thinkers. We use or abuse it whenever we give a meaning to a sentence. Embryonic thought is not very different from the most developed. We shall indeed find the protocol writers needlessly tiresome unless we see in their still largely inchoate divisions the incipient foreshadowings of those differences in outlook and assumption from which all the movement, dialectic and drama of unfolding human consciousness derive.

The first section of my exhibit, however, displays only types and samples of the problems as far as they concern Simple Sense. Closer studies of some of them come later; the Analytic Contents will help to make the plot clearer.

### JUSTICE

Was Mr Biaggini's comment fair? Most readers decided that it was not, and their reasons are what we have to study.

First may come those who held that he mistook (unwittingly) the nature or purpose of the passage. Citations with an asterisk are complete comments, and I have left spelling and punctuation as I found it.

1.1.* There is not much use in examining 'the simple sense of what is stated in a passage' if the passage does not set out to make a statement—is not intended to have 'sense' in the strict meaning of the word. There is no reason why love should not, in a series of metaphors, be compared to five different things. These metaphors are not statements of *fact* about love. And the different things to which love is compared are not incompatible. The fact that the sun is like a round yellow plate does not prevent it from being also like a furnace.

'As if one argued that a motor car was a bag of potatoes' etc.—the writer of passage I is not *arguing* or *stating,* he is making a series of emotive utterances valuable, if at all, only as feeling. This kind of criticism is therefore beside the mark. That all this about love and music is rubbish is no doubt quite true, but for other reasons than the ones alleged.

As for 'demonstrating rather than expressing unsupported opinion,' the critic does not even begin to do so. He simply says that the five things with which love is compared are incompatible and leaves it at that. He does not begin to examine the validity of any single one of the comparisons—to see whether it makes the desired emotional impression.

As to the demonstration point, this reader has missed the phrase 'in this book' which widens the scope of Mr Biaggini's remarks.

1.11.* The critic is subjecting his text to tests which the author never intended it to stand. He is studying it as a statement of fact in which every connection must be scientifically true, verifiable by the happenings of everyday life; whereas the author intended it as a myth.

The passage is not nonsense, though it may not be common sense; that is, it is possible to explain and elucidate the connection of ideas, though not in terms of scientific truth. It is not 'much as if one argued that a motor car was a bag of potatoes etc. etc.'; for the author is not 'arguing' anything.

In his last sentence it is the critic himself who is deliberately bamboozling, by using an ambiguous term 'satisfactory statement.' Nobody, except one whom many, perhaps the majority of people, would call insane, would accept the first passage as a 'satisfactory statement' *in the sense in which the critic here uses the words.*

I have begun with two very straightforward and intelligent comments. If all the writers were at this level and could state their opinions with this clarity, there might be no occasion for inquiry. Alas it is not so! Even here however the phrase 'a series of emotive utterances valuable, if at all, only as feeling' and the reference to 'myth' rather conceal than elucidate difficult questions. They may, I hope, cover useful points, but they may be *vacua.* We shall be returning to them.

Similar accusations were brought by many. Here is one which better shows the wilder possibilities of the problem:

1.12. The insistance on 'simple sense,' which is not defined, seems to mean phrases taken in as literal a way as possible. The man ignores the possibility that in a non-logical sense, Love might equally well be identified with morning star, rainbow etc. (though it is *not* done in the passage he is commenting on). His own 'as if one argued' seems to give the clue: he is 'arguing,' whereas the (successful) poet—or writer—would not be. He would be creating the identification. The comments he makes as a result don't seem particularly helpful. He is saying something quite obvious in one sense and equally questionable in another. His use of 'statement' in the last sentence seems to me to show that he is not clear what he is trying to say about passage A.

*Identification* is always a difficult word to interpret. Two things when identified cease in some respect to be two. This is a summary reference to deep parts of the theory of metaphor in which there is a wide choice of doctrines. (See Chapter VIII, p. 121.)

1.13.* The critic is doing what is known to journalists as 'debunking,' and he seems at first sight to carry the day. It is not until one begins to examine his criticism that certain gross errors are discovered. He 'makes it a point' to ask students to examine 'the simple sense of what is stated in a passage.' Good. But he makes no attempt to define what he means by simple sense. Later we find that here at least it means 'dictionary sense,' and we are told that the writer of the extravagant passage on Love and Music says that 'Love is a rainbow' etc. He does not. The tone of the passage tells us that it is going to be metaphorical—he *compares* love to the rainbow etc. And a rainbow, the morning and evening star, etc. are not such *incompatible* things.

'Dictionary Sense' here is fairly plainly what a word has *when it is a name*—the Dictionary being taken to be the book which tells us of what things, acts, processes, events . . . a word is the name. This is a simplification, for the questions 'What are Names?' and 'What does a Dictionary do?' are full of tricks. However the writer makes his point here well enough.

1.14. The writer is applying standards of logic to the criticism of 'poetic prose,' with the result that it is his own passage that is

inane. . . . He never gets down to considering the fundamental false-
ness or truth of the emotion expressed in the passage. His sense of
logic is outraged and that is enough. He does not understand that the
'simple sense' of a passage is not always easy to perceive.

Just how an emotion may be fundamentally false or true, and
what are the limitations to the permissible application of the standards of logic are here the questions to raise. It might be, for example,
that logic here was not inapplicable but merely misapplied.

And what sort of thing is the 'simple sense' here? Has such a
passage as this a 'simple sense' at all? Or rather, shall we so define
the phrase, 'simple sense,' that the passage must have one, good or
bad? On these points a number of alternative assumptions appeared:

    1.15.* In his impatience (with which one sympathizes) the critic
has treated two different uses of language as the same. The statement,
'Love is the evening star etc.' is fairly obviously not of the same kind
as 'A motor car is a bag of potatoes.' The first writer is not really
saying anything about Love at all, but building up, for the right
reader, an attitude of vague emotional warmth. And the critic, objecting to this attitude, has fallen into the trap of treating the passage
as scientific prose. He might however have concluded something from
the fact that the imagery is unrealized, and that the separate metaphors
have little or no interaction with one another.

*Unrealized* is a word worth attention. It is one of those blanks
which are frequent enough in criticism—they may mean much or
little or nothing. The teacher's business is to guess at and help
forward whatever may be stirring, unexpressed, behind them. Here
there may be a lot, as the rest of the sentence indicates.

But the main interest of the comment is in the suggestion that
a passage can say nothing, and have no sense, without therefore
being entirely empty; that it can be approached like a stove, which
does not have to tell us about therms to warm us.

    1.151.* In the first place it seems illogical to apply a logical method
to a passage of a kind which would appear to be an attempt through
the medium of the emotive power of words to express the inexpressible. For the majority of people there is no necessity for such a
logical sequence as is here suggested and they find no inconvenience
in the apparent incompatibility of the symbols employed. The rhythm
of the passage is evocative of these feelings to which it is impossible

to give expression. For the writer Love and the word 'Love' were beauteous and he attempts to give us a feeling of beauty by conjuring up in a natural sequence objects of beauty—rainbow, clouds, stars, horizon, birth, life, death, dawn—all pervaded by an air of mystery which adheres to the intangible and indefinable.

Where are we now? The clarity of our earlier extracts is gone. This is a far more typical comment, and harder to handle fairly. We need, say, Socrates' description of the Sophists to remind us that we have to see, if we can, what the writer means, not merely have our fun with his words. It is no use ejaculating, 'Objects of *beauty*— birth, death!—express the inexpressible!' Not so. There are other things to note. Whatever *we* may think of the example, it has, for *him,* brought up, out of the depths, an ambiguity in 'utter' or 'express,' on which, for everyone, at one point or another, our conception and use of language must turn. But by 'inexpressible' he may, in part, be denying that the passage had any simple sense—or any simple sense which included something said about love.

1.152. It is not a statement at all, at least, not about Love and Music.

Instead of being a statement, and so having a sense, it is assumed to work by an 'emotive' and 'evocative' power in its words, exercised partly through their rhythm but more, as some pictures work, through the things they represent ('conjuring up in a natural sequence objects of beauty') offering them for contemplation without 'saying' anything about them.

This analogy tends to overlook the variety and subtlety of the modes of presentation of objects by pictures, a matter that repays an investigation on parallel lines to the present inquiry. Current opinion and practice is even more confused about the place (places rather) of *representation* in art than about sense in speech. But though the language modes of painting afford a useful field for a corroborative parallel analysis, it must not be entered here. The conception, however, of writing as a mode of evoking pictures in the mind is directly relevant.

1.153. This author, as I see it, was illustrating 'How beauteous is the very word' and he attempted this end by a lengthy string of metaphors. This I believe to be a reputable device if each image adds to the vividness of the picture. Whether or not each image does this, I have not decided, but certainly I could conceive 'worse nonsense.'

Such a passage may have little value, but it is scarcely a 'pitfall.'
I wasn't 'bamboozled' at any rate.

This writer may himself be using his phrase 'the vividness of the
picture' metaphorically. The next is not.

1.154. As a criticism it treats too seriously something which would
be read as a piece of emotive writing and left as such. It takes no
account of the fact that it was written under great emotional stress,
describing a picture—at least in the author's mind—highly coloured
and belonging to a distinct type. Emotional and intellectual writings
can hardly be fairly lumped together and criticised by the same rather
hackneyed method. The author is entitled to write a description in
the words he considers will most nearly reproduce his state of mind
or experience.

Quite so; but the reader is entitled to make comments too. Among
them would be a query about the 'great emotional stress.' True that
the passage professes, by its manner, to be so uttered. But it is putting the cart before the horse to suppose that we know this 'fact'
otherwise than through what is uttered. An over-charitable readiness
to take the will for the deed betrays itself everywhere in this
comment. And where is 'a piece of emotive writing' left if we do
leave it as such? In a mental picture gallery? If so, it would be not
surprising that it is treated as necessarily immune from criticism,
since no one man's private mental pictures are often at all like
another's.[1]

The 'rather hackneyed method' I take to be the aggressive literal-
ism.

[1] Nearly all readers are keenly interested in this problem of the place of mental
pictures and other imagery in reading, and many teachers make a practice of drawing attention to individual imaging. If we do not leave the matter there—but insist
a little upon the inevitable differences between readers, pointing out that imagery
in itself is *not* the meaning, and has no authority that it does not derive from the
meaning—this approach may be helpful. It may be made an excellent way of
directing attention to more important aspects of meaning. Exercises for this purpose
are easily devised. Moreover, from this we can go on to point out the unfortunate
ambiguity of the word 'image' (visual image and figure of speech) and therewith
pass over conveniently into the study of metaphor. It is important to discourage
*early* the identification of imagery with meaning, for this is one of the strongholds
of that crude associationism—natural to all early reflection—which prevents, so often,
any helpful self-critical meditation on interpretations. See *The Philosophy of Rhetoric*,
Lectures I and II; and pp. 86-7, 101, 117, 124 below.

Others took a middle view on the question of 'simple sense' and, not assuming that the passage was without sense, split the sense off as a quasi-independent, adventitious and subordinate part:

> 1.16. To examine the simple sense of a passage is to say that prose is, simply and solely, a medium by which actions, thoughts or instruction can be conveyed to the reader. It allows nothing further. With simple narrative prose, this idea is perhaps quite correct, but in a passage like this, when the sense is not the most important thing, why look for it? The writer has been carried away by his emotion and is endeavouring, without great success, to express his emotions by copious images and illustrations. Surely the writer of prose is allowed the use of images and of the other technical ways which the poet uses to such effect? This is not commending the qualities of the piece, but deploring a lack of sensibility in the critic. In the piece itself the adjectives are laboured and the style artificial, but why look merely for sense in a passage which is obviously primarily emotional and essentially an attempt at the decorative.

The stiffness, lack of articulation, and disorder of the first sentences here is something with which every teacher is too familiar. Usually the writer knows that something is wrong, that he has not said what he thought, but he cannot see how to put things right. He has still too little access to his own notions; he has had too little exercise in separating them from his words. To help him in this is one of the tasks of Grammar.

'Why look for the sense?' We may reply, 'Have you got it already? Is it perhaps in your hand? And does the rest of the effect of the words turn on it or not?'

> 1.161. The critic quite evidently begins with the assumption that 'the simple sense of what is stated in a passage' is the most important element in it. He appears to make no distinction between passages dealing with scientific fact, and those which are concerned with imaginative ideas. It so happens that the particular passage with which he is concerned consists largely of imagery written down in what may loosely be called 'terms of fact.' He chooses to regard the various ways in which 'Love' and 'Music' are described as so many definitions of these words, and concludes that the passage is nonsense, since the definitions do not coincide.

'Imaginative ideas' and 'imagery written down in terms of fact' here give a deceiving impression of precision. There is the usual trouble of the ambiguity of 'image' (figure of speech, mental picture, metaphoric linkage, speculative venture etc.). And perhaps what he is saying with them is not very different from what others would say by means of terms like 'emotive' or 'evocative.' The use of the word *definition* is worth notice. It is near to the 'Dictionary meaning' we met with above. We shall see later that there is hardly another word about which more difficulties currently arise. *Coincide* here seems to mean 'articulate as do Dictionary definitions.'

References to imagination were frequent:

> 1.162. It is a pity that the two paragraphs of romanticism should be judged by one whose attitude is so relentlessly unsympathetic. The realist makes no attempt to appreciate the imagination of the writer he criticises.

The perfect hostess surely!

> 1.163. To appreciate a literary effect, one must feel as the writer felt when he composed it. Obviously the first passage is a highly emotional purple patch in which the author has worked himself up to a pitch of feverish imagination, and to appreciate it, or at least to do it justice, the critic in the second passage should have at least used his imagination—if it were possible judging from his criticism. Instead of that, however, he criticises it from a purely mundane point of view. . . . Of course, two people looking at an object from different angles, see the object in different settings which holds in the case of the passage and the criticism as well. The criticism is thus unfair because the critic does not see eye to eye with the author.

This writer is 'at least' indignant. Would he otherwise have failed to notice and feel uneasy about the enormous implications of his last sentence? He teams up with 1.154.

> 1.164.* It is rather unfair to criticise a flowing piece of rhetoric as if it were trying to be a logical argument, and to treat an orator's expressions of love and music as if they were definitions in the Oxford dictionary. When a prose writer uses similes he must be treated with a certain amount of imagination.

Very often a turn of phrase tells us more about the commentator's view than what he professes to be saying. 'An orator's expressions of love and music' has a tranquil slovenliness, an easy-going ineptitude that shows us how shallow the writer's 'commonsense' thought has been. This is a complete comment. I wish I could reproduce the neat round script and the green ink in which it is written. I may take this opportunity of remarking upon the invaluable sidelights often thrown by the handwriting of the comments. Typescript may be a rest to the teacher's eyes, but so is a fog-bank.

> 1.165. The critic seems to be utterly devoid of anything like imagination. If literature were to be without the quality of imagination and rhetoric, it will be merely a shopkeeper's account book, containing statements of plain facts. . . . The critic who condemns the passage does not seem to appreciate love and music to the extent that we expect a normally healthy and intelligent human being to appreciate. Otherwise he would not have tried to ridicule natural emotional outburst.

The syntax and the omission of an article will make us suspect perhaps an Indian or Chinese writer. But others brought the same charge and offered various explanations for the lack of imagination:

> 1.166.* This passage is obviously written by a man who is either a sceptic or completely insensible to the music of words. He has not adequately conceived the passage in its true setting and context. His bare statement at the end, which may appeal to an academic few, would not, I think, appeal nearly so strongly to the masses both rich and poor. He pours scorn on the very vivid imagery of the first passage, which may be of a rather oratorical nature, and tries to ridicule it by exposure. I do not consider that the opinions, as expressed in passage I, are really unsupported; the whole imagery in the first passage hangs together quite suitably. The fact of 'being bamboozled by specious writers' is surely one of the delights of literature for most readers. The second writer is obviously only too interested in literature that is informative, and not imaginative; whilst the first writer tries to capture the rapture of love and music by his words.

This amateur of 'the music of words' perhaps writes 'poor. He pours' and 'capture the rapture' to illustrate his taste, as he illumines his conception of scepticism by his use of 'bamboozled.'

> 1.167. In disagreeing with the writer of the second passage one immediately lays one's-self open to the charge of being one of 'the masses (rich and poor).' But at the risk of this—and the risk is all the more apparent when one considers the amorous inanities of the present day song-ballads—I cannot agree with the writer's sweeping

aversion for simile and comparison. Perhaps the poor fellow was never in love himself—the which would explain his outburst as partly ignorance, partly envy. . . . And as it is obvious by the 'motor car' passage that the author has no eye for anything but colourless and prosaic objects, we will leave him to stew in his own juice until he finds love.

Amorous inanities indeed!—and nearer home than in the song-ballads!

1.17. Critic is attacking the abuse of metaphor and its acceptance by 'the majority of people.' If however, the simple sense of what is stated in a passage were to be the only consideration metaphor surely would be impossible.

He has ignored the fact that the writer, rightly or wrongly, being in a certain state of emotion, has allowed his imagination to lead him into an atmosphere or place where we cannot follow him.

Must not the credit that would thus accrue to the lost writer therefore remain doubtful?

In the first paragraph here, we meet again a snarled cross-thread that is often a main lead in this tangle—the equation or identification of 'the simple sense' with 'the literal sense.' It seems evident enough that a metaphorical phrase, e.g. 'the legs of the table,' may have a simple sense that is not the literal sense. No one doubts this if the question is put by itself, but in the distractions of critical debate it is easy to neglect a distinction which is not so much forgotten as covered over by the coils of other interests. And to illustrate this confusion between sense and letter was a prime purpose of this exercise. It is important. If we confuse the sense with the letter [1] we lose sight of what should be thought of and innumerable cross-purposes and complications ensue. To prevent this blundering what is needed is probably practice in interpretation with material (such as the passages used in this experiment) which will show our errors to us clearly, rather than elaborate theoretical dissections. These have their place however, which is in the background and will be visited later.

[1] Compare pp. 135-9 below. The notion 'literal sense' when closely examined will be found to be itself greatly in need of clarification. Metaphor is mounted upon metaphor, wheel within wheel in language. What is literal for the purposes of one examination is metaphoric for another.

The confusion and the struggle to amend it are well shown in the following:

> 1.171.* The first writer, in a lyrical outburst, has not expressed himself accurately enough and thus has given his opponent an opportunity to make fun of his statement. The first writer *does* actually say that Love *is* a rainbow, the morning star, the evening star etc., whereas he really *means* that Love is revealed in these things. On this point the critic censures him justly for not meaning what he says. The critic, however, seems to go too far; his analogy of the motor car and the bag of potatoes applies as little as most analogy: the first writer was enumerating the qualities of Love rather than defining it. But on the whole the criticism is just; the *simple sense* of what is stated in this passage is nonsense.

The ambiguities of 'say' (sounds or shapes uttered—meaning normally given to them in most contexts—meaning specially given through some abnormality in the context) could hardly be better illustrated. So too, the ambiguities of 'is' (some of which follow 'say'). In his tussle with these, the commentator loses sight, I think, of his critic, and makes him do mainly what he finds himself doing. All the general features of this comment deserve the closest and most sustained attention. The principal procedures of misinterpretation are evident in them. What may be meant by 'accurately enough' we will study in Chapter IX. (See 'definite,' Sense VIII, p. 154.) And what is being discussed in the remarks on analogy and defining is a topic the Logic Section must tackle.

In the end, the writer does identify *simple sense* with literal reading, and concludes that it is nonsense.

Others, taking the simple sense to be carried by the metaphor, decided that it had been missed:

> 1.172. I am *not* full of admiration for the second passage as a criticism of the first. While it is obvious that the author of statement 1 has 'spread himself' rather more than 'good taste' demands, yet author no. 2 has entirely forgotten that 'love' and 'music' are things which naturally admit of this. I consider that author no. 1 has hit upon a number of most happy metaphors—love *is* comparable with his five, so called, incompatible things. The critic in his anxiety 'to boil everything down' has ignored the true sense. He is so anxious to make his crack about motor cars and bags of potatoes that he fails to

realise that love and music can be all these things the author of 1 claims for them.

As to what the simple sense, that has been missed or ignored, would be (and whether it would be simple) there was difference of opinion:

1.173. The critic in the second passage lays entire emphasis on the lack of sense throughout the first. It does not seem necessary for him to use the phrase 'simple sense'; unless he were to make a distinction between simple and complex sense. Complex sense the passage criticised might indeed contain [Present arms!], but would it then be sense? . . . [As you were!] Such a passage would not pass as a satisfactory statement to most people. It would give them probably what they would call 'just an impression,' like the blurred lines of two photographs which have been, by some slip of the camera, confused together.

1.1731. If we examine the 'simple sense' in the literal way applied in passage 2, we do indeed discover some remarkable things about Love and Music, but surely the first passage is nothing more than a lyrical outburst equivalent to 'Ain't Love Grand!' and 'I like Music.'

This seems, though, an even more drastic process of 'boiling everything down.' (1.172.)
So is this:

1.1732. The first passage is unusual and possibly distasteful to educated people. It makes the statement that Love adds to the bright side of life. The writer of passage No. 2 has completely failed.

Against such extreme simplicities we may set this, in which again the sense seems in danger of evaporating into airy nothing:

1.174. With all his solicitude for the integrity of his student's logic and sensibility, the writer of the second passage is a greater offender than the rhetorical rhapsodist of the first. The first, at any rate, has no pretensions and no schema; he rants as he will. But the second (presumably a schoolmaster or a professor) has been captured by the suasive attractions of clear, consistent, logical and 'punctuated' thought; and his standards and conclusions are indeed specious. What he insists on discovering—the 'simple sense' of the passage—he has no conception of, for the simple sense of a metaphorical passage such as this (and of all such, including those far superior to this forced ecstatic paragraph) can never consist in the meanings of the various words and phrases. The writer of the first is more successful: he uses a rapid and vague series of figures and tropes which he is persuaded will be effective—in fact, their power has been tested long before his use of them, for they are the stock in trade of all such writers. . . . The second is 'analytical' etc. etc.—he uses words like 'bamboozled' to declare his unrhetorical and unhampered method of criticism. But he misses the point completely, for the phrases in passage 1 are not incompatible, since they are never on the level of discourse in which ideas are compatible or incompatible. A motor car is not a bag of potatoes, nor a hollyhock, but its 'not being so' is not the same as Love's 'not being' a rainbow: Love may be a rainbow for the purposes of a writer of the first type, and his readers will never stop to question it, for metaphors and similes are alike, to them, a pleasant flow of vaguenesses, and substitutes for the reality of Love, which is something quite else. The iconoclastic critic . . . reveals a gravely limited perception of what un-sensible and unlogical literature *can* be made to do.

With this subtle and penetrating analysis this first section of my exhibit might come to an end. But I will add, in side-cases, a few further specimens.

1.18. The object of the first piece is clearly to induce a certain pleasant, if morbid, state of emotion in a sentimental and miseducated section of the population and, judging by the resemblance of its phraseology to that of the more egregious film-captions, it might easily succeed.

The style of the second is certainly suitable as a criticism of this or anything—for since it is (besides being obviously recognisable) that appropriate to thoughtful and dispassionate inquiry it leaves the reader inclined to consider and judge rather than to accept unquestioningly.

I have no clue to the 'recognisable' point. If we could still be surprised, we might well be here by this conception of a 'dispassionate' style.

Sincerity doctrines, as usual, produced some queer comments:

1.181. If a writer has an idea of Love as five different things, and if he feels sincerely, there is all the truth in his statement that can be demanded. The scientific truth of his writing must not be considered, but only the sincerity and value of his feelings and the quality of his expression. If a man sincerely and passionately feels that a motor car is a bag of potatoes or hollyhock etc., there is truth in his statement that it is these things.

A reference to asylums would be but a controversial trick here. Probably this is primarily a revolt against the stern limitations proposed by Mr Biaggini's comment. But teachers have ample occasion to note how obstinate and frustrating such ardent muddling can be, and how much it may prevent the development both of intelligence and of feeling. It defeats the very causes that it professes to support, blurring discriminations that are urgently needed, and precluding the free play of 'the sunshine comparative power.' With it goes a contemptuous attitude towards every mode of thought that can be labelled 'logical'—which may be *excused* but is not to be justified by the trivial conceptions of logic displayed by some 'logical' writers.

1.182. The 'sense of logic' would scarcely help in an investigation of the nature of Love or Music.

But apart from an adequate method (which may as well be called Logic) no investigation of anything is possible. Those who misuse the logical manner have thus a heavier responsibility than they are aware of. To simple minds they discredit not merely *bad* logic but thought itself.

More often than we know our opinions are due to excessive reactions against opposed opinions which are equally inadequate. Error causes error in our pendulous minds. Several of the commentators averred that Mr Biaggini's remarks induced in them an unexpected sympathy with Gantry:

1.19. Though the total effect of the first passage was one of nausea, the second passage, in attempting to detract from it, in its strongest point, had the unfortunate effect, from the writer's point of view, of making me more in sympathy with it. This superior summary criticism has a want of logic rather surprising considering the demands it makes on the first passage.

It will be only fair then to supply an opportunity for prejudice to swing back again:

1.191. The 2nd passage is in the strictest sense impertinent. It has reference to an entirely different sphere of discourse (and that entirely apart from the faults of the 1st—certainly worlds distant from the positive content of the 1st). When a Mahommedan prostrates himself in the dust, we might expect the author of the 2nd to say 'He will probably get his face dirty.' It is obviously an inadequate, incom-

mensurate, impertinent comment. It is half-witted because the author
has by certain ingrained dogmas come to deny the existence of one
half of his mind. That is perhaps the 'meaning' of the one-eyed
cyclops. They could perceive a finite object but permanently blinked
an eye at infinite awareness. It is when an infinite and a finite meet
that mysticism is born and humour (as Coleridge notes of Tristram
Shandy). Love is such an ultimate and rightly produces wonder when
perceived informing the finite. But unless Love is taken as infinite the
passage is seen in the light of the author of the second.

Better than this, we may think sadly, would be even a wholehearted
devotion to these scorned methods of detraction. For they are discussable, their error is corrigible and inquiry into them is instructive.
But this opposite flight, I fear, cannot be studied with much profit.

To round off the documentation on the 'Justice' aspect of the
experiment, I should add that several members of the jury thought
Mr Biaggini too mild:

> 1.192. The author of the criticism is certainly too serious in his
> comments on this love-sick piece of prose: his criticism is too gentle-
> manly even to disturb the distant rustle of the wings of the Cherubims,
> which haunt the Holy Music. His sense of humour is kept chained
> up except for a few flying bolts. Surely nonsense is too pleasant a word
> for such a piece of writing? The English Language hardly possesses
> a word to qualify such 'utter rot.' The five incompatible things are
> fantastic enough in themselves, but when music is said to be the
> perfume of flowers—

Others held that he was 'deliberately side-tracking the issue . . .
and taking the easiest way of damaging the passage,' 'fastening on
the quickest and most obvious line of attack' or 'having the shortest
and cheapest cut' at something which did not deserve fairer treatment.

Another, that he was afraid of the first passage:

> 1.193. He shows a curious kind of fear of I. Why shouldn't readers
> be bamboozled? If a writer succeeds in making readers forget 'original
> sensibility and a sense of logic' he has succeeded in what he aimed to
> do—if he can be said to have aimed at all.

Finally, since an undue number of my citations have been from
the more intelligible layers of the protocols, and as a reminder and

forecast of the more desperate tasks that await a theory of interpretation, let me add:

1.195. 1st passage is a piece of poetic prose in adulation of Love, creating effect by cadence, rhythm, and diverse imagery.

2nd passage makes no attempt to analyse or value this, but attempts to point out the effect it will have upon the minds of the majority. The critic singles out the characteristic of imagery for special treatment and demonstrates that many people are unable to perceive any likeness of essence or single characteristic in several diverse objects. He ends by saying that their incompatibility is insurmountable for the majority of people—but does this mean that he asserts that a quality is not there for a few because there are many that cannot perceive it? Can he prove that the writer whom he criticises was not aware that many would condemn his prose, or that it was not written for the few.

Not that this would be an ideal state, but the writer might have been aware of the limitation of his appeal.

If we could guess what this wrong-headedness came from we should be well on our way! The writer is utterly at a loss with a set of sentences hardly more difficult to construe than the simplest with which we might attempt to approach and help him. He is not alone, he represents a larger proportion than it is pleasant to observe. But I am postponing exemplification and discussion of this large scale ineptitude in the apprehension of arguments until later.

# *Chapter Two:* The Scope of Metaphor

> *Unless we take care to clear the first principles of knowledge, from the embarrass and delusion of words, we may make infinite reasonings upon them to no purpose: we may draw consequences from consequences and be never the wiser. The further we go, we shall only lose ourselves the more irrecoverably, and be the deeper entangled in difficulties and mistakes. Whoever therefore designs to read the following sheets, I entreat him to make my words the occasion for his own thinking, and endeavour to attain the same train of thoughts in reading, that I had in writing them. By this means it will be easy for him to discover the truth or falsity of what I say.* BERKELEY

Thus far I have illustrated chiefly opinions and assumptions as to the division of the language functions, the diverse aims for which language may be used. I have omitted the most curious and the most enlightening products of the venture—the attempts to grapple in detail with the suggested parallel between Love's relation to the rainbow and a motor-car's relation to a hollyhock. These take us deep down into the theory of metaphor, and the writers' wanderings in this dim subterrene realm are to me the most interesting part of what this experiment has to offer. They are also a much sharper challenge to our ability to follow them. Inadequate though such terms as 'emotive,' 'evocative,' 'imaginative,' 'lyrical,' 'poetic,' 'statement,' 'simple sense,' 'expression' . , . be as a means for indicating differences in the uses of language, they are clear and precise and their ambiguities are well understood in comparison with the terms of art which, the protocols show, are most likely to be introduced in discussing these parallels.

Suspecting that the 'Justice aspect' in the first experiment would be a powerful and distorting distraction, I followed it up quickly with an exercise in the translation of metaphors in which a comparison was invited between an elaborately metaphoric passage and a translation into 'direct language' which claims to be clearer and more definite. (See Exercise Two.) This brought up again, by the way in which it was presented, the questions about the language functions that we have been watching. The same tendencies appeared again to treat metaphor as *only* appropriate in writing that endeavours to move rather than to state, or as appropriate only in the degree to which the arousal of feeling is the aim. And the same disabling lack of clear terms in which to discuss the grounds, the modes, and the functions of metaphoric shifts and to compare parallels and analogies was still more evident. I was reminded of the agonies of strained attention that came when I was first invited, as a beginner in Philosophy, to contemplate and compare not things but the relations between them, and to observe differences not merely between relations but between the relations of relations to one another. What a struggle that was to distinguish between relations and what they related, between what I had been accustomed to call a relationship (relations being cousins and sisters-in-law) and relata! Those were moments when the effort to increase the span of abstract thought seemed almost to snap one's mind. And yet there was no difficulty in observing such relations in the concrete. I knew that if John was James's brother, James in turn was brother to John; but if John was James's grandson, James couldn't be John's grandson. I knew that 'A = B' ran like 'brother to,' and 'larger than' like 'grandfather to.' I knew that in kicking a football I did something to the football, but that in fearing a spider I did nothing to the spider; and that when I threw something, when I said something and when I saw something, my relations to whatever was thrown, said and seen were different. Like everyone else I used such knowledge all the time without staying to reflect that I had it or being aware at all of what it was that I had. Only when the effort to abstract once again the already abstracted—the operative principles of our normal awarenesses—is forced upon us by philosophy, do these convenient skills become a burden threatening giddiness and nescience. We can recognize the same strain in many of the struggles with metaphor that fill these pages. They are the same effort, the same return of the mind to take stock of its own powers and achievements. 'And alas!', as Coleridge said, 'the largest part of mankind are nowhere greater strangers than at home!'

The sameness of the effort explains why in what follows we shall seem so often to be circling back in merely novel phraseology about the same point. I complained above that the vocabulary available in discussing metaphors, analogies, parallels and comparisons is even worse—more confusing and more slippery—than that for distinguishing the language functions. But to say so may be misleading. This is no matter of a shortage or a vagrancy of terms, of gaps to be filled by a happy introduction of technicalities, of order to be restored by a little firm discipline, a regimentation of picked words with fixed meanings. Would it were! If *that* were all, it could soon be put right, as it always is, without trouble or delay, in new crafts, new techniques, new games, new branches of the sciences. We are never long without the useful handy word or the apt and steady record of the convenient distinction when once what it is wanted for has become clear and where no special factors or forces are preventing . . . what?

It is well to halt here with the sentence unfinished while we consider what we would be doing by completing it. 'Clarification?' 'Separation and fixed segregation of single meanings?' 'The crystallization of what is amorphous, indeterminate, variable, fluid, indefinite . . . into a distinct systematic structure of ordered thought?' However we finish the interrupted sentence, however we try to say what we need to say here, or however we describe the condition of the topic which is its difficulty, we find ourselves therein employing devices of metaphor and parallel, or introducing fictitious units and operations of thought to be treated by analogy with quite other matters. And however we try to avoid this seemingly awkward, unsatisfactory and regrettable 'accident,' we fail. We only substitute another metaphor—recognized as such or not—for the one we are eluding. There is no escape. What we are attempting to dispense with is no accident but the essence of thinking. Thinking is radically metaphoric. Linkage by analogy is its constituent law or principle, its causal nexus, since meaning only arises through the causal *contexts* [1] by which a sign stands for (takes the place of) an instance

---

[1] See *The Meaning of Meaning*, Chapter III, and *The Philosophy of Rhetoric*, Lecture II. To distinguish this sense of 'context' (the connections with past events which make $x$ a sign) from a 'literary context' (other signs $yz$ accompanying and co-operating with $x$) I shall write of literary contexts as 'settings.' The two are closely connected. Any group of signs, like a word or sentence, is artificially selected from its accompanying and preparatory sign-field. It is the sign-field which deter-

of a sort. To think of anything is to take it *as* of a sort (as a such and such) and that 'as' brings in (openly or in disguise) the analogy, the parallel, the metaphoric grapple or ground or grasp or draw by which alone the mind takes hold. It takes no hold if there is nothing for it to haul from, for its thinking is the haul, the attraction of likes.

I have made these metaphors here very evident—merely by putting less usual words for the semi-technical words we most employ. But, the same would appear to close inspection if I were to write instead about the theory of 'cognition' in terms of 'attention,' 'apprehension,' 'abstraction' and 'intellection.' An obvious misunderstanding is possible however. My point is *not* that language is full of metaphors, or even that, as Darmesteter wrote in *La Vie des Mots,* 'In none of the languages whose history it is possible for us to study is there an abstract word which, if its etymology is known, is not resolvable into a concrete word.' My point goes deeper, and these well-known characteristics of language are among its consequences. It is that thought is itself metaphoric—not merely that it expresses itself in linguistic metaphors. The metaphor that a thought is using need not correspond to the metaphor that its language displays, though it usually does, and the thought will often adopt the verbal metaphor when this is noticed. But equally often we discount and disown the metaphors in our speech, treat them as dead, or kill them as we go. We may then easily suppose that we are no longer using parallels and analogies because we are avoiding a particular set that our language might seem to bring in. We shall find none the less that we are using another set. *Our thought in all cases is being guided by its causal context;* and this is only another way of putting the matter.

Yet another way I used above when I wrote that all thought must take its object *as of a sort.* Nothing for the mind is a mere *it:* each thing is a *what:* the most unqualified, unrestricted *it* is merely a *what* of the extremest general sort. Its *what* is *how we think of it,* and *how we think of it* is not another question, except verbally, from *in* (or, *as of*) *which sort do we take it?* The classes, kinds or sorts by which we handle the things we think of are, otherwise described (and there is no superiority in one mode of description

mines interpretation. The multiplicity and interdependence of the meaning of words, so much insisted upon here, becomes obvious and necessary as soon as we conceive of interpretation in terms of sign-situations.

here over another that is equally intelligible), the parallels, analogies, recurrent togethernesses, contexts, or equivalent others with which we separate what we are taking from what we are not taking. And the vast apparatus of qualities, attributes, characters, relations, functions, orders, types, etc., etc. with which logic conducts its divisions and compares its distinctions is again nothing but yet other language in which the same sorting operations can be conducted, studied and checked. Most of the traditional squabbles in logic and epistemology are about precedence between different mixtures of these languages; though those who indulge in them and maintain them—being speakers of one logical language only—naturally enough often suppose them to be about nothing less than the foundations of the universe. (See Chapters XXI and XXII, below.) Neither the real ground nor this supposed bearing should be overlooked if we were inquiring into the causes of philosophical vehemence. Fortunately here we are not so concerned. But it is very much our business to persuade those who are temporarily adherents of one logical language that anything useful that they have to say may be said in several other languages as well. This persuasion is to be effected not through argument but through exercises in translation and the accompanying studies in comparison. Only so can the mind acquire the confidence to unstick itself from its formulations. Clinging is usually a sign of timidity if not of despair. The last few pages then may be taken as no more than a note, in advance, of the speculations which comments on parallels between metaphors open up.[1]

We have, before we begin to watch the efforts of the protocol writers to disentangle for themselves the complexities of metaphor, to make every effort we can to understand what in general the difficulty of the undertaking is and why they should have so much trouble. The way towards a solution, as I have insisted before, is not by a lucky choice of a right answer to the many very difficult

[1] To give the fully extended sense to the term 'metaphor' on all occasions would of course be inconvenient. For other purposes we do need to distinguish metaphor from what is not metaphor—without however forgetting the likeness of all modes of thinking, to stress which I have been stretching the term here. Only when metaphor (in narrower senses) is seen as a special type of the mode of operation of all language (and all signs) does a study of it become really fruitful. In metaphor, more narrowly defined, we cross sorts to make new occasional sorts; but the sorting operation is fundamental. See below, pp. 59, and *The Philosophy of Rhetoric*, Lecture II.

questions that arise about metaphor. It is rather by a more discerning understanding of the reasons which make these questions themselves so difficult. We shall even see, in some cases, that there is not, and cannot be, a right answer—because the questions themselves are wrongly put. To empty these questions then, rather than to answer them, is the way to an improved command of the interpretation of metaphor. For it is the assumptions which give rise to these wrong questions which chiefly lead us astray, assumptions we may not know that we are making, assumptions that are no more than analogies convenient for one sort of purposes allowed by inadvertence to guide us in other undertakings to which they have no relevance.

Why are the terms with which we must attempt to discuss metaphor so tricky? No short answer is useful; it would only be an exploitation of some of their tricks. What we have to do is to watch them at work tricking us and our fellows into supposing matters to be alternately much simpler and much more complex than they are.

# *Chapter Three:* Love and the Motor Car

> *The greatest thing by far is to have a command of meta-*
> *phor. This alone cannot be imparted to another: it is the*
> *mark of genius, for to make good metaphors implies an*
> *eye for resemblances.* ARISTOTLE
>
> *Eppur si muove!* GALILEO

Was Mr Biaggini's parallel between Gantry's Love-similitudes and his own suggested utterance about a motor car fair and was it effective? All four main divisions were represented. Some held

    (i) That it was perfectly fair and made mincemeat of Gantry
    (ii) That it was fair but pointless and only showed that Mr Biaggini had no imagination, for, of course, one might very well on occasion call a motor car any of these things
    (iii) That it was not fair; but was a good way of getting at Gantry's admirers
    (iv) That it was unfair and ineffective.

As regards the last point of (ii), I pay my compliments to those who made it. I remember a Professor of English at Harvard who acquired an ancient Ford and christened it Thaïs (after the heroine of Anatole France's story). When asked why, he replied that it was because she had been possessed of many! If we can do *that* to a car, successfully, what limits can we confidently set to metaphor?

If the motor car-hollyhock parallel to Gantry's metaphors for Love was unfair or inept, why was it? I may insist perhaps that this is a very normal, natural, typical question, of a kind that is summarily decided hourly by all of us when we decide for or against any comparison that may occur to us. It raises no issues that we do not commonly assume any moderately intelligent person to be capable of dealing with. And yet! Here is what happened when the protocol writers tried to answer it.

Rather more than one fourth set it to themselves as a reasonable and relevant question (I did not suggest it in any way). Among them may, I suppose, be found the pick of the commentators? What is the difference between saying that Love is a rainbow and that a motor car is a hollyhock? A majority chose as key terms in which to discuss it some contrast between the *abstract* and the *concrete*. My specimens range from apparently simple to evidently complex.

2.1.* The critic is wrong in supposing that five things incompatible in themselves cannot be likened to one abstract thing, and in his argument about a motor-car he makes the mistake of comparing the concrete with the abstract. Music, undoubtedly does have qualities which can be likened to the voice of love, a magician who makes humble people kings, the perfume of the flower, and the strength of the athlete.

2.11.* The criticism to the effect that the statement that love and music are each several incompatible things is unsatisfactory seems to me to be unjust. The parallel drawn between that statement and the statement that a motor-car is a bag of potatoes, a hollyhock, a flying cloud, and the sound of the sea, is fallacious as in the first abstractions are described in concrete terms, while in the second, a concrete object is described in terms of other concrete objects, so that the absurdity is obviously apparent.

2.12.* Love, or music, being abstract, may quite well be said to be several things which, because they are concrete, are themselves incompatible. To say that one might equally well say that a motor is a bag of potatoes is not logical, because a motor car is concrete and cannot be said to be anything else.

2.13. The example of the motor car is not to the point; even if it were true it cannot be taken as a decisive blow to the first passage, for what is true of abstracts cannot always apply to substantial things.

So far there is little to comment on except the remarkable blanketing power of these terms, and the stiffness or limitation by which the writers are unable to read *is* here except (following Mr Biaggini) as 'is numerically one with and the same thing as'—instead of taking it as 'is in some respect like.' The whole question of the uses of *is* I discuss in Chapter XIX, below; and the *abstracting* problem in Chapter XXII.

The writers now begin to let us see a little more what they mean by *abstract* and *concrete:*

2.14. It is quite legitimate to compare or identify love with innumerable incompatible things provided that each image strengthens or clarifies. The writer's example of a motor car is not convincing because he uses a concrete object which is not made more vivid by identification with other concrete objects.

This *may* be saying that it just happens that a motor car and a hollyhock don't, or that *no two concretes* do, become more vivid by identification. The second would be the more interesting point. 'Identify' is, I think, merely the writer's word for 'compare in the elliptic form which puts "is" for "is like." '

2.2. The remark that Love is likened to five incompatible things is true. However there is no reason why an abstract quality should not be linked metaphorically to five or more incompatible things. I agree that in this case it is done extremely badly. The comparison of Love and Music with the Motor Car is unreasonable. The first is an abstract; the second is intangible; while the third is a purely physical contraption. No real comparison can be made.

I suspect the capital *L* in *Love* of some responsibility here. Love is for this writer an Abstract Quality in some further sense than that in which 'being music' would be an abstract quality of music, or 'being a motor car' would be an abstract quality of cars. What this is and why it should be supposed to make this difference is our problem. The limitations of motor cars as subjects for metaphorical description were insisted on by others too:

2.21.* Just as there are two angles of approach to the first piece of prose, one from the heart, the other from the mind, so there are two corresponding angles in the second piece.

In the passage on Love we have to make up our minds which attitude to adopt, the cold logical critic of the intellectual sense of the words or that of allowing the heart to assert its rights in our awareness of a certain, if rather effulgent lyrical beauty in the passage. The passage itself is reminiscent of some Roman Catholic Church in a manufacturing town, full of cheap tinsel and stale incense, yet, despite that, containing nevertheless evidence of the beauty and glory of worship.

Intellectually, then, the second passage is quite an adequate criticism of the first and to a scientific logician love is indeed a unity and not a five in one, music also a unity and not the four things the first writer makes it. But even in this eminently logical piece I can see a faint trace of illogicality, for the writer props up his argument with the assertion that to give love and music such attributes as does the first writer is as if he (the second) were to compare a motor-car to a bag of potatoes and a hollyhock. But a motor-car, he should have realised, is a concrete manufactured article, whereas music and art have much of the inexplicable about them.

And that is just where B (the second writer) trips up. Had he presented a firmer brief for his case we might agree more closely with him; but he fails to make providence for the inexplicability, the very intangibility of the lyrical qualities of love and music. Intellectually even he is unsound, as I have tried to demonstrate. Emotionally he seems cold and dead and I cannot help feeling that A (the first writer) is not only the most attractive piece of writing, but also comes best out of a mutual comparison, and that A has more appeal to us, however lush, effulgent, fulsome and grandiose it may be.

Here not the 'Abstractness,' but the 'inexplicability' and 'intangibility' of love and music are the ground alleged. I do not think, though, we are really moving far from the thought of 2.2. What they have both in mind, I fancy, is nothing much more subtle than is put in the italicized sentence of the following—which adds a personal aberration of a familiar and interesting type. Truly Love (in a special sense) takes all things for its food. He, or she, however, is perhaps on the way to more understanding of the whole matter than has been *shown* yet.

2.22.* The first sentence of the criticism, down to . . . 'from the evidence,' arouses no antagonism in me. I also agree with the critic in disliking the first passage, but for different reasons. I see nothing incompatible in love being 'a rainbow, the morning star, the evening star, a miracle that shines around the cradle of a babe, and something which shines round the quiet tomb.' To anyone who is really in love it can be all these things. Love has little to do with logic, and hyperbole is its usual medium of expression. The critic is too literal. Music does exalt one to a realm inhabited only by kings, it is magic. I cannot see it as the perfume of a flower, or as the strength of the athlete, but am willing to believe that the author does so. The introduction of the motor car and the bag of potatoes, does not seem to me to provide the parallel which is intended. *A motor car can never be anything but a motor car—a concrete object.* Love and music live in the effect which they have on us, not in what they essentially are. Even so, I have no objection to comparing a motor car to a bag of potatoes, if I can be shown any attribute which they have in common. It is not to be found. Whereas Love and music have the same power of exciting wonder before beauty as the things to which they are compared.

Another and a big step forward is made in the following:

2.23.* Abstract qualities and a definition of their splendours difficult to convey except by concrete terms. Such a quality as Love can best be conveyed by an assembly of visible objects thro' which a feeling of Love works on or from human beings. In using metaphor Love as morning star and evening star is saying they are symbolic of that abstract feeling which as stars they arouse.

Meanwhile motor-car is concrete and difficult to link with potatoes because both concrete terms. Absurd to say motor car = flying cloud and motor car = sound of sea; but if abstract qualities involved the writer justified.

Purr of engine of motor car = sound of sea + speed of motor-car along a road = flying cloud [1] purr + speed the abstractions.

Here the writer does manage, in his last paragraph, to give the word 'abstract' a use which is helpful. It has quite another in his remark about the abstract feeling which the stars arouse and had a third meaning in the first sentence. The doings of 'a feeling of Love' cut perilously across; but still—towards the end—the right thread in the tangle has been found. The abstract is no longer simply taken as such, its derivation from the concrete has been observed. The answer is no longer in bare terms of an unresolved concrete-abstract opposition. 'What is being compared with what?' has given place to, 'How, in respect of what qualities, are they compared?' as the formulation of the question, and the writer is prepared to see that abstracts, instead of being *data* to be compared with each other and other things, are themselves the products and at the same time the instruments of comparison.

This is no slight triumph; the great steps in the history of thought are taken again, or fail to be taken, in every growing mind; the obstacle of uncomprehended verbiage must be passed or it will be used only as a shield and a protection; it is not ridiculous to hail with a moderate applause every such instance of intelligence.

This is, however, the best comment I have from the users of 'concrete-abstract' divisions. We are well behind this with the next:

[1] I understand that one of the motor-cars of America was called, by the manufacturers, the Reo-Flying Cloud, Trade Mark, U. S. Patent Office, etc.

2.24. Why is it incompatible that love should surround the grave as well as the cradle, should brighten both the morning and the evening, both happiness and adversity? If this had been said directly no one could have challenged its reasonableness. But the critic shuts his eyes to the real meaning. He professes to deal with the 'simple sense of what is stated,' but what he is really dealing with is the logic of the imagery. He attempts to explode it by parody; but only shows his insensitiveness by choosing a comparison that is completely inapplicable—something as concrete as a motor car, to compare with something as abstract, as variable and as all pervading as the emotion of love, and the beauty of music.

Also, the tone of his criticism is snobbish and superior to a disgusting degree.

'Abstract' here, I think, means hardly anything more than 'vague, intangible, and ineffable.' And my next group will show how the ineffable, the emotional, the inexplicable, the inexpressible, the all-pervasive, the omnipresent, the sublime, and the immaterial, as ingredients in current notions of the abstract, can intervene to distort the question. They even turn it into a comparison between Love and a motor car!—instead of between parallels in which Love and a motor car take part.

2.25.* While the writer is examining 'the simple sense' of the passage he is sound. When he comes to his observations he seems to be obsessed with the idea that the thing must have a literal sense. How else can we express what we mean by love than by analogy? Different types of mind liken it to different things, and the same type of mind under different circumstances. To liken love to a motor-car is to liken an abstract quality to a material object. The point could be better made by likening love to another abstract quality.

2.26. The comparison of the motor car obviously falls through, on his grounds; for he himself is comparing love and music to a mechanical conveyance.

2.27.* The writer, though hinting at his own original sensibility and 'sense of logic' takes his stand in this passage on an examination of the 'simple sense' of the piece he is criticizing. However it seems that he is unable to understand, himself, the 'simple sense' for surely the original prose states not that Love is a rainbow but that Love is like a rainbow illuminating the 'dark clouds of life.' Similarly the other phenomena to which Love and Music are likened are qualified with the word 'like.' The critic states that these comparisons are incompatible, though the Love envisaged here, the Divine Love, is, presumably, so vast, so many-sided that innumerable comparisons would but reflect its different facets. Further on we see what is perhaps the source of the error, Love the abstract quality is compared with a motor-car a concrete object. The author himself needs a lesson in logic. We may agree that the passage on Love is not a satisfactory statement but that is not to agree with his argument.

This way of writing as though Mr Biaggini were comparing Love and Music to a motor car is confusing. It may be mere ellipsis but, if so, it is a dangerous brevity, and had more than a little to do with the confusions in which it occurred.

2.28. The 2nd passage makes only one criticism—that love and music are said to be both several incompatible things. But the writer of the first made it clear that he was speaking of Love as a divine presence so that to some extent he was justified in calling it a rainbow etc. What is intended to be a crushing analogy of a motor car does not succeed because few people would attribute divine presence to cars.

The muddle here, being grosser, is easier to dissect. The question is not 'What properties does Love (as envisaged by Gantry) share with a motor car?' It is not even 'Are the links between Love and Gantry's similitudes for it the same links as those that might occur between a motor car and Mr Biaggini's oddments?' It was, or should have been, 'Are the links *within* either group good enough to support the similitudes?'

As to this, it is, I think, plain enough, if the question is put separately, that a mere recognition of Love as a divine presence would be insufficient ground by itself for any of Gantry's metaphors. It is too universal and indiscriminate a ground and would link too much, unless qualified or supported by other links which in fact Lewis makes Gantry supply in each case—either explicitly or through an obvious and trustworthy special setting that is hinted. He is in fact as careful to provide them as Mr Biaggini for his purpose was careful not to supply them; and there, in a nutshell, is the all-important difference. It is no special, peculiar, mysterious, bonding power of Love which is at work in the metaphors here, but linkages of the order of those which, as we shall see, could easily enough come into action, *with suitable settings,* between motor cars, holly-hocks and the rest. It is not a mere all-pervasiveness of Love that justifies the metaphors and makes them intelligible. As all-pervasive, Love would make all things only *instances* of itself, and metaphor (in the restricted sense of the word) would not be occurring. Cats and dogs are instances of animal life; we should not ordinarily say that metaphor was present in such exemplification. The parallelling by which we range them together as examples of a class, naming their common property, has become so simple, so detached from rival groupings, that the limit has been crossed. In metaphor (in the restricted sense) there is a cross-grouping and a resultant tension between the particular similarity employed and more stable habitual classifications, which would be absent here.

2.29. Metaphor often unites apparently incompatible things by some one resemblance. Here all these things are pervaded by a unifying spirit of love which the writer is feeling.

I am a little doubtful as to how this should be read. He may be saying

(i) That it is the writer's (Gantry's) unifying spirit of love that pervades them.
(ii) That the writer feels that *they* are so pervaded.

The second seems the likeliest. In either case I suggest, as before, that although such a general link may be in the background, there are much more special links than this between Love and the rainbow and so on. And that it is these special links which control the interpretation of the metaphor. It is these links, therefore, which we must take account of in our comparisons.

One further point—I believe an important one—before I leave this large group of 'abstract-concrete' commentators, for other wanderers in the theory of metaphor. It will have been noticed that most of them are in the grip of an assumption that metaphor is only suited to dim, vague, mysterious, inexplicable, intangible, and indefinite matters. That it is only in place when we are not at all sure what we are saying, have nothing perhaps precise to say, or are dealing with the inexpressible, or the ineffable. We can guess at the sources of the assumption. It came from sad experience of the misleading effect of random dreaming vagaries in metaphoric thought, where 'the sunshine comparative power' is suspended; from rebukes, perhaps, for fuzzy arguments in which unexamined analogies have had full play. It is fostered also by the disheartening mystery in which the topic of metaphor is left by most current discussion or instruction. If we add the notions that metaphor is not a serious way of thinking, that metaphors are merely decorative, not structural, in thought, that they are fanciful and, unless used by Poets (and perhaps even then), flimsy, frivolous, irresponsible and unreliable: add in too the associations of the word 'concrete' (hard, solid, heavy, detailed, business-like, suitable for foundations, brute fact) and those of 'abstract' (thin or hot air, remote, empty, invisible, intangible, not to be grasped, sublime, remote) this common assumption or prejudice is not difficult to understand. That it is deplorable and disastrous, that it hinders its victims in acquiring control of an immense range of the most important uses of language and modes of thought, that it deprives them of powers which they badly need, will, I take it, require little showing. The assumption enters here to persuade the writers that metaphor is of no service as between concrete things, that one or other or both the things linked together must be, in some sense 'abstract'—and this view was not due merely to confusion with the relevant fact that the linkage is always in respect of some common character or quality, i.e. something which, if taken apart, would be an abstract. This subtlety was out of sight for most. They were simply thinking that since a motor car is a motor car (a concrete object and that's that!) it cannot usefully be compared to (or said to be) anything else; whereas a spirit of love, being not a concrete object, can like some monstrous disembodied chameleon, turn mysteriously into almost anything and be said to be anything that it pleases us to call it. All our minds doubtless are haunted by such Protean ghostly beings, relics of our childhood and of our magic-ridden social inheritance. But, if we cannot keep them in their places—on the borders of sleep, for they are evidently products of the dream type—if we let them intervene in hours in which we should be awake, then good-bye to 'the sunshine comparative power, the distinct contra-distinguishing judgment of Realities as other than thoughts.' The teacher's first and last duty is to help the mind to clear itself from this 'somnial magic' which is the enemy (as Keats said) not less of Poetry, than of any other self-ordering development of intelligence.

> Art thou not of the dreamer tribe?
> The Poet and the Dreamer are distinct,

Diverse, sheer opposite, antipodes,
The one pours out a balm upon the World
The other vexes it.

The notion that metaphor will not link together things that are concretes and cannot make definite and clear statements through their linkage, appeared in scores of the comments. I ventured, in my lecture, to suggest that I could demonstrate its groundlessness by remarking that these writers were owls! Both the writer of a protocol and an owl are things as concrete as any we can find, yet the metaphor quite evidently worked. Given a suitable setting, there are many more links of resemblance, available as discriminated grounds of comparison, between concretes than between abstracts. The higher the abstraction the fewer the different *varieties* of metaphor that can be made to or from it. But the modes of comparison between concretes are inexhaustible. They become the more numerous the more we know about the concretes. Similarly, two unutterables cannot be compared. Only their common unutterability would be available as a link between them. But with any two concrete familiar things we may make as many metaphors as we can find links—that is, enlist efficient focusing contexts to serve as their grounds.

The ground, for example, of the owl metaphor here, if I may be permitted to detail it, was that an owl is a bird not able to see things in broad daylight, dazzled by excess of illumination, preferring obscurity and with a reputation for wisdom that, if these other peculiarities are stressed, is comically not deserved. Similarly, those who suppose that metaphors between familiar things will not work are being blinded by what is overwhelmingly evident, by what is illustrated and illumined by everyday conversation every few minutes; they too prefer obscurer topics, and their discernment there may be ranked too high.

For this to be not only a possible ground but an operative ground —that is for the metaphor to be understood—parallel interpretative contexts must be guiding the speaker and his audience. When we think of anything we do so only through and with a context in which it has its place, and the most powerful controlling contexts are those that are so constant that there is no need to allude to them, those that can be taken for granted. I wrote above that Mr Biaggini in speaking of a motor car was careful not to supply a special setting. That leaves it to us to take it in whatever setting we may or will. We cannot think of a motor car without a context, and we understand the words 'motor car' only through a context. Which context it goes into depends on its setting.[1]

Left to ourselves by Mr Biaggini, we read 'a motor car' and give it a sense, take it in a context, think of *it* as,—well, a number of the protocol-writers were at pains to say how they took *it*. 'As a mechanical contrivance,' 'as a means (varying only in efficiency and comfort) of going from one place to another,' as 'a purely physical contraption,' . . . and so on. One, we have seen, even took it upon himself to say how Mr Biaggini should have taken it! 'A motor car he should have realized . . .' (2.21). There will be a variable range of ways in which *it* can, equally properly, be understood. None of them will, without a special setting, allow *it* to be linked with a bag of potatoes or a hollyhock, if they too are understood without special settings (i.e. by the action of the general habitual contexts). Supply a special enough setting and anything may be linked in metaphor with anything.

Now let us consider this comment.

2.3.* The analogy between a Motor Car and Love and Music which is the concrete foundation upon which this criticism rests does not appear to be a wholly adequate one. A motor car, I would suggest, presents itself to the senses of all human beings (apart from savages who are not acquainted with its nature) in approximately the same way; not as a potato or a hollyhock, but as a means (varying only in degree of efficiency and comfort) of going from one place to another. Love and Music however do not depend upon external qualities for their value so much as on the constitution of the individual mind. In different people there can be no doubt that Love and Music will make up different emotional states, and find their level on different planes of emotion. For our critic each must be for everybody a rigidly fixed quantity—'a simple sense' obvious only to those with 'original sensibility,' for that is 'how the masses think' and any contrary suggestion will not 'pass for a satisfactory statement.' In the case of the writer criticised Music hits him on a plane of

[1] The usual phrase would be 'depends on its context.' See Preface and footnote on p. 48. In my technical sense of *context*, 'which context we take it in' = 'how we understand it.'

Emotion, a facet of his personality if you like, which is delineated by the four ideas or experiences mentioned, which the critic denies to have any connection, as likewise with the five 'plotting points' of Love which are outward manifestations of the contour of his reaction.

Lest somebody after looking very closely feels that this is too good to be true, I repeat here that there has been no tampering in the least particular with any of these quotations. I have never even cut them short when I thought it possible that the rest might change an interpretation of the sentences I gave.

This writer has illustrated, of his own accord, all my points (and some I have not yet reached). And he has done this in a leisurely Olympian style which makes it hard at first not to think that one is misreading him.

He begins with the assumption we have already considered that the ratio, Love : Rainbow :: Motor car : Hollyhock may profitably be studied merely by examining Love and a motor car and pointing out differences between *them*. But his choices of differences lead him into still worse trouble.

'A motor car I would suggest presents itself to the senses.' How? 'As a means . . . of going from one place to another.' 'The senses' are brought in, I would suggest, to mark the motor car down at once as a material, external, sensory object, something concrete, invariable and public in contrast to mind-dependent Love and Music. Very well, but what do the senses as such give us? Coloured, resonant, smooth and hard configurations? Perhaps. Tin and wheels and leather seats? No. Certainly not—without the intervention of the mind, which recognizes these things, interprets the sensory signs, and builds up on them the most variable and delicately poised structures of knowledge and expectation. 'The fool sees not the same tree that a wise man sees,' said Blake—deliberately, I think, choosing an example which would make his point as outrageous as possible. We will all take his point much more easily about motor cars. Where I see just two cars, my 14-year-old nephew sees two things so unlike one another that he puts me in my place with ease. If only we could remember what Blake told us, what an immense deal of nonsense we should all avoid! That 'concrete' thing we call a car, how mind-dependent it is, how different to the owner and to his friends, how painfully more scratched to one set of eyes than to another; and how it changes as a buyer turns into a seller. It is the concrete car that is variable in these disconcerting ways, and its changes are part of its concreteness. What stays dependable, reliable, unchanged and permanent is, as Plato taught us, the abstract car—the thing which this writer has so luckily presented to us 'as a means . . . of going from one place to another.' What could be much more abstract than that? But, according to him, it is *the senses* that present this. Alas! Poor Plato and all his progeny! How little of that elementary apparatus of clear and useful distinctions which you introduced and have handed on, that apparatus upon which the whole weight of Western Culture has ever since been carried—no metaphysical abstruseness but the handy daily instruments of intelligence—how little of all this has reached—I won't say the ordinary reader—let me rather say the average reader of *The Criterion* or *The New Republic*.

However, to return to the teacher's problem. How salutary it would be for some of the writers I have been citing, if they could be brought to notice the reversal of the applications of 'concrete' and 'abstract' that this last commentator brings out! But the process of abstraction and how to teach something about it are topics for the Logic Section.

Much of 2.3's difficulty is traceable to the fixed setting, 'as a means of conveyance,' he has imposed on the motor car. While that setting is fixed similarities involving other settings may be temporarily barred out. One or two commentators noted that a motor car might be like a hollyhock in brightness, or like a bag of potatoes in bumpiness or like the sound of the sea in its purr or like a flying cloud for swiftness. It is a frequent complaint of poets and critics that too many readers refuse to allow themselves to understand comparisons which are novel in type, that they will only follow metaphors of kinds with which they are familiar. The following may illustrate this complaint. It is also of interest in bringing up the very important matter of *motivation*.

> 2.31. The critic's parody of the metaphors . . . shows that he has not grasped the point of metaphor at all, and has merely chosen his descriptions at random; of course one might connect the sound of the sea with a motor car, but hardly a bag of potatoes or a hollyhock.

One might suppose that this writer was an enthusiastic motorist and a lover of the sea-side! But that I think would be too simple an explanation. Would it not be that such comparisons as with the sound of the sea (or with a flying cloud) are of a kind frequent and familiar in certain sorts of verse, and so are supposed to be *in themselves* in some way poetic? And that metaphor is similarly supposed to be in some way a peculiarly poetic use of language, and that therefore the writer has been willing, in the hope of poetic gratification, himself to supply in imagination a suitable setting here? He would find it easy because such settings are old literary friends. With the potatoes and the hollyhock he was less willing perhaps and perhaps the effort required would be greater.

However this may be, such a reluctance to explore novel types of setting is, very often, what is so much cursed by fashionable critics—under the misleading headings of Romanticism or romantic preconceptions in the judgment of literature. I may take this opportunity of remarking, in passing, how much more useful in promoting sane reading a little more study of this question of familiarity *versus* novelty in contexts would be than further class-room discussions of Romanticism. This study would turn largely upon precedences as between merely literary (verbal) settings and larger supporting settings in non-verbal experience. In other words, on attempted segregations of literature from life, and thereby it would cut right across the Romanticism versus Classicism (is it?) or Realism divisions. For, to take only an obvious point, a generation brought up on, and familiar with, so called Romantic Poetry, takes that as its literary norm; puts it, that is, into the place occupied, for Classicist critics, by Vergil and Horace. Thenceforward, for them, departures from this pattern—whether in choice of subject, in tone, or in any other literary feature—have some of the strangeness which was the superficial enticement of the initial departures of Romantic writers. In such a topsy-turvy situation, discussion of the historic problems of the Romantic Revival would require a mental agility that is not to be expected from any but a few lively yet experienced readers. On the other hand, to restate the matter in terms of familiarities with literature and life is to bring it, comparatively, within reach of everyone.

# *Chapter Four:* Motivation

> *Fortunately, however, for my uncle, his godfather, Mr Benson Earle, was a sound classical scholar, and had been a ward of the celebrated James Harris, the author of Hermes. This book Mr Earle put into the hands of his godson, then about fourteen years of age, and the young student, on opening it, felt as if his mental eye had been couched, discovering with surprise that the lessons which appeared to him, of all his scholastic tasks, the driest and most unmeaning, involved many profound speculations of intellectual philosophy.*
>
> WILLIAM HAZLITT, on Sir John Stoddart

An interlude of general reflections may be in place here before I continue my documentation with further exemplification and discussion of theories about metaphor. We cannot too early consider the part played by the expected satisfaction, the inducement, the motivation which is behind and guides every process of interpretation. No writer supplies the full setting which controls the reader in his reading. He cannot. Always the major part must be left to the reader to bring in. This is perhaps the truism which in practice we most neglect. The writer can at best only use a small selection from the whole setting—taking this as the total situation, all the conditions governing what is going on. What he uses has a nucleus, namely what he explicitly mentions. Round this is a sphere of relatively stable factors, those things which all, on reflection, would agree to be implied, to be necessarily co-operative with what he has actually mentioned. Round these, less and less dependable and stable, are sphere after sphere of more and more doubtful factors which spread out, if we carry our speculative description far enough, to include the whole past experience of the reader. If, and in so far as, communication occurs, vast ranges of these free or unimplied factors must still be somehow ordered so as to secure some correspondence

66

between those active in the reader and in the writer. They are so ordered, if at all, by what Coleridge called 'the all in each of all men,' the common principles of human life and the routine of normal experience. It seems a shadowy thing on which to depend unless we recognize that it is rooted in our biological continuity one with another.

From this common principle evidently branch all the specialized similarities that training and common studies can induce. It makes them possible, but without them we could go no great distance in understanding one another—as all who have resided, say, in Japan know too well. Hence, since a language is our chief controllable common training, the paramount importance of studies in English for English-speaking peoples. Hence innumerable morals —e.g. the importance of a common body of literature familiar to all—for the teacher and the framers of a curriculum. (That we can no longer refer with any confidence to any episode in the Bible, or to any nursery tale or any piece of mythology is a clear and well-recognized sign of the urgency of taking these things more advisedly in hand.) Hence too the inaccessibility, to all but specially trained readers, of most literature of past ages. We perhaps as a rule can give only enough training to our pupils to hide this inaccessibility from us and from them, without giving enough to build a genuine bridge across the gulf.

The writer, relying upon the common linguistic training, and on whatever other common controlling factors in experience he can, offers at best a skeleton or schema to be filled out by his reader. Looked at from a distance it may seem a miracle that he should succeed, and our wonder must be that understanding is achieved so often and goes so deep, not that it so often fails. But, looking closer, the explanation is perhaps to be found in the extreme interconnectedness of the processes of any single mind. If we thought of experience (as the cruder exponents of associationism used to think of it) as merely a series of impacts on a passive mind, linked together only by frequencies of concomitance and by resultant habit sequences, communication might well seem inexplicable. But such a theory, though it haunts more than a little educational theory— recommending, for example, drill as a mode of improving composition!—is now merely an intellectual curiosity like astrology. It is now agreed, beneath all their differences in phrasing, by all schools of psychology that the mind (or whatever they put in its place) is not a passive substratum, that mental process is from the beginning selective. In other words that experience is not just suffering things to happen to us but a mode of ordering our lives. From this self-ordering, organizing, principle comes the sameness upon which communication depends. In addition to the uniformity of experience conceived as offered to us *from without,* there is its uniformity as organized by us *from within;* and here is where the control of inducement over interpretation comes in. We choose, in brief, and the laws of choice are alike in us all, though their outcome, of course, is not.

What we arrive at as our interpretation is what we are satisfied with as the meaning. To write 'what gave us satisfaction' might mislead, but, if guardedly taken, it would make the point more vigorously. We may be well content to find an author's remarks 'unsatisfactory.' There is an inner movement in the process that is easily described as our tendency to find what meaning we please. If sometimes we teachers are inclined to blame this—as whimsicality, wantonness or obstinacy—when things have gone wrong, we should not forget that we have it equally to thank whenever things go right. For if we ask, Upon what can an author rely to guide his reader to his meaning? the broad answer fundamentally must be this: he must rely upon the right reading being more satisfying than any other reading.

I have left out all sorts of qualifications; 'satisfying to whom and in what state of mind and for what purpose?' we must hurry to ask. But that is my point obviously enough here. We must never, if we can help it, forget that nobody ever reads anything for no purpose or in a state of utter indifference as to what he finds it to mean. And we must never pretend that aberrations in interpretation can be considered apart from distortions in the reader's appetitive process. This is why the question of inducement, of motivation, goes to the heart of all the teacher's problems, and all problems of interpretation and expression.

No slight stress has lately been laid upon this doctrine in discussions of the principles of English teaching, but sometimes in an unduly onesided fashion and without recognizing its manifold implications. It is often urged for example that it is no good making backward writers do composition at random, in the blue, merely *as* composition, that unless they are writing about something that interests them, unless they have something they care about to discuss, they will have no genuine impulse to write, no steam behind their wheels, and, with nothing to express, no cause to improve their expression. Well and good so far as it goes—but that, I think it can be shown, is no great distance. Granted that composition-exercises without *any* motive, and interpretation-exercises equally, would be absurdities, this recommendation assumes altogether too simple a view of interests. It has, I suggest, a fatal and obvious defect in that it identifies them with what the psychologizing moralists used to call 'involuntary' appetitions and overlooks the immensely important domain of voluntary actions—those namely in which something is done not for its own sake, not for the immediate satisfaction in the action, but for the sake of remoter consequences. The vast majority of the interests on which education depends are plainly of this voluntary type and it is a commonplace of morals and psychology alike that the successful exercise of such voluntary activities, that is the process of attending deliberately for an ulterior purpose to a task which is not intrinsically alluring, generates an *in*voluntary intrinsic interest, if not in the work itself, at least (and it is quite as helpful) in its successful prosecution. In brief, *pride,* reluctance to be beaten, self-esteem are enlisted, no stronger motives than which can be engaged. And with even a slight satisfaction to these—and the least sense of success with the work will yield it—the work itself, becoming identified with an activity of the self, picks up a derivative attraction.

I am here, of course, merely echoing the homilies of innumerable moralists. But there is a more immediate reason for doubting whether the policy of utilizing only or chiefly a pupil's own personal interests is advisable, or for thinking that he will advance best by writing about his hobbies or reading only the literature which has already caught his fancy. It comes from the central place of linguistic ability in man's being as a social creature. Without ability to speak we have no standing, our rank depends upon our capacity to understand and to express ourselves so as to be understood. The incredible intellectual feat that the child achieves in learning to speak had as its chief motive just this enhancement of its self-esteem. If the motive lapses later with the development of a partial command of interpretation and expression, that is because the performer is suf-

fering from a relaxation of the social criticism which originally
drove him on. Ideally, his own self-criticism should take its place;
failing that or pending this moment of maturity, it is the teacher's
business to arrange for the stimulating challenge.

He has to contrive that the pupil becomes clearly aware that he
is as yet unable to interpret or to express things that others, whom
he regards as no more than his equals, succeed with. A painful
process to recommend no doubt. But if it is true that the main
reason why any of us can talk or understand speech at all was that
we each so hated feeling a fool, this recommendation as regards the
motivation of English studies is obvious. It seems that the adver-
tisers who undertake to make us impressive public speakers have
been better psychologists than the Drill school of educationists!

Guardedly used, what I may perhaps call the 'protocol method'
might be employed more widely with advantage. Nothing is more
stimulating than to see how others have succeeded with the same
task. Nothing more quickly transforms a problem from a mystery
to be guessed about into a practical matter that can, and must, be
understood. Like other powerful methods it is open to grave abuse;
it can bewilder, wound, and frustrate. I should be loath to see it
employed without the protection of anonymity. Unless ample leisure
for meditation is allowed, specimens of other students' work will not
be illuminating. To hear random comments read out soon induces
a nervous crisis. But, if these obvious dangers are avoided, I believe
that a process of presenting to the class the varied views that any
set of comments will supply, might do much to freshen English
studies and, by restoring candour and humility, redeem what is too
often a dreary and hypocritical ritual.

I assume then, as a general motive which should be dominant
both in expression and in interpretation, a desire to esteem oneself
as a person capable of saying and of reading things adequately—
an unwillingness to be patently silly or inept in these activities. It is
this motive which more than any other holds in check the vagaries
of the active and passive uses of language. The merit of a literary
exercise must, I believe, be judged by the degree to which it invites
this motive to overrule adventitious, distracting and more limited
interests. No doubt the general motive can be reinforced by special
interests, and there is here some weight in the 'Let him write about
what he dreams about!' doctrine. If he feels that a subject is impor-

tant, he is more likely perhaps to take care in saying things, or in discovering what is being said, about it. On the other hand this is evidently truer of factual matters than of imaginative. In general, exercises for which revealing tests of adequacy are not able to be applied take up time on which there are better claims.

It is a narrow view of motivation which supposes that an exercise in interpretation or composition merely as such, and taken apart from the special enthusiasms, pursuits or curiosities of the individual, must be devoid of interest or lack incentives. Such a view overlooks the fascination of puzzles and omits to consider how these special interests themselves originally developed. In most cases perhaps they would be found to have grown at first as modes of self-enhancement; developing, with growth, their peculiar intrinsic attractions. But of course the exercises must be well chosen, they must present themselves as reasonable challenges, as tasks that the learner feels he ought to be able to succeed in. Above all they must call for a kind of effort from him that reassures him as he achieves it; they must not, and here is the fatal objection to most drill, make him feel that he is merely submitting to the compulsion of an unintelligible command. That feeling numbs intelligence at once and deadens just what we are most anxious to awaken. It reverses the right order as between habit formation and insight. Here modern psychology can do the teacher a service. Nothing is more impressive in recent studies of learning than the overthrow of the assumptions on which the drill recommendation rests. We learn by *seeing* how to do things, not by blindly going through the motions. *After* insight, repetition will develop habits that may usefully take its place, but not before. It is strange that these obsolete notions of how learning happens should find such a stronghold in teaching practice, since nowhere should the waste they entail be more apparent.

'When I had once found the delight of knowledge and felt the pleasure of intelligence and the pride of invention,' said Imlac, 'every hour taught me something new. I lived in a continual course of gratifications.' It is these gratifications that are the fundamental incentives to all study. Good teaching offers them incessantly, bad teaching witholds them: and perhaps there is more bad teaching in English than in any other subject. Mathematics used to be notorious too and a comparison might be useful. I understand that methods there have improved,[1] and that more teachers now can transform a dark mystery operated only by mechanical dodges and tricks into an intelligible field for reason.

We must not forget that blind rote and drill kill the teacher as surely as his pupils. Unless we can see a mistake as a problem we cannot make it fruitful for its victim. And only so can we raise the occupation of the teacher of elementary English into a profession that can, without self-sacrifice, attract the talented. The correction and analysis of interpretation and composition can and must be developed into a study worth pursuing for its own sake. But there should be no difficulty in doing this once we realize that it is nothing else than literary criticism descended from its windy heights and restored to contact with its actual facts.

The class-room indeed offers unique opportunities for criticism, including self-criticism. The literary critic who wonders, as he must often do, whether he is of any service to the world, and whether his efforts make any difference to anyone, can find there, if he will modestly descend to minute particulars, an inexhaustible field to cultivate. There, living in the flesh, are all the types of the human spirit; there all the steps which the historian of culture would like to trace are being taken anew; there all the literary discoveries are being made again. There too, and more evidently, the heresies, the confusions, the outworn, exploded, exposed-to-death assumptions that have frustrated so many possible poets and prophets, are being reinvented. Who would be only a paleontologist if the dinosaur still roamed the swamp?

To be more temperate, the varieties of interpretation which a well-chosen passage can elicit do sometimes astonishingly repeat in miniature the characteristics of vanished literary epochs. They are, I suggest, if carefully examined, capable of presenting a fascinating synopsis of intellectual history—not less interesting for being more compassable. As a word or a grammatical form may contain the germ of a whole philosophy, so certain ways of reading carry implicitly with them a characteristic outlook or culture. And apart from these attractions, the detailed study of interpretations has its interest as showing us, again in miniature, many facets of human nature which we ordinarily perceive only as traits of character. On

---

[1] Certainly, if such a book as Professor L. T. Hogben's *Mathematics for the Million* were taken into the schools we might expect great gains.

these grounds alone, it would be capable of some justification as a part of general education aside from the help which it may give to the development of linguistic ability. But centrally its value derives from the insight it may give us into how our minds work, into their difficulties, their weaknesses, their temptations and the means of overcoming them. And this insight, which the discerning and skilful teacher can share with and induce in his pupils, is the only source of advance and its chief reward.

# A First Landing Stage and a Recommendation

*Man, being the servant and interpreter of Nature, can do
and observe so much and so much only as he has observed
in fact or in thought about the course of nature: beyond
this he neither knows anything nor can do anything.*

*Novum Organon*

One very simple and broad observation—with an obvious accompanying recommendation—can, I think, be made at this stage. It is that a whole literature seems to be missing from the library of pedagogics. The literature namely which would describe plainly and candidly actual procedures followed by teachers in correcting or discussing the compositions of their pupils, and detail the explanations they venture to give of their corrections. The technical journals of the teaching profession compare extremely badly with those of dentistry in this respect. They bulge with repetitive discussions of principles, but where can we find case-histories detailing the treatment recommended for a given confused paragraph? The dentist is ready to tell his *confrères* how he rights a rotting tooth. The teacher seems as yet oddly unwilling to confess in equal detail how he criticizes a bad essay. To do so is of course to invite comment that may be disconcerting, but the man of faith will not flinch from that. The literature that would result if studies of interesting confusions and misunderstandings became as regular features in the professional literature as descriptions of procedures are in the dental journals would soon revolutionize practice. We should begin to profit, as dentists have long been profiting, from one another's mistakes.

It is one thing to insist (as we have all been insisting for years) that the pupil's great need is to attain a mastery of clear and ordered expression. It is quite another *to show, in detail,* how a given paragraph fails or how the pupil can best be helped to see that it fails and to put it right. The first sounds like the end of the matter, which lapses into universal agreement. The second may well be the beginning of a lengthy and valuable dispute. Doubtless for the layman stupidity and bad writing are not things he would willingly linger over. Their study is, he may think, no more his concern than the horrors of pathology—which he leaves to the medical profession. But just who is the analogue to the pathologist here? Who does study misconception with the care it deserves? The teacher at present does not; but who else should? And is the layman's position really as well taken as he thinks? Stupidity is a complaint from which no one can claim immunity, and adults must commonly be their own schoolmasters.

Stupidity is an unduly harsh name for the misinterpretations and frustrations of expression with which we are concerned here. In their less gross and palpable forms they are ceaseless, and we flatter ourselves if we think we escape them ever. Who, asks the moralist, is the just man and perfect? Who, asks the alienist, is not psychopathic? Who, we may ask, interprets, or expresses himself, as well as he might? They are all equally rhetorical questions. The real questions are as to the extent of our loss and the power of the available remedies. That both are much greater than we ordinarily suppose will, I hope, be established in the course of this discussion. That they are strangely neglected is implied. I doubt indeed whether there is another matter as important to mankind which receives as little systematic study, or in which so much might evidently be done if we set to work to do it.

The obvious recommendation which follows from the shortage of detailed case studies of failures is that the professional journals should reserve sections—perhaps under special editorship—for such communications from teachers, and encourage, in correspondence columns, a critical discussion of them. This would provide openings for much thought which at present has no very useful outlet; it would stimulate interest at the very point at which the teacher is apt to feel most need for such stimulation (the correction of papers) —the point at which his work is most apt to seem merely disheartening; it would give him the support of a co-operative venture; he would be able to compare his own troubles with those of his fellows. Instead of a mere *ad hoc* struggle with a single difficulty, he could feel that he was taking part in a general effort to improve technique and that his thought had a wider usefulness than the ordinary limitations of the school setting present it as having. And there would be a further and obvious use in these communications. They would in time provide an abundant supply, in a prepared and developed form, of just those exercises in interpretation which are a chief need in teaching. They would give us both model problems and a technique of discussion. At present if we offer our pupils a passage to comment upon we are making a somewhat incalculable experiment. Only after watching its strange adventures as it passes through mind after mind are we in a position to see clearly what may best be learnt from it. The experiments which I am reporting in this section of my statement were obviously of very different value from this point of view. They all made, perhaps, too exacting a demand to be of general use. I had to risk this because too easy an exercise would—given the conditions under which my audience submitted itself to me—have cost me more interest than I could afford to lose. But exercises of this type—through which students must come to see for themselves that what they regard as adequate reading and writing is not adequate—exercises which will prove to them, apart altogether from a teacher's opinion, that they have not nearly mastered the arts of reading and writing, and that without further improvement a large part of their intellectual life is mere folly, such exercises, I am convinced, are a prime need. No one can sit down to invent such exercises. You have to wait until one is revealed to you by what at first seems a happy accident of your own or someone else's stupidity. Then you have to satisfy yourself that it is no mere individual accidental lapse that has occurred but that the troublesome passage is a natural and general matrix of misunderstanding.

To discover the most useful exercises must be a large corporate undertaking. Moreover they must be suited not only to the pupils but to the teachers, and what may sometimes be an arduous process of preparation is required before they are ready for use. The communications and the critical correspondence would both prepare them for the teacher and, which is perhaps even more important, would, whether good or bad, be a valuable exercise *for him* in the considerations which this kind of work entails—exercise which ordinary school work by no means necessarily supplies. Doubtless the editor of such a section would receive plenty of queer letters.

The teacher's desk has no virtue to protect him from misinterpreting. But once the point has been granted that the study of almost any misinterpretation may be profitable, the source of the blunder is unimportant. It may even humanize the subject to realize still more often that Fate has us all in its hand here!

# *Chapter Five:* The Fidelity of a Translation

> '*Disorders of intellect,*' *answered Imlac,* '*happen much more often than superficial observers will easily believe. Perhaps, if we speak with rigorous exactness, no human mind is in its right state. There is no man whose imagination does not sometimes predominate over his reason, who can regulate his attention wholly by his will, and whose ideas will come and go at his command. No man will be found in whose mind airy notions do not sometimes tyrannize, and force him to hope or fear beyond the limits of sober probability.*' SAMUEL JOHNSON, *Rasselas*

The detailed discussion of my next batch of protocols is on a scale which the foregoing chapter would, I hoped, explain. Of the opposed risks—of being intolerably trite in my comments and of being indefensibly mistaken—I have taken the one, I expect, about as often as the other. It is in the nature of these risks that we run them most when we suppose we have escaped them.

My second experiment offered to my audience a short paragraph of highly elaborated metaphor and some critical comments upon it with a translation into 'direct language' by Mr Herbert Read. It came from page 29 of his *English Prose Style.* If, as I believe will appear, it is itself an example of defective interpretation, its occurrence in the work of a writer of his reputation makes it the more instructive.

## EXERCISE TWO

The following passage shows the use of merely decorative metaphors:

> The Oxford Movement may be a spent wave, but, before it broke on the shore, it reared, as its successor is now rearing, a brave and beautiful crest of liturgical and devotional life, the force of which certainly shifted the Anglican sands, though it failed to uncover any rock-bottom underlying them. It is enough if now and then a lone swimmer be borne by the tide, now at its full, to be dashed, more or less ungently, upon the Rock of Peter, to cling there in safety, while the impotent wave recedes and is lost in the restless sea.
>
> M. A. CHAPMAN, in *Blackfriars,* April, 1921.
> (Quoted by Stephen J. Brown, *The World of Imagery,* p. 308.) [1]

By translating this passage into direct language the meaning could be preserved without any loss, and even clarified. Because of their vagueness, it is not always possible to be sure that exact equivalents have been found for the metaphors; but this only reveals the weakness of metaphorical writing. The translation which follows may not be so pretty as the original, but it is more definite, and to be definite is the proper aim of expository writing:

> The Oxford Movement may belong to the past, but before its end it produced, like its successor of today, a fine sense of liturgical devotional life, the force of which certainly had some effect on the looser elements of the Anglican Church, though it failed to reach any fundamental body of opinion. It is enough that the Movement, when at its height, led a few desperate individuals to become converted to the Church of Rome, and there these remained in security of mind when the Movement, losing its force, became a merely historical phenomenon.

[1] The reference appeared by my *incuria* in the sheet as issued to my audience. It led some to suppose that the name of the critic and translator was Brown. A few, however, had read *English Prose Style* and recognized the passage.

The first impression given by my 200 odd protocols is that the task as set was found much too difficult by more than half the audience. Too many separate points of interest were raised simultaneously; general questions interfered for them with the examination of details, and *vice versa;* theory and practice competed. Some discussed only the argument, others only the example. Those with a span or grasp of attention capable of holding both aspects together and bringing them into order were few. To stretch this span is, without doubt, one of the main purposes of such exercises, but here the strain imposed was too great. It would therefore be better on another occasion to divide the experiment into two stages: to give first simply the original paragraph and Mr Read's translation with some such question as: 'Do you consider that the second version adequately reproduces the meaning of the first?' As we shall see from the protocols, any formulation of this question which includes words such as 'meaning' or 'say' will raise, for many of the writers, serious theoretical difficulties. And indeed it should and must. We cannot avoid these difficulties and it is our business to bring them into the focus of attention, but gradually and in the form most favourable to reflection. So at this stage the less we distract the readers from the close comparison of the two paragraphs the better.

After the comparison has been made and the extremely diverse opinions which it elicits have been displayed and discussed, we might go on to give the whole paper (as I have printed it) with perhaps some further paragraphs from Mr Read's discussion on the preceding page (see Appendix, p. 402) to assist perception of the assumptions he is allowing himself to make. We could then invite comment upon the argument and on the general questions.

I propose, in my citations from the protocols, to follow this order, and to give, first, evidence of the ways in which the original and its translation were read. I follow that up with reflections upon some who failed to read *either* closely enough to have anything to say; and then pass on to larger and more confusing questions, such as the limits of the literal, an alleged impossibility of translation, the rivalry between the metaphor and its meaning, the coherence of Mr Read's argument, and the readers' struggles with it and with the senses of 'definite.' But advance samples of all these troubles appear in this first collection.

Almost every phrase in the translation gave occasion for differences of opinion among the commentators, so various that the last of the protocols were still adding novelties to the collection. What two of them intended to say, in noting the possibility of many interpretations, was thus irresistibly borne out:

> 2.11. Various other paraphrases into direct language could be made, which would provide other definite meanings: but in no single one of them would the meaning of the original metaphorical passage 'be preserved without any loss.' The essence of the first passage is that it is vague, that several definite meanings could be abstracted from it, and all of them be right. The writer apparently did not require or intend a very high degree of precision.
>
> The critic admits all this himself, apparently without knowing that he has done so: he says 'it is not always possible to be sure that exact equivalents have been found for the metaphors' etc. Of course it is not. It is the essence of metaphor that while it gives a precise image,—in this example a visual image—it is capable of various interpretations, can include various different but related meanings.

The repeated phrase 'the essence of' is not perhaps to be taken seriously here. It is a trick of the writer's phrasing rather than of his thought—a 'tic' of expression. 'Some metaphors give precise images . . .' was all he needed to say. The over-emphatic phrase hid from him, momentarily, that there are others which do not. We can already see that 'vague' and 'precise' are words needing special attention. A multiple meaning, or an alternation of meanings, is not necessarily a vague one.

> 2.12. The difficulty of finding an exact equivalent for any metaphor is the same difficulty that we encounter in paraphrasing any passage of poetry. It is impossible in paraphrase to find one correct meaning and exclude all the other possibilities. The Writer probably means every meaning that we can suggest and more besides.

I do not think he would hold to his last remark if he read through the protocols! Over-emphasis has betrayed him too. A naïver critic took a juster view here:

> 2.13. The 'corrector' of the first passage speaks of 'translating this passage into direct language.' This is really impossible, for no two people regard the paragraph from the same point of view. We all derive from it meanings which are different. Therefore, the transla-

tion of the passage into 'direct language' cannot be accomplished to the satisfaction of everyone, especially as the passage in question, owing to a liberal use of metaphor, cannot be pinned down, so to speak.

Another, more warily, said:

2.14. In certain kinds of writing the various mental images brought to mind by a metaphor, though they lack precision in themselves, and one person may obtain a different mental image than another person, yet they are an asset and not a liability. . . . Metaphor extends the range of meaning and opens endless combinations and possibilities, but in so doing it is never less exact because of that, but rather its exactitude covers a wider range of meaning.

I now take the two passages phrase by phrase:

*may be a spent wave*                    *may belong to the past*

2.21. The inference of 'has been' remains, while the overtone of force and splendour (reinforced by the later images) has vanished.

2.211. A 'spent wave' implies more than a 'past' movement—because it also has the idea of force, progress and depth, also of something greater than man, which is important to the exponent of the Oxford Movement.

The next develops, and so explains this.

2.212. A metaphor such as this conveys so many new values of the fact that it appears to present several new, separate, yet welded together, facts, e.g. the translation 'the O.M. may belong to the past' conveys far less to me than 'the O.M. may be a spent wave' which presents the O.M. in the following ways:
(1) as an outburst of energy (not stated, but understood)—the wave has uprisen.
(2) as a part of something much bigger—the sea or the Catholic (universal) Church.
(3) as an effort which has achieved its aim—i.e. broken on the shore.
(4) a spent wave flows back and seems to feed the successor which breaks over it.

2.213. A spent wave suggests momentary power—present ineffectiveness; possibly, probably, some enduring result. 'May belong to the past' is simply a scientific statement, impartial and cold.

'Belongs to the past' might be (Cf. 'its end'); but 'may' is surely rhetorical and, together with 'but before its end,' has here lost the connecting, antithetical force it had in the original.

2.214. 'A spent wave' carries a suggestion of momentary crisis and of hopelessly transitory beauty, which makes 'belongs to the past' seem obtusely bald.

2.215. 'A spent wave' conveys sensations (partly through remembered sights and sounds, partly thro' past metaphorical uses) which cannot be conveyed by 'belong to the past,' e.g. exhaustion, faintness, flagging etc.

The point about past uses is well observed.

2.216. If the Oxford Movement is a spent wave, it not only means that it belongs to the past but that its power is exhausted and cannot be revived.

2.217. 'spent wave' implies a duty performed.

A dark saying to me, and not so profitable to inspection as:

2.218. He seems to be an enthusiast, and therefore has to avoid emotional irrelevance. What would be otherwise irrelevant can often be well combined in a metaphor: its frequent vagueness is not due to what the critic terms its 'weakness,' but to its numerous emotional and sense-implications. Thus it seems more accurate, more 'definite' in fact, to describe the Movement as 'a spent wave' rather than in the phrase 'may belong to the past'—which has an entirely different meaning. For the metaphor 'a spent wave' may (can) have only one (set of) implication(s), but 'belong to the past' has many.

What seems puzzling about this is explained by evidence of the process of composition in the Manuscript. He wrote at first ' "a spent wave" may have only one implication.' Then noticing, probably, that this hardly accorded with what he had written above, he changed 'may' into 'can' and made it 'one set of implications.' He does not save his sentence by this, I think, for how 'belong to the past' has many implications (in the sense he requires) has to be explained. Was not his point really that 'belongs to the past' has *no* implications and so will not link up with what follows as 'spent wave' will? However, the self-contradiction, and the changes, show that the writer is in touch with the chief difficulties that come from the ambiguities of 'definite.' He is in a much more hopeful position than scores of others who ran into no such troubles and the rest of his protocol (2.2581 below) contains acute remarks.

He serves me as an excuse for another moral. These detailed comparative studies of the 'scatter' of interpretations, while we keep to the readings that depart little if at all from normal paths, become all but insufferably tiresome and monotonous. The erratic case comes as a relief, and we sit up refreshed to take notice. But the inexplicable absurdity is a mere distraction; what it yields is not to our purpose. It is the deviation whose origin can be traced that is interesting. When traced it loses its charm as a 'howler,' and a temptation to read it in the more amusing way has to be watched for and firmly resisted. Craziness enough remains in the protocols without our collaboration.

*before it broke on the shore*                                            *before its end*

    2.22. Came to its inevitable predestined end.

    2.221. More happens when a wave breaks on the shore than when a Movement just ends. This may be meant to be implied.

The next details some of this:

    2.222. This is not correct, for a wave breaks when it reaches shallow water, and then sweeps in and up the shore. 'Before the end' does not give anything of this meaning—whilst the metaphor produces a definite picture of the author's meaning, the second 'definite' phrase merely gives the reader the satisfaction of knowing that the sense of 'devotional liturgical life' came somewhere between start and finish of the movement.

Just how far these implications are to be followed up is discussed later. 'Not too far yet,' I am inclined to urge. The 'breaking wave' metaphor does, I think, carry over this much, and its effect is left out in the translation. The next comment touches on a different aspect of meaning and accuses the translation of an addition:

    2.223. Perhaps an added tone of sheer inanition in the translation as against a fine climactic end in the original.

*reared . . . a brave and beautiful crest*          *produced . . . a fine sense*

Here the scatter was wider and more instructive. Let the last speaker continue:

2.23. Here it is plain that all the sense of a fine and perhaps tragic striving has departed. 'Fine' alone is a half-ironic term, no equivalent of 'brave and beautiful,' the crest is a symbol of an impossible but courageous instability; and Mr Brown's combination of 'liturgical devotional' is apparently designed to imply that the devotion was only liturgical.

The last remark is an ingenious explanation of a change that seems (otherwise than as the typewriter's doing) hard to account for. But just where are we getting to with 'impossible instability'? Almost certainly Mr Chapman intended nothing of the sort and if he has really implied it then metaphor is even more a double-edged weapon than it is supposed to be!

2.231. The mingled admiration and condescension of this phrase is lost in the translation—as is the suggestion of a forlorn pre-condemned hope. (2.213.)

2.232. The devotional life was the crown and top of the Movement and was also as quick to vanish as sea-foam.

These three commentators, I may remark, perhaps, without prejudicing any particular question, were those who, on their general performance in the protocols, as I realized long afterwards, most clearly would have gone into a 1st Class had I been marking their papers in a Tripos Examination at Cambridge. I regret that I know nothing more about them.

2.233. Though the phrase 'brave and beautiful crest' is rather self-conscious it implies that liturgical and devotional life was the chief glory of the Oxford Movement, and an intrinsic part of it, which the attempted equivalent does not convey.

2.234. There is a much more definite sense of the depth of religious feeling in the phrase 'a brave and beautiful crest,' etc. than in the corresponding 'fine sense.'

The versatility of these metaphors of spatial degree is notorious. (Compare the 'shallow water' of 2.222.) Transpose the signs on our co-ordinates, 'and the hollows and heights of the world are as one' to use the words of a great expert in wave metaphors. But little risk of misunderstanding, however, is, as a rule, introduced by these superficial contradictions. They are clumsinesses of expression only. A defter writer may escape them and yet be much more erratic in his thought.

2.235. The metaphor 'a brave and beautiful crest' etc. legitimately conveys much more than 'a fine sense of,' because it conveys pride, or perhaps aspiration. The translation into plain terms has missed this.

I miss it too; and take it to come here as an echo from quite different metaphoric uses of 'crest.' Aspiration, of course, might properly come from 'devotional.' This echo process by which words take over powers from other uses is of great importance and will be considered below. (Cf. Chapter XIV, 242.)

2.236. There seems to be some hint of a gleam of light through the wave, which associates with Light, the religious symbol in stained glass windows.

Here a visual image (in the sense of an actual picture before the mind's eye and not merely thoughts of things which might be so pictured) has probably come in. (Compare the Ruskin paragraph quoted on page 181.) This associative enrichment or development, though, does not *here* pass out of the control of the main sense. Too often it does, which is the danger of such flights of fancy. Mental pictures are mentioned by the next writer, but, in spite of this, I see evidence that he is no visualizer himself:

2.237. The passage gives its meaning vaguely to the mind of the reader, but has none of the force of the translation.

General opinion, as we shall see, is vigorously opposed to his. Probably the ambiguities of 'force' are responsible. It is perhaps here no more than a term of praise, implying that something approved of is more present in the translation. He continues:

The use of a metaphor is to enforce the meaning by calling up a mental picture which, with its analogies and suggestions, would impress it more forcibly and more fully on the mind. In order to do this, it must not only be a careful comparison, which can be tested at each point (like Milton's similes) but it must be capable of arousing some suggestions and memories in the mind of the reader. For instance a metaphor describing an arctic sunrise could have no meaning whatsoever for most readers.

His last remark is in part why I think he is no visualizer. This is indeed a drastic appeal to a doctrine of 'experience.' How firmly a crude theory can suppress common knowledge! We should expect him to be a pedant when he comes to detail, and we are not disappointed.

> The force of the crest of the wave is said to be the power of the movement—true regarding the facts of the Oxford Movement, but a weak metaphor, because untrue.

It is the case that Chapman has made the crest, not the whole wash of the wave, do the work. Most readers, though, took this in their stride as an ellipsis. If we do not, there is again a danger of developing the metaphor too far (cf. comment on 2.23) in a fashion in which it would conflict with the purpose it is being used for. There is no metaphor which we cannot, if we wish, break down by over-development. The question to be discussed later is 'How is the limit of proper development set?'
Here is another who shared this literalist's trouble.

> 2.2371. Really good metaphors are not applied so externally as these, which are not always fitting, e.g. The crest of the wave disturbs the sands. Where fact, as it so often has, must be tempered with emotion, then metaphor may serve a very useful purpose.

Whether this last remark is intended as an apology for Chapman or is about something else and thus whether its own metaphor is *not* applied 'so externally,' I am not able to decide.
Here is the humble but baffled enquirer. He is the man we most want to help so I give his protocol in full.

> 2.238.* At a first reading, the meaning of the original passage appears to be fairly clear, but a second reading and a comparison with the version in direct language reveal its vagueness. No precise meaning seems to be conveyed in the words: 'it failed to uncover any rock-bottom underlying them.' I am quite prepared to believe that the

translation, 'it failed to reach any fundamental body of opinion,' is an accurate expression of the author's meaning, but it happens the impression I gained from the phrase 'rock-bottom' was of a 'basis of belief' rather than a 'body of opinion,' and it seems to me that the original formula of words admits equally well of either interpretation, and of others. Similarly, it was with slight surprise that I found 'sense' put forward as a translation of 'crest,' as it seemed that 'crest' should convey a more definite meaning than that contained in this use of 'sense,' but what that definite meaning is I cannot discover. Most surprising to me was the transformation of the 'lone swimmer' into 'a few desperate individuals.'

There are occasions when metaphorical language can be used to convey a clearer impression than direct language could do, but this is not one.

He needs more courage. But here is a very confident writer who is, I think, in a worse case, though he does not know it.

2.239.* The first passage uses such images as are carried to their logical conclusion. One knows what to expect. The spent wave, breaking, rearing, shifting the sands, and rock-bottom. Such would be the fate of any wave that reared its head. Perhaps its obviousness goes to prove that the simplicity or straightforwardness of the second passage is more convincing. To an audience of rather sentimental people a passage like the first, read in a chanting voice, would prove more effective.

The first passage reveals a person interested spiritually in the subject, conversant with the average taste. The imagery is carried too far: a lone swimmer, tide, dashed upon the rock, clinging, lost in the restless sea. Before one reads a line of the passage one knows the sequence and end.

The second, like a newspaper report, is a disinterested report. Its purposes, however, are far-reaching. 'A fine sense' seems to me better than 'beautiful crest.' Sense of life has more meaning in it. As prose the first sentence of the second passage does not read as well as that of the first. It seems too long, a little out of control. The second sequence of the first passage does not translate quite in the same way.

Preconceptions about 'style' are often a heavy hindrance. This reader knows too well 'what to expect' to notice much of what happens. I return to these 'distancing' effects of superior literary attitudes below. (See pp. 95-7.)

*shifted the Anglican sands . . .*          *had some effect . . . looser*
       *rock bottom*                    *elements . . . opinion*

Here interpretation scattered widest, as we would expect. I will begin this time with a helpless reader:

> 2.24. The first sentence fails because it is more of a statement than an attempt to evoke emotion and there is thus. every reason for banishing rather than introducing metaphor. Certain metaphors do not confuse the sense of ordinary expository prose; such metaphors as 'regard, uphold, grasp, uplift' etc. are generally harmless. But in the sentence before us the metaphor is so long sustained that it conceals the sense and so laboured that it spoils instead of improving the sentence. The sentence, for instance, which describes how 'the force of the wave certainly shifted the Anglican sands, though it failed to uncover any rock-bottom underlying them' verges on the ridiculous and is quite useless, since it cannot be understood. By saying that the wave 'had some effect on the looser elements of the Anglican Church, though it failed to reach any fundamental body of opinion,' the translator has exhausted only one of the possible interpretations.

How does he know what the first sentence is trying to do? How does anyone ever know these things? How do we tell joke from earnest? Scores of others arrived as confidently at the reverse opinion.

Only from what a passage does can we gather what it is trying to do. And, when it fails, only its failure can tell us what it failed at. Certain general characters, harder to discuss than points of detail, guide all interpretation—showing us with what kind of purpose we have to do. Failure to interpret these general characters aright ruins everything. But *intention* can rarely show itself directly, and must be divined through the things the words do in its service. (See pp. 103-4, below.) This writer assumes (with Mr Read) that the intention must *either* be to convey emotion *or* to state fact, and that while emotion may require metaphor, statement requires direct language. These assumptions oversimplify and are extremely misleading; to dissipate the confusions which give rise to them is one of the teacher's longest tasks.

The 'cannot be understood' point is much more manageable:

> 2.241. The phrases about the shifting of the Anglican sands 'though it failed to uncover any rock-bottom underlying them' is vague—it

might refer to doctrine, to the effect on the membership, opinion, ceremony, or almost anything connected with the Church.

If it did refer to all this, what then? The next reverses the charge:

2.242. The metaphor is clear, but the definite term 'looser elements' vague. For in what sense is 'looser' to be taken? Freer from conviction, less erudite in dogma, easily swayed by strong emotional appeal: to quote but a few of the possible interpretations.

The next writer is prepared to come much closer:

2.243. In support of the original passage it may be alleged that it is not expository in the sense accepted by S. J. Brown; that the metaphors are not 'merely decorative,' that decoration is a subsidiary function in this passage, and that the difficulty of being sure that exact equivalents have been found for the metaphors is at once the strength and the main purpose of them as they are used here. The author of the passage might point out for example that if to the majority of Anglican readers 'the Anglican sands' conveys only 'the looser elements' of that church, as the words do to Stephen J. Brown, to his Roman Catholic readers they may suggest the whole Anglican Church; and that in close conjunction with the word 'rock' and in a religious discussion he can depend upon the word 'sand' to evoke derogatory memories of the house founded upon it in the parable. In fact, the metaphors are of use to him in two ways; first and most important in that they are more open to variety of interpretation than more direct expressions and therefore fewer readers will be inclined to disagree with the passage—since they will probably take it to mean what they would like it to mean; and second, that they provide him with an opportunity of reinforcing his argument by the evocation of an authoritative and sympathetic background, which will enable his article upon forms of faith to escape from the ill-suited one of a newspaper.

Less acquaintance with the Bible did make things harder:

2.244. The 'Anglican sands' do perhaps seem far-fetched and as if they had been scattered on this special shore that this special writer might use them specially for this meaning. But do they mean what the second writer would have them mean—'the looser elements of the Anglican Church'?

2.2441. 'Decorative' metaphors—Yes. The 'sea' image running through the passage does not clarify the thought, it merely gives the passage a kind of unity, that does not seem particularly necessary. The writer probably thought of the Oxford Movement as a 'spent force,' decided to make it a 'spent wave' and then thought of making the finest results—the 'crest'; the Anglican Church the 'sands' (though I cannot imagine why! Surely the Oxford Movement came out of the Anglican Church, therefore given that the O.M. is a 'wave' the Church must be the 'sea'); Cardinal Newman, etc. lone swimmers, apparently 'on the wave.'

Those who knew something about religious differences (or at least brought their knowledge to bear in their reading), and they were fewer than we might expect, had yet a further advantage. It made some of them nervous.

2.245. Without entering a religious controversy, the first writer seems a Roman Catholic, and he would regard the Anglican religion as all sand and no rock—no firm foundation of belief. If I am correct in my interpretation, the first metaphor means much more to me than any clear statement—the idea is flashed on to the brain.

Another finds himself (herself?) so enthusiastic over the paragraph that she is careful to add in a footnote, 'I am neither a Roman Catholic nor an Anglo-Catholic.'

2.2451.* 'The Rock of Peter' means far more than 'The Church of Rome.' It reminds us how Christ renamed Simon, and called him 'Petros,' or 'Peter,' which is the Greek for 'Rock.' It reminds us that Peter was the first Bishop of Rome, and that Roman Church assumes its infallible authority on the grounds that Christ gave Peter the Keys of heaven and of hell. It reminds us that modern Catholics may still speak of the Pope as though he were St Peter himself. The translation in this instance does not preserve the meaning of the original passage; it makes it clearer by making it weaker. 'The Anglican sands,' also, is badly translated to 'the looser elements of the Anglican Church.' By 'the Anglican sands,' Mr Chapman means the whole body of the Anglican Church; it is a term of contempt, used by one who seems to despise the Anglican Church for its lack of authority. Metaphor, when used competently, is a far more pregnant and powerful medium than literal statement. It enables the writer to communicate more in fewer words. It is also a more sensitive and subtle medium; it makes possible the communication of fine and delicate shades of feeling. It becomes dangerously vague in the hands of someone who uses metaphors without knowing. But Mr Chapman does not make this mistake; by a supreme intellectual feat, he is able to preserve one metaphor from beginning to end, to expand it into every possible detail, to wring from it every possible nicety of meaning, and to make his images fit exactly and continuously the literal facts that they are meant to represent. His images fit his ideas so nicely, that the further Mr Brown wanders from his original, the less exact he becomes. His apparent exactness is specious and false.

In other cases it was the readers who did this expanding, wringing and fitting:

2.246.* The translation is not only not so pretty as the original, but fails to say what Mr Chapman does succeed in saying. The aim of expository writing may or may not be to be definite, but the passage from Blackfriars is one in which it is the emotion behind the sense that is more important than the plain statement of what is meant. One arrives at one's knowledge of that feeling largely through the metaphor; the consistency with which it is maintained, the choice of correlates to its different parts and the rhythm which sweeps us from one part to the next. One learns from it Mr Chapman's admiration for the more Roman Catholic aspects of the Oxford Movement: his contempt for the Anglican Church generally, and his certainty of the necessity of the Rock to all men.

Little of this survives, or survives in its original intensity, in the translation: and it is perhaps the emotion in the passage which leads one to quarrel with some details of that translation. Surely the rock-bottom underneath the Anglican sands is not just 'any fundamental body of opinion'—but the same rock as the Rock of Peter. This interpretation conveys a sense of tragedy, as one feels how near the wave was to uniting itself with the Rock, and squares with the feeling of striving to a great purpose which informs the passage.

2.2461. The Anglican sands were shifted implies that the accumulations of Ages, which were hiding and destroying the true church were at least disturbed though not removed—this cannot be interpreted by 'looser elements,' the idea of the rock as the true church is lost.

These, I feel, support the opportunist suggestion in 2.243; they 'take it to mean what they would like it to mean.' More knowledge and reflection gave a better result.

2.247. Shifted the Anglican sands—the metaphor of sands is a pregnant one and the writer may hope to stir various associations and obtain his desired result—the introduction of a vague suggestion of the insecurity of the Anglican Church by this Biblical metaphor of the house built upon the sands leading his hearers to expect the antithesis of the "Rock" of Peter which is skilfully deferred until the conclusion of the paragraph. 'Anglican sands' suggests the whole Church and is really richer and more comprehensive than 'looser elements.' In fact 'looser elements' is the vaguer of the two expressions. 'Any rock-bottom'—again is more suggestive than 'any fundamental body of opinion.' In fact a 'body of opinion' can hardly furnish a rock-bottom, since opinion suggests uncertainty, eclecticism, contradiction. 'Rock-bottom' may stand for more than conviction and probably includes validity of Orders and Sacraments in the writer's mind.

In case this should now seem 'the only possible view,' let me append:

> 2.2471. He has given an adequate 'scientific' rendering of the metaphor of the shifting Anglican sands and the rock-bottom of opinion.

> 2.248. 'Had some effect' is less definite than 'shifted' and the whole phrase in the earlier passage, implying 'created a general change in,' is not borne out in the later one. 'Uncover any rock-bottom' is not adequately translated by 'to reach any fundamental body of opinion,' since 'failed to uncover' implies 'did not discover, if there *was* anything *to* discover.'

The sarcastic intention is rightly noted; the other point is more doubtful. 'Shifted,' did it apply to *sands,* would be more definite. But, as saying something about *the basis of Anglicanism,* who can decide how definite it is, since there is no means of knowing what it says? It could hardly be less definite than 'had some effect,' however, and the loss again of the derisive gesture in 'shifted' is—one would like to write—'unmistakable,' but all such words, 'obvious,' 'evident,' 'undeniable,' and the like, may seem at this stage to be turning into extravagant tropes.

'Looser elements' proved to be as ambiguous as 'sands':

> 2.49. What is meant, for example, by 'looser elements of the Anglican Church'? Only if the reader knows the character and opinions of the men who were affected and has gathered that Mr B. considers the word 'looser' appropriate to these men and no others does the phrase become in any way 'definite.'

'And no others' (words or men?) is a very representative muddle. Will the suggestion of another that Mr Brown

2.2491. supplies us with an idea of unruly and turbulent members amongst the clerics of the Church

help us at all here?

| *It is enough . . . Rock of Peter* | *It is enough . . . Church of Rome* |

2.25 The difference between these two passages is due to the different aims of each writer. The former is concerned with expressing the glamour of the Oxford Movement per se and not so much with a plain statement of fact. And yet the facts are there, underneath the images. The former passage contains all the facts which the latter has, is rather shorter and, at the same time, expresses more. For example 'a lone swimmer' does at least reveal some sympathy and admiration on the part of the writer, but to translate this by a few 'desperate individuals' completely changes the tone and gives it a patronising rather strong and silent flavour.

2.251. 'A few desperate individuals' does not seem to me an accurate translation of 'a lone swimmer.' The paraphrase does not convey the idea of a single lonely individual floundering in a sea of conflicting opinions.

2.252. Nowhere does Chapman imply desperate individuals—as though all 'lone swimmers' were bent on suicide— . . . The danger of poor metaphorical writing is precisely what has occurred here—it can be made to mean all things to all men, If one imagines a pleasant and sunny sea, the 'lone swimmer' has just gone rather too far out. If one imagines it stormy he is obviously 'desperate.' In the quotation given the metaphor is muddled—not clear enough.

The last writer is playing with one half of the metaphor and ignoring the Oxford Movement. But there are always the two sides and though the main transference may be one way, what is given is governed by what receives it. (See Chapter VII.) In this case the action between the O.M. and the wave image is reciprocal. The O.M. determines what sorts of waves etc. they shall be which represent it—nearly as much as they, in their turn determine how it shall be represented. But metaphor is a famous decoy for the clever, the more captivating to them the further it is followed. If the writer may easily forget what he is writing about under the spell of his image (and I shall examine in the next Chapter some accusations of this that were brought against Mr Chapman) so equally may the reader forget what he is reading about—as, I take it, this reader has forgotten here.

**2.253.** The wresting of will from the individual is ignored in 'led a few desperates.'

A good point, put more explicitly by

**2.254.** 'led a few desperate souls' does not imply, as does 'borne by the tide,' that some men were carried, actually in the movement, not as reaction from it or as a result of it, and 'to become converted' is a poor equivalent of 'be dashed, more or less ungently,' which gives an impression of the unwilling and unexpected conclusion. The general meaning is abridged and weakened in the later passage.

'More or less ungently' was a phrase complained of by several, who were too busy detecting what they regarded as a weakness of style to consider just what was being written of or what might be implied. This peculiar 'literary' or 'stylistic' interest frequently accompanies, if it does not cause (by distraction), an imperceptiveness of more important matters, and I quote at greater length from several protocols to illustrate it:

**2.255.** 'The following passage shows the use of merely decorative metaphors.' Well, perhaps; though 'decorative' is hardly the term which fits them, for here is a piece which needs some careful dissecting in order to see which metaphors are decorative, which simply horrid and which not metaphors at all:
'Reared, as its successor is now rearing.' The phrase to rear a crest is one which does not bear too close a scrutiny. Separating the 'reared' from its 'crest' by the parenthesis draws much too much attention to the phrase and makes it appear ungainly.
'To be dashed, more or less ungently.' Here again, the love of that trick of style of inserting a little qualifying phrase has brought about a piece of clumsy writing. 'Dashed' is a good strong word and ought to be left to itself, but dashed 'ungently'—too absurd.

The writer is very confident and his 'superior' attitude is a clear warning. What is wrong with 'to rear a crest'? It is surely familiar enough in connection with waves (cf. White horses). 'Crest' has been in use from Middle English on for 'the curling foamy ridge of a wave'; and for 'the ridge of the neck of a horse' since 1592. (O.E.D.) Usage, as I shall be arguing in my Second Section, is not in itself the final authority it is often taken to be; but it is evidence that a phrase has seemed appropriate, and in such a case as this it is sufficiently conclusive. And as to the attention drawn by the parenthesis to the phrase, if there is nothing wrong with the phrase there is no reason why we should not attend to it.

Behind the next complaint may be just the silly but common notion that a writer should use as strong words as he can. ' "Dashed" is a good strong word.' Yes, and if we were being asked to think only of breakers, 'dashed ungently' might well be absurd. There is nothing about a natural wave and a natural rock to make gentleness a relevant idea. But the writer is thinking about something else, and in his wider context gentleness has its place. Peter was to be a shepherd as much as a rock. Further, 'more or less ungently' (especially when it is backed by 'now and then') does carry the rather important suggestion of a *succession* of converts and of the varying modes of their conversion. The same preoccupation with trivialities and the same false confidence over verbal niceties accompany a similar complaint in another:

> 2.2551. In spite of the value of its metaphors the texture of the first piece is so bad that the second is clearer and more vivid. This is quite apparent from the number of commas, 7 in the first sentence! 'More or less ungently' is a vague and muddle-headed way of expressing 'roughly.' 'Impotent wave' implies that the wave had no power, what actually it should imply is that it has lost its power.

From comma counting, he turns to settle as easily a point that nearly always asks for delicately balanced judgment. 'Near,' 'not far off'; 'much,' 'not a little'; 'harshly,' 'unkindly'; the choice between these alternatives which English provides us with so generously is usually an occasion for instructive reflection.[1] Apart from a setting nothing of course decides between them since neither is in use. In some setting, when the complex word or phrase is preferred, that will be because its positive component adds or indicates something which the negative word would miss. Frequently the implication is that things are not as we would expect, or not as we would have them to be and this implication is present here. The

---

[1] Opportunities for useful interpretative exercises are thus provided.

phrase contributes to the feelings of nearness and sympathy that the sentence carries.

The explanation of this rough reading is here, as usual, a restriction of the context. Relevant factors are being overlooked; more specifically, like 2.255, he is thinking only of the wave. The baseless bit of dogmatism about 'impotent' which follows confirms, I think, this diagnosis. But he may be trying to make any one of several points, or some of them together. He may be complaining that Chapman did not write 'the *now* impotent wave'—to which a sufficient defence would be that the critic could supply it. Or he may, more probably, be declaring that 'impotent' is being misused, that it means 'powerless from the first,' not 'having lost its power.' If so the Dictionary is against him. But what 'actually it should imply,' means—whether Chapman's phrase or a supposed 'standard use' is being talked about—I cannot decide.

The next comment is an objection to Mr Read's phrase:

2.2552. 'Impotent' means here, I think, inherently without force, quite as much as 'losing its force.'

By adding 'here' this reader leaves 2.2551 far behind; but his correction raises the question 'powerless to do what?'—to pursue which indiscreetly would be damaging to Chapman's metaphor. Powerless to dislodge the convert but not powerless to lodge him? Powerless, as all waves are, in themselves, to save him. We will do well to leave it at that.

Now comes the troublesome temporal problem:

2.256. The 'impotent wave recedes' refers not only to the 'spent wave,' as Read takes it, but also to its 'successor,' and possibly other successors.

2.2561. 'The tide, now at its full' surely refers to a present, not a past condition? The Catholic writer is influenced by a spirit of faith and hope of which his critic appears to have no inkling.

2.2562. The next is 'When at its height.' The original writer is envisaging the two movements as two waves of one tide (not very clearly) and the second sentence refers to the present (and to all time) not to the past days of the Oxford Movement. 'The tide is now at its full' he says distinctly. That is a careless mistake to make. Nor did the Movement and such Movements 'lead' an adventuring and despair-

ing 'desperate' individual or two to Rome. According to the first writer
the tide itself threw them, and 'lone' (which is not truly equivalent
here to 'desperate') means rather 'even one only,' 'singly' and such like.

Mr Chapman's 'historic' or timeless present, like his possibly relative 'now,' would allow us to date the conversions as Mr Read dated
them if we had not a general intention to guide us. The evidence
that can make us reasonably certain, on reflection, that Chapman is
referring to the present also and not to the past only is fairly complex. No single phrase does it; and 2.2562 may be going too far, I
think, in asserting that he 'says so distinctly.' He only says so, if we
are satisfied, on other grounds, that we are to read 'now at its full'
in that way.

2.2563. Again it was not when the Movement was at its height
that individuals were converted to Rome, but at any time: especially
now when the tide is full, and the Movement dead.

2.257. In my opinion the Critic has created his greatest error in the
sentence 'It is enough if now . . . cling there in safety.' In the first
place he makes the Tide equal the Movement forgetting that the
Wave is the metaphor assigned to that task. The Tide is the force of
Religious experience and expression. Again 'to be dashed ungently' is
the hardships and mental difficulties attendant on conversion.

The writer seems to be suggesting that Mr Read has a special creative gift for misrepresentation. The tide, however, is certainly a
more inclusive thing than any of the succession of waves. Wave
and tide collaborate to lodge the convert, and a relation between
Roman and Anglo-Catholicism is thereby rather wittily assumed.
This, though it is not the prettiness Mr Read was thinking of, is
equally left out by his version.

Just how the swimmer is related to the wave and its crest was a
matter several wisely thought would be best not inquired into.
Some were forgiving:

2.2571. 'Desperate individuals' for 'lone swimmers' is, in my reading,
an error. It reveals in the mind of the translator an assumption that
desperation alone leads a man to Rome. The 1st writer would rather
suggest that among many 'desperate' folk only a few self-propelled,
not mass directed, people . . . etc.

2.258. If there is a certain confusion between the shifted sands and
the lonely swimmer, which would call to mind the discrepancy between

a weak vacillating creature and a kind of aquatic Hamlet, then let the connection between the rock-bottom and the Rock of Peter pardon this. It is really an excellent idea, and if the passage is read with the breathless devotion which Cardinal Newman might hope his readers to employ, then it will convey, so much more clearly than the analysis, an idea of what the Oxford Movement was.

The Rock, though, was by no means a peace-offering to others. So far from appearing as 'really an excellent idea,' it became a stumbling block:

> 2.2581. The chief weakness of the first passage lies in its difficulty, not in its vagueness: although the complication of the metaphor,—the use of 'rock-bottom' for 'fundamental body of [Anglican] opinion,' and of 'Rock of Peter' for 'the Church of Rome' (the second use of the word being taken from a context outside the metaphor itself)— is also a defect. Nor indeed, should the critic stress 'the weakness of metaphorical writing' when in a passage of attempted purely expository writing he uses the phrases 'the Movement, when at its height' and 'security of mind,' which are both concealed metaphors. (2.218.)

'A context outside the metaphor itself'—that is the crux. The writer seems to be excluding the parable, if he recalls it at all. And yet

> 2.2582. It seems that the whole metaphor has been suggested by the phrase 'The Rock of Peter,' and so has been loosely constructed to connect it with the text of the passage and build it up into one metaphor.

Many, as we have seen (e.g. 2.245, 2.2451, 2.247), remarked upon the central position of the Rock in their reading of the passage.

> 2.2583. It is the insertion of the Rock of Peter, the use of a metaphor within a metaphor, which again forces the attention of the reader on the actual metaphor and not on what it is expressing.

This well records a phase of the process of interpretation when the reader realizes that the author is inviting him to make more linkages than he supposed. If, on the other hand, he has let himself forget that the passage is not a marine view but a piece of religious propaganda, he may be jerked back uncomfortably:

> 2.2584. The imagery in the first is too entangled. Our associations with waves may allow us to follow the Oxford Movement breaking on the shore and shifting loose sand. Beyond there we cannot easily

go without constant glances back to see just what has gone before. And the bringing in of the traditional Rock of St Peter is another strain—mixing up real sea with artificial rock—bad stage-scenery (as Addison points out). The malicious dig at lack of rock-bottom in Anglican Church also confuses the issue so that all is very mixed up indeed.

If he feels so, he is likely to think that the complexities of the metaphor are distracting. He *is* being forced to attend to the 'how' of the expression, rather than to what is being expressed. But, as 2.247 shows, not all readers—and none of those who recalled the parable—felt this jerk. The moment recorded in 2.2583 passes, and, as the form of the metaphor becomes familiar, what is being said shows through. When it is realized that not just any sea shore, but a sea shore already metaphorized, is being referred to, the connection grows clearer.

The last writer certainly missed the references to the parable and did not supply, as some did, anything to take its place. Nor does the next who, in spite of his 'religious associations,' seems equally ignorant. Some confirmation, perhaps, for the opinion that these complaints against the Rock are not very sound, may be drawn from the other evidence in the protocol of his acuteness and span.

> 2.2585. Chapman is using it extremely carelessly. He claims to be working out one metaphorical image but, in fact, he changes his meaning and brings in new significances. First the connection is extremely vague between the crest at the top which shifts the sands at the bottom, which is later turned into a tide at its full. I think we are justified in treating these metaphors literally, for since the whole claims to be the same metaphor, we should expect literal consistency all through. As another example 'Rock of Peter' is not really of the same type as Anglican sands and rock-bottom—it has a new significance of its own as a stock phrase from the Biblical sentence, and has general religious associations. It is out of place in this literal type of metaphor. Lastly—restless sea is not part of the metaphorical sense at all—it is useless and is in merely for decoration and rounding off.

We have seen that it is Read, not Chapman, who turns the wave into a tide. Whether the whole is, or claims to be, the same metaphor, depends upon how we decide to read it, upon what we are counting in it, and what leaving out. And why should Chapman not change his meaning and bring in new significances? It is the critic who has introduced the rule that he must not; and, with his last complaint he shows that he is not even willing to recall old significances—which brings us to the last point in this comparison— 'the restless sea.'

> 2.259. The whole metaphor seems to me to be unified by a hint that the world is a 'sea of troubles.' This would have evaporated if the author had used a plain method. The point is, is the author quite competent enough to use metaphor? Has the sea a deeply felt response for him? I think he has not quite sufficient grasp and that his metaphor has some similarity to the chalk and water metaphors, which abound in elementary and popular science.

Here critical theories, even more than the accidents of his own metaphors, interfere with the writers' expression of what are, after all, two very sound observations. His first sentence does point to the ground of the whole metaphor; and the last reflects the uneasiness that very few failed to feel. But any weakness in the passage has nothing whatever to do with Chapman's attitude to the *sea!* The critic may not have meant to ask 'Has the sea a thrill for him?' any more than he meant to say that the author by using a plain method would have boiled the world away. What he meant was probably, 'Has Chapman a deeply felt response to the sea?' And *that* is a question which is utterly irrelevant here. The critic has imported out of the 'sincerity prattle' in current theory of poetry, a notion which has no work to do here.

Writers with all sorts of interpretations of 'restless sea' agreed that the translation gave no interpretation for it at all. Here is one in whom we can trace a growing tolerance for the passage as he re-reads it.

> 2.2591. True enough it is difficult not to be repelled by the passage, which is rather overburdened with imagery so that it is impossible to read it without forming a mental picture of an actual swimmer clinging to a rock etc. It would seem that a metaphor to be successful must not be too long, otherwise the passage appears to be written, and tends to be read, more for the sake of the metaphor qua metaphor and pretty writing than for the sake of the sense behind it. But granted that Chapman wished or thought it expedient to use this particular metaphor to describe the Oxford Movement, what has been

gained? Certainly something not to be gained from the very bald paraphrase. An instance or two:—the very last image 'the impotent wave . . . lost in the restless sea.' The phrase 'restless sea,' evoking a clear impression (? because it is stock image?) of the turmoil of religious opinion and philosophical speculation out of which rose the Oxford Movement and which still went on when the Movement had spent its force, finds no equivalent in the critic's paraphrase. There is something rather suitable about the choice of metaphor; each part of it has some meaning behind it and is not merely decorative. Yet somehow the whole passage does not ring true; there is a suggestion of artificiality about it.

Another in whom the same change seems to be occurring:

2.2592. The translator has failed to translate the bias conveyed by the strong imagery of the first passage, 'A lone swimmer, borne by the tide . . .' may approximate to 'a few desperate individuals' but there are possibilities in the first phrase, not covered by the word 'desperate.' I do not think the metaphorical passage merely decorative, because all the time one is reading one is tempted to amplify certain phases as though they were capable of real growth. '. . . the impotent wave recedes and is lost in the restless sea.' Is it the sea of lesser creeds, like the turmoil of little waves, or does it merely mean time as the translator has taken it? Also the description of the swimmer 'dashed, more or less ungently, upon the Rock of Peter' calls into mind at once the circumstances of Newman's conversion in a way the second passage does not.

A third, as reluctant, is more severe on the translator's prose, and tries to use my *Practical Criticism* distinctions to expose him:

2.2593. The failure of the 2nd is most serious at the very end where an overt cliché—'historical phenomenon' is considerably more impotent than the metaphorical cliché—'restless sea.' The latter is somewhat transformed by a preceding succession of marine imagery, and really does suggest the great awesome deeps of unplumbed human sub-consciousness which occasionally causes a storm in the upper consciousness. The 'feeling' of the translator is as different as his 'tone.' Whereas his 'intention' is not personal communication of a directly experienced set of ideas, but simply a 'translation' of those ideas. His intention is expository, the other's is, perhaps dangerously, suggestive as well.

The 'impotent overt cliché' was called other names too.

2.2594. It is doubtful whether the turgid journalese of 'when the Movement, losing its force, became a merely historical phenomenon' means anything.

We have been concerned in this chapter with the detail of the varied interpretations put upon the two passages, and this has required over-much attention to particulars. It is important that in the process of comparing them and turning them about we should not forget that our interpretation of a particular phrase can never be justified by that phrase alone, nor, indeed, as a rule, by any demonstrable combination of 'fixities and definites.' Interpretation constantly responds to the pressure of imponderables. In all our reading we are controlled by considerations which we cannot formulate, however hard we try, by signs we cannot explicitly notice, by forces whose direction or source we cannot indicate, and whose resultant alone is known to us. By this time, we are more intimately and more variously aware of the possibilities of this passage than we perhaps have ever been of any similar thing. We have looked at it through scores of different eyes. We have re-examined it *ad nauseam*. Moreover it is cut off artificially from its supports, which would normally solve many problems for us. It is brief and incomplete. Its two sentences are linked only by an 'It is enough if' which does little to help us to put them into significant connection. And yet in spite of these disabilities it shows us how it is to be read. But just how it does so we must not expect to be able wholly to track down.

These unusual circumstances heighten and make more evident, for this particular example, the general truth that I am endeavouring here to stress. It is as well to stress it, especially when so much close dealing with the detailed interpretation of single phrases may have drawn attention away from it. My point is that it is a general truth. In nearly all reading, we are guided by factors of which we could give no satisfactory account if we were challenged to justify our interpretation. There is nothing, of course, peculiar to reading in this. It is true of all interpretation. How do we sometimes know that a stranger is telling the truth? 'By the look in his eye,' shall we say? But what look? Can we describe it? Can we say just how it differs from 'shifty' looks? We can no more give a satisfactory account which would allow of classification and explicit inference, than an infant can say just why it knows that its mother is annoyed with it. It is the wide controlling influences which most escape and defy reflective, explicit analysis.

This does not mean that our interpretation of them is necessarily less discriminating and accurate. But the situation has this consequence for the teacher. He must recognize that mistakes in the interpretation of *intention* are not to be rectified as easily or by the same means as mistakes about *neutral sense;* and that when mistakes about sense derive from misinterpreting the intention they are also peculiarly difficult to attack. Argument, explanation, the process of pointing to overlooked factors, by which we can try to correct aberrant interpretations in more detailed matters are harder to apply.

It is important not to force them, for nothing induces more distrust of reasonable inquiry than an application of its methods when they will not work. They must be confined to the cases, which are never lacking, in which they can really throw light upon what has happened and upon what should have happened. What we must do is to separate as clearly as we can the points of interpretation that *can* be argued from those that cannot, and show why we leave some alone and argue others. Those we leave alone will include a large proportion of the most typical points of literary criticism—especially the large problems of poetry. We should concentrate instead upon those problems for which we can attain something like convincing evidence of the superiority, the greater adequacy, of one interpretation over another.

Already, in watching the efforts of these readers to compare the passages, we have seen various *general* difficulties getting in their way. Some arise from theories about metaphor or from divergencies in the meanings of terms. These I discuss in later chapters. But beneath these relatively interesting and profitable problems, there are a range of troubles less tempting to examine; cases in which the obstacle is *an attitude of the reader to the whole task of interpretation*. To study these would lead us into characterology and away from our main theme, but I may not omit some slight notice of factors which are perhaps the most decisive, if the least modifiable of all. This is my excuse for the next chapter.

# *Chapter Six:* General Attitudes Preventing Approach

> *The other, taking the booke in his hand, would under-*
> *stand nothing at all, being as meete to reade Aucthours as*
> *an Asse to play on the Organnes.*
>
> SIR THOMAS WILSON, *The Arte of Rhetorique*

All but a few of the citations I have given above were from protocols whose authors found themselves, for good or evil, able to say something in detail about one or both of the compared paragraphs. I should give a misleading impression if I did not follow them with some examples from the writers who did not succeed in coming to close grips with either. They were many. About half my audience remained at a remarkable distance. Some were evidently timid; others disguised their aloofness in various manners, were haughty, affable, humorous, whimsical, politic, theoretical, literary, pompous, discursive; in fifty different ways they found excuses for not committing themselves to detailed opinions about what was before them. This in spite of an explicit suggestion from me that they should do nothing else.

They were under no necessity to write at all, and they were anonymous. I do not doubt that in most cases this remoteness was involuntary, that they were trying, in a fashion, to come nearer, and that these queer circlings and avoidances were due to obstructions of various kinds. If so, these obstructions merit attention. Every teacher knows that mis-workings of the mind are incomparably easier to deal with than failures or refusals to work at all. It is the minds which wander everywhere except in the field they are invited to explore that are hardest to help. To get them to attend closely and yet freely to something put before them is the great first step and often the aim and end of our whole undertaking.

The closeness or remoteness of thought from its subject matter is extremely easy to remark in other people. Whatever it is that we can so describe—and no less metaphorical description of this difference seems to be any more helpful—the way in from remoteness to closeness is certainly the secret and Royal Road to intelligence, understanding, sagacity, insight, and all the useful and creditable modes of learning. What the difference is, or rather upon what it depends in a given case, and why it should vary from one minute to the next, and how ability to approach can be increased, are key-problems in all education.

The best way to help our pupils is to make them more aware of and more reflective about this difference between closeness and remoteness. I have insisted already—and may again—that it is not any mere correction of their mistakes which relieves them, but an understanding of how they came into error. Methods to facilitate such understanding work through heightening this sense of the difference between being close to a question and being at a distance from it. Their virtue will be in the cunning by which they provide suitable opportunities for the mind to ask itself "What have I been doing?" "Am I near or far from the real problem?" An excellent way is to show them *other minds* at work from different distances, and the results—leaving them to draw their own morals in act rather than in words.

What follows is a brief comparison of some types of remotenesses.

2.3.* Emotion blurs the vision of most authors, even when it is held at arm's length (as here to a certain extent) and fixed, so that it becomes the emotion aroused by the memory of an emotion, which the writer is still trying to find words to express.

These two passages are obviously saying different things, because of the different intensity and emphasis. The first is vague, yet impressive, as a gaunt tree seen through a mist is impressive. This awe is emphasised by reference to the sea.

Though the second passage may be more satisfactory as an account of the Oxford Movement, it does not translate the first. There is no warrant for the feeling of disinterestedness aroused by the words 'desperate,' or 'a merely historical phenomenon.' To most people the sea is not merely a scientific phenomenon but a miracle, so the passage has been changed.

A healthy immaturity seems to be shown in these irrelevances, in the super-subtlety, for example, of the first paragraph, as though the writer were practising *the motions* of terrific critical feats rather than actually attempting them. The cloudy edge of play time has not really been crossed; the world of free-fantasy that the child should pass half its time in has not been left. Things for his comment happen as he wants them to. (As the child's savages are 'dropped' by his marksmanship every time. Meanwhile the sparrows escape however closely he aims!) And, as a tale he has been told may become, temporarily, the child's own life, so here, though he does not know it, some other comment by some other person, (perhaps Wordsworth) has been taking its ghostly way through this writer's head.

The same independent, private-world existence attaches to the 'gaunt tree seen through a mist,' it has nothing really to do with Chapman's paragraph: the word 'impressive' and the appetite for 'an emotion aroused by the memory of an emotion' have brought it up. And he is a little nervous about its relevance, as his remark about the source of the awe shows. Before he gets near the Oxford Movement, sea-feelings again take him in charge. He resents their dissipation by the second passage, and he has really nothing else to say against it. For 'disinterestedness' though it might with another writer indicate a *mis*interpretation of Mr Read's attitude, is not, I think, here registering any detailed interpretation at all. He merely dislikes that sort of writing as carrying him away from the seaside.

The remedy, I suppose, is growth, which will occur if testing occasions enough force the adolescent survivals of the child's dream-world habit to withdraw into their proper place. Unluckily, private reading—when it is only a partially controlled form of dreaming—is a protection from such tests. It too often becomes a romantic preserve for mental processes which are relatively extinct in fully waking life. Whence the importance, in such cases as this, of finding the right way of making the reader realize what he has been doing.

Allied to this case is that of the, temporarily, one-idea'd man, the hobby-horse rider. A reader who has recently had what seems to him an important thought, here finds chiefly an occasion to apply it.

2.31.\* Whether a metaphor is a powerful and vivid or merely a decorative metaphor, it will make a deeper impression on any reader. If a speaker wishes to convince his audience, he will achieve more success if he uses metaphor. There are many reasons for this.

One reason is that pride exists in every mind; and when a speaker uses terms of metaphor—'The Oxford Movement may be a spent wave'—the listener feels, consciously or unconsciously, that he is highly considerable in the eyes of the speaker. He feels that his mind is one with the speaker's: that the two minds are running in a single (and an intellectual) groove. If his mind can so follow that of the speaker, he will be automatically convinced.

With regard to 'exact equivalents'—if an exact equivalent has been attained, the thought will be conveyed the more powerfully. If it has not been attained, the eagerness of the hearer to follow up the train of thought of the speaker, and to satisfy his pride in believing himself to be one with the speaker (or writer), will go a long way to clarify the particular point.

It is true that the translation on the sheet is not so pretty, and true that it is more definite, but surely the first leaves a more vivid impression on the mind.

This perception of the importance of self-esteem in motivation, and of its bearing on interpretation, is not a thing of which I can afford, after Chapter IV, to speak lightly! It may, in time, be useful to this reader. Here, I take it, he would have done better to have put it aside. It has prevented him from looking at what he might have noticed without it. But the reiteration of the other notions too, and the mechanical repetitions of pattern are discouraging. The excitement of a train of thought, though not intense enough to spread to other ideas, seems unable to die down and give place, so that he overlooks the most awkward inconsistencies and wrests his reading to his preconception.

I have no suggestions as to a remedy for such a pronounced case as this, but a moral is plain enough. The exercise was much too difficult to be useful. And the frequency with which scripts of this order turn up for the dismayed contemplation of Examiners for the English Tripos at Cambridge, for example, justifies me in putting some weight upon it. No experienced teacher of literary subjects fails to realize that, as we teach them at present, they provide this sort of reader with nothing that does him the least good. They give him endless opportunities to beat the air—usually with such vigorous and sustained gestures that he gets a Third Class Honours Degree. Often he is a hard worker and his Degree cannot be denied him without confessing openly that the whole programme of his studies has been one vast futility. On the other hand there seems no reason to suppose that studies which are not concerned with, or conducted through, language will give him what he needs. A different earlier discipline with words is the only hope.

These dreary reflections unfortunately recur in connection with my next group of protocols. Here, however, the conjectural causes of defeat seem sometimes rather more remediable. But the treatment must be applied before the victims arrive at the University. This is the group of the fence-sitters, the hedgers, who reconcile without considering what has to be reconciled.

> 2.32.* The first noticeable point about this is the fact that M. A. Chapman must be, or must have been in 1921, a very clear thinking gentleman, or he could never have produced such a string of metaphors without getting them mixed. Actually, I think the use of metaphor is here carried a little too far. The passage is flowery and highly decorative, and might sound very inspiring if delivered from a pulpit, but it hardly seems necessary to squeeze twelve or so metaphors into eight lines. It is only fair, however, to agree that they are good ones.
>
> The translation is certainly direct and I think it does, as the middle paragraph suggests, clarify the meaning. True, it is far less imaginative than the original, and so far from being, as the original is, rather emotional, it is distinctly 'brass tackish.'
>
> Frankly, I don't think either of them would make very good reading, for the simple reason that they are extremes, and extremes seldom satisfy. The elaboration of the original would (assuming the writing to continue) soon become sort of sickly, while the hard 'rock-bottomness' of the translation would cause it to come to a standstill for want of oil, as it were. There is nothing like a well balanced compromise.

Quite so! But . . .

> Confucius said, 'They are only your good careful people of the villages, at whom I feel no indignation when they pass my door without entering my house. Your good careful people of the villages are the thieves of virtue. I hate your good careful people of the villages, lest they be confounded with the truly virtuous.' Mencius, when asked why Confucius hated these people, replied:—'If you would blame them, you find nothing to allege. If you would criticise them, you find nothing to criticise. All men agree with them, and they think themselves right, so that it is impossible to proceed with them to the principles

of Yao and Shun. On this account they are called the "thieves of virtue." ' Moreover he said, 'Confucius, not getting men pursuing the true medium, to whom he could communicate, determined to take the *ardent* and the *cautiously-decided*. The ardent would advance to seize their object; the cautiously-decided would keep themselves from certain things. It is not to be thought that Confucius did not wish to get men pursuing the true medium, but being unable to assure himself of finding such, he therefore thought of the next class.'

The great teacher's words [1] are not out of date yet. These followers of a false middle way that is no way to anywhere, lacking both the ardour, which might land them in truth or in discussable absurdity, and the self-critical caution which would tell them when they were out of their depth, make the poorest pupils.

2.33.* The first passage loses much from lack of clarity, directness and power, through the use of a rather heavy and clumsy metaphorical style. It has a distinct tendency to become obscure, especially in the later lines. The piece seems to be too top heavy with metaphors, and cannot be understood quickly at first sight, and so it defeats its end, for the reader gets tired and gives it up in disgust. It is the last four lines that present the real difficulty, especially if the reader does not at first grasp that the 'Rock of Peter' is the Church of Rome, and the reference to the 'impotent wave' at first is inclined to present a little difficulty, but when a little thought is put to the matter it becomes quite plain. But should this passage be read aloud rather quickly to anyone who did not know it, I feel sure that if you asked him afterwards what it was all about he would not be able to tell you very much. It is just a 'clanging of brass,' which very easily might be taken at its face value without excavations were undertaken to find out its real meaning. The critic is quite true—it is very inclined to become vague, because it has been overloaded with metaphors. The author has not hit the 'happy mean!'

The writer doubtless feels that he is discussing an important aspect of the matter, and perhaps several of his sentences are true. But how carefully he has kept at a safe distance, and refrained from telling us, himself, 'what it was all about,' in spite of no slight challenge, as Chapter V has shown, from Mr Read. He shares with the last writer a trick of perseveration—'heavy,' 'top-heavy,' 'overloaded,'—

[1] I am pleasing myself about their interpretation. Mencius' discourse on them is incomplete and seems to have suffered in transmission. Cf. *The Works of Mencius,* Legge's Translation, pp. 374-377.

and a habit-ridden phrasing—'distinct tendency to become,' 'is inclined to present,' 'is very inclined to become,'—which perhaps allows us to hope that an earlier training which gave more place to
reflection than to composition might have helped him.

Now comes an example of a very well-known type—the dealer in
homely 'common-sense' parallels.

2.34.* The question is whether there should be plain writing or
metaphorical writing? I think there should be a compromise. The
question is just the same as whether there should be plain food or
spicy food. I should prefer food with some spices in it. But if the
food contains more quantity of spices than it should, it will produce
dangerous results. Extremes must be avoided. The given passage is
overflowing with metaphor, and so it is an extreme case. If any writing is overcrowded with metaphors its meaning becomes obscure. The
main purpose of language is the expression of our thoughts, and if
we express our thoughts in an obscure and unintelligible way, we
defeat the very purpose of the language. Then, some might argue that
we should use only plain and necessary words and that metaphors
should altogether be done away with. The reply is that plain food is
certainly good for health, but the same food with a bit of spice in it
gives better taste. If we are to read page after page of plain narrative,
it will surely be a very tedious and dull affair. Just like walking in the
plains on a straight road without trees or scenery, or even milestones.
I think the journey will be simply dreadful. Life, with its dull routine
is bad enough, then why should Literature be made dull?

It was very largely because this sort of handling of a question—
through a remote, inessential or irrelevant analogy—is so frequent
that I decided to give exercises in metaphor and parallels a prominent place among my experiments. Traces everywhere appeared in
the protocols of the effects of past warnings from teachers as to the
dangers of analogies in composition. The warnings did not seem to
have been effective, and what effects remained were not entirely
healthful. A merely scared suspicion of metaphor was the commonest, a distrust not justified in understood grounds. Many felt that
there was 'something wrong' about using parallels without having
any further notion as to where parallels might be in place and where
not. I have argued repeatedly that if we reject the use of parallels
we thereby renounce thought. We think by parallelling; and to think
better, to be more intelligent, is to use better parallels. How can we

develop a more relevant choice among the infinite variety of parallels that every question offers? How but by comparing parallels in their turn? Some parallels are condensed and summarized in general words; others, of a less routine order, have to be expressed in metaphor or simile or overt analogy; but there is no essential difference (though habits of interpretation may introduce big practical differences) in the linkage they effect. All alike require 'an eye for resemblances,' to quote Aristotle again, and a complaint against analogies can only be against the use, in thought, of resemblances that do not do the work we require from them.

Here we have one pair, direct and metaphoric writing—compared to another pair—plain and spicy food. There is a resemblance undoubtedly,—for one kind of writing and then only under one aspect —a resemblance which does even have the implication that the writer draws, does even imply that a moderate use of metaphor would be best—all other things being equal. An ingenious mind, looking closely, might, I dare say, invent further resemblances, with further implications, that would break down this last restriction. But he would have to detail them; without that the comparison does not assist with the problem, for here all other things are *not* equal. We are asking about the virtues of direct and metaphoric writing with regard to a varying set of conditions which have no parallels—or none that we can fix—in the use of plain and spicy food.

All this is obvious enough, even though my account of it may not be; but my point is that the exploration and criticism of parallels should be, and could be made, explicitly, a central part of the discipline of intelligence. This victim of a facile analogy is suffering from its neglect. His other parallel of the walk—with his weak yielding to the milestone temptation—shows the strength of the habit. I doubt whether it could be broken. But it has grown through the lack of a training that could, if we realized its value, very easily be given.

The criticism of false parallels is a class-room subject ready made to our hands. Specimens for examination are supplied by every batch of essays. Let it merely be known that a selection of the more doubtful ones will be submitted to the class later for dissection and by that alone the crucial step will have been forced upon those who most need to take it. For the same movement of the mind which finds a bad parallel will also recognize its badness, if a sufficient additional motive is supplied to remove premature self-satisfaction.

The last of my middle-course men is suffering from a verbal disease.

2.35.* It is the aim of any writer—in the use of language to establish an exact congruence between, on the one hand, the received associations of the words used and the manner in which they are related to each other, and, on the other, the ideas drawn from the world of 'experience' which he is attempting to express. And in that process he will find that at times the meaning he has to express is so profound, so subtle in its perceptions, that it, as it were, bursts the bounds of literal statement and assumes the more heightened and vivid form of metaphor. That is the justification of metaphor. That is what we must apply to the two passages before us.

Therefore, the effect of metaphor on the mind of the reader will be increased by a wise forbearance in its use, and debased by an injudicious excess. And this consideration will force us to steer a middle course, as it were, between the two passages. We can say that the subject of the first demands the use of metaphor; but that the metaphor is sustained so long that what began as a method of conveying a heightened impression of truth terminates as a mere piece of virtuosity in the use of words. The metaphor takes its rise in a comparison which is by no means original. For the wave breaks repeatedly, eternally and monotonously in every History Text book. The metaphor is sustained at great length with considerable ingenuity, but with no little violence to that increased definiteness which is the only end and justification of metaphor. Turning to the second passage, we have other reasons for our dissatisfaction. The second passage is not more definite than the first, but it fails for a contrary reason.

The first two sentences are no ordinary achievement in circumlocution. 'A writer tries to say what he means; in metaphor if he can't do it literally.' Is his remoteness from the texts due to the lumbering sentences on which he rides in his approach? Or the other way about? Impossible to say without more evidence. He will, however, seem both snappy and to the point, 'ardent' and 'cautiously-decided' too, if put next to

2.36.* The main question arising for me is whether the weakness of metaphorical wording really is revealed only because it is not always possible to be sure that exact equivalents have been found.

Taken from a philosophical treatise and cited without preliminaries, the first passage might appear unsatisfactorily. The meaning of the sentences is not definite enough to be understood in an irreproachable way, but, after all, one can't judge about such a profound question only by reading a mere passage taken from every connection if this passage is written in indirect language. In doing so with a poem, you would fail in the same way. Most probably the expository wording appears clearer in direct language, but it is, in my eyes, throughout possible to write about certain subjects of a philosophical nature (and the Oxford Movement would be among them) in metaphor as well as in direct style. The length is practically the same, and regarding the fact that nearly every author of philosophical writings likes to write in a certain style due to the nature of his subject, it might be that the way of metaphorical style is as well justified as the proposal to be 'definite' in writing direct.

I would be over-exasperating if I continued this show further on these lines. Complete unfamiliarity with the sort of topic—blank inexperience of the kind of interests which the Chapman paragraph exemplifies—seems the likeliest explanation of this inability to enter at all into what is going on. But that explanation only pushes our wonder back upon the modes of his past reading and his invulnerability to former impacts.

# Chapter Seven: Detailed Problems of Interpretation. Tenor and Vehicle

*As to metaphorical expression, that is a great excellence in style, when it is used with propriety, for it gives you two ideas for one.* SAMUEL JOHNSON

The last Chapter was an interlude or reminder to preserve pedagogic perspective, to keep us from losing sight of the wood in the trees.

I now come back to a series of *detailed* problems in the 'Hows' and the 'How nots' of interpretation. Most of them have been touched on in Chapter V; this is an attempt to show more amply and clearly the factors from which the divergences of view, in each case, derived. I will begin with the allied questions 'Did Chapman forget what he was writing about?' and 'How far was the metaphor mixed?'

The suggestion was frequently made

2.4. that the exposition of the Oxford Movement is lost in the metaphorical expression:—after a not-too-careful reading the thing that remains with me is a visual image of the lone swimmer, unrelated to the Oxford Movement. It is possible to get some such meaning as is given in the comment out of the passage by re-reading it carefully, but this should not have to be done in reading expository writing. The mental attitude of Chapman, judging from this passage, seems to be not:—how can I best explain the significance of the Oxford Movement CLEARLY?, but:—how can I explain it beautifully, "artistically"? Chapman may be quite unconscious of this attitude but that does seem to me his approach to the task.

The delicate question is whether the responsibility for any loss of the Oxford Movement lies with the writer or with the reader. The following complete protocols will show how delicate it can be:

2.41.* The faults of the original passage (and it undoubtedly is faulty) are due to the mass of the metaphors submerging instead of revealing or accentuating the writer's intention. Our interest in the Oxford Movement is forgotten in our interest in the metaphor. 'The spent wave' excites our interest and wonder until it is finally 'lost in the restless sea.' In the meantime the converts to Rome have completely failed to take root in our minds as an idea.

In so far as a metaphor colours a passage and helps to clarify to the reader the writer's intention, in so far a metaphor is valuable. It is not necessary that metaphors should make us *know* more about the subject, but that they should make us *feel* more. When a metaphor is carried to the extent of that in the passage under consideration we discover that the *feeling* inspired by it—i.e. the rise, wash and return of a wave—has actually nothing in common with the matter to be conveyed. We may agree intellectually with each constituent part of the metaphor but to feel its likeness we cannot. The fullest value is obtained from a metaphor when the amount we *know* more about the author's meaning is coincident with what we *feel* about it. If the senses respond too fully to the metaphor the sense is lost, while if the mind is the more affected one is liable to become enamoured of the author's cleverness.

Next to this, I may set an enthusiast who, it will be noticed, swallowed all the inconsistencies others noticed in the translation, but managed to supply a good deal that was lacking through his ignorance of the parable:

2.42.* The whole thing depends on the validity of the commentator's summing-up; is 'to be definite' the proper aim of expository writing?

The answer must be in the affirmative, for all prose should be definite; but why isn't the original passage quite definite itself? It is. The commentator is a man who likes to see facts or statements laid down in straightforward reality, so that the meaning can never be in any doubt.

Where our original writer has the advantage over his criticism is that his work is both clear and metaphorical. No one could help grasping the subject in hand; and then what mental joy he can experience in imagining the situation as set down.

The idea of the movement sweeping along like a wave until it meets some hard opposition like a wave does the rocks.

Next, how the followers of any movement which suddenly is scattered do actually escape into the huge infinite mass of people, just like the waves rebounding into the sea.

Again, what a lovely picture he has drawn of the convert floating and then swimming—striving so hard—to reach the stronghold of Rome, where the scattering of their means of getting there will scarcely matter to them.

The imagery here is so complete in its concentration—it is like a French metaphorical passage—that the definite facts which were being set down by the original author include the implied realities translated by the commentator. And in addition the ornamentation of the metaphors, which increase the value of those bare facts.

'Because of their vagueness, equivalents have not always been found for the metaphors'—well, that is unnecessary, as only the use of Anglican *sands* is at all uncertain; they might be the surface matter concluded or developed from the fundamental 'rock,' or the shifting uncertain parts of the whole movement. Give me the first passage every time.

Two ideas for one are well and good for minds that can manage them at once. It seems unfair to blame an author because all minds cannot. The writer of 2.41, I think, can manage two ideas himself and he seems to be speaking on behalf of less fortunate persons, such as:

2.43.* 'Good words in good order' was Coleridge's definition of Prose; and 'the best words in the best order' his definition of Poetry.

This passage is neither the one nor the other. The words are in good order but are themselves singularly unfitted to prose, and would be more suited to a poetic setting. The object of prose should be to make a statement, to communicate a decision or a fact—this passage, unless carefully translated is nothing but a medley of beautiful sounds which communicate nothing.

It does, in fact, evoke a picture of a storm; and this picture spoils its possible success as a symbolic passage. This picture was the only result of first reading the passage—no other communication or emotional result was present.

Here, as 2.41 remarks in his acute last sentence, the senses *have* responded too fully. Imagery has its risks, which should not be forgotten when its function in reading is stressed as too many teachers stress it.

2.41's own trouble, however, seems to be not to combine two ideas but to link the wave *feelings* on to the *idea* of the Oxford Movement. And here a further and important subtlety in the situation is brought out. As the contrast with 2.42, I hope, shows, Mr Chapman is not to blame for this. Others can do just what 2.41 will not do. Blame, if blame it be, lies elsewhere. Those ready to feel wave-feelings about the Oxford Movement, do so. 2.41 is not ready; he 'finds nothing in common' between 'the feeling inspired' and 'the matter to be conveyed.' The subject is controversial, and he is, I fancy, on the other side. He is, if I am not mistaken, crossing two very different questions about the success of the author's intention and about his own approval of it. If so, he would be only doing what more eminent critics have done. T. S. Eliot, to take a recent example, when he objected to Bertrand Russell's very successful advocacy of atheism, preferred to do so by calling it 'bad prose.'

Fewer than I expected were conscious of this controversial aspect —or perhaps cared enough about the Oxford Movement or the Church of Rome to bother about it. The most pronounced intervention of this interest was in the following:

2.44.* There are many criticisms which one might make on both the passages for consideration. First it would be interesting to consider what is the purpose in the writer's mind (of the original prose selection). If, in the first place, he is endeavouring by the use of metaphor to compose a piece of what he considers to be beautiful prose, he is singularly unfortunate in his choice of subject. On the other hand if he is writing an apologia for the Roman Catholic faith, he is not employing language calculated to inspire the reader with the truth which he believes himself to be urging.

The manner of his communication, then, does not fit its matter, although the metaphors may be beautiful it is not certain that they are desirable and even less certain that they are true.

Before commenting on the second passage it may not be beside the mark to comment on the truth of the first. It is, on the whole, not true, this may, or may not, damage it as a piece of writing, but it certainly does as a statement which it proclaims itself to be. The metaphor is well sustained but it is difficult to be impartial and to admire what is not true. If one could divorce the writing from its subject, which is, of course, impossible, it would perhaps be less unpalatable to its present critic.

In the second version, as is noted, the vagueness of the metaphors has caused difficulty. The translator has no technical knowledge of ecclesiastical nomenclature. Thus he cleverly has linked liturgical and devotional life together and called it *liturgical devotional* life, which

is an inaccurate description of the metaphor in the first passage, the
two aspects of worship not being exactly the same.

One could continue—lone swimmers are not always desperate—
here, the translator has not quite kept to the truth of the first statement.

N.B. (This passage is obviously written by an ardent Romanist and
it is not a *very possible* thing that a Cleric of the Anglican Church
should criticise it fairly.)

I did not know 2.44 was among my audience when I issued the
sheet, and had I known I would probably not have expected this.
He may serve at least to remind us that we are not here concerned
with the confusions and bewilderments of schoolboys only, and
that such work as this has bearings on the life of the world at large.
Another was concerned with its controversial aspect in a different
way.

2.441.* If one inquires too closely into the metaphor it does not
entirely hold good.

The wave that dashes one lone swimmer upon the Rock of Peter
must surely dash many more upon the Anglican sands, and this, the
writer has no intention of conveying.

For such a simple subject, the style is too grandiose, too pompous.
The translation shows more desire to drive home a statement than the
first passage, which seems to be a poetical exercise rather than heartfelt conviction.

What does the writer mean by 'uncovering rock bottom'? Is it that
the Oxford Movement did not succeed in striking fundamental tenets,
or that the sand was sifted, and nothing more weighty than a pebble
was found? This passage is so steeped in treacly metaphor that I
find myself using it unconsciously, and probably quite as vaguely.

The translation is incomparably better, because it gives one something to fix one's teeth into, which it should, as the subject is controversial. The first writer sounds as if he loves to hear his own voice,
without caring much who listens, or whether what he says is worth
listening to or not. I should not care to meet him in debate.

I suppose the author would reply that the sands, unlike the Rock,
are no safe abiding place; and the subject, we shall agree, has been
proved to be hardly 'simple.' More important is the first point. No
metaphor, I have urged, entirely holds good if one enquires too
closely. How about the critic's own uses? 'Something to fix one's

teeth into!' Who wants to be bitten in a controversy? Is not there some confusion here between a feast and a dog-fight?

We return to the main question with the penultimate sentence. What about the heartfelt conviction and the writer's concern for his subject as opposed to its expression?

> 2.45. Taking the first passage as one intended to be of an expository nature, I fully agree with the comment that much of its force has been lost by the introduction of decorative metaphors.
>
> One ought, I think, to discriminate, however, between a metaphor in which the force lies upon what is intended, rather than upon the image chosen for the metaphor. In this example there is little wrong with the 'sea' image except the fact that the writer appears to be working with his mind more upon the image than upon the statement he wishes to make. This is seen in the length to which he protracts the 'sea' metaphor. I cannot help feeling that for him the images and the underlying idea were out of proper proportion. If he wished to be at all forceful he would have confined himself either to direct statement or else to statement which allowed metaphor to clarify and not decorate and confuse, as seems here to be the case.

On 'force' see 2.237 and my comment: there are all sorts of forces. The second sentence here raises the interesting point. If we extend it we have the suggestion of a scale. At one extreme would be metaphors in which one of the two 'ideas' would be focal and the other peripheral; at the other extreme their positions would be reversed; in the middle would be the case where both are equally central in attention. We suffer evidently here from the lack of a handy technical vocabulary. Only clumsy and confusing descriptive phrases—'the original idea,' the 'borrowed' one; 'what is really being said,' 'the thing it is compared to' and so on—seem available, unless we make confusion worse by saying simply the 'subject' and 'its expression,' or 'the meaning' and 'the metaphor.' Both 'subject' and 'expression' may, and sometimes must, be used to cover both.

This may seem harmless enough—until we begin seriously comparing and reflecting upon metaphors. Then we find too often— as in many of the classifications of Shakespeare's 'imagery' that have recently come into vogue—that the metaphors are being sorted in respect to one only of the pair of 'ideas' which every metaphor, at its simplest, gives us. The protocol writers by the dozen were ready to sniff at the Chapman passage on the ground that 'its metaphors' were 'trite,' could be found any Sunday in Mr Garvin's leading article in *The Observer*, were merely a stock collection which can be used anywhere to suggest a dramatic situation, that 'this wave has foamed its way through the pages of innumerable history books,' and so on. They were counting as 'the metaphor' only the one member and ignoring the other—behaving like the people who choose a hat and disregard the head it is to sit on, or pick colours without considering what they are to go with.

The ambiguity is not merely inconvenient; it contributes to and protects these and more frustrating confusions and false simplifications. Worst of all it blurs the whole topic and makes analysis, which would otherwise be a clear step by step· process, feel like trying to extract cube-roots from the head. The mere inconvenience of a shortage of fixed terms showed everywhere in the protocols and indeed it is so familiar that its continuance through centuries of studies in rhetoric is a puzzle. I consider some possible explanations in the next Chapter. However that may be, it is curiously difficult to suggest acceptable terms to stand respectively for what is transferred and for what it is transferred to—for the spent wave here and for the Oxford Movement. Without much anticipation that others will do likewise, I shall here use *vehicle* for the spent wave and so on, and *tenor* for the Oxford Movement.[1] I hope so to avoid whatever malign influence it is that develops ambiguity in most terms that imply representation of the one by the other ('representation' itself is the typical specimen).

I can now restate my point about the scale. At one end the tenor is in the forefront and the vehicle in the background; at the other the vehicle is in front and the tenor behind. In the middle case, tenor and vehicle are equally prominent, neither is subordinated to the other. This mid-case is often described as 'a fusion,' or 'identification,' between them, with an implication, as a rule, that this is a specially desirable state of affairs, above all in poetry. But that is an assumption of a kind which holds up inquiry and is at least premature. A taste for the fusion metaphor in discussing metaphors, and the implication that fusions are superior, is perhaps connected with the feelings behind the word *creative*. (See *Coleridge on Imag-*

[1] I discuss these terms and apply them to the analysis of other material in *The Philosophy of Rhetoric*, Lectures V and VI.

*ination,* pp. 32-3.) Tenor and vehicle are like two men acting together. We do not understand them better by supposing that they somehow fuse to become a third man who is neither. Moreover, equal prominence and fusion (if we take fusion strictly) are not the same, and it is obviously best to make as few assumptions here as possible.

It seems probable that metaphors could be arranged according to this scale, if we could decide how the metaphor in each case should be read. But *that* is evidently a great difficulty. As we have seen, different readers here gave very different positions to the tenor and the vehicle. They varied from 2.451 to 2.452.

2.451. The metaphors of the original passage are decorative in much the same way as are the metaphors of the less successful metaphysical poetry. The writer is at least consistent in his use of imagery. The 'spent wave' breaks upon the shore, and shifts the Anglican sands—the lone swimmer borne by the tide is dashed upon the rock of Roman Catholicism, etc.

But these metaphors are not functional, as is brought home when one contrasts the original with the plain sense of the translation.

They are metaphors for metaphor's sake, spun out ad absurdum. In themselves they are not vague. Their vagueness is due to the fact that the writer forgets historical data in his absorption with an ingenious conceit. Instead of metaphors and plain sense running parallel, from the moment 'the wave' is mentioned they diverge rapidly.

2.452. The metaphor of a 'wave' used of some intellectual movement is stale, and all the elaborations with which it is surrounded—'spent wave,' 'reared a crest,' 'shifted the sands,' 'rock bottom,' 'lone swimmer,' 'dashed upon a rock,' 'restless sea'—all these are stale, too. Consequently, the eye passes flatly over them and the brain receives no more stimulus from them than from the matter-of-fact translation given below.

In 2.451 the tenor is said to be forgotten through absorption in the vehicle. In 2.452 it is the vehicle which is said to be overlooked and passed unnoticed. The last, it will be noted, in bringing his charge of staleness, avoids the over-simplification I alluded to above. He adds the phrase 'used of some intellectual movement' to guard himself from it.

Three more:

2.453. The first passage is cloudy, extravagant; it lacks precision but it has movement. It carries you on so that you are interested in the rise and fall of the wave, but to my mind, just as a wave, not as the Oxford Movement.

2.4531. I get the impression from the first passage that the writer of it probably smiled with glee when he found the metaphor he had chosen could go on and on.

2.454. The metaphor is vivid, and through the imagery of the wave the mind *sees* what the passage means.

And three more, which I give at length to illustrate the complexity of the factors that may enter in to decide such an apparently simple question as 'Is the figure perhaps too obtrusive?'

2.455. 'To be definite' (for what the phrase is worth) should be the aim of all writing, and not the exclusive property of expository writing—that is why most of Shelley's poetry is so bad. An exposition will be vague or definite according to the clearness or obscurity of the writer's mind, and not according to whether he uses metaphor or 'non-metaphor' (I put this in inverted commas because non-metaphor scarcely exists).

B. has as many metaphors as A. only they are the unconscious, natural metaphors which have become part and parcel of the plainest prose. We will call this ingrained unconscious metaphor 'non-metaphor' for argument's sake, and only consider as metaphor, the deliberate method of A. (e.g. 'shifted' the Anglican sands).

The critic B. then, is vague himself in not knowing what metaphor is. He is prejudiced by the combative impulse, which I, in the freshness of having only just now been warned about it, hope to avoid, in biting the biter.

Now for the respective merits (or more likely, demerits) of the two passages.

Apart from the question of suitability to its subject, I hate the laboured, piled-on, *painfully consistent* use of metaphor in A. It is metaphor at its cheapest. The writer works himself up into such a state over language that, not caring if he *says* anything or not, he fills his head and the paper with a succession of *juicy* expressions, all following one another in perfect order. But it is much more readable than B, there isn't time to say why.

I had been making some remarks about the influence of indignation upon Mr Biaggini's handling of the Gantry passage and warn-

ing my audience that the combative impulse was a notorious dis-
turber of interpretations. 'Says' has an interesting specialization here,
and there is real resentment behind the phrase 'in perfect order.'
The analysis is taken further in the next.

2.4551. It is very easy to find fault with the first passage. There is
something desperate and wearying in the determination with which
the 'pictorialising' is carried through. Every phase in the history of
the Oxford Movement is forced and cramped into the sea-image,
which was at first only an overtone from the metaphor, almost dead
and fossilized, of the 'spent wave,' and the even less evocative symbol,
'Rock of Peter.'

The result of this wholesale dyeing of the clothes to match the tie-
pin, is that the reader, detecting the process, immediately takes a dislike to its artificiality and painstaking insistence; the device is here
too obvious and too obstinate.

We are at a lower level with

2.456. The comparison of the Oxford Movement, decadent and lacking in fervour and zeal, to a spent wave breaking on the shore, is
by no means odious to our notions. As a simile, though commonplace,
it is pretty and quite apt. Unfortunately the author seems less keen
on expressing his thoughts than on the manner of expression. And
this passage is a perfect example of an ornamental style. It suffers
from the same vice which marred so much of Victor Hugo's work.

His imagination, not a creative one in the sense of Shelley, but
merely a decorative one in the sense of Hugo, is not big enough to
conceive of anything better. The image though not unpleasant is
worked to death, and the crest of the wave, enthroned with the light
of liturgical and devotional life (both of which adjectives are far too
ponderous and ugly to suit the sense) is too much for our perhaps
limited visual faculty . . . but the image is strained still further; with
what results . . . it is almost the ridiculous to the absurd.

Then he elaborates on the idea; and the conception of the lone and
desperate swimmer borne by the tide of fortune to the Rock of Safety,
is to my mind, the best image in the passage. By carrying on a metaphor or simile too long, or by elaborating, the force of the figure of
speech is lost, even as the actor who rants King Lear from beginning
to end, and has no high water mark; it is full out all the time. Of
course, the second piece of writing makes perfectly clear what the first
conveys only in a nebulous manner.

But it is the expression of a more materialistic and precise mind. It has no literary value beyond conciseness. It might be an article for the 'Encyclopaedia Britannica.'

This is full of odd details of interpretation due to wavering between exclusive attention now to tenor, now to vehicle. Something extraneous seems to be brought in by 'decadent and lacking in fervour and zeal' and something essential left out in 'tide of fortune.' 'Enthroned' beats me: I do not think visualizing, in the strict sense, played much part. The remark that Mr Read's version has the merit of conciseness is also puzzling. But the main point is as to the rivalry of tenor and vehicle. This is the explanation of the queer objection to the adjectives 'liturgical' and 'devotional.' If 'the sense' is the tenor, then it is hard to see what other adjectives he could have hoped for. But he is thinking, for the moment, of the wave; the vehicle has come into the foreground and, naturally enough, they do not well describe wave-crests. Why should they?

The length of the metaphor was often given as the cause of its obtrusiveness, also an alleged distraction due to a difficulty in 'working it out':

2.457. The metaphors are so involved that they are confusing, and the reader is forced to be too much occupied with their literal meaning in order to grasp the sentence as a whole. Thus his attention is misdirected, and the metaphors do not serve their purpose of impressing and clarifying what may be called the 'full meaning.'

'Literal meaning' here seems to be the structure of the vehicle.

2.4571. In this passage clear expression has been sacrificed to a very ambitious form of metaphorical pomp, which does not convey an enormous amount till about the fifth reading, and then with the aid of translation below.

2.4572.* There is no doubt that no part of the translation is indefinite, whereas in reading the original, it was essential for me to pause several times to decipher the imagery.

Therefore, if lucidity is a reader's first demand, he may discard the original passage.

There is little doubt, however, that a reader can get a more vivid impression of the sense from the metaphorical passage.

Chapman has developed intensity by complexity, although I believe he could have done better by modifying the metaphor. After a while, a reader is more likely to become impressed with the metaphor *as a metaphor* rather than as a vehicle to facilitate the idea which the writer wishes to convey. One is tempted to believe that Chapman's original scheme was to add force to his sense, but in carrying the metaphor on and on and on, he became intrigued by his own ingenuity, and attempted to swim further in his sea of metaphorical waves, than he should have.

'A figure,' said Longinus, 'does best when it escapes one's notice that it is a figure.'

But some, so far from resenting this puzzle aspect, allowed it merits on its own:

> 2.4573. The metaphors are not 'merely decorative' nor do they obscure the sense; they are rather an alternative interest.

> It is perhaps a low form of entertainment to excite the reader's curiosity as to how the metaphor is to be worked right out, but it is certainly preferable to the flat dull style of the translation.

One made it more than this mere sporting interest:

> 2.4574. Metaphor logically carried out; produces in the reader a certain intellectual excitement, which can be very pleasurable.

And while most who found difficulty accused the passage of disorder and Chapman of carelessness, one took the opposite view—

> 2.46. At first sight the generalization about the weakness of 'pretty' metaphorical writing seems true. But the second passage is as metaphorical as the first; the difference is that in the first, *one definite image* has been adopted and used to the full throughout, while in the second there are hints and implications of assorted metaphors—vaguer than the wave-image—suggested by such phrases as 'looser elements,' 'at its height,' 'insecurity of mind,' 'losing its force.' By 'clarifying' the first passage, the writer has introduced fresh difficulties of interpretation, which are not so noticeable as the image of the first, but are there all the same. . . . The claim that the meaning has been preserved 'and even clarified,' therefore only holds good on the surface. The new version is only an approximate translation. For example, there are several implications in the words 'the *impotent* wave recedes and is lost in the *restless* sea,' that are. not at all apparent in 'the movement, losing its force, became a merely historical phenomenon.'

> Again, the whole idea of waves breaking one after another, and receding after washing objects about aimlessly, surely suggests some-

thing of the nature of historical movements that the writer of the first passage intended, and the writer of the second was obliged to ignore. . . . Because the wave-image is worked out so fully and carefully, it may make it difficult to see exactly what the writer is referring to all the time. But the first passage is not emotional writing, but imaginatively-conceived intellectual writing.

Complaints that the metaphor was mixed will have been noticed. They were often, but not always, associated with the opinion that Chapman had been led into it by too exclusive an interest in his vehicle, or by prolonging it unjustifiably. Here is yet another:

2.461. Metaphor should not only be used to ornament the sentence, nor even merely to express the meaning intelligibly, but it should bring out the meaning in strong relief, enhance it, so that it impresses itself strongly upon the mind of the reader. Straightforward, direct language is all right in text books where it is read in small doses and learnt like a parrot by unfortunate schoolboys, but metaphoric language is much more likely to be unforgotten in the course of everyday reading in an arm-chair.

As for the first piece on one sheet, the metaphor is run to death and completely drowned by its own waves. It is permissible up to 'devotional life' where it does present a vivid picture; when it comes to 'Anglican sands,' however, we are beginning to flounder. There could well be a full-stop after 'life,' and a clipped sentence will carry more weight to bring out the rather important point of the 'Anglican sands' and 'rock bottom.'

Any merit the metaphor may ever have possessed is ruined, when with an awful twist, we have to consider the survivors of the Oxford Movement as lone swimmers wrecked upon the Rock of Peter.

This is overdoing it and it takes some mental adjustment to realise what has happened, and the 'lone swimmer' really gives no sign that he represents the survivors of the Movement.

'Wrecked' comes from a runaway pen merely. The 'unfortunate' schoolboys have a better ground.

2.462.* There is some inaccuracy in the first passage. For example, a member of the Anglican church ought, surely, to be a grain of the 'Anglican sands.' When, however, he is to be converted to the Roman church, he becomes a swimmer. The metaphor, in fact, is altered, without the reader being told.

There is, too, a good deal of vagueness. It is by no means obvious whether the Anglican church is represented by loose sand and solid rock, or by sand only. The main disadvantage of the second passage is that it has to put its own interpretation on the first. The word 'restless' is not paraphrased at all.

Rhythms, too, are lost, though the rhythm of 'the impotent wave recedes, and is lost in the restless sea,' is admittedly no loss.

Is it the case that the metaphor is altered? Some significant limitations on the part of its defenders may help to make the answer to this question clearer. Thus 2.46 wrote *'one definite image* has been adopted and used to the full throughout' and another who wrote,

2.463. The passage employs one sustained image.

changed 'metaphor' to 'image.' The change brings out yet another ambiguity in the word that is a frequent source of trouble. Have we one metaphor here? Or have we eleven, as a hostile reader counted them? The following rather acute discussion, if we follow its thought, not its phrasing, analyzes the situation and describes very well the struggle between tenor and vehicle.

2.464. The metaphorical power is 'constructional'—just as Donne compares the body of his mistress to a continent, or Shakespeare moulds the texture of a dramatic around punning associations of one word, so the author obtains complete meaning by squeezing as many allegorical coincidences from his picture and from his idea as he can. *Yet,* the picture he gives us is rather like a snapshot; it seems to have crystallized and lacks fluidity. Donne's dialectic, we remember, was a little more fitful in its resort to imagery, so that his argument was not stifled or rendered static as this tends to do. Moreover, the passage is historical, it seems. It intends explanation rather than persuasion— and so it differs from Taylor's prose significantly.

The danger of any metaphorical writer is that the metaphors subvert the matter, and that faculty which should come to qualify, to elucidate and emphasize takes (loses?) priority in the writer's process of composition. Now by a power of suggestion, in the author's mind, the faculty which creates the first metaphor may set up a logical yet irrational process of its own, and imagery may become reiterative, or succeeding images may share some quality (e.g. luminosity), whilst they have no other affinities (Shelley's poetry in particular).

This will be most pernicious to prose which aims at clarity. We may find a suggestion of this fault in the procedure of the argument—

'spent wave' and 'lone swimmer.' A change of metaphor-subject would have refreshed us and prevented the one suggestion overlapping the other.

(For 'takes priority' I read 'loses priority': two possible phrases overlapping in the writer's mind—'loses priority' = 'takes a back place.')

The development of different metaphors out of one 'picture' or 'metaphor-subject' is well noticed. The metaphors are changed; what is sustained and continued is 'the field of imagery,' as another termed it. The vehicle (or set of vehicles rather) has a unity, but its interconnections by no means correspond to interconnections between the parts of the tenor which are severally linked to it. But there is no necessity that they should, since the tenor here is independently organized. Our apprehension of its structure does not have to be derived from the unity of the vehicle.

But I leave the last word to a writer whose enthusiasm makes him open with a rash statement, follow it up with a test whose difficulties we have already considered, proceed to a shrewd observation and yet conclude whole-heartedly in Chapman's favour.

2.465. No one can deny that the first passage is a metaphorical tour de force of sustained vigour. Expository writing is a species of rhetoric, of which Aristotle, to go no further, declared Metaphor to be a driving force and not a mere ornament.

The test of a metaphor, or analogy, or interconnection of fields of imagery, is how far it can be followed without coming to some patent absurdity. Most metaphors are only a partial inter-illumination of ideas, and good writers give them up or adroitly slip into a different one before the strain becomes apparent. In this case it is evident that the author had a clear complete image of a whole process in his mind.

# Chapter Eight: The Influence of Theories

*Without Unceasing Practise nothing can be done. Practise is Art. If you leave off you are Lost.*   BLAKE

I pass now from practical difficulties in the way of the interpretation of metaphor to discuss some of the notions and theories about how metaphor works that appeared in the protocols. Some seem to be preconceptions, habitual assumptions rooted and operative before the experiment: in other cases we may suspect them to be intellectual improvisations evoked by the challenge, and in that case we need not suppose that they had so much influence upon the actual reading. At times they intervene vigorously and lend support to the gloomy opinion that imperfect doctrine is worse than none at all. But where no doctrine is stated we should not assume that none is at work, though practice, for good or evil, does not readily follow theory. In yet other cases these sketched principles are attempts to describe or account for something obscurely felt about the passage or about its treatment in the translation.

Most literary perceptions of inadequacies begin with a dim discomfort, as uncertainly located and as characterless at first as the malaise that marks the first step of an infection. Between this groping sense of something wrong somewhere and the fully articulated complaint come various stages. At some of these the discomfort will borrow any handy formulation—much as the sick man with the medical book is said to have found ALL the descriptions 'Very exact!' Later, perhaps, in some cases, the critical opinions offered gain a different sort of precision and rest upon more extended and more reflective comparisons and eliminations. But, especially with these rapidly formed and hastily expressed decisions and explanations, it is prudent to premise that few theoretical pronouncements mean what they say (could we agree even upon *that*), or are any more reliable, than ambiguous agents serving rival powers may be expected to be.

A widespread opinion, sometimes expressed with great confidence, was that metaphor is *in its own nature* untranslatable. And many of the interesting theoretical comments were attempts to support it. 'Can metaphors be translated?' is a notoriously difficult question—though more difficult to state unambiguously than to settle when its parts have been clearly stated. The attempts made here show us, in an incomplete series of no doubt distorted sections, something with which we are highly familiar, as a living process, in our own reflection.

I will begin with the extreme uncompromising position:

2.5. There would surely be no justification for metaphorical language if, as the critic claims, it is ever possible to find exact equivalents in direct language for it.

An easy line of escape from this is soon found:

2.51. The ideal metaphor has no 'equivalent' in plain prose.

Of the IDEAL anything, much may be safely said. Here, probably, that metaphor is 'ideal' which is untranslatable (by acting definition); so what we are to read into 'ideal' depends upon how 'equivalent' (or 'translate') is taken. That is the real crux; so I will continue with those who attacked there.

2.52. Speaking generally, it is clear that metaphor would have no service in literature were it possible to express in 'direct language' what metaphor expresses. Contrary to being inexpressible through vagueness, metaphor in general is untranslatable through close accuracy of resemblance.

Definiteness, far from being foreign to metaphorical expression, is its purpose.

This echoes enough authoritative judgments to feel impressive. Critics as diverse as Wordsworth, Shelley and T. E. Hulme have said it and no doubt a little hunting would bring it out from many earlier pages. I will quote only Hulme, who is brief: 'Plain speech is essentially inaccurate. It is only by new metaphors . . . that it can be made precise.' [1] Incidentally it is refreshing to observe how boldly

[1] *Speculations*, p. 137. A further discussion of these remarks will be found in *The Philosophy of Rhetoric*, pp. 127-134.

this stern restorer of Classicism rediscovers the essential tenets of the Romantics! With so much authority behind it, we may suppose that the doctrine says something that is true. It can also say things that are not true. To separate them explicitly is a delicate job involving a struggle with some of the worst ambiguities in language.

How has 2.52 taken it and just what is he saying? That he is an acute reader is proved by the rest of his protocol. He also shows that he can be 'cautiously-decided,' for he guards himself, with 'speaking generally' and with 'in general,' from being supposed to be covering *all* metaphors. The two points at which he is not 'cautiously-decided' enough are with 'express' and 'accuracy of resemblance.'

'Express' is, of course, among the trickiest words, and I am not here so much alleging a fault in this writer as complaining of the language. 'Close accuracy of resemblance' asks to be completed by a mention of the two things between which the resemblance holds. For that evidently is the point upon which the doctrine turns. Which pair we choose (among several possible pairs, see page 138) makes all the difference. Similarly, for Hulme's sentence, a parallel question arises for 'inaccurate' and 'precise.'

Is it a resemblance between tenor and vehicle he is thinking of? It might be, but I do not think it is purely that here. This is a frequent misreading of the close accuracy doctrine, mistaken and misleading because there need be no 'close accuracy of resemblance' between them. Try to say what resemblance is the metaphoric ground in

Thou still unravished bride of quietness.

No ready answer is forthcoming. Still less need we see what the resemblance (if any) is. Tenor and vehicle may be extremely unlike one another—as in William James' favourite example, 'blotting paper voices.' And often the operative ground of the metaphor is not a resemblance at all but some other relation. This relation may be obscure, as James thought it was here, even too obscure to be discovered. That does not prevent tenor and vehicle working together to produce the required resultant; and the extent, intimacy and adroitness of their co-operation does not necessarily at all depend upon our supposing that we know what the ground is.

I will labour the point further because the assumption that the service of a metaphor depends entirely upon our perceiving points of resemblance or correspondence between tenor and vehicle is such a common over-simplification. It is often broadly true for plain neutral expository writing but even there close examination will show us action through disparity as well as through likeness. A slight and remote link brings in a vehicle which then picks out the aspect of the tenor to be attended to through other relations than direct resemblances.

For example, 'picks out' in the sentence I have just written: there is a slight resemblance between what happens and an act of picking out, and if we hunt for them we will no doubt find more, since in these matters we normally find what we look for. But the action of the vehicle is very much more complex than a mere invitation to regard the tenor as, in some respects, like it. Even in such case as this, its unlikenesses come in; we do not, for example, lend the vehicle a hand to pick with, or make it a choosing agent, a miniature mind; we discount these possible resemblances. A set of ghostly invisible quotation marks hangs over the phrase, warning us not to take it strictly or without letting the differences count too. Indeed, we might say that every exposition that is not technical and is trying to keep close to its points must play an incessant game with the discrepancies in its metaphors.

In technical writing we are relieved from this necessity; a system of definitions is doing the work. But there are very few technical words yet outside the sciences. Technical words, if they are really fixed, give no trouble; nor do free words, to good readers. As so many have insisted, it is the half-technicalized words—and this includes the whole vocabulary of philosophy, criticism and the allied subjects—that make even the most careful readers and writers scratch their heads in despair. All the words with which Mr Read, the protocolists, and I are attempting to explore the niceties of metaphor are semi-fixed, and that is responsible for more of the trouble than is the inherent difficulty of the subject.

To return for a moment to my 'picks out' example: if I had written instead 'determines,' or 'defines,' or 'stresses,' in each case, what happens to the tenor would at least have run a risk of misapprehension. 'Determines' is a typical semi-technicality and might easily make me have said much more than I meant—for the aspect (feature, character, point) to be attended to in the tenor is determined (if this word is technicalized) by much more than the vehicle. And 'defines,' which is less technicalized, might have misled with an unwanted 'sharpens the edge of' suggestion, and 'stresses,' worst of all, might have brought in an 'enforcement' notion. These would have misled because the action of a vehicle can be very far from either a sharpening or an emphasis. Its virtue is often to blur, to generalize, or to mitigate. My phrase, 'picks out,' fails to hint these and I am far from thinking it a triumph. I took it as an excuse for noticing the points about semi-technical language as well as to be an example of metaphoric action through disparity. It is a minimal case to show that even in the most neutral writing, where purposes beyond that of exposition have barely any influence on the choice or interpretation of words, disparity operation can still be noticed. The conduct of even the plainest, most 'direct' untechnical prose is a ceaseless exercise in metaphor—as many of my audience pointed out.

When other purposes are dominant—and with this we return to 2.52's problem—action of the vehicle which does not derive from its 'close accurate resemblance' to the tenor has vastly more scope. We notice the effects due to resemblances more readily and they are far easier to analyze and detail. The process of *following* a metaphor is largely one of looking for resemblances, and, as the protocols show, most arguments about a metaphor are mainly about the degree of correspondence. Resemblances are commonly the ostensive ground of the metaphor; but the operative ground is usually much wider. We overlook this through the influence of the assumption that metaphors only work through correspondences of vehicle to tenor; and this assumption, hazily mixed with a number of others which are very rarely brought into the focus of attention, is responsible for much crude reading.

Dissent from this view has two main sources. We may restrict metaphor (by definition, see Chapter XXIII) to action based upon resemblance. If so, then I am writing here about something else; and the point to make is that this other action is sometimes as important as resemblance in interpreting figures of speech. Alternatively, we may—through paucity of terms and distinctions in this field—*call* any co-operation between tenor and vehicle 'correspondence,' or 'resemblance,' or 'identity.' If so, there is again no dispute; the point to make then is that there are very different modes of correspondence. There is the paralleling which gives us Logic (pp. 15,

112): that is the main mode of metaphor. But there are innumerable other modes active in fluid speech.

Turning back now to 2.52's doctrine. If it is mistaken, the right *teaching* policy, I suggest, is not to begin with an abstract analysis of the assumptions which are pooling their powers to betray us. That, by altering the focus, transforms the whole problem and hides what has been happening. The better plan is to begin at the other end—not with the sources of the mistake but with its outcome—and then trace the actual process back into its cloudy origins. What are the consequences here? Are they not the implications (1) that no good metaphor can be 'translated' in direct language, and (2) that to attempt translation is waste of time? Are not both these plainly contrary to common experience?

Before we can be quite happy in saying 'Yes, of course!' we must look at his word 'express,' and distinguish between two things it may be doing. First, we can stretch it to cover everything. Then, what a metaphor expresses could not be expressed in direct language (or, for that matter, and this is nearer the point, in other metaphors) unless the other language did *everything* exactly in the same way that the metaphor does—had *all* the effects and no others, that the metaphor has. Now that transparently will not happen.

2.521. In the alteration of the words it seems almost impossible not to alter the meaning as well, even though it may only be slightly.

'Almost impossible' is too weak, if we are taking 'meaning' as 'what is expressed' unrestrictedly. Change the words and in some respects the effects, the meaning, what is expressed, will be different. If 2.52 is taken as stretching 'express' so far, his remark becomes almost an idle tautology. So we must put some limitations on 'express,' and when we do so, common experience tells us firmly enough that what a metaphor expresses can often be expressed in other language. We can put varying sorts of limitations on 'express'; they give us different kinds of meaning—mere sense, sense and implications, feeling, the speaker's attitudes to whatever it is, to his audience, the speaker's confidence, and other things.

Sometimes the translation will now 'express' only one of these kinds of meaning. Perhaps mere sense alone. Sometimes it contrives to 'express' several of them fairly well, with only minor losses and distortions. That is, we get different kinds of translation. All are partial; they express part of the meaning, not the unrestricted whole effect of the original metaphor. This is especially clear in the case of translation into Basic English when the magical 'identification' feeling that comes from the use of language which is not a fully comprehended living medium to us is cut out.

'Untranslatable,' in Basic English, reads, 'not able to be put in other words with the same effect.' No two things can be the same in all respects; unless they are different also they become not two but one. This, which is unmistakably obvious with 'the same,' gets hidden when we use words like 'express,' 'translate' and 'meaning.' Whence, for example, interminable troubles for the readers of Croce's 'intuition is expression' doctrine and, nearer home, for half the protocolists in their approach to metaphor.

So much for the first implication; we escape it by noting that all translation must be partial.

Now for the second: Are not partial translations extremely useful? Undoubtedly they are. Without them indeed we could not analyze any metaphor, much less expound it. The process of considering a metaphor critically is largely one of comparing it with possible partial translations, to bring out the differences between *its* total meaning and the partial meanings *they* more or less express. But there may be many good reasons for using a given metaphor even when plain or less metaphorical language as efficient for most recognized purposes is quite as easily found. For example, to compress, or to avoid insulting obviousness, to hint rather than insist, to flatter the reader with a 'you, of course, will take me' glance. As to all of which I have been under a self-denying ordinance in much of the above. These last effects of metaphor are parts of the total meaning and if 2.52 seems to be overlooking them here, that would be because he is including them in his unrestricted sense of 'express.'

I have started from the outcome of the writer's view and tried to trace it back to the origins of his mistake. The path has led us to the unrestricted use of 'express.' But this surely is too simple and glaring a mistake to be made unless there is some further obfuscating influence. There is, and it is a systematic ambiguity in language, so extensive, so multifarious in its appearances and disguises, that very few remarks in this topic escape its snares. The ambiguity protects itself, as such things do, by reappearing in most attempts to distinguish between the different things that the guilty phrases may mean. All the other ambiguities of 'meaning' and its synonyms are its allies; and with none of them does it do much permanent good to try to clear them up one by one. It is better to make friends with them and charitably study their ways; for they are, after all, the ways of our own thought and we should not amend them roughly or until we know them.

The obscuring or distracting influence comes from a merging, in the unfocused formless background, of the harmless view that a successful metaphor does what it should do, with those very questionable assumptions about likenesses between tenor and vehicle which I discussed above. The harmless truism says that the utterance hits the mark; it seems to say that tenor and vehicle must have a 'close accuracy of resemblance.' And reciprocally, that tenor and vehicle have this resemblance seems to be guaranteed by the truism. By introducing these technicalities, 'tenor' and 'vehicle,' I have made this quasi-identification of two different things (of several pairs of different things it is really) less plausible. If we recall the ambiguity of 'metaphor' that I discussed when introducing them, we shall see why the confusion is so hard to avoid. In one pulse of thought we take 'the metaphor' to stand for the vehicle only—that is the 'image' or 'figure' which is co-operating with a partner, namely the tenor, to produce the meaning. In the next pulse of thought all is changed; 'the metaphor' now stands for the whole thing (vehicle and tenor together) which is then set over (as an 'expression' or 'carrier'—'vehicle' in quite another sense) against a meaning which it conveys or expresses. And the old tenor now frequently follows round in the dance to masquerade as this meaning.

One has to be intolerably prolix in describing these manoeuvres. A diagram puts the change with much more perspicuity.

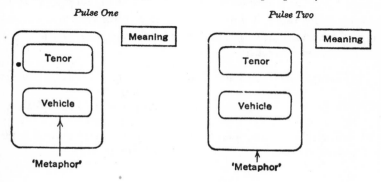

*Pulse One*                 *Pulse Two*

A diagram is itself, of course, a species of metaphor—a representation, a figure—with severe restrictions upon how it should be read. It must not be taken too far. With caution, however, its services in exposition may be immense; and I should not be surprised if, in time, most of the theory of language came to be expounded chiefly through diagrams. Most people, perhaps, if they try to redraw this diagram, after a little interval, will find that fixing the incidence of 'metaphor' is a process which reproduces all the opportunities for making Pulse One represent Pulse Two, and *vice versa*.

These alternating pulses of thought which shift the disposition and the nomenclature of the pieces so deftly, follow one another very rapidly. Anyone who is accustomed to watching how he thinks may notice several changes a minute. Physiological causes may even be conjectured for the alternation—as in the case of those geometrical outline figures which fall into alternate reliefs as we gaze:

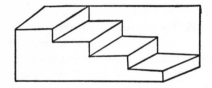 

To watch oneself shifting one's interpretation of 'the metaphor,' of 'correspond,' and of 'meaning' in

'The metaphor must correspond with its meaning'

is the quick way to mental ease in this topic. It makes the confusions I have been discussing no mystery. The mystery is rather in how we avoid them. Their systematic interconnection and mutual support are the things to notice. I will tabulate some of them for convenience of reference:

I. *Vehicle: tenor* confused with *metaphor* (i.e. *vehicle + tenor*): *meaning*

II. *Tenor* confused with *meaning (or a limited kind of meaning, sense)*

III. *Total effect or full meaning* confused with *any of a choice of limited kinds of meaning*

IV. *What a phrase*   confused with *what the author hoped it would do*
*does or actual*                 or *intended meaning.*
*meaning*
(for the standard
reader or for any
one reader)

This brings us back to Hulme and to my next examples from the protocols. Hulme's 'inaccurate' and his 'precise,' if we disentangle them from suggestions as to vehicle and tenor likenesses, may best be taken as having to do with correspondence between what the phrasing will actually do to a suitable reader (or to you) and what he calls 'the exact curve of the feeling or thing you want to express.' On the one hand there is what the phrase does, the action of that segment of the language in that setting, which may as well be called its meaning; on the other, there is whatever it is that the author wanted to express, the author's meaning. And Hulme says, at some length, that the nearer the first comes to the second the better. But in insisting upon this, he runs into much peril, with remarks such as 'the whole of the analogy is necessary to get out the exact curve.' I cannot help feeling he was perhaps then not very far from 2.52 in confusing the tenor-vehicle relation with the relation in IV above. What is *the whole* of an analogy? Where do we stop it? The important thing however that he was joining with Wordsworth and Shelley in saying is that the controlled use of metaphor is frequently the indispensable means to nearness or precision of expression ('definite,' Senses IV and X, see Chapter IX) and thus has a justification apart from 'mere decoration.' That is true of the writer, and it is equally and as evidently true when we turn to the reader's side of the venture. Without a controlled use of metaphor in interpretation he gets nowhere; or anywhere, which is here the same thing.

The following touch upon various points in the above discussion and will need only brief further comment:

2.53. It is doubtful whether the translating of metaphorical into 'direct' language ever clarifies the meaning. . . . The 'metaphorical' passage conveys its meaning by subtleties of association and suggestion which cannot at least be used to any great extent by the direct method. It is only fair to the author to suppose that the wave metaphor was chosen deliberately to express something which it alone could convey.

It can clarify parts, and thereby, if properly done, clarify the whole. Certainly, in any translation a large part of the actual effect of Chapman's passage would be lost—either by change of vehicles, in which case much would probably be added too, or, if we try to keep the use of metaphor in the translation at a minimum, through the discursive expansion that would then be required. We might try to include the missed points serially one after another: but that would change their interaction. Compression is no mere economy; it produces an explosive mixture of a different stability.

As to the 'fairness' remark, we may have our doubts. Confusion No. IV seems not far off. What the passage does *in toto* may be untranslatable. Whether another mode of writing could have conveyed equally well, or better, what the author intended to convey is another question. The deed and the will are not so simply interchangeable.

2.531. Surely the use of metaphors indicates that the author has some special aspect of his subject to express, which he can convey in no other way. This theory is not invalidated by the weak use of metaphor by many writers.

'His subject' may be the tenor, or it may be the whole meaning or a part of the meaning. If it is the tenor, or if it is less than the total actual meaning, then it may very well be conveyed otherwise. Metaphor which is translatable *need* not be weak; it may do its work as well as possible and yet be easily replaceable by other language. In the most highly concentrated and intricate contexts, a metaphor is, of course, often irreplaceable by any other. That gives it an adventitious rarity value to be distinguished from the merits of its work. If there were only one mathematician in the world we might make a great fuss him but he wouldn't be a better mathematician for being irreplaceable. These 'ideal' = 'no substitute' assumptions (cf. 2.51) come in part from Confusion I.

Various attempts to split up Total Meaning with reference to the purpose of the passage now follow:

2.54. Is not it the strength rather than the weakness of good metaphorical writing that no equivalents can be found for the metaphors? and is not vagueness on this point merely a sign of the weakness of weak metaphorical writing?

The translation gives the plain sense of the passage in so far as that can be completely extricated from the other uses of language. Plain sense is the only thing that one wants from such a passage, unless the author has a precise and individual attitude to his theme which can only be conveyed by means of imagery.

Every sentence here contains at least one assumption that has been shown, I hope, to be misleading. The last sentence also dictates an aim to Chapman, and in its use of 'individual' is echoing much current 'personality,' 'sincerity,' 'individuality' and 'self-expression' talk, which has as little basis in fact or in desirable assumption as the rest. Imagery is not in the least need of such justification; it can equally serve the most general and impersonal purposes.

Juster reading and better theory appear in:

2.541. In the first place the metaphors in this passage do not seem to me to be 'merely decorative.' The critic and translator seems to have taken an unduly limited meaning for his phrase 'expository writing'; Chapman is attempting more than a summary of the history of the Oxford Movement; he is attempting to convey his own sympathy with it by the tone and attitude of the passage. This tone is to a great extent maintained by the metaphors, and is completely lost in the translation. . . .

The use of metaphorical language means that a great deal of the sense of the passage will depend upon the unconscious association of ideas. Here for instance the metaphor of the impotent wave and the restless sea indicates quite plainly that Mr Chapman considers the Church of Rome a very satisfactory haven.

Finally the fact that the critic's admission of his failure to discover an exact equivalent in direct language for the metaphors is a complete justification for the use of metaphors, and not in the least a weakness of metaphorical writing.

'Tone,' 'attitude,' 'sense,' 'ideas'—we understand in such a case, perhaps, well enough what we mean by them. There is a long step forward in the analysis of these factors ready to be taken and its results before long may have a very direct bearing upon teaching.

The second paragraph here calls attention to an obviously important point. Metaphor, through the wider field of possible linkages which it opens as compared to explicit literal statement, may allow a freer and more delicate intervention of more remotely relevant factors. The writer's last sentence is the muddle of a runaway exaggerating pen rather than a surrender to our confusions.

2.542. Is the aim of the original to be merely 'expository'? This may be so, but it is not clear from the passage as it stands; the metaphors suggest the attitude of the writer to his subject—possibly unintentionally, possibly unflatteringly—but, if *in*tentionally, with an effect the paraphrase is of necessity incapable of reproducing.

Of course, the paraphrase contains abundance of metaphor, too,—possibly unrealised by the writer:—'force,' 'at its height,' etc. This suggests a wondering as to how far 'definite . . . expository writing' is a possibility—certainly not, I imagine, for anyone with a positive emotional attitude to his subject such as the writer of the original passage.

It is *never* 'possible to be sure that exact equivalents have been found for metaphors.'

Another paraphrase might not be 'of necessity incapable of reproducing' the attitude, whatever it was, intentional or not. This writer is trying to handle too many threads at once and crosses them. His wondering about the possibility of non-metaphorical writing shifts as he turns the sentence to a wondering about 'definite . . . expository' and again to *neutral* writing. Whether, or to what extent, writing may be without metaphors, in some limited sense, is a difficult question. The others are not: definite and neutral statements are certainly possible—if we do not set ridiculous 'absolute-zero' standards of definiteness and neutrality. And unbiassed writing from men with the most vigorous private, personal, positive emotional attitudes towards the subject we surely expect—not only from Supreme Court Judges. The last sentence probably implies, I think, that it is also impossible to find equivalents.

The use of 'logical' is the most interesting thing about the next; otherwise it has been covered already.

2.543. This quotation reveals the attempt to interpret such a complex and subtle phenomenon as the Oxford Movement in prosaic and severely historical terms. It is obvious that the author's so-called translation of Chapman's passage entirely falsifies the original statement by omitting all the meaning which is not purely logical. He reveals his inability to understand the passage by his unqualified assertion that metaphorical writing must be inadequate because no exact translation can be made, whereas metaphor is of the utmost significance in literature simply because by it we can convey to others perceptions which cannot be expressed in merely logical statements. In this case Mr Chapman is not only recording an historical event—in fact that is of least significance—but he is trying to describe the spiritual and psychological effect of the religious revival. That aspect is passed over by the author of this book. To be 'definite' merely means to limit one's ideas to those which are apprehensible by logic alone. But the author has not only omitted, he is also guilty of unjustified addition. What warrant has he for the use of the word 'desperate'? That does not correspond to a lone swimmer.

It would be highly useful if we could satisfy ourselves—so far as the natural dimness of the topic allows—as to what 'logical' means here. Plenty of other words can be used as partial equivalents; but most of these—'intellectual,' 'scientific,' 'plain sense,' 'thought,' 'rational,' 'non-emotional,' 'positive,' 'factual' are favourites—have equal troubles of their own. They may seem to offer single and secure footholds to their users. To an uneasy and questioning reader it is otherwise. Yet whether they seem simple or covinous, what they deal with is the matrix out of which helpful disciplines must be drawn. In all interpretation some sort of selection of 'sense' or 'thought' for special handling, which sets it temporarily over against our feelings about it or about other things, is taking place, and how this selection is made is all important. What one puts into sense another takes as feeling. Here the writer seems to be segregating *as sense* the historical event, making that alone amenable to 'logic,' and to be taking the description of 'the spiritual and psychological effect' as somehow not fact and as not 'apprehensible by logic alone.' But his use of 'logic' as 'the mode of contemplating fact' is crossed with another use coming from the 'plain language—metaphoric language' distinction. Perhaps I am unfair to him—he may be merely complaining that Mr Read was doing these things. He serves me as an occasion to note again, for fuller treatment later, the haziness of *all* the terms with which a Boundary Commission on the provinces of the modes of meaning would have to work. Least of all, perhaps, is 'the facts' to be trusted, as the next writer shows:

2.544. The chief difference between the passage from Chapman in its original form and in translation is that although they both have the same meaning, taken in its narrowest sense, the former invokes admiration for its subject, whereas the second leaves us impartially considering the facts. If the sole aim of the writer were to give clear, uncoloured statements of facts he would have succeeded better by leaving his metaphors alone; one cannot help feeling however, that his aim was to give these facts plus the interpretation in his own mind and the admiration consequent upon it. If this is true, it is a mis-statement of the case to say that it is purely expository writing.

Even 'meaning, taken in its narrowest sense,' is elastic—as a theoretical conception and as a container in practice. Here, if exercises can induce meditation and meditation can clarify, we have a great opportunity. Fortunately neither premise is doubtful.

# Chapter Nine: 'Definite'

I pass now to assumptions and theories about 'definiteness' which naturally turn, in part, on the limitations that are variously set on 'meaning.' It will have been noticed that different writers not only take very different views as to the 'definiteness' of the two passages but seem to use 'definite' in varying senses. It is a very puzzling word. If we try to distinguish different senses for it, we are likely to find ourselves merely muttering over 'exact,' 'accurate,' 'precise,' 'having fixed limits' and so on, without thereby gaining much insight into just how it shifts its sense in differing incidences. The protocols show that it does so and in more ways than the dictionary can easily take note of. The writers, I repeat, do not merely call different things 'definite' (or 'vague,' to take *that* as its opposite); they mean different things by so calling them. And these differences are important. Not a little of the difficulty that was felt, and the helplessness shown and the bewilderment suffered, came from them. And with innumerable other topics it is the same. We should expect —should we not?—that uncontrolled fluctuations in what we mean by such a word as 'definite' will be a bad hindrance to the development of general intelligence.

From this point of view it may be stimulating to observe how very far from definite our notions about its meanings are! Definiteness seems a landmark, or initial point for surveys, and when we recognize that we and our neighbours have a practice of removing it freely, we seem at least in sight of one of the causes of confusions. These seem then more remediable evils; though here again, as always, we have to bear in mind that our business is not to tell people how to use the word, but to give them the best occasions to notice for themselves, and reflect upon, how it will, in fact, continue to be used, and why it is variable.

Indeed my original reason for choosing Mr Read's page as the subject of this experiment was to find out what would happen with this word. I knew how confusing the topic of *definition* is in Logic. I wondered whether the adjective would play as troublesome tricks in a fairly full setting. It does; and its behaviour here is a means of introducing considerations which deserve fuller treatment in the Logic Section.

The very difficulty of thinking about what 'definite' means makes it an excellent subject for study—*if* we can keep the difficulty from becoming paralyzing. The thing seems too simple, at first, to be thought about. ' "Definite?" Why, it means *definite,* and that's that!' represents an unavoidable movement in approaching it. And we suffer, as we approach, from a distressing feeling that we must know the answer in order to ask the question, that we are bootstrap-lifting or trying to see a light wave or to carve an atom with a pen-knife, as Mr Wells suggested in his 'Scepticism of the Instrument,' cutting at the irreducibly simple and ultimate. But our use of 'definite' is not a simple matter at all; it is a tricky way of playing with likenesses, and differences, and implications. To think about it usefully we have to recognize this complexity. Once we can do that, the feeling of helplessness subsides, and we have merely to watch a number of different things—that can be talked about with the same words and can be very easily mistaken for one another. And here other people's uses of the word—especially those that seem to us, for the moment, odd and inexplicable—are our great help. The best way to teach the meanings of 'definite' (and its fellows) is *via* other people's uses of them, rather than through an attempt at direct exposition—a Dictionary Article with detached examples. The setting and the drift of the remarks in which the word occurs, open up what is happening as an analytic description hardly can. In any case we need some much fuller treatment than any extant Dictionary provides; and devices to induce a much more prolonged, leisurely and lively meditation of it than is customary when we consult the Dictionary. Before turning to the protocols I shall sketch in here a very rough outline of some wanderings of this word—a preliminary draft of a possible Dictionary Article—as a guide to what may be observed when we come to them.

There is an old and bitter controversy in Logic as to whether we define Words or Things, and this gives us a clue to a first main division of the senses of 'definite.' There is a group of senses in which we are saying with it something about a thing; and another in which we are saying something about some representation of a thing, about a statement, or an expression, or an idea of it, and comparing this representation of it with others. The second is the more interesting and important group here. I will try to get Group One out of the way quickly.

## GROUP ONE

Here are some of the senses in this group in an order proceeding from general to more specific, from wide to narrower: I put the minimum sense first, the sense in which we are saying as little as possible with the word, and indeed it is almost nothing at all.

*Sense One: distinct, having some character differentiating it from other things.*

I will give examples, though any I give run a risk of being read with some of the other senses: 'This is a definite trait in his character,' 'a definite phase in the disease.'

In this sense every distinct thing is definite by being distinct, by being a thing, and 'thing' is taken in the most unrestricted way. 'Every thing is what it is and not another thing,' said Bishop Butler, safely enough. He was saying, 'Every thing is definite' in *this* sense.

*Sense Two (a specialization): having limits.*

This introduces quantity; spatial quantity, temporal quantity, or numerical quantity. By metaphor it is extended to qualities; and by complication to form.

Examples: 'a definite area,' 'definite duration,' 'definite colour,' 'definite temperature,' 'definite shape.'

*Sense Three: having fixed limits.*

This is the usual main head in the dictionaries; its defect, as such, is that 'fixed' changes its sense as it follows 'definite' round in *its* changes of sense, and so reproduces the very ambiguities we need to discover.

Examples: 'Every brick has its definite size.' Here persistent spatial configuration, fixed limits, are implied. But compare 'Definite clouds now form.' Here, I am supposing a setting which makes the meaning to be that the vapour now acquires limits which remain constant enough through a duration to be treated as being fixed. But with both these examples the question of our modes of measurement threatens to come in, and if it does we pass over to a Group Two sense of 'definite,' concerning the appropriateness of this or that account of the thing, rather than the thing's own size. The more we consider this, the more we may be tempted to doubt if it has one.

Now compare: 'That was a definite flash of lightning. But I couldn't say where it went.' This takes us back to Sense One. No *fixed* limits are implied, and physics would decline to say where we put them either in time or space. Like other events, a flash of lightning has limits if we like to set them, but, if we stress *our* setting of them, we are again going over to Group Two senses. In my instance, we are just talking, not doing physics, and such limits are not giving it the character in respect to which we are calling it 'definite.' What we care about is its 'being a flash of lightning,' a distinct thing.

The difficulty about the senses in Group One is that in *discussing* any example of them we have to assume that questions about the language we use do not come in, and that is never a matter about which we do well to be certain.

## GROUP TWO

It would be possible to distinguish an enormous number of these; since the comparisons they turn on between our perceptions, thoughts, ideas, feelings, attitudes, hopes, wishes, intentions, resolves, commands; our words, descriptions, statements, suggestions, evocations, expressions are all but inexhaustibly various. The profitable thing to do would be to list as separate senses just those main varieties which experience shows are likely to be confused with one another and whose confusion leads to trouble. I will take *statement* first, since its problems have been thoroughly discussed in the Logic books and it may serve as a model for other, less studied, cases.

A cunning pitfall awaits us here, into which the wariest may step.

It is by no means easy to get out of, and a few minutes in uncovering it will not be wasted. Since 'definite' in 'a definite statement' has seemingly to do with how the statement represents whatever it does, there is a great temptation to put, as its sense, something like *corresponding more or less closely to what it represents,* i.e. 'This statement is definite' = 'it corresponds closely to what it represents.' But if we do, we are deep in troubles; for example:

(a) What is a statement? (b) What does it correspond to, or represent? Both terms between which the correspondence holds are hard to get at. The statement is not just the mere sentence, the marks written (or any more complicated thing derived from them, such as the system of their letters in whatever handwriting). To get at the statement which might do the corresponding, we have to add in an interpretation of it. It is the sentence, *as understood in some way,* that corresponds to—well, what? Equally on the other side we have to be careful what we put. We cannot make it simply the facts being talked about or we would have crossed our problem about 'definite' with a problem about truth. A definite statement is not necessarily *true* by being definite and we must not make it so. What then is it that the understood sentence corresponds to—when it is definite? Does it not have to be, not 'the facts' but 'the facts as they are thought of'? And is not this just the way the writer thought, what he put in his sentence to be understood by us? And, if so, are we not back at the other term and has not the correspondence, whose closeness was to be definiteness, vanished? Instead we have one thought—the thought the statement is to convey—which is simply, in itself, more or less definite (Sense One), or, to use metaphor, fuzzier or sharper (Sense Two).

I have gone through this favourite old conjuring trick here partly because something of the sort is inevitable, as an incident, often a recurring movement, in every meditation on 'definite.' I am not going now to spend time discussing which cards were palmed when and exchanged for which where. It is more to the immediate purpose to notice how this sleight of mind favours a merging of Group Two with Group One, and confusion between Relative and Absolute Definitenesses, and also to recall how upsetting such a movement may be to the effort to think out the problem. No wonder, if it often remains obscure and is shunned as some will shun a Goofy House. Fear, indeed, of we know not what—of being lost in words, or between them, of losing hold on realities—explains many refusals to think, and many seeming *inabilities* to think reasonably and persistently.

If all this seems uncomfortably and, for our purpose, unsuitably like the first few passages in a maze, I would remind the reader that we have all been in this maze all our lives, that we live there and that these are just those current problems which all thought is incessantly *dealing with in specific forms*. They are being discussed here in general terms. It is not necessary to teach people this general study, it is no part—unless immensely simplified and improved as only practice in teaching can improve it—of class-room subjects. On the other hand it has an undeniable bearing upon them, which is my reason for exploring it here. The abstract mapping can help us to understand the concrete perplexities and to find better ways of helping others with them. There is no doubt that a sense of bewilderment due directly to the inherent complexity of the situation we are in when we communicate is a main cause of stupidity. Conduct may lie, as Bridges wrote, 'in the masterful administration of the unforeseen,' but that should not prevent us from encouraging foresight by any means we can.

But to return towards a formulation of Sense Four: between what must the comparison be made in terms of which this sense of 'definite' is written?

Last time I began with too simple an answer—thought and things —and then developed complexities to correct it which led us back in a circle. This time let us start with two statements, or (to cut out a troublesome gyre) make the comparison be between two thoughts:

(1) The thought the sentence conveys (which, to simplify everything, for the moment, as much as possible, we will take to be the same for the writer and for the reader—a happy fate to which things will approximate as writer and reader and the use made of the language are all good).

(2) How we choose the other thought to be taken as the standard with which the writer's thought is compared, and by which its definiteness is measured, can be seen most easily from some examples. Here are three statements of increasing definiteness: (A) 'This stuff is coloured,' (B) 'This stuff is red,' (C) 'This stuff is scarlet.' They are so related that if C were true, B and A would be true; but though A were true neither B nor C need be true. In

point of fact the stuff might be green without that making any
difference. The sense of 'definite' we want here is one not involving
that what is definite is true. It involves only these implications.
Moreover 'definite' here becomes frankly a comparative term: B is
definite with respect to A, but not with respect to C.

It is from this sense that uses of 'definition' in optics come. From
the more definite image the less definite images could be derived
but not *vice versa*. From the view given by a telescope the view
without it could be constructed, but not the other way about.

I can now write:

*Sense Four: one Statement is more definite than another when it
implies the other, without the other implying it.*

We extend this sense by grouping statements about different
things together as having roughly the same degree of definiteness
on parallel scales of implication. Thus: 'There is something in the
box,' 'There is a coin in the box,' 'There is a farthing in the box,'
can be put parallel to the colours example, and we can say that 'This
is scarlet' is more definite than 'Something is in the box.' So we can
say that one essay 'On the Constitution' is more definite than another 'On the hibernation of bears.'

In all uses of this Sense Four of 'definite,' whether direct or extended, we are making covert references to other statements which
might be made instead of the statement we are judging. Sometimes
these references are to more definite statements we feel we could
reasonably expect the writer to make instead; sometimes we recognize that it would not be to his purpose to do so; sometimes we
admit that no more definite statement is available. 'Definite,' thus
is, in these uses, short for 'definite enough, enough things considered,' and any charge that a given statement is 'not definite,' or
any praise of it as 'definite,' depends for its validity on how far
enough things have been considered. What is definite for one purpose may be hopelessly indefinite for another.

What I have just said can be transferred from statements to
thoughts, ideas, conceptions, notions, or whatever we like to call
them. The same sense of 'definite' applies to them, for a statement,
even the most long-winded, is (as I am using the words here) an
idea or conception spread out and an idea is a theory or discourse
writ small. One conception, then, is more definite than another if

it implies the other; or, indirectly, as with the farthing and scarlet, if it implies conceptions of the same order as the other. These implied conceptions may contradict the other. For example, a physicist's idea of combustion is more definite than that of the person who supposes that sunlight puts the fire out, and it implies ideas of the same order as that idea which contradict it.

Since conceptions are theories compacted, so that they may be uttered in a word instead of in twenty pages, the bearings of the purpose in hand on the choice of *ideas* is rather different from its bearings on the choice of *statements*. Whereas over-definite, explicit *statement* may and often does distract from, or clog or otherwise impair, the execution of the purpose, over-definite *ideas* behind the words have no such disadvantages. No man's *ideas* of anything can possibly be too definite: he need not use them in their full definiteness all the time; he uses only the part of their implication which suits his purpose. And he can do so the better for having the more definite idea to guide him; it can serve as a very delicate hidden control over his use of words even when he is talking broadly and simply. To value and recommended the utmost definiteness attainable in ideas is one thing. To clamour for definiteness always in statements is quite another.

This brings me to a different sense of 'definite,' which has been hovering near throughout the last paragraph.

*Sense Five: explicitly, or fully, stated; detailed.*

Example: 'He is in London just now, I had a talk with him yesterday' is less definite than 'He was in a broken-backed chair in the upper front bed-sitting room of 71 Marchmont Street at 4.30 yesterday and remains in it for periods varying from 2 to 16 hours most days, though he goes into the country some week-ends. We discussed . . .' The confusion of this sense with Sense Four, in which 'This is a fruit' is less definite than 'This is an apple,' is easy—and may be made over any examples.

The important difference between them is shown in this. We can discuss the definiteness in Sense Five of a statement without regard to the purpose for which it is made. It can be treated as a mere matter of the number and articulation of the items presented for separate attention. But with Sense Four 'definite' is always short for 'definite enough for a purpose in hand.' We can take any sentence and make it more definite in Sense Five by filling in details and expounding conditions. A full statement of what 'the cat sat on the mat' means might involve a course of anatomy. What then resulted would, of course, *say* something that was not the same as is said by 'The cat sat on the mat.' It would probably be more definite in Sense Four, as well as in Sense Five, but such combinations of the two senses should not make us forget how different they are. If we do the protocols will remind us how far confusion between definiteness as *explicitness* and as *implication* may lead astray. Sense Four turns on the implication between thoughts; Sense Five on the relation of the thought to its expression—i.e. on the explicitness or compactness of the expression of one thought.

This last summary, and especially the phrase 'relation of the thought to its expression,' will illustrate the next sense to be listed. Coming in this setting and at the end of my explanations, it may itself be definite enough in Sense Four, though not at all definite in Sense Five, but in a sixth sense it is highly indefinite.

*Sense Six: unambiguous, able to be reasonably interpreted in one way only.*

How any utterance is interpreted depends, of course, upon a setting, in part provided by the writer and in part supplied by the reader. But still, for a given setting so present, phrases vary enormously in their capacity to be interpreted in one or in a number of ways more or less diverging from the intended meaning. And there is a very recognizable sense of 'definite' in which a definite statement is one which can only be read (without gross blundering) in one way, and an indefinite statement is one which can reasonably be taken as possibly saying a number of more or less different things. And this is Sense Six.

The phrase I picked out, 'relation of the thought to its expression,' as highly indefinite in this sense (I will not do more than hope that it is worse than its neighbours) needs a more than ordinarily strong setting to keep it from being misunderstood.

It might suggest, for example,

(1) That the point was the faithfulness of the expression to the thought; as, if I happen to say *Wilkins* when I am thinking of *Wilkinson,* my expression is not faithful.

(2) That the point was some similarity between the expression, as a

mere set of marks or sounds, and the thought. But there is no such thing. The word 'relation' was only hinting that we have to do, in Sense Five, with one thought and various sentences related to it as its expressions.

(3) That the point was about some correspondence between the thought as spread out in a detailed expression and the same thought as compacted in a short form—a puzzling matter I am not entering into.

I give these tedious specimens of possible misconceptions partly by way of clearing up what I may have left doubtful, partly as typical examples of the ambiguities which all discussions of this topic of meaning inevitably present. They cannot be cleaned up verbally since the instruments (the words or the logical machinery) we must use in all cleaning up processes themselves introduce them again. But this is no ground for despair. We have a remedy in the fact that we can familiarize ourselves with them and as they become more familiar they give less trouble. Definiteness in this Sixth Sense, absence of ambiguity, is not, even in the most multiferous contexts, unattainable. But to attain it a kind of training for readers and writers alike that we hardly as yet so much as attempt to give directly, must be deliberately undertaken and developed.

We may contrast with indefiniteness in this Sense of ambiguity—when we do not know which *one* of several different meanings we are to take—mere multiplicity, when the sentence means many things at once, all of which are to be taken as, collectively, its meaning. I will not list singleness as a separate sense of 'definite'; though, as the protocols (to look no further) show, people very commonly use it so, and, resenting the invitation to think of several things at once, try to attach a stigma with the words 'indefinite' or 'vague.' A subheading, VIa, *Singleness,* will take care of it. And I will not do more than mention in passing a way of describing as 'indefinite' sentences containing alternatives: 'He is either in the Chapel or the Buttery.' Probably a mixture of Senses Three and Four is present. I am anxious to reach the senses that arise apart from statement; but there is still another important statement sense to be listed.

*Sense Seven: clear, at once certain, evident, obvious.*

This, though commonly combined with other senses, is a separate sense. To make it imply others is, for hasty readers, an endless temptation to be unjust. How long it takes or how hard it is to decide what the meaning is settles nothing in itself as to whether the statement is definite or not in any but this Sense Seven. Difficulty may be accompanied by evidence of ambiguity, but it is this evidence, not the difficulty, that proves the ambiguity. Conversely I may remark, arriving instantaneously and without doubt at a meaning is no proof of definiteness, in any other sense, in the statement. It would be paradox-mongering to insist that the vague is very often the clearest, but to see as clear and to see clearly are not the same. Hasty clarity may show definiteness in an Eighth Sense in the *reader*—and with that I pass on from statement-senses to others that have to do with the will and the emotions. Fortunately they can be dealt with more simply.

'You are very definite about it!'

With this last use we have taken one of the most familiar semantic steps or straddles—from a description of what is done to a description of the doer—and often the suggestion is added that to do so is a habit, and, as a habit, likely to lead to mistakes. So, as a description of the doer's character, it is usually derogative. Compare 'certain,' 'confident,' 'positive.' Most of the neighbour words take the same step. So we arrive at:

*Sense Eight: decided, quick to resolve, confident of being right, unwilling to admit doubts.*

As a description of a person's way of behaving—whether in adopting opinions or in choosing his ties or in giving his orders—the word accepts a very wide range of secondary suggestions from varying settings and, through them, allows us, in using it, to express all sorts of attitudes to the person we so describe. These make it seem to have different senses implying approval, disapproval or amusement as the case may be. I am not listing them as such, since the word takes them from the setting, is submissive to it, and is rarely if ever, I think, able to impose one of them on a neutral occasion. The same sorts of secondary suggestions hang about the other uses of 'definite' in connection with attitudes and their expressions. (I use 'attitude' here as a term conveniently wide enough to include feelings, interests and wishes etc.)

In beginning to list these last Senses, we seem to be led back to

Group One. We have to distinguish the case when we are attempting to describe somebody's attitude *in itself,* from the case when we are describing *his expression of it* with respect either to it or to other expressions of other attitudes. Sense Nine would therefore be a specialization of Sense One—Sense One in its application to people's attitudes. The justification for it would be that we experience, or have, attitudes ourselves; and therefore seem able to consider their intrinsic definiteness in themselves, apart from descriptions of them. But things or events which are not modifications of the mind —clouds, stones, and the like—are harder to get at. (I am, it will be observed, trying to write linguistics here, not epistemology; and so make what assumptions seem most convenient, leaving discussion of them to other occasions. We may, in an inclusive view, resolve these distinctions between mind and its objects, without denying ourselves the use of them for more restricted purposes.) The point briefly is that whereas a cloud or stone seems to be just what it is and unable to become *more itself,* whatever it does, an emotion, say, does seem capable of being more or less definite in itself—to have more or less distinct character differentiating it from other emotions. I am not prepared to deny that this may only be a matter of greater or less approximation to some type of emotion we happen to have recognized—thus a matter of the relative merits, as to what they imply, of different descriptions, which would make it a Group Two sense of definite. But the other speculative possibility seems to remain—that in experience, our most intimate insight into the growth of living things, we can see sheer increase of absolute distinctness taking place. This however is hardly the occasion for dealings with the abstrusest problems of biological ontology, complicated as they are by the difficulties mentioned in Chapter XIX, below, in connection with the is of Modification.

*Sense Nine: highly organized.*

Usually perhaps when we ask, 'Is his attitude, feeling, resolve . . . definite?' we are supposing that a process of increasing organization is going on, or might go on, by which the attitude can become more definite. We seem to be asking what stage it has reached. And a complaint that it is not definite seems to imply that it ought to have gone further, or that, if it had tried to, it would have become something very different, not on the same lines at all.

With the next sense we are unquestionably back again in Group

Two, we are saying something about the *expression* of an attitude: 'a definite indication of his regret,' 'a definite hint,' 'a definite cry of alarm.' Is it such as to communicate the utterer's attitude? This looks a perfectly harmless question and one worth asking and I cannot help listing as a sense:

*Sense Ten: communicating the utterer's attitude.*

And yet! My impression is that the questions and the assertions that this sense lends itself to are among the most confusing and misleading things in all literary discussion. Such gross assumptions ally themselves with it. For example: that when an emotion is conveyed to us we must share it. Easily seen to be contrary to fact when focussed, but covertly assumed by innumerable people and used in the strategy of all sorts of pursuits. We feel what Iago's attitude to Othello is, we don't share it. Drama, of course, defends us from such mistakes. More personal-seeming poetry—appeals to faith, denunciations . . . most literature into which emotion enters—invites us to confuse understanding with sharing. We can share if we wish; but sharing is *not* a condition of feeling what the attitude is. And this is true however strongly we distinguish *feeling* an attitude from mere intellectual recognition of its character. We can feel, and in that sense enter understandingly into an attitude, without therefore having to take it up and make it ours. We all know this very well but unfortunately forget it just when it would be best remembered. If it were the case that we could not understand without sharing, then the chances of human intercourse ever reaching a tolerable level would be bad indeed!

Finally there is

*Sense Eleven: really, he means it, to be taken seriously.*

Examples: 'I gave you definite orders,' 'Mussolini's intentions are quite definite: he may not know what he wants but he is going to try to get it!'

This last sense comes out more clearly with the adverb—though that, of course, like most adverbs, has tricks of its own. 'Definitely the last appearance'; as with 'really,' the secondary suggestion is negative—'Perhaps not after all; you have good reason for being doubtful.' So too with 'He gave a definite denial.' The suggestion may be 'How could he, what a liar!'

The peculiarity of this use is that the word acts as an intensifier, and so has rather a gesture than a sense. (See *Mencius on the Mind,* Chapter IV.) But gestures can be translated into senses. When translated—into 'and he meant it too'—it contrasts readily with Sense Ten, which says that the expression and what is expressed accord, and which commonly enlists Sense Nine to say that what is expressed is specific (to use another word which dances round with 'definite' through most of its figures). Sense Eleven, on the other hand, merely *enforces* whatever it is that may be going forward. 'He gave me a definite promise to do something about it, though he couldn't say what it would be.'

In the above, there is much that is arbitrary; its justification would be convenience—a balance of advantages that would need rather elaborate testing. A parallel study of the partial synonyms of 'definite'—'specific,' 'exact,' 'precise,' 'clear,' 'distinct,' and so on—would be helpful. Sense Ten and Senses Four to Six, at certain points duplicate one another, though at others their distinction is useful; there are other overlaps, for example, between Eight and Eleven; and Nine is awkwardly out of place. But no set of distinctions can be considered apart from the uses we propose to make of it. This set is designed to assist in reading the protocols, and is evidently no more than a very rough sketch of an oddly neglected topic. I have omitted such senses as enter when we contrast the definite and indefinite articles in Grammar or definite and indefinite descriptions in Logic.

I append a summary Table of Senses to facilitate reference.

*Group One*

  I. Distinct in itself.
  II. Having limits—literally and metaphorically.
  III. Having fixed limits.

*Group Two*

| | | |
|---|---|---|
| IV. | | Implying other statements. |
| V. | of | Explicit, full, detailed. |
| VI. | state- | Unambiguous, able to be interpreted in one way only. |
| VIA. | ments. | Singleness. |
| VII. | | Clear, at once certain, evident, obvious. |

  VIII. (of a person or his acts) decided, quick to resolve, confident.

IX. (of an attitude, or experience or perception) highly organized.
 X. (of an expression) communicating the utterer's attitudes.
XI.            Forceful, to be taken seriously.


Let us now watch some of these senses interacting with one
another and distracting thought in the protocols. Most of these
comments spring from an incomplete perception that there was
something queer about Mr Read's use of the term. In what follows
we have two things to watch: shifts in the senses of the word, and
changes as to the fields in which the word is applied. I begin with
some who remarked on the restriction of the word to *statement*.

2.61. Is 'to be definite' the proper aim of expository writing? The
critic has certainly given a 'more definite' version of the original but
in doing so hasn't he lost the spirit of it? The aim of the first writer
seems not to be to convey a definite meaning so much as something
of the essential spirit of the religious movement surging through the
century. In translating it, it is not so much the weakness of metaphorical writing (even though it may not be particularly good metaphorical
writing) that is revealed as the inability of hard scientific and rather
heavy prose to express the same sentiment. The metaphorical passage
gives a very good idea of the emotional element of the movement and
the removal of the metaphors has meant the removal of the emotive
appeal.

Here we have 'sentiment,' 'the emotional element,' and 'the essential spirit,' as something *in* or belonging to the religious movement;
and, at the same time, 'the emotive appeal,' that is to say, the feelings of someone contemplating it. The writer is not keeping them
very distinct, nor need he here; but he is contrasting them both with
a meaning which is separated as being *definite* in a fashion in which
they are not.

2.62. More often than not it is safe to say the aim of expository
writing is to be definite, i.e. presumably, make a scientific statement
with as little garnishing as possible. But this is one of the few kinds
of writing which justify metaphorical rendering. It is an emotional
or religious idea that is to be conveyed, and ordinary language cannot
suggest this as metaphor can. It does not set out to be a definite statement—as soon as it does so, as in the 'translation,' it loses its 'inspiration' and becomes a record of an historical event rather than the suggestion of the emotional effect caused by such an event.

Here is the same limitation of *definiteness* to statement, the same withdrawal of 'suggestion' and 'inspiration' from its sphere, and the same, or a closer, merging of the emotive with the metaphoric. Both writers are on the defensive. They accept a use of 'definite' by which its sphere is severely restricted. They don't specify the restriction except by the implication that 'what someone does' or 'facts' would be capable of definite description but not what he felt (feelings not being 'facts'); historical events but not emotions. They don't challenge it, they take it over, unexamined, from Mr Read and merely press the claims of the rest of meaning to be not overlooked.

This readiness, shown by both, to let feelings be treated as though they and their expression were inherently vague, *while insisting on their importance,* is one typical outcome of the confusions my account of 'definite' was designed to exhibit. Here the writers recognize that the senses in which a *statement* may be definite are different from those in which *expressions of feelings* may be definite; but they do not take the further step of comparing the attitudes expressed in the two passages, and they altogether overlook the very definite (Senses IX and X) attitude of the translation and its difference from that of the original. They are hypnotized by their perception of the difference between direct statement, and the expression of attitudes, into ignoring the more interesting questions.

Statement and the expression of attitudes are, of course, by no means so separate from one another as these writers (and scores of others with whom I could back them) seem to assume. Their close interconnections—which are usually blurred by such favourite terms as 'inspiration,' 'spirit' and 'emotive' of which the last is the worst—I can illustrate with

2.63. I agree that definiteness (IV?) is one of the important aims of expository writing—but is it the only one? Something seems to be lacking in the second piece, and it seems to have suffered from the abrupt lopping off of its green leaves. The change is this—that whereas the first piece challenges and stimulates the imagination, the picture remaining in the mind for a long time, the second piece leaves one cold and unresponsive. It has lost powerfulness. (XI)
One can study for a long while, and delight over, all the little implications present in the metaphors of the first piece. Of course, they could not be adequately translated into direct language, not on

account of their vagueness (—IV [1]) as the second writer suggests, but because each reader sees a little more of the metaphors, or views them from a different angle. (—VI)

He makes the point, which others so often miss, that a passage expresses an attitude *through* what its statements imply. What seem to be feelings mysteriously carried, as if they were smells, commonly turn out to come from quite simple implications.

The next writer has a more prolonged struggle with the problem.

2.631. The explanatory note in this passage states that 'to be definite is the proper aim of expository writing.' That is, then, that Mr Chapman, with his development of metaphor is not definite (IV?) enough —*but only* for Mr Stephen Brown. He cannot vouch for others.

He accuses Mr Chapman of 'vagueness' (—IV?) in his metaphors. He, however, understood them sufficiently to give a very fair representation of what they conveyed to him. Why should he presume that others could not do the same?

And if others were to do the same, the result would possibly not be identical with that of Mr Stephen Brown. (—VI)

Conceptions as to the meanings of such metaphors would differ. And that surely is the point of metaphors such as Mr Chapman's.

This passage, because of the metaphors, may hold beauties for some people, invisible to Mr Brown. His translation is clear-cut and rigid. It conveys a meaning which could hardly be misunderstood—or, perhaps, understood differently. (VI) For nothing can be 'read into' Mr Brown's translation. Mr Chapman is, presumably, writing a serious, propagandist and even devotional piece of work.

For that reason, he is entitled to use metaphor as his medium, for, in doing so, his prose comes very near to poetry.

The passage, he thinks, while *not* definite in Sense VI, yet will yield to different readers meanings which *are* definite in Senses IV and X. This leaves the question uncomfortably unsettled which of these Mr Chapman is to be credited or debited with, some only or all. And we may doubt whether the translation is either so rigid and clear cut (? Senses VIII and VII) or so unable to have things 'read into' it (VI).

It is instructive to compare with 2.63 the following:

2.632. Expository writing has its proper aim in making a passage clear and definite (VII, VI), and may be best done by a simple

[1] —IV = 'not definite' in Sense IV.

explanation; but surely it loses something of its very 'definiteness' (XI, V) if the explanation is too sparse and cold. It then merely becomes a statement of facts. Exposition attempts to weave the data, which statement merely gives, in a coherent and attractive whole.

Here 'clear and definite' seems to be VII and VI; and 'definiteness,' XI and V with perhaps a hint of X. The writer takes metaphor to be facilitator, a mere convenience, a tempting outer case which will make something, that may be discontinuous, *look* one.
The third sentence of the next feels as though it hit some mark.

2.64.* The writer is wrong, in my opinion, in seeking exact equivalents of metaphors in direct language. Metaphor, properly used, often expresses what could not nearly so well have been said in any other way.
Expository writing has not so much to be definite as clear. Explanations are not always most easily made in direct language, every speaker of any skill knows how often a metaphorical illustration of a fact or an idea gets his meaning home to his audience.
What follows is, I am afraid, mere carping, but it is a pity that the writer should get away without it.
The 'translation' is not clearer than the original. It gives the impression of confused thinking in the 'translator's' mind probably caused by a word by word attack. 'Looser elements of the A. Church,' 'fundamental body of opinion,' 'desperate' (to which the original holds no clue)—these might have been avoided with an increase of clarity. Although I am not particularly attracted by the first I think its meaning is much easier to come by. Decoration is almost always preferable to the bare wall.

He is taking 'expository' in a restricted sense, I think, for writing which is expounding the meaning of a passage not just setting forth a subject in view. What is the contrast between 'definite' and 'clear' he has in mind? I do not feel sure that it is between any pair of my senses. Perhaps, from the penultimate sentence ('easier to come by'), 'clear' means predominantly VII qualified by XI ('gets his meaning home') and 'definite' means just IV. But I fancy both are more complex; a 'bare facts not feelings' component may be added into 'definite' and a charge of X be added to 'clear' as the carping develops. What is interesting is that a distinction apparently so plain and simple at first sight, 'not so much definite as clear,' should, on close examination, turn out to be really very far from either. The truth is that we are more at ease with shifting mixtures than with 'fixities and definites' as Coleridge called them, and it is the supple metaphoric life in 'definite' and 'clear' that makes us take them as so readily intelligible.

Two who have a fight with Mr Read's argument now follow.

2.65. Metaphor should be a short cut to the reader's mind but in Mr Chapman's piece of writing the short cut is longer than the normal way round, and as such must be condemned. The commentator quite rightly seizes upon this point; he is almost too kind in his second sentence. When they are vague (—IV, —VI), surely it is certain that exact (IV, VI) equivalents have not been found for the metaphors. The commentator's paraphrase is, as he says, 'more definite,' because Mr Chapman's incapability to use metaphor effectively makes him obscure (—VII) rather than enlighten what he wishes to say with his use of it. If Mr Chapman had produced a good piece of metaphorical writing, it would have lost not only its prettiness but also its 'definiteness' (VI, IX, X) in the straightforward paraphrase of the commentator. The commentator implies in his last sentence that as the proper aim of expository writing is to be definite, therefore metaphor must not be used in it. But metaphor well used increases the 'definiteness' of the passage.

This opens with an interesting assumption. One feels impelled to ask, 'Yes, but a short cut to *what* in the reader's mind?' Both V and XI may have their bearings upon it. Actually, as we have seen, a full explication of these metaphors would need a translation very much longer than the original. But the writer has been too busy attacking the argument to find time to examine either passage at all carefully. His objection turns on a pretty ambiguity. 'Vague,' as he uses it, is, I believe, —IV, —VI; and 'exact' IV/VI, the contrary. This seems to make hay of Mr Read's remark; but 'exact equivalents' has another equally plausible reading—as 'expressions exactly equivalent.' It is surely possible to reproduce a vagueness and often easier to do that than to reproduce a highly implicative movement of the mind— as we all have ample occasion to notice. Later on, 'obscure' is probably —VII crossed with —IV and the later 'definitenesses' are straightforward VI/IX/X.

2.651. If metaphors are so vague that it is not possible to be sure that their exact equivalents have been found, it can't be possible to translate a highly metaphorical passage into 'direct language' preserving the meaning without any loss. As is proved by the actual translation. Is definiteness, at the cost of saying what you really mean, the proper aim of expository writing? To 'belong to the past' is not the same as to 'be a spent wave'; 'a lone swimmer' is not 'a few desperate individuals.' The translation seems to prove that the metaphors in the original passage are not 'merely decorative' since through them M. A. Chapman has expressed something apparently untranslatable into 'direct language.' Does 'direct language' mean absolutely void of metaphors? If so, isn't that almost impossible in description?

The first argument is almost as the above, but he goes on to cut deep. The contrast between 'definiteness' and 'saying what you really mean' is a good way of bringing out the shiftiness of the notion. 'Definiteness' I suppose to be IV + VI restricted to mere statements of events and 'saying what you mean' to be IV + X with, perhaps, —IX.

As I am dealing with comments on the argument, I will add here one which shows what preference for one's own senses of words (preserve us!) can do.

2.652. In Stephen Brown's comment there are two assumptions:

That direct language is unmetaphorical
That metaphorical writing is vague

Neither of these is true. I mean—and I suppose he means—by 'direct' language that language whose sense is most immediately clear to the persons to whom it is addressed. ('Sense' I am using in an extremely broad way, to include not only 'prose' sense but emotional content.) The parables of Christ are one illustration of language of extreme directness and simplicity which is metaphorical. There are countless instances of this fact that the most direct language can be, also, the most 'metaphorical.'

Mr Read made clear and certain enough how he was using 'direct.' It was as the opposite of metaphorical. The writer might if he wished have complained (as the last and many others did) that direct or unmetaphorical language is harder to find than Mr Read supposed. Instead he introduces a quite new sense of his own for 'direct' (incidentally, as VI + X + VII) and then pretends that he has knocked Mr Read out by showing that this other sort of direct language is frequently metaphorical. His parenthesis '—and I suppose he means—' is little better than brazen impudence under the circumstances.

Others dealt, if not more kindly, at least more fairly with this argument.

2.653. 'To be definite is the proper aim of expository writing': yes— but please, there are 100s of ways of being definite. Metaphor proves often one of the greatest.

2.654. The most provocative passage on the page is the one between Mr Chapman's and the 'translation' of his precious passage: it abounds in assumptions, and reveals the weakness which is to be found in 'direct' as well as in metaphorical language: one is easily seduced into the belief that words such as 'equivalents,' 'definite,' 'clarified,' with all their fine latinity, are the sane and clear weapons of discourse, while phrases like the 'Rock of Peter,' and 'the 'restless sea,' are to be avoided as lush, unvirile, and precious. It is true that the first passage is hardly what one hopes for in an account of the Oxford Movement (unless one happens to have a taste for admirably sustained 'comparaison à la longue queue') but neither will translating it into impressive historical Latin work.

But to come back to our 'definites'; here is one who in spite of his syntax and his exceedingly risky uses of 'beauty' and 'logic' yet manages to keep senses X, XI and VII in good order.

2.66. I do not believe that the 'translation' of it 'into direct language' in any way clarifies its meaning. But perhaps that is because I belong to that class of persons who sees more truth in beauty than in logic, and is able *to see* the meaning of a passage like Mr Chapman's (or at least *think* I see), while the 'translation,' taken alone or in comparison with its parent, leaves me muddled and cold. I cannot agree that 'to be definite is the proper aim of expository writing.' If the writer means 'to achieve a clear, unconfused effect in the mind of the reader is the proper aim—,' I can agree immediately. But from his translation I do not believe that this is so. . . . Is not the metaphorical stronger, and clearer in its meaning? Does not the translation pervert the writer's sense? It must appear so to an impartial judge.

Contrast with that this hasty, definite VIII, reader:

2.661. The commentator on this passage rightly considers that its meaning could be clarified by translation. The use of metaphor is here inappropriate. The author's purpose is to give an analytical survey of the effect and value of a movement, and his attitude is a scientific one. In that case no emotional effect is desirable. The prose passage does not exist in order to convey the author's state of mind;—the author, as a critic, should adopt as detached an attitude as possible. Metaphor may be used to clarify abstract thought by means of concrete imagery, but here the thought is simple and direct, chiefly the statemen of facts. These facts are greatly obscured by the metaphor. For instance, there seems to be no gain in calling the church of Rome the 'Rock of Peter,' and the 'Anglican sands' is sufficiently vague to be applied either to people or to instability of doctrine—the meaning is not at once evident. The first three lines of the metaphor might be effective, but the subsequent continuation of it is forced, and demands some effort on the part of the reader for interpretation.

How does he know all this about the author's purpose and his attitude? And why should no emotional effect be desirable from a survey of the value of a movement? The writer is as arbitrary as a jackdaw in the things he has picked up and the uses he makes of them. 'Clarify abstract thought,' 'not at once evident,'—it looks as though (apart from his objection to 'Anglican sands,' which is —VI) Sense VII were his only weapon.

2.67. 'To be definite is the proper aim of expository writing.' This is one of the aims, but not such an important one as that of giving a definite impression. Expository writing with only a background of definiteness is inclined not to hold one's attention or interest very long. Metaphor is precisely what remedies this fault: its combining strength outweighs the supposed weakness of uncertainty of exact translation. Christ's method of clarifying his argument was to make a parable, just as Socrates or anyone else illustrates his meaning with pictures. The loss entailed by translating metaphor into 'direct language' apparently inexistent for the writer of the centre passage—consists of this uniting force, which connects each limb of the passage.

The second 'definite' here has more of XI behind it than anything else; the first might be IV. The metaphor in 'background of definiteness' seems to work though I do not know how. I think, though, I know what he means. 'Precisely' = 'just' and is merely an emphatic (XI). The theory of the parable is a favourite one, but we may hope over-simple, if the 'combining strength' and 'uniting force' here envisaged (compare 2.632) only bring in the chocolate-box view of metaphor again.

I add two to show that with well-controlled settings 'definite' may be freely used without confusion.

2.68.* I should comment first on the last phrase of the short criticism: 'to be definite is the proper aim of expository writing.' What does 'expository writing' mean here? The exposition of an argument, a 'statement' appealing to reason? If this were so, I suppose non-metaphorical definiteness (IV, VI) would be to be desired. But it is not the only sort of 'definiteness': equally great (greater?) definiteness of *impression* (X) might be created by emotive means, and yet be in place in 'expository writing.' The passage quoted from Chapman seems to be a case in point. In dealing with matters of religion (in whatever sense) the final appeal cannot be to reason; therefore the criterion of 'definiteness' is definiteness of total impression (X) (convincing as poetry convinces) for which metaphorical language works more successfully.

2.681. Besides his failure to understand the first passage is the critic being really definite? Do vague phrases like 'the looser elements of the Anglican Church,' or 'became a merely historical phenomenon' convey as much (X), even as mere statement (IV), as the precise and familiar metaphors of the first writer? The familiarity is important; an esoteric image may succeed in being emotively significant, but a metaphor which has to condense not merely emotional suggestion but also a variety of implied statements (as these metaphors, I think, do) must be taken from 'familiar matter of today'—from something which will have a widely common meaning to all readers.

The last sentence is a sagacious retort to those whose 'sensibility' recoiled from triteness.

The next, a little unwillingly, but with 'a clear distinction,' separates some things that the integrity of the mind requires united; and so his last word need not surprise us.

2.69. Chapman gives a sense of religious experience—the tone of the second passage is that of the history book. One is devotional, the other critical. The first expresses a religious state of mind not to be expressed otherwise than by metaphor. Sir Th. Browne could combine the merits of both passages in one piece of writing but today it seems we must have a clear distinction between the two. Chapman's passage is successful because it expresses his state of mind (X).

Is the second passage more definite? (IV, X?) I do not think so. It is not even an accurate paraphrase. Chapman has one dominating thought, for the moment, the vast importance of the Roman Catholic church. This is not at all clearly brought out in No. 2. For to cling in safety upon the 'Rock of Peter' is very different from remaining a convert to Rome when the Oxford Movement had become a social phenomenon. No. 2 puts the Church of Rome in its proper place— No. 1 regards it as a thing divine and no fit subject for prying analysis. Thus forceful writing may say something more definitely (X, XI) than clear (VII) writing—Witness Hitler.

Finally, and not so opposed to the last as it may seem on the surface:

2.691. To be definite (IV) is not necessarily 'The proper aim of expository writing.' A bogus company promoter may issue an admirable and eminently successful prospectus which would never have been so admirable or so eminently successful had it been at all definite.

# The Second Landing Stage

*If, then, it seems to you after inspection that, such being the situation as it existed at the start, our investigation is in a satisfactory condition compared with the other inquiries that have been developed by tradition, there must remain for all of you, or for our students, the task of extending us your pardon for the shortcomings of the inquiry.* ARISTOTLE, De Sophisticis Elenchis

This will be a good place to stand back a little distance to consider what are the main points that this close study ought to bring out. These are firstly that over a large number of questions, which, if they are clearly stated, must be agreed to be of immense importance in the everyday working of every mind, our pupils are in a state of gross confusion. Such questions are: Is metaphor a trick for expressing feelings or may it be also a way of making statements? If it expresses feelings, how does it do so? Can what is said in a metaphor be said otherwise? Can a metaphor be definite in its meaning and, if so, how? What do we mean by 'definite' in any answer we may give? Is what is definite necessarily clear? Is what is clear necessarily certain? Is what is certain felt to be so or can it be shown to be so? Is strong feeling incompatible with clear insight? Or is it necessary to it? Can we seek the truth about what we really care about? Or can we unless we care?

That these questions are practically important must be granted if we agree that metaphor is all but indispensable in our speech; that we are endlessly retranslating and retranslating it in the motion of our thought; that a large part of the effort of education is just to induce definiteness (in some of its senses) in our pupils' attempts; that 'definite,' 'clear' and 'certain' are in our mouths as teachers all the time; and that (to look beyond the schools) today's battle for the cultural domination of the world is being conducted upon strategic principles implied in the rival answers to the last questions. Neither Mussolini nor Hitler have underestimated them.

It is easy to talk eloquently about freedom in the pursuit of truth and the democratic method. But what we need is to induce the struggle between the rival forces repeatedly on a small controllable scale so that the different outcomes of the choices shall become apparent. The world crisis, 'Shall we accept others' views (good or bad) or learn to see?' is reproduced inside every genuine experiment in interpretation. Appeals to principles are very well—*after* the principle has grown into something to appeal to. And so are right answers, theoretical analyses and demonstrations—*after* the learner has shaped in himself the terms in which they must be read. There is no short cut, and none is recommended; but to say so is not to leave things to nature. In other subjects we do not. To teach English is no doubt more difficult than to teach Mathematics or Chemistry; English is so very much more complicated. But that is no reason to despair or to think that the learners may therefore be left to master their language unaided. Some of these confusions about metaphor— from which larger helplessnesses come—are like haziness as to which is addition and which multiplication, or uncertainty as to the difference between an electron and a molecule.

The last point of this retrospect concerns the gap between theoretical analysis (of the mechanics of metaphor, say, or of the variations of 'definite') and the practical handling of language in the conduct of thought. But this gap is only serious if we overlook it, or think that further analysis *by itself* will fill it. It becomes easier to cross as we examine it, for study of the gap is itself the bridge. This study must be made from both sides. To build the bridge and induce his students to build it with him is the teacher's business.

# *Part Two:* GRAMMAR

*Sentences in scripture (says Dr Donne) like hairs in horse-*
*tails, concur in one root of beauty and strength; but being*
*plucked out one by one, serve only for springes and snares.*
                    COLERIDGE, *Omniana,* 172

# *Chapter Ten:* What Is Grammar?

> *When our ancestors have fairly gained a conquest over
> the natural enemy of writers, which I take strict grammar
> to be, I do not see why we should give it up.*
>
> CHARLES JAMES FOX

Grammar has, historically, a prestige in teaching that needs some explanation. If we have any respect for authority, we should believe that Grammar—or, at least, something which traditional Grammar attempted to give—is what we need. And yet, at present, few teachers are looking hopefully in that direction. For some time grammatical studies have been passing into ever deeper and less regretted neglect. But by this we may well be losing something of peculiar value, and the problem is to separate it from the other things we may be glad to lose. So one aim of this Section is negative. It attempts to distinguish between the different subjects (with different purposes) that share the once honoured name of Grammar. When they are separated, it can be seen, I believe, that confusion between them has been the source of innumerable false problems and unnecessary mysteries. These confusions are removable. Until they are removed there is no open field here for the learner's meditation. With their removal many traditional questions and their answers, that have been little less than outrages to intelligence, fade away—or become themselves valuable illustrations of bad procedures, occasions for diverting and fruitful thought about language.

It will be noticed that notwithstanding its title there is very little discussion of the usual topics of Grammar in this Section. The Parts of Speech and their relations, the comparison, classification and analysis of constructions are hardly touched on. This does not imply that in an *ideal* English Course these things should be omitted. If we could illuminate the problems which such treatment covers we should do so. But grammatical theory is not yet ready for this. As many modern linguists (Brunot, Jespersen, Bloomfield and Sheffield are varied examples) have for some time been pointing out, the definitions and the analytic concepts we are still forced to employ introduce worse troubles for the reflective student than those they profess to set in order. Grammar here has borrowed from Logic just those very instruments that can at present least safely be used. A more helpful study of the classes of words and their inter-actions will only follow, and cannot precede, a better understanding of the logical machinery we use in their discussion. Otherwise we merely import logical perplexities into part of Grammar. Mean-while naïve trust in traditional Grammar is the main impediment that the logician suffers from. The two problems are very closely connected, and this interdependence is my excuse for postponing discussion of sentence structure to another occasion. The barrier to thought about how language works much resembles a log jam; too many questions are piled up across one another. The first step will be to locate, if we can, the key log.

In discarding Grammar—taken as an ambitious normative *science* —the teaching tradition has increasingly put in its place a doctrine of *usage*. The larger part of the Section consists of attacks from various angles upon this doctrine. I believe it to be, on the whole, the most pernicious influence in current English teaching, doing more than all other removable errors together to inhibit the course of self-critical and profitable reflection about the conduct of thought in language. It is a product of reaction against illegitimate applica-tions of logic and philosophy to language. The effect has been to discourage, and often to exclude, all intelligent reflection about language. In attacking the *usage* doctrine, I am, of course, not recom-mending a return to the modes of treatment against which it was a revolt. They are rightly discredited. A lot has happened since the days of Lords Kames and Beatie, of Withers and Harris. Both in philosophy and in philology we are a long way from the Eighteenth Century. We are now in a very different position to understand, and to help others to understand, how language works, and to make this understanding an aid in its use. But since thought upon such matters must, in the growing mind, incessantly recapitulate past history, and go through stages in which supposals appeal that we might take nowadays to be mere historical curiosities, I have added, in the last Chapter of the Section, a slight discussion of some miscon-ceptions of the relations of Logic to language.

The proposal I make in the Section is briefly that as a school subject we replace Grammar by a study of what Grammar is. It will perhaps seem odd that anything so notoriously difficult and recondite should be seriously recommended. My reply is that it is now capable of becoming neither difficult nor recondite. And is it recondite? It is already and inevitably a pressing immediate interest in every learner's mind. '*Why* is this sentence right and that sentence wrong, or this arrangement of words better than that?' are questions all want to ask. We damp curiosity when we insist that they must just learn *which* is right. And to fob them off with an answer in terms merely of *usage,* 'It's right because good writers write so! That's *why!*' is a quick way of destroying just that movement of the mind which would be of the most value to it. As to the difficulty of the theory of what Grammar is, confused theories are usually difficult—especially when they mix very different things under the same terms. A clarified theory—in the degree to which it is clarified—becomes incomparably easier. We have only to think of the history of Mathematics and consider the fashion in which teaching in the developing subjects (the sciences) becomes easier and can at once go deeper when theory advances, to feel that the theory of the interactions of words need not for ever terrify the class or the teacher. Here again, a beginning in the attempt to teach it seriously would soon yield experience guiding us towards improved teaching.

Some elementary drill in the forms of language will, of course, always remain a necessity. It need not be much, except in special cases. Its chief drawback, as part of *general* education, is the damping effect I have just spoken of. The natural curiosity about how language works—which the young share with primitive races—struggles hard before it chokes. Formal descriptive grammar generates a resentment against the grammarian, which is traditional in the subject. I believe that this resentment can be made use of, and that it would be excellent pedagogy to open a course on the theory of grammar with an exhibition of some of the odd arbitrarinesses and mistakes of grammarians—to serve as a sort of animated cocoanut-shy for our pupils. To offer some of these absurdities for criticism, early, relieves the resentment, and to ask about them 'What on earth has been happening here?' sometimes opens a path into the subject which leads towards its very centre. The terminologies with which professional grammarians make such magnificent play had perhaps best be left out, or introduced only for picturesque effect. Amateur spectators need not be expected to wield such weapons.

I begin then with some curiosities—chosen to introduce the Usage problem—before proceeding to a dissection of the different purposes that are combined under the general head of Grammar. And the order of my progress is from the frivolous to the profound.

Some specimens of pedantry come first; all cases, seemingly, of wilful and near-sighted niggling. A lively warning against arbitrary carping is useful; my protocols show a numerous class of pedants-in-the-bud who need it. A first effect of inviting attention to the *detail* of writing is to offer everybody an almost unlimited supply of remarks that seem to be to the point. All those many, whose difficulty is that they cannot find anything whatever to say, flock gaily through this new gap in the hedge, and I anticipate that to show them others doing so may have its uses. Secondly, as Stevenson remarked somewhere: 'Every word looks guilty when you put it into the dock.' The students may well be accustomed from the start to accept this guilty air and allow for it.

A third effect is less easy to explain. There may possibly be at first a decline of natural perceptiveness when we turn from assuming unconsciously that we do know what things mean to examining them critically. An alarming but probably apocryphal story is told of the Boy Calculator, Zerah Colburne, who earned vast sums by extracting immense cube roots in his head and performing other wonders. His father was anxious to discover how these feats were accomplished, so he and the youngster sat up many nights enquiring into the matter. At last, one midnight, young Zerah called his father in with the good news that he had discovered the secret. They put it down on paper in full detail and went to bed happy in the belief that Time's teeth were drawn. Alas, next morning the gift had vanished! Neither could now understand the account of how it was done, and poor Zerah no longer knew how to do it! The moral is not as grim as may appear; the loss in verbal perceptiveness is not great, is temporary, is abundantly recovered; but it may be well to give our pupils ample time to make up what they may lose. All through this first display of pettifoggery the general moral for interpretation is about the endless dangers of ignoring or mistaking or arbitrarily imposing verbal settings. At the same time, the comparisons thus pointed are a good exercise in sentence building.

My specimens come from a mixed collection of school books and Handbooks for Teachers. There is no special significance in the choice; there is no lack of similar examples, similar models of criticism. My difficulty is to refrain from putting in a bookful.

## EXERCISE THREE

### I

My author, who, incidentally, wrote after long service as one of His Majesty's Inspectors of Schools, takes the following sentences from Matthew Arnold:

> The reader will see how, through all the dubiousness and involved manner of the Greek, Mr Long has firmly seized upon the clear thought which is certainly at the bottom of that troubled wording, and, in distinctly rendering this thought, has at the same time thrown round its expression a characteristic shade of painfulness and difficulty which just suits it.

He then comments:

> What is the modifier 'through . . . Greek' attached to? Perhaps *through* should be *penetrating;* then the modifier would be attached to 'Mr Long.'
> And a 'shade' is not 'thrown': a body interposed between a light and the ground casts or throws a *shadow* on the ground, and an object placed within the space between the shadow and the body is in the *shade*. A shadow has a definite shape on a surface and is two-dimensional. The space deprived of light—the shade—is three-dimensional.

To this he adds a footnote:

> The connotation of the terms is clear cut. Both belong to optics and to art. The O.E.D. is not sufficiently critical of the loose usage of the two terms. Arnold's use of the term *thrown* suggests that he had some notion of the connotation, though he was evidently not familiar with the terms as technical terms. Shade is sometimes used in the sense of a *trace* or a *trifle,* but it is improbable that Arnold meant this.

His own improved version of Arnold is this:

> The reader will see how Mr Long, penetrating the obscurities of the Greek phrasing, has succeeded in divining the underlying clear thought; and how, in rendering this thought clearly into English, he has contrived to throw over its expression a shadow of painfulness and difficulty that seems to be characteristic of the original.

The questions that arise are all but endless:

Why should not the modifier be attached to 'Mr Long has seized'? Cf. 'I went to her through the gate' or 'Through the water Mr Long lifted the pearl.' If the reply is that this is not as the critic is using the word 'modifier,' then he needs a wider notion in describing Arnold's sentence.

But more important points are:

(1), *shade* and *shadow* have had centuries of non-technical use which is perfectly as appropriate to our reading of Matthew Arnold as any technical uses could be. Johnson's Dictionary gives,

> *shade* the figure formed upon any surface corresponding to the body by which the light is intercepted: the shadow.

Example, 'Enviable merit or its shade pursue' (Pope); and, inversely, for *shadow,* Johnson gives,

> opacity, darkness, shade:

Example,

> 'By the revolution of the skies
> Night's sable shadows from the ocean rise' (Denham)

There seems no great need to be more correct than Johnson; but, for our pedant, he too, with poor Pope and Denham, must join Matthew Arnold on the same back bench, for Denham's shadows unfortunately leave the ocean on which he would have them thrown, and Pope's shade seems only pursuable as a shadow.

(2) Even technically a shadow would be part of a shade (as a wall is of a city); therefore the simplest of all forms of metaphor, Aristotle's whole for a part, could very well, if we wished to indulge a favourable form of pedantry, be supposed to be at work. And an equally obvious metaphor would make a shade be *thrown*. Neither, however, is in the least need of such justification.

(3) It is not the business of the O.E.D. to be critical and allege loose usages, but to record all usages as far as its limited space permits; the great work none the less in this instance scores over its critic, and he would have done well to have consulted its article more thoroughly, for it gives 'A shade of annoyance crosses his face.'

(4) Why should not Arnold do what he is evidently doing, combine *shade* as a volume, *shadow* as a surface hue, and a selection

of the metaphoric senses—a trifle, a fleeting impression ('under a cloud'), all in his single word? There is no one-at-a-time rule for meanings; a good writer can mean half a hundred different and distinguishable meanings at once with a phrase, just as a determined enough pedant can make any number of gross confusions and crude mistakes in his efforts to 'distinguish' between them.

II

The attitude of the professional zoologist to the amateur field worker is sometimes misunderstood. You find belligerent field-workers who know their subject extremely well who contend that the academic authority is based solely on access to works of reference and type specimens, and that the seat of true learning and observation is in the open air rather than pickled in formalin.

Editorial Note, *Discovery*

The critic comments:

The sentence contains several faults of construction, and its last phrase is flippant. The general meaning seems to be:

Amateur field-workers in Zoology sometimes possess a sound knowledge of their subject, and are inclined to resent the rather patronizing attitude of their academically qualified brethren. They maintain that, after all, the seat of true observation and learning is in the open air, and not in the library, the laboratory, and the museum.

(1) Why not be flippant?—'Nothing like a little judicious levity!' as Michael Finsbury observed.—Especially when, as here, a rather spirited dispute is being summarized.

(2) It is flippant—this I suspect is what has upset the critic without his clearly seeing it; such things do. There is a rather robust joke in the background—something to do with the use of the word *seat* (always a temptation to jokes)—a remote suggestion that the field worker and his 'academically qualified *brethren*' (who by the way are *the critic's invention*) are waiting somehow to catch one another bending!

(3) Taken more literally—where the critic thinks it is flippant, it is exact; and a failure to mention formalin and its pickling, i.e. distorting, effect would (and does in the rewriting) miss a main point.

(4) The 'general meaning' is not what he gives:

    (a) 'belligerent' toned down to 'inclined to resent'

(b) 'know their subject extremely well' is not equal to 'sometimes possess a sound knowledge of their subject.'

(c) The whole ironical implication in academic authority being 'based solely on access . . .' is left out.

(d) The critic contrives somehow in his turn to patronize the field-workers. We can see on which side of the controversy he would be found!

Under the cover of correcting 'faults of construction' he will not allow the Editor to say what he had to say. Divergent sympathies are masquerading as grammar, and concentration upon the articulations of the sentences, as so often, enables him to neglect their meanings.

### III

Again, as respects the form of breakers on an even shore, there is difficulty of no less formidable kind. There is in them an irreconcilable mixture of fury and formalism. Their hollow surface is marked by parallel lines, like those of a smooth mill-weir, and graduated by reflected and transmitted lights of the most wonderful intricacy, its curve being at the same time necessarily of mathematical purity and precision; yet at the top of this curve, when it nods over, there is a sudden laxity and giving way, the water swings and jumps along the ridge like a shaken chain, and the motion runs from part to part as it does through a serpent's body.                    RUSKIN

This rouses our critic to put the following queries:

What is an 'even' shore? What do we know of the appearance of the 'hollow' surface? Is 'curved' or 'rounded' meant? Can there be mathematical 'im-purity'? Can a curve 'nod over'? Does the top of the curve become 'lax'? Can water 'swing'? Does motion 'run'? Does the form of the breaker cease to be mathematical when the curve 'nods over'?

Let us try to see what these complaints come to. The difficulty in doing so is that the disease is catching. It is easy to invent more doubts about the import of the pedant's queries than he has invented about the meaning of Ruskin's passage. By 'even' what could Ruskin be supposed to be meaning—except such a configuration of the shore as would permit the formation of the very breakers that he is in the paragraph so successfully describing? 'Even' takes its whole force, in other words, from its context. We know that waves on a rocky, steep, irregular, *uneven* shore do not break as they break on level sands or shingle (but, perhaps, I am not allowed to use 'level' so!) and to remind us economically of this is the word's duty, which it performs. The commentator pretends that for him it will not do this. A pre-occupation with some supposed 'only correct use' of the word, derived from other settings, must be distracting him, but it is the business of a reader not to be distracted. Next 'hollow'? He must be hypnotized by the sense in which an empty egg-shell is hollow, but has he never looked into a hollow oak or cave and observed it to be hollow? At what point would he refuse the word to a *portion* of a concave surface? But the word has a specific use, as Ruskin knew: 'in the hollow of the wave.' He asks, 'Is "curved" or "rounded" meant?' Can he possibly be in any real doubt as to whether Ruskin's surface is convex or concave? (He tempts one to stop and explain that, of course, I don't mean here Ruskin's own superficies!) As to 'mathematical purity' there are many kinds of purity and 'mathematical' comes in both to single out the abstract formal character of this purity and to hint at the simplicity of the equations determining the curve. When the curve 'nods over' the change of metaphor indicates just the very change in the character of our apprehension of the form that the critic is remarking and complaining about. The top of the curve does *not* become lax, it may be noted, but at the top the surface does. This feels lamentably like plying back to the critic with guns from the same workshop. But though this is a queer game, one may as well play it properly.

As to his other queries, they show very clearly what he is doing throughout. He is refusing to allow the setting in the passage to intervene in his interpretation of the words. He is putting them into settings of his own which are chosen to exclude the sources of the powers which these words are here exercising. He is thereby providing examples of the fatal obstruction to understanding that crude notions about 'proper usage' and 'correctness' can become. When we find them being invoked to exclude so innocent a thing as flippancy, their danger should be evident. But flippancy evicted has its revenge. Seven Devils of Frivolousness seize on the bailiff. Here we see him in their grasp, jumping to their motions. Naturally the man is in grim earnest, saving the language from its corruptors. But the more closely we examine his objections the more they resemble those of the schoolboy who has just discovered that language can be interpreted in various ways. It is an exhilarating discovery. We all know the boy who finds it fun when you remark, 'That's a nice picture on the wall,' to reply, 'It's not on *the wall,* it's on paper!' A promising trick, but, if he never grows out of it, he is likely to become this sort of grammarian. And what began in fun ends by being rather more than a joke.

All this in an 'academically qualified brother' witnesses to very odd ideas about language. Just what they are, and how powerful they may be in producing less absurd and therefore more dangerous aberrations, is what we have to find means to make our pupils consider.

'Speech' wrote Ben Jonson, 'is the only benefit man hath to express his excellency of mind above other creatures. It is the instrument of society, therefore Mercury, who is the President of Language, is called *deorum hominumque interpres.* In all speech words and sense are as the body and the soul, the sense is as the life and soul of language, without which all words are dead. Sense is wrought out of experience, the knowledge of human life and actions or of the liberal arts.'

The liberal arts are in neglect. Jonson was near enough to the spirit of the Scholastics to feel no strangeness in making them equal partners with the knowledge of human life and actions as the material out of which sense is wrought. But they did not fall into neglect without good reasons, which modern instances may suggest. They will not be restored unless we take due and full note of the travesties by which they may be degraded.

What can the explanation of these travesties be? A superficial one is that this is 'Grammar.' The word has been pronounced, its influence descends upon the scene, and with it a strange and deadly cramp seems to spread over the intellectual faculties, afflicting them with squint, making them unable to observe all sorts of things they are perfectly conversant with in normal life. This attacks the greatest along with the least, and men for whom we must have the utmost respect. Even scholars as great as Jespersen and Kittredge do not escape. It is a healthy moral that not even such men are immune; talk about language is always on the verge of nonsense, and the discovery of absurdities need not lead us to respect them less. Their greatness does not prevent our giving their work, here and there, as a fly may to a mountain, a close local inspection, and what we find will only seem a considerable flaw to those who are unable to see the mountain in its proper scale.

How about this?

> It may not be amiss to call attention to the fact that in ordinary parlance we understand the use of the word 'thing' so as to include what should not properly be called a 'thing,' as in: I shall speak to him the first thing in the morning, The only thing left for us was to run away, He hath wrought folly in Israel, in lying with Jacob's daughter; which thing ought not to be done.　　　*Linguistica*, 309

Jespersen gives further examples from Carlyle, Shakespeare and miscellaneous novelists. How odd it all really is! A grammarian, a bold and thoughtful one, a man who has spent all his life on the study of how words are used, finds it 'not amiss' to speak so about 'what should not properly be called a "thing." ' He is not addressing the mob in a book the size of *Linguistica*. It is evidently aimed at champions worth such a weighty missile. But, 'what should not properly be called a "thing" '! As though he knew some thing which shouldn't! How are we to make our students—or grammarians, but that is another matter—see what a manoeuvre occurs in that 'properly be called' and in the phrases that are equivalent to it? But this last example about 'thing' has led us from the pedantry cocoanut-shy to a different alley in the fair, where the thimble-rigging and the three-card trick are going on. Here we ask, What are grammarians trying to do?

To open this up it is convenient to take one of the traditional 'hard questions' of grammar and insist that they are hard mainly because we will not stop, before asking them, to inquire, 'What are we asking?' Like many other invitations to controversy, they would disappear if we learned how to separate their confusions and deal with the points one at a time.

Grammarians battle with one another in such arenas as: 'What is the true construction of

> *What I have written, I have written?'*

One says, '*What I have written* is the object of the principal clause *I have written*' : and he goes on, 'It is particularly misleading to write (as Sonnenschein does) *what I have written (that) I have written* for the interpolated *that* completely alters the significance of the principal clause.'

If it does alter the significance somewhat, what about it? We should then have different interpretations of the sentence fitting into different settings. The sentence, in fact, can be taken in many more than two ways, as we all, when we are not under the spell of grammar, know, in practice, well enough. If we compare

*What I have written, I have written*

and

*What I have written, that I have written*

we can feel more or less explicitly and clearly from occasion to occasion that neither has in itself one fixed interpretation; both shift not merely from one position to another but *through several;* and to try to notice and describe the differences between these positions can be made a fascinating pursuit, is the practice of criticism, and should be a main part of the business of grammarians. But to assume, as both these authors seem to do, that there is one proper interpretation and that any other 'is misleading,' is to indicate again that there is something radically wrong with this variety of the grammarian's interest in and dealings with language.

What could 'misleading' mean here? This is a question that could very easily be used controversially. But let us ask it calmly and reflectively, for to follow it may help us to discover why grammar, which, one would think, must be the very discipline of interpretation we need, is so often not merely useless but destructive to intelligence.

There are two main ways of taking 'misleading' here. The first reading would be simply that, if we took the sentence as Sonnenschein takes it, we should misunderstand it (be misled by our interpretation). But this assumes that there is a uniform context in which alone the sentence is used. And this assumption we can any of us smash without trouble experimentally, by saying, *What I have written, I have written* in different settings, and noticing that we are sufficiently well understood in each—in different ways, of course, since we are saying different things. To take a few only,

we may be saying something similar to what Mr. Ezra Pound said
in one of his earlier poems:

> When I behold how black immortal ink
> Drips from my deathless pen, ah well a-day,
> What matters it at all what others think?
> There is enough in what I chance to say!

Or we may be saying something equivalent to

> Let's have no more shilly-shallying!
> No more haggling! Take it or leave it!

Or we may be saying,

> It can't be helped now.[1]

Or finally (for this must stop), we may be saying,

> I am as the Medes and the Persians.

The alternative sentence,

> *What I have written that I have written,*

seems more fitted (in most settings) to the last; but it is not hard
to invent situations in which it would convey the others without
strain or unnaturalness. The part that intonation and stress would
play should be noticed. A change in intonation changes the causal
contexts through which the sentence works. But, in all cases,
whether the utterance was *misleading* or not—if by that we mean,
'was it justifiably misunderstood?'—would be a question about the
particular occasion and the relations between the speaker and hearer.

But this, though relevant, was not, I am sure, what my grammarian was thinking about. By 'misleading' he probably meant one
or other, or several together, of the things which may be meant by
'grammatically incorrect,' or 'contrary to my grammatical theory,'
or 'not analogous with other sentences I have in mind,' or 'not historically so,' or 'not psychologically so.' Let me consider briefly

---

[1] Again a sentence apt to start a grammatical rough-house. The use of *help,* here,
looks like the exact opposite of *help* in 'Grammar can help us,' and so is by some
said to have the sense of *hinder* or *prevent.* But obviously everything depends upon
what *it* stands for, which depends upon the setting. Compare 'I can't help it' (of a
sneeze) and 'I can't help it' (of a toy boat out of reach); or 'Grammarians can't
help it' and 'Grammarians can help interpretation.' See Henry Sweet's view, p. 261,
below.

some of the assumptions that might be behind *grammatically correct.*

A common undiscussed assumption is that for every sentence in a language such as English, an account (in the strictest view, *one and only one* account) can be given, in terms of a limited number of primitive ideas, which is *the correct grammatical account* of its construction. The analogy supporting this assumption is perhaps an analogy with that vague and philosophically hazardous assumption that if we knew enough about the laws of Nature we should find that they could all be stated in terms of a limited number of ideas or axioms. Another analogy might be drawn from the attempts made recently by logicians to derive all mathematics from an initial set of primitive propositions or operations. But it is perhaps unlikely that this analogy is at work here.

Whatever analogies could be rallied in support, the inappropriateness of such an assumption to an enquiry into the working of language should need no stressing; but unluckily it does. Grammatical theory cannot possibly be a closed system. The facts it attempts to order are a selection of the acts of men. So too, it may be said, are the facts of mathematics. But mathematical thought restricts itself to certain clearly defined aspects of things, their numerable and quantitative aspects, or in the case of geometry, to properties which can be defined *ab initio.* It proceeds only in virtue of these definitions. But grammar has no such definitions to support it. If it had, it would no longer be an enquiry into the uses of language; it would cease to be an empirical comparative enquiry and become a deductive symbol system.

Grammarians strain endlessly to produce what they call 'definitions' of their terms—of nouns, verbs etc.—but if we enquire what they seek in a definition we find that it is usually something of a kind which the sciences have renounced.

They are seeking descriptive formulae which will happen to cover just the items that seem to be sorted in common-sense classifications. It is much as though a zoologist should strain every nerve to find a formula which would apply to, and only to, what the common housewife calls a 'fish' (i.e. crabs, oysters, whales and mackerel) and yet should refuse 'lives in the water' as being 'not scientific enough'; or as though we were trying to define 'pretty things,' or 'nice things,' or 'objets d'art,' or 'knick-knacks'! It is like trying to refine upon common-sense metaphoric anatomy, e.g. 'fingers.' Has a star-fish fingers? And are the chimpanzee's fore-limbs furnished with fingers or toes—and if with fingers, just when do toes begin and fingers stop, between him and the two-toed sloth? Or, 'Is the valve of a submarine a window, a door or a chimney?' These absurd queries are not very far removed in their type from some of the puzzles grammarians have set themselves, through not considering first what they will want the answer for. They would do better to follow the example of a recent Tutor of Magdalene. He sent for an undergraduate whose parrot was disturbing the neighbours, and said, 'Mr W.! I must ask you to keep your bird under better control. Otherwise I shall have to consult the Dean as to whether it is to be regarded as a gramophone or a dog.' Both these being objects which College Rules permit us to exclude, the Tutor (who is a mathematician) would have known perfectly for what purpose he needed his definition.

Too many efforts of grammarians to define 'adjective' or 'verb' have been more like struggles with conundrums than like the orderly classifications by systematic, interlocked definitions that are used in the sciences. A definition for science fixes a use for a term and then explores the consequences: it is not upset by finding that the use is not exactly that of everyday users, but the grammarian's game has mainly been that of finding awkward words or sentences that won't fit in and have been overlooked by his rivals. There is no reason to think that this game could not be carried indefinitely far, but however far it were carried it would not thereby become more scientific. It would not, that is to say here, bring out deeper connections, or thereby assist us in control over anything, or give us increased power of prediction. The mistake has been that grammarians, like most early natural scientists, have assumed that the common-sense differences visible in language must correspond, somehow or other, to a set of exact distinctions of thought. But, as we shall see in Chapters XVII and XXII, there are good reasons why such correspondence between language-forms and thought-forms should not be found. We can also see why it should be expected.

Carried further, the traditional grammatical treatment will become no more useful than, in its relatively early stages, it has long been. With this we turn to the merits which the grammarian's

classifications—parts of speech, constructions and so on—undoubtedly have. When left at a simple early stage they have had, and
still have, enormous and evident uses. To be as clear as possible
just what these are, and just what they are not, is the important
thing. A glance at the history of the subject may help.

In his endeavour to classify the parts of speech and the constructions the grammarian was early successful—particularly with Latin
Grammar. He arrived at a description of the main types of words
and of the ways in which they are put together to be effective
in communication—but effective only with reference to a given
sort of setting. Obviously, with Latin the settings were primarily
those of written uses of the language. As has often been pointed
out, if the early grammarians had had to do with spoken Latin instead they would have found things not so easy. But what is a
'successful' description here? It is a system by which, for any sentence which we need to examine, the mutual relations of the words
in it can be described:

(1) By reference to a limited number of notions—those of verbs,
pronouns, prepositions, modifying, case, etc.

(2) So as to satisfy a certain purpose. The fewer the notions required, if the purpose is satisfied, the more successful the description. But what is the purpose, with grammar?

With this, we come, I think, to the reason which has always
prevented grammar from being as useful as it should be as a discipline for interpretation. Its purposes have always been mixed, and
usually even conflicting. Bundle them up in a phrase like 'To explain how sentences work,' and we can see very quickly how easy
it is to confuse them. Here are some obvious purposes which may
interfere with one another.

(1) To provide a machine by the aid of which a language may be
taught, a method by which gross differences between sentences and
between the work done by different words in them can be quickly
and clearly pointed out even to stupid learners. (The prime use of
Latin Grammar. See close of Introduction.)

(2) To establish a norm of good use with which practice may be
compared. (The chief aim of early Grammars of English and of much
18th Century Work.)

(3) To give a psychological analysis of the different mental processes and operations supposed to accompany the use of different words

and sentences. (For this psychology and linguistics wait on one another.)

(4) To examine the logical form of the statements made with different arrangements of words. (See Chapters XVII and XXII.)

(5) To provide a machine by which changes in the meanings and forms of words can be systematically presented so that laws of change may be inquired into. (The Semantic, and historical aims, which used to be simplified by a belief in one original Garden of Eden Language; now being put on a more respectable basis.)

(6) To provide apparatus by which languages can be compared as regards (here would follow a list of aspects such as range of use, precision, ambiguity, facility, subtlety of discrimination, pregnancy, etc.—aspects not necessarily best considered with the same network of distinctions).

(7) To inquire into and measure the influence of the forms of language upon the ways—social, political, moral, philosophical—of thought.

(8) To aid training in interpretation by which our use of language, both active and passive, might be improved.

The list is very incomplete, but it will suffice for our aims here. To suppose that these different purposes can be simultaneously forwarded by one set of distinctions is really not unlike supposing that a footgear equally suitable to the battlefield and the ball-room, for rolling logs and climbing rocks, can be found. 'Only connect' is an excellent maxim. 'But discriminate too!' we must feel inclined to add. Certainly, ordinary language seems to do more than enough connecting. Any, some, or all of these purposes we must expect to find sheltering under such phrases as: *gaining a sound understanding of, a thorough grasp of, a true sense for, a real insight into, a genuine mastery of, a language.* And the word 'explain' (its uses provide important matter for the Logic Section) covers every purpose. To put the trouble with grammar succinctly: it has tried to *explain* language without sufficiently considering what it wanted the explanation for. It took 'explanation' to be a word with an absolute meaning—corresponding to one Truth about language—as it took so many other words.

How easily any one question that the study of *interpretation* wants to ask may be mistaken for others, which need have nothing to do with it, may be shown by asking it:

*Just how is the word being used?*

Here are some of its translations:

(1) What other words will—from setting to setting—take its place?

(2) What are the effects of using it?

(3) What is the situation in which it is used?

(4) What happens in the mind when we use the word?

(5) What account does the word or sentence itself seem to offer of 4?

(6) What other words and phrases are used in parallel ways and so can be classified with it?

The grammarian's traditional technique is appropriate to answering 6 and, less successfully, 1. For grammar has hitherto consisted primarily in the collection and sorting of words and word-groups which behave alike. But questions 2 and 3 push in now to ask 'Behave alike? How? When? Why? In what settings? And for whom?' And these challenges (as my remarks on the first reading of 'misleading' were intended to suggest) bring out two things. (A) The grammarian's word and sentence groups are composed of specimens which behave alike only in certain general settings. Consider any two specimens in sufficiently special settings and you will find them possessed of powers which no longer seem parallel. (B) 'Behave alike' for the grammarian primarily means 'stand *to the other words* with which they may be put in similar or analogous relations.' As we all know, in

'Timothy likes strawberry jam'

and

'Edward hates wedding cake'

'Timothy' could take the place of 'Edward' and 'likes' could take the place of 'hates' and 'strawberry jam' could take the place of 'wedding cake'; but, inside these last two groups of words, 'wedding' and 'strawberry' will not change places, though, if we crossed them out, 'cake' and 'jam' could. The relation between 'strawberry' and 'jam' (for the standard supposed setting) is not the same as that (again for the standard supposed setting) between 'wedding' and 'cake.' One way to show this is to substitute (Cf. 'How is it used?' (1), above) for 'strawberry' the word-group 'made from strawberries.' We cannot similarly substitute for 'wedding,' 'made from weddings.' This incidentally reinforces what has been said about the importance of the supposed setting, for strawberry jam might not in fact be made from strawberries, and yet be legally sold as 'strawberry jam.'

But this is only the ground floor level of the grammarian's sortings. On top of them he erects storey after storey of more generalized classifications. Or rather he should do so, for historically he has started at the top or near it, and has ever since been trying to fit in the lower storeys under his assumptions. And the endeavour is immensely complicated by the efforts of questions 1, 2, 4 and 5 to take charge—as is shown in the endless struggle of grammarians to combine and reconcile form and content and function in their treatment. Only through form and content can we collect the words whose *grammatical* functions are classified in constructions; but, equally, a word with no function—taken alone without *any* supplied construction—has no content. *In strict isolation,* it is a meaningless sound or mark. Its *grammatical* functions are classes of settings, as its content (or *lexical* function) is another name for its context. (See p. 49.) Grammatical and lexical questions are inseparable, yet the traditional formulations of grammar separate them. For example, when it is said that an adjective may be used as a noun. The protests of Jespersen and others against such things are encouraging, but they need to be carried deeper. The theoretical requirement is a radical re-conception of the order of the abstractions by which we have arrived at that convenient fiction whose name is the word *word*. Even then, the systematic survey of languages which has hitherto been Grammar's main task would be no great help to the study of interpretation. It would tell us about our *use of words* in a sense in which we know, practically, almost all about it already. It would not necessarily give us that increased insight into our *use of words* (in another sense: how to make them work) which is our need. The systematic ambiguity of most of the phrases with which we try to draw this distinction ('what we may do with words,' etc.) is noteworthy.

Return now to the teaching problem at the point from which these reflections on 'grammatically correct' branched off, to the typical 'hard problem' of grammar,

*What I have written, I have written.*

An obvious exercise is to collect a list of parallels and to explore the differences as to how anyone would interpret them if he introduced a 'that' in their middle. The point, however, would not be merely to give practice in a detail of the use of language. In the background there is a much more important general lesson. To bring this out, a passage such as the following from Jespersen may be chosen. It gives a good opportunity for raising that central and most puzzling question to which so much that comes later in this Section and in the Logic Section must address itself: when is a writer showing us, or reminding us of, the distinctions he is making, and when is he telling us something that, without changing his distinctions, we can disagree about?

> Examples of relative clauses as primaries are 'Who steals my purse steals trash,' 'Whoever says so is a liar,' 'What money I have is at your disposal,' 'You may marry whom you like,' 'You may dance with whom you like.' Unfortunately it is not quite superfluous to state expressly that it is the whole relative clause that is the subject, the object of the verb, or the object of the preposition, in such cases, and not an imaginary *he*, etc., to which the relative clause is an adjunct.
>
> JESPERSEN, *The System of Grammar*, § 35

What is Jespersen saying here? Is his sentence, 'It is the whole . . . in such cases,' only short for, 'As my definitions go I allow myself to describe the whole relative clause as etc. . . . in such cases,' or, 'Let us then call (and in doing so we shall not be departing from the analogies which make the terminology convenient) the whole relative clause the subject . . .'? Or is he saying that other views would impair our use of the language—would not merely lead to a different systematic description of the language, but would, if we allowed them to become operative, make us fail to express our thought or fail to interpret others?

To *decide* this last question, that is, to enter so thoroughly into Jespersen's system of grammar as to be able to decide whether his treatment does or does not imply such drastic consequences,[1]

---

[1] The answer, I take it, is that no such consequences are entailed. But this answer is not arrived at without disproportionate trouble. Jespersen's chief point is, of course, that no ghostly *he*, etc., need normally accompany such sentences: a psychological point; question (4), rather than question (6).

would require a study of formal and functional parallels throughout
the language that would be quite unprofitable for our pupils. Even
if they had time to make it, it would not in the end yield so much
gain as the mere three hours that may be required for making out
just what sort of a question it is. To get the difference between (1)
matters that are settled by definition, and (2) matters of fact, even
momentarily clear (it never stays quite clear, for good reasons)
helps the mind to get it clear again. And all intelligent thought
and argument depend upon the attainment of such clarity. It is
not a compliment to grammarians to say that they give us so often
such magnificent specimens of the confusion. None the less these
things are a side reason for some study of Grammar. As an exercise
ground for displaying these definition *versus* fact manoeuvres, it is
too convenient to be neglected.

More specifically, however, to get the very technical and limited
nature of *this* sort of grammatical question recognized by the
learner as something not for him, not his business (any more than
the classification of inks would be for him in learning to write),
would be enough gain by itself to justify some introduction to the
theory of grammatical aims. Among these aims are matters that
are vitally his business and he should be attending to them. He is
prevented because other aims, which require a lifetime of specialized comparative study, are crossed with them. The distress that a
normally honest mind feels at being utterly unable to see what the
point is in such a pragraph as I have cited from Jespersen, is not
healthy. Too often, since he supposes that it is the sort of point he
should be able to see he is convinced of stupidity, and the strain
forces into a foggy and uncertain background things that seem
allied to it that he should and hitherto could see. For example, that
(a) *You may marry whom you like* and (b) *You may marry him
whom you like* can mean utterly different things, though they need
not; that *whom* may = (1) 'anyone whom' (being short for 'whom-
ever') or (2) 'that (already identified) one whom,' and *like*
may = (1) 'choose' or (2) 'feel warmly towards'; and that the sentence in form (a) invites the understanding of *whom* and *like* in
senses (1), whereas in form (b) it invites an understanding in terms
of senses (2). But 'Who steals my purse ( ± he) steals trash,' = 'If
anyone steals my purse, he steals trash'; and 'Whoever says so is a
liar' may = 'The person who sets this story going (whoever he is)

is a liar (though those who repeat it in good faith need not be).'
To make such comparisons may be a useful exercise in interpretation. To puzzle over relative clauses as subjects and so on, without realizing that these are questions of another order, is nothing of the kind; and to clear up this confusion must be a first step towards any profitable study of grammar as a part of teaching discipline. But we do not clear it away by dodging the problem. The better plan would be to take some time at an early stage for explaining it.

# *Chapter Eleven:* Basic English in the Study of Interpretation

*The error is both in the deliverer and in the receiver. He that delivereth knowledge desireth to deliver it in such form as may be soonest believed and not as may be easiliest examined.˙ . . . As in the courts and services of princes and states, it is a much easier matter to give satisfaction than to do the business.*

FRANCIS BACON, *Valerius Terminus*

After the foregoing Chapter, I shall not be supposed to be offering now a set of fundamental definitions to rule all the modes of language study. None the less, reflection suggests certain divisions in the task which language performs and with them certain analytic procedures which are especially useful as training in interpretation—the last of the purposes listed on p. 190, and the Cinderella of the language subjects.

We may divide the duties of words for this purpose under four main headings:

1. To point to (or name) things.
2. To express our feelings about them and our attitudes to them.
3. To represent our acts.
4. To indicate directions.

This scheme will at first sight seem to leave out much that language does; but if we take account of the omnipresent processes of metaphor, and of the compression of language by which many different phases of meaning are telescoped into the work of single words, this very simple apparatus of distinctions will be found to supply a surprisingly powerful analytic instrument with which to compare the meanings of sentences and control our interpretation of them. Only a sustained use of this technique for comparisons will reveal its powers, and, after a brief explanation of the four divisions and their grounds, it is best to proceed by detailed consideration of examples.

1. *Pointing to things.* It is argued in Chapter XXIII below that unless the words in a language are at many points equivalent to acts and not merely to other words, the connection between lan-

196

guage and living on which their service depends would fail. Chief among the acts to which words are equivalent and from which they draw their meaning [1] are pointings. The word takes the place of the movement of the hand, or eyes, which can then be dropped out of the context. Next the actual presence of the thing—there before us to be pointed to—can be omitted. The word means or metaphorically points to a thing of that sort in its absence. It has become a common name. Names of visible, tangible, separate, physical things are the most evident type of pointer-words: *chair, table, tree, sand* . . . and such 'things' are the fundamental or primordial type of objects. We extend this pointing use of words by analogy, contriving fictions towards which words like *power, heat, act, feeling* seem to point in a similar fashion, though we are perhaps always aware, with differing degrees of clarity, that these fictions are 'things' of another order. To call them 'fictions' here is not necessarily to throw any doubt upon their importance. It is merely to mark differences in their status as objects from that of a stone or an apple. But we use their names just as we use *stone* and *apple*. The pattern of the pointer rules the ordinary use of language with all names—whatever the physicist or psychologist may, for Purpose IV, p. 190, above, need to say further about the differences [2] in the syntax *of science* between the uses of names of different types of objects; or however students with other purposes, in that list, may find it convenient to subdivide them. The greater part of the English language consists either of names pointing to tangible and fictional things, or of words which, if we expand their meaning, have an indirect reference to such things: as *embark,* for example, points to a ship.

When our single pointer names do not enough distinguish, we support them with descriptive adjuncts. We use pointing phrases: *the grey paper, not the white*. Often our names over-distinguish, as we see with the legal problem whether the word *man* includes women also. Pointing is sorting, and our pointer may be governed by a sorting operation which limits its selection beyond our needs

[1] Through the causal interpretative contexts which control all our behaviour with signs. See *The Meaning of Meaning*, Chapter III, and *The Philosophy of Rhetoric*, Lecture II; also p. 48 above.
[2] See Rudolf Carnap, *The Logical Syntax of Language*, Part V, on the formal aspects of some of the dangers of confusions between the languages of science and of everyday life.

of the moment. 'Human being' here may narrow down to 'adult male human being.' We can imagine a language in which all the differences of meaning between nouns were taken over by adjectives.

2. *Expression of feeling*. Some of these adjuncts derive from differences we discern in things: *great, little, grey, green, hot, cold*. Others come from differences in our feelings under different circumstances towards things which may not themselves change: *good, bad, beautiful, dull*. The division is not watertight, of course; language would lose most of its subtler powers if it were, and no line between what belongs to something in its own right and what we have lent to it can ever be easily drawn, so supple and indispensable is the metaphoric interplay of thought.

> Since that all things thou would'st praise
> Beauty took from those that loved them
> In other days.

So too with many things that seem to us in themselves blameworthy. The politics of the passions make us put the effects that things have upon our feelings into the things themselves. It is a way of making our opinions about them seem more compelling (see below pp. 366, 369). But their validity depends elsewhere. For linguistics (taken apart from politics), we sort things with our pointer names not only according to their own differences but according to our different feelings towards them, and these two principles incessantly interact. Whether the day is hot or not can no more be settled by a thermometer than a girl's beauty by a tape measure. Thus interrogation of the meanings of words and phrases commonly throws us back from the so-called 'objective' or intrinsic qualities of the things pointed to, into considerations about the nature and the causes of our feelings about them. And this both for sentences which are explicitly *talking about* (pointing to) feelings and sentences which are merely manifesting them. These are some of the points hinted at in the separation of questions (4) and (5) on p. 191. Face values and deeper values are being balanced against one another in the interpretation of any but the thinnest, flattest speech. A sensitive, active or passive, handling of vocabulary is mainly the perception and control of the related sets of possibilities of the word at that place in the discourse. Our task is to devise the simplest comparing apparatus to assist self-training in that perception. Our risk is to add encumbering machinery, useful perhaps in dissection, but not in forwarding the growth of controlled awareness.

3. *Acts*. Thus far we have been on well-trodden ground, though the notion of the projectile adjective as a pointer to root feelings has not yet been put to enough service in teaching. The novelties which ensue are not to be so summarily expounded. Acts of pointing have been taken as fundamental in the use of names. What of the verbs? They too can be taken as names: as names of acts. Moreover, experiment shows that a very small group of systematically related acts is sufficient to provide an analytic instrument subtle enough to allow us to compare the work done *in their settings on an occasion* by any two verbs in English. Proof of this rests upon Mr C. K. Ogden's demonstration of the translating capacity of Basic English. The immense scale of that demonstration justifies and makes evident a contention which would otherwise have to be considered as no more than a bold piece of speculation. The contention can be put briefly in this form: the meanings of all verbs can be exhibited in terms of a very small set of names of acts combined with the names of directions and with a limited set of names of things, qualities and relations. In practice, *give, get, put, take, keep, let, make, come, go, be, do, have,* prove to be an ample supply of names for key acts. The list could be cut down—at the cost of undesirable prolixity and unprofitable over-elaboration in analysis. For the same reason, it is convenient to add *say, see, seem* and *send,* as luxuries, though on occasion, as Chapters VIII and XIX illustrate, that innocent-looking word, *say,* may be in great need of critical examination. In Basic English only these words go through the inflections of the verb and play the verb's part in the sentence. The other names of acts, *fall, move* and *test,* for example, remain nouns.

Basic English is thus a sub-language into which—at a varying cost due to reduced compression and to disturbances of the emotive functions—sentences of Complete English may be translated. As with all reductive or analytic translation the process is accompanied by a heightened awareness of the meaning of the original.[1]

---

[1] I have discussed, in *Basic in Teaching: East and West,* this aspect and the advantages, so far as the mother tongue is concerned, of Basic over imperfectly known foreign languages. See p. 136 above. We should especially note that in all transla-

But there is much more than this behind the recommendation of Basic as a training in interpretation. Before taking that up, I must complete my outline of its structure as a language.

4. *Names of directions.* The key acts whose names are *put* and *take, give* and *get, keep* and *let, come* and *go,* have to do with movement. This is evident if we consider their use with physical objects; and movement implies direction. We may arrange them in pairs, as here, when various oppositions in the directions they probably imply become prominent.[1] (This makes them peculiarly easy to teach to speakers of other languages, since the first steps in learning their chief or root use may be made through acting them.) But each of them is used with a variety of prepositions (direction words) and Basic classifies the phrases that result—though always as they would occur in complete utterances—and separates those that are fully intelligible, given the root uses of the words that are interacting in the phrase, from those that depend upon accidents of linguistic history, and are 'idioms.' That the 'prepositions' are names of directions is surprisingly often a surprise to speakers of English. The least obvious examples are *of* and *for.* But *of* is a softer *off,* as in:

A chip off the old block
A bit of(f) the cake

and *for* has complex connections with *before.* (We must not confuse etymology here with semantics.) *For* is the greater replacer among the direction-words, as witness:

Let me have Goliath *for* my *champion* = *in front of me* to give and take
the blows
Let me have Goliath *for* my herald = let him go *before me* to say I am
coming
Let me go *for you*                = *in your place*

tion we select an aspect of the meaning and find an equivalent for it (compare questions (1), (4) and (5) on page 191), we do not reproduce the integral meaning.

[1] In Basic: 'have to do with motion. This is clear if we keep in mind their use in talking of material things; and motion is not possible without direction. We may put them in groups of two as here, when different ways in which the directions which most naturally come in may be opposite to one another become more marked . . .' and so on. Here Basic makes us take note of the fact that 'imply' goes through a change of sense.

| Send him *for* a paper | = *to get* a paper |
|---|---|
| This will be ready *for you* | = when you are (*before you*) |

Its centre or key senses for Basic are 'in the place of,' 'in the interests of,' 'in front of.' The use of these direction words with the names of fictions (*in love, for freedom, to the good, well off, from fear,* . . .) is an exercise in the simpler modes of ellipsis and metaphor affording endless opportunity for the development and explicit study of skills with language that we hardly, as a rule, realize that we possess.[1]

These four classes of words: *names pointing to things,* whether material or fictional; *quality words,* by which we further determine what we are pointing to, whether as having a quality or as the object of our feelings; *names of the key acts* in terms of which complex meanings having to do with change may be built up; and *names* of directions in which things are put in motion—these are the categories which Basic offers, in place of the traditional noun, adjective, verb and preposition with which to open up better modes of training in interpretation. Even after the last Chapter, I should insist again upon the risk that the range of purposes served by this analytic instrument will be confused with the other purposes of traditional Grammar. Experience shows that ample and gross misconceptions must be expected, and that etymological, historical, logical, psychological, syntactical, normative, philosophical and other presuppositions supporting other aims of the study of language will be advanced against this method, until its different intention and the novelty—as linguistic principles—of its guiding principles are understood. Its principles, *outside* the theory of language, are, however, the oldest and most indubitable of all, for they are those by which we maintain our vulnerable bodies unharmed in a world of hard, moving, impenetrable and excarnificatory objects. The root or central meanings of the Basic operators are what we and our prehuman ancestors know most about—in the sense that they name the acts which we know best how to do. Compared to our competence in giving and getting, in putting and taking and going, all our other intelligential feats are insecure,

[1] *The Basic Words,* an account of those senses to which the 850 words of Basic English are limited for international purposes, is a good starting-point for these games.

problematical and conjectural in their nature and their achievement. Divorce any receptive or contemplative process from its outgoing controlling partner in the whole act and its standing soon comes into suspicion. Even seeing or tasting, if taken as giving us the matter of our premises, are now so clouded by philosophic doubt that we are not certain whether it is a table or sense-data that we see, an apple or olfactory percepts that we taste. All convictions based on introspection are uncertain, being dependent upon the very process we know least about, can least predict and are least skilful in. Any thought about thought is itself a thought, and any theory of meaning is itself a meaning. And there is no secure foundation to be won in the certainty of any one intuition.

But if theories of how the mind thinks and perceives are specially doubtful, of what are we more certain? Of how to put and take and go; of how to get out of the way of an oncoming car. Perhaps the word 'certain' changes its sense here, with the great change of its application, but if so, it has gained, not lost, in the kind of meaning we require it to have. With these acts, we are certain in the sense that we trust them and stake our lives daily on them. These motor adjustments may seem odd places in which to find what is ultimately trustworthy; but that is perhaps the fault of philosophic tradition. However this excursion is intended only to explain why manual acts and not Locke's 'clear and distinct ideas' or any other products of cogitation were found to be the necessary key terms [1] in this method of interpreting language. The experience which is fundamentally necessary to living is not our experience of how it feels to be, not pleasure or pain, or any suffering or any pure reception, but our knowledge of how things are put in motion, of how, as Hobbes has it, 'by the application of bodies to one another we may produce the like effects.' Throughout the whole fabric of our meanings the pattern they set persists as essential structure, however much linguistic cross-connections, through metaphor, compression and repeated substitutions, may overlay it. And that in part is why Basic with so few words is able to render the essentials of any English sentence—though frequently neither its feeling nor its sensory charge.

We may now turn to consider more precisely what uses may be made of Basic as training in interpretation.

[1] See *Bentham's Theory of Fictions*, by C. K. Ogden, p. xlvi.

First may come its power to elucidate and display—not as theory, but automatically and inevitably in practice—that mutual depend- ence between the words in the sentence whose recognition is in- terpretation. In making a Basic version you incessantly find that if you change one word you must change another because its sense has already been altered by what you have done. You find too that in Basic there is hardly ever a safe, mechanical, single word equiva- lent, or a regular phrase equivalent, for even the most frequent English clichés.

An alert questioning of the whole intention of the original must be maintained throughout. Routine, word-for-word translation—of the de-coding, mechanical type—soon fails in Basic—through not making sense. The first necessity in handling this restricted though supple medium is some definite (IV, X) view as to the meaning of the original. This may be provisional only; a common result of the search for a Basic version is to suggest other possible inter- pretations. The choice then and the clarification of the indications that the original offers is work in interpretation of the kind that is most needed.

The superstition that every good sentence or paragraph should have one and only one meaning suffers heavily in this process. We are forced to see that a word (or a sentence) works by relating itself in various ways to various other influences in the passage—as a strut in a bridge has various tensions and thrusts to take from the other members. We cease to think of it as an isolated, self- governing addition. We realize instead that it is a component. And with the dissipation of the cloudy magic-charged concept of the proper or true meanings of separated words, the way is open to a fruitful experimental exploration of the structures of meaning.

In much of this we find ourselves examining the versatilities of the words in the Basic list as much as those in the original. Thus such a sentence as:

*This is one of those amusements from which I get no amusement*

sets a pattern of fluctuation (from cause to effect) which can be followed, through partly parallel sentences, via *pleasure, comfort, profit, music:*

*There is no music in this music,*

(see p. 340 below on *song*) to the more important problems that *knowledge*:

> *Such knowledge gives us no knowledge,*

or *doubt* offer. With *doubt* the shift from the point that may be doubted to the condition of doubting is still partly like that from a cause of amusement (in someone's opinion) to the amusement given:

> *Those doubts are no doubts for me.*

And *question* may go the same way; but *love* and *desire* make, in most settings, a different step: from the name of the feeling to the name of the thing towards which we have it. That thing need not be in any important respect the cause of the feeling. It may be merely the occasion. Here a simple, familiar and very convenient verbal shift, of a kind which we are always making without the least difficulty in everyday speech, leads us to the brink of some of the most important of all general practical problems.

There are scores of games whose formula is 'Make statements with words from the Basic List which go like ——.' And they can be graded from very simple parallels to tasks which will strain the resources of the most ambitious lexicographer.

In considering them it may be stressed once again that their value does not lie in any new knowledge that such and such words may be used in more ways than were supposed. That knowledge is generally possessed already. The value comes from the reflections which accompany the processes of comparison, and the increased span of awareness of the factors (never mentioned, it may be, in the original) which govern the meanings in the supposed settings.

A few specimen exercises may make the possibilities in this work more evident:

*Easy*

1. After making a clear comparison in your mind between:
   (a) The destruction of the town took three minutes.
   (b) The destruction caused by the attack might still be noted after twenty years.

make up parallel sentences using the words: *invention, building, change, answer, question.*

### Moderately Easy

II. We may equally well say, with the same sense:
  (a) 'The water is boiling in the kettle.'
  (b) 'The kettle is boiling.'

Is this because *boiling* or because *kettle* has different senses in the two statements? What is the change if any? Make up other statements in which a word has the same trick of changing its sense, such as 'Those were happy days,' 'The boys have 5 hours of English a week.' Are these tricks in all ways the same?

### More Difficult

III. A. I went on *foot* to the foot of the mountain.
  B. Come with a *bright* face and in your brightest colours.
  C. This is one of the amusements from which I get no amusement.

The above are examples of different forms of expansions of the uses of words. Which of the following would you put with A, B, and C as having in them parallel or nearly parallel expansions?

  1. These *tinned* fruits are in *glasses.*
  2. The machine worker becomes himself a *machine.*
  3. If we are going for this *sail,* up with the sails!
  4. The *thunder* of the guns was louder than thunder.
  5. His looks were *blacker* than the night.
  6. He gave the suggestion no *support.*
  7. He gave us a *stiff* answer.
  8. The payment made a *serious hole* in my *pocketbook.*

I insert a sample answer to this last question, in Basic English:

Most statements may be taken in more ways than one, so there may be more accounts than one of a change in the sense of a word. What we have to do here is to say how the two uses of a word are different, and by what sort of step we go across from one sense to another. In doing this we have first to get one sense for it (in this connection) as clear and fixed as possible, and then make a comparison between that sense and the other.

A. A man's foot is normally the lowest part of him. So the part of a mountain which is lowest may be named its 'foot' *as having the same relation to* the mountain as his foot has to a man. Part : mountain :: foot : man. It will be noted that 'foot' first has its sense narrowed down to 'lowest part' and then comes an expansion of its use to be the name of lowest parts of mountains, pages, trees and so on.

B. Bright colours (other things being equal) make us happier. A bright face *has the same effect,* normally, as bright colours, lighting up the minds of those who see it.

(Other accounts are equally possible: a bright face may seem as if a light were inside it and so may bright colours.)

C. 'An amusement' may be equal to 'a cause from which (in the opinion of some persons) feelings of pleasure, rest of mind, good humour, and so on, come; or it may be equal to 'those feelings themselves.' The step is from the use of a word as *The name of a cause* to its use as *The name of the effect.*

The forms of these changes are:

In A, *having the same relation.*

In B, *having the same effect.*

In C, *name of cause becoming name of effect.*

It will be noted that if two things have the same effect on me (or on some one thing) then B becomes an example of A.

1. *Tinned* is normally short for 'put into an air-tight tin to be kept for later use.' So *glassed* fruits (bottled fruits) would be 'put into glasses, bottles. . . .' The man who is talking is giving an expansion to *tinned,* stretching it to take in 'put into any air-free vessel to be kept for later use.' He is conscious of the stretch and that is the point of what he is saying. The step then is from one named way of doing something with a certain effect to any way of doing it with the same effect and so is in that respect parallel to B.

2. *Becomes a machine* is short for 'becomes like a machine in some respects'; the worker's motions become like the motions of a machine. These motions are to a man's normal acts as those of a machine are to men's acts. Machine motions : acts in general :: machine worker's motions : his normal acts. The change is parallel to that in A.

3. The sails are the cause of the boat's motion, and we take *sail* as the name for the motion. Parallel to C, but going the other way. 'These are sails from which I do not get a sail.'

4. The name for one loud noise (*thunder*) is taken as the name for another (made by guns). The effects are in part the same. In that respect parallel to B.

5. Parallel to B.

6. Parallel to A. A support keeps something up or going. What he didn't give would have been to the suggestion as a material support (a leg) is to a body.

7. The root or chief sense of *stiff*, as in 'a stiff card,' or 'a stiff bit of iron wire,' is 'not bent (changed in form) without undergoing a certain degree of force.' *Stiff* in 'a stiff answer' does its work because a stiff answer has to our desires the same relation that a stiff wire has to our hands when we are attempting to give it another form. In that respect it is parallel to A.

Such things as stiff wires give us trouble and seem to go against our desires. Taken so, the change is parallel to that in B.

8. Here, as with 6 and 7, doubt comes in because the sense of the word with which we have to make a comparison is not certain. For example *serious* is not normally used in quite the same sense in 'serious thought,' 'a serious look,' 'a serious view,' 'a serious feeling,' 'a serious attempt' and 'a serious decision.' But in special connections some of these uses may be the same. The sense in common to 'serious thought,' 'a serious attempt' and 'a serious decision' might then be something like 'taken or made with care and attention because important effects may come from it.' A serious feeling may be sad or full of fears, and a serious view may be one in which we are not forming a good opinion of something. A serious look is normally one which is a sign of serious thought or feeling. A serious attempt may be one made with force, and a serious decision may equally be one coming from serious thought or one which will have important effects. Serious decisions may not be seriously taken! The sense of serious here in 'a serious hole' might be viewed in comparison with any of them, and different parallels with A.B.C. would come into view.

*Pocketbook* and *hole* give less trouble. A pocketbook is one place in which money (notes) may be kept. Any other place where money may be kept has the same relation to money. So this is in part a parallel to A. But other more complex parallels are present: through a hole things may go out of view; money has gone out of view after the payment; a parallel to B turned round the other way? Or: a pocketbook is any place where money comes from, any cause of the same effect—the coming of money; another parallel to B. Or, by another step, *pocketbook* becomes the name of money itself; effect named from cause; parallel to C.

As it stands, the sample answer is too elaborate, and too hard for most classes to follow. A good teacher would break it up into questions, giving time for each point to be thought out. But it may serve here to illustrate the ways in which Basic can make us consider 'in slow motion,' to borrow a label from Mr. Lawrence Conrad, the essential processes of apprehending meaning. Translation into Basic forces attention to the patterns of sense shifts as the use of Complete English never does. And these patterns are the key patterns of thought.

In most talk and reading these shifts of sense are made so smoothly that they are never noticed. The mind takes them in its stride, adjusts scores of complex rival relations without hesitation (as it balances its body on one foot) and is surprised when it discovers what wonderful things it has been doing. To those who feel that I exaggerate the fluctuations of the senses of words and their interdependence, a course of exercises of this type may be suggested as an experimental mode of inquiry. A good example to try might be:

Trace the parallels and note the divergences between:

(1) A simple statement is not always simple to make and

(2) A serious step is not always seriously taken.

Similar exercises can and should be conducted in Complete English. But Basic, since it has to exploit its few words to the most varied advantage, turns them and twists them and gives us good reason to see what they will and will not do. There are very strict limits to their use, which must be observed or the value of the exercise is lost. A chief principle of the system is 'If it is bad English, it is bad Basic'—obviously an important condition for its general use as a world language. This necessary restriction makes translation into Basic and free composition in Basic (exercises in composition should come first) about as difficult as the easiest types of Crossword Puzzle.

And, if we take into account the phrases, and the notions that are attended to, compared, modified, redisposed, exchanged, recombined, compared again and rejected, as well as these that are put on the paper in the fair copy, we shall see that learning to write in Basic, under the disguise of a game, is an exploration of the most important devices of English syntax. They are the most important tricks of the writer's trade because they are the most indispensable; Basic deserves its name, because its constructions and vocabulary are the foundation of the language.

The fear that Basic may lead to the substitution of crude approximations for exact statements, and so blur discrimination, is soon dispelled by actual practice in it. After the first few fumbling steps, the exercises in comparison that it compels come into effect, the writer finds himself distinguishing between meanings that he would formerly have taken to be one and the same, and stepping up and down the ladder of generality with a new freedom. As he grows familiar with the powers of the Basic words, he gains confidence; its simplicity in comparison with complete English, and the incessant recurrence of problems of the same types in its handling, encourage him to look critically into how it works. Certain experiments with Basic as a method for remedial reading and writing courses show this very plainly. The backward boy feels as though he had been taken out of the New York Central Telephone Exchange and put in charge of a village line; his heart leaps up and his pen dashes over the paper. It is well, though, when he comes to *translation* into Basic, to mix the work by asking him from time to time to say *in Complete English* how his translation seems to him to fail in doing justice to the original.

A number of other delusive fears as to the effects of translation into Basic are often expressed. Most of these fade away at once under the sunshine touch of actual experience with it. The fear that the pupil will exchange his ordinary English for Basic, for example. Those haunted by this notion little know how the mind, after a spell of Basic, aches for release into a wider vocabulary. The monotony inseparable from a formally limited word-list wakes a hunger for fresh words.

Another fear is that the practice in analysis which Basic gives will turn all those who undergo it into logicians. Some even seem to think that this is the aim of those who recommend it; that we wish our schools to turn out the little Mills (of the James or John Stuart models) of whom Blake was perhaps prophesying in his most Memorable Fancy. There could be no idler fear or more utter misapprehension. Logistic, if studied enough, may leave some such effect; but Basic analysis, with its insistence upon the versatility of words under mutual control and its recognition of metaphor as the ruling principle of language is an influence in the opposite direction. Logic pins its words to fixed definitions. Basic enhances and clarifies our sense of the dependence of any word's meaning on the other words present with it and on the purpose which, together, they are attempting to fulfil.

An allied but heavier dread is that Basic may kill the natural poetry in the young. Locke's advice to an unhappy father whose child betrayed a poetic vein is well known. Here it is:

> Methinks that the parents should labour to have it stifled and suppressed as much as may be; and I know not what reason a father can have to wish his son a poet, who does not desire to have him bid defiance to all other callings and business.

Coleridge, at one time, chose to spell The Philosopher's name Lock —'the great LOCK,' he called him. This aim with which Basic is sometimes charged seems to be that of *locking up the baby poets!*

The accusation hardly seems to deserve reply. If to increase awareness of the fugitive reverberations between words and sensitiveness to the structures of meanings would be damaging to poetry, then Basic would plead guilty. Not otherwise. A Basic version stands to a passage of poetry somewhat as a photograph may stand to a painting. Is it the case that comparison between the photograph and the painting is likely to make us less conscious of the part played by colour?

A more deeply grounded doubt may derive from comparison between the intricacies that analysis of such a word as 'serious' details and the seeming simplicity of our use of it. The doubt is whether close examination *reveals, uncovers, displays* these complexities, or whether it imposes them; whether they were in some sense, present (latent?) before the analysis, or whether they were brought into being by inquiry. The difference between these views is not perhaps so great as appears at first sight. It is the familiar difference between feeling something and expounding it, or rather between the thing which is felt and the thing which is discursively expressed. There is never any profit in *identifying* things (in taking 'them' as *one and the same*) when our modes of apprehending 'them' are very different. *Proof* of identity, as innumerable problems of perception (including the Body-Mind problem itself) have sufficiently shown, is unattainable. What is useful is a criticizable technique of translation between them. We have that for the case of the hand and the eye, and have started on the way to it for the mind and the body. We are on the way to it for the felt meaning and the explicitly articulated account of a partially equivalent meaning, though the way is endless.

So much for the theoretical doubt; the practical fear is an easier matter to settle. It is that practice in pondering minute particulars of relationship may interfere with the adroitness of summary handling. In its crudest form, the fear is that analysis might replace vision, that we might become unable to see the wood for the trees. But there is no warrant for it in experience. The danger will only seem alarming if we do not notice that this exercise in analysis relies throughout upon skill in the swift 'intuitive' perception of the unanalyzed. The aim of translation into Basic is never the Basic version, or the articulated analysis, for its own sake, but improvement in the normal reading of Complete English.

# *Chapter Twelve:* Elementary Difficulties in Reading

> *The true mode of interpretation is the precise opposite of what Glaucon mentions. Critics, he says, jump at certain groundless conclusions; they pass adverse judgment and then proceed to reason on it; and assuming that the poet has said whatever they happen to think, find fault if a thing is inconsistent with their own fancy.*
>
> ARISTOTLE, Poetics
>
> *It was only a question of not, by a hair's-breadth, deflecting into the truth.*
>
> HENRY JAMES

In my experiments I introduced the whole topic of Grammar abruptly by issuing the following excerpt from Campbell without any preparatory discussion and with merely an invitation to discuss it as doctrine and as argument. The results, which I now begin to analyze, are partly my reason for thinking that some preliminary exercises and explanations would make it yield more. It was chosen partly as a vigorous statement of the ruling assumption—that 'usage,' and 'usage' alone, governs 'correctness.' I wanted it to bring this assumption out into the fullest daylight so that there might later be no doubt as to what I was attacking, and, I hope, demolishing. But I wanted it for another reason too—as a specimen, or text, on which to discourse about arguments which depend upon opposing two or more different senses of a word, here 'grammar.'

## EXERCISE FOUR

It is not the business of grammar, as some critics seem preposterously to imagine, to give law to the fashions which regulate our speech. On the contrary, from its conformity to these, and from that alone it derives all its authority and value. For, what is the grammar of any language? It is no other than a collection of general observations methodically digested, and comprising all the modes previously and independently established, by which the significations, derivations, and combinations of words in that language are ascertained. It is of no consequence here to what causes originally these modes or fashions owe their existence, to imitation, to reflection, to affectation, or to caprice; they no sooner obtain and become general, than they are laws of the language; and the grammarian's only business is to note, collect, and methodise them.

The truth of this position hath never, for aught I can remember, been directly controverted by any body; yet it is certain, that both critics and grammarians often argue in such a way as is altogether inconsistent with it. What, for example, shall we make of that complaint of Dr Swift, 'that our language, in many instances, offends against every part of grammar'? Or what could the Doctor's notion of grammar be, when he expressed himself in this manner? Some notion, possibly, he had of grammar in the abstract, an universal archetype by which the particular grammars of all different tongues ought to be regulated. If this was his meaning, I cannot say whether he is in the right, or in the wrong, in this accusation. I acknowledge myself to be entirely ignorant of this ideal grammar; nor can I form a conjecture where its laws are to be learnt. One thing, indeed, every smatterer in philosophy will tell us, that there can be no natural connexion between the sounds of any language, and the things signified, or between the modes of inflection and combination, and the relations they are intended to express. Perhaps he meant the grammar of some other language; if so, the charge was certainly true, but not to the purpose, since we can say, with equal truth, of every language, that it offends against the grammar of every other language whatsoever. If he meant the English grammar, I would ask, whence has that grammar derived its laws? If from general use (and I cannot conceive another origin), then it must be owned, that there is a general use in that language as well as in others; and it were absurd to accuse the language, which is purely what is conformable to general use in speaking and writing, as offending against general use. But if he meant to say, that there is no fixed, established, or general use in the language, that it is quite irregular, he hath been very unlucky in his manner of expressing himself. Nothing is more evident, than that where there is no law, there is no transgression. In that case, he ought to have said, that it is not susceptible of grammar; which, by the way, would not have been true of English, or indeed of any the most uncultivated language on the earth.

It is easy then to assign the reason, why the justness of the complaint, as Doctor Lowth observes, has never yet been questioned; it is purely, because, not being understood, it hath never been minded. But if, according to this ingenious gentleman, the words 'our language' have, by a new kind of trope, been used to denote those who speak and write English, and no more hath been intended than to signify, that our best speakers, and most approved authors frequently offend against the rules of grammar, that is, against the general use of the language, I shall not here enter on a discussion of the question. Only let us rest in these as fixed principles, that use, or the custom of speaking, is the sole original standard of conversation, as far as regards the expression, and the custom of writing is the sole standard of style; that the latter comprehends the former, and something more; that to the tribunal of use, as to the supreme authority, and consequently, in every grammatical controversy, the last resort, we are entitled to appeal from the laws and the decisions of grammarians; and that this order of subordination ought never, on any account, to be reversed.

GEORGE CAMPBELL, *The Philosophy of Rhetoric*, Book II, Chapter 1.

Both purposes would have been better served if it had followed (1) some illustration of the different things 'grammar' might mean and (2) an example suggesting the need for wariness when two views of a subject are being controversially opposed. As it was, no doubt, the experiment better represented the normal responses and so may be more instructive to us—if it was not to those who took part in it.

One special circumstance I should explain. I combined this experiment with another, in which they were invited to criticize, and construct sentences parallel to such things as, 'Meaning is an arrow which reaches its mark when least encumbered with feathers.' (See Appendix, pp. 397-402.)

Whether through some fault in the form of my invitation, or because such parallels really are very difficult to consider, this task, which most writers chose to take first, absorbed an enormous amount of the energy I expected would go into examining Campbell. I have rarely seen more apparent signs of intellectual torture than during the three-quarters of an hour that elapsed before I collected the scripts, and I was hoping that some very penetrating observations on the doctrine of usage, as Campbell expounds it, would result. But when I looked them over, I found that not Campbell but these parallels had been causing the agony. I consider them later, in the Appendix: they were very curious and rather disappointing. The technique of that kind of exercise obviously needs much improvement, though I still think it a hopeful line for experiment. I mention all this here to explain why the comments on Campbell are mostly short, show evidences of fatigue and content themselves frequently with the first thoughts that came. This makes them perhaps no less representative of common cursory reflection on the subject.

They divide in general into those which might have been written by people thinking for the very first time in their lives about Grammar; and those reproducing a standard conventional set of views in which little or no interest is felt. And this may in fact correspond to a difference between those for whom grammar teaching had been entirely omitted in their education, and those who had had at least a talk or two at school about it. I have no way of checking that.

Before illustrating this broad division, I will pause to show once again that with an almost perfectly straightforward (and as some said, I think, rightly) very lucid and forcible piece of debater's prose, an appreciable proportion of the readers failed at certain points to make out *in the least* what was being said.

One sentence which held up several and even threw some of them right off the track was,

'Nothing is more evident, than that where there is no law, there is no transgression.'

Campbell is using it, rather neatly, to show that Swift could not have meant that there is no law, for an offence must offend against something; but several readers jumped over this and supposed him to be himself saying that there is no law in the language. Thus:

4.1. This seems to me a clear and true account, but it is hardly right in saying that 'where there is no law, there is no transgression,' for there is the law of custom in language. It may be altered just like fashion in clothes, by general custom and particularly by the influence of the best people. It may be altered suddenly by a great writer, just as the Prince of Wales can suddenly introduce the boater. It is possible for the ordinary man to make a change against the law of custom. A great writer may also offend if his change does not make itself worth while.

This is worth more study than such things, being so common, are wont to get. We shall hardly find a better example of one of the most frequent mishaps in reading. 'He that cannot contract the sight of his mind, as well as disperse and dilate it, wanteth a great faculty,' wrote Bacon in *The Advancement of Learning*. This reader has limited his purview for the moment to that single sentence and ignored the sentences before and after. Ability to disperse and dilate, to stand back and take a general view of what is going on as a whole, is at least as much in need of exercise for many as the power to contract and concentrate upon detail. Perhaps it is more in need of development, though a relaxed and distant vision, incapable of focussing on anything in particular even to misrepresent it (see Chapter VI), is distressingly common. The phoenix, the Mogul diamond, the rare and invaluable mind, is the one which can expand and contract itself at will in one movement of thought, stand back or go close to detail without forgetting in one vision what it has seen in the other. Some deliberately planned exercise in shifts of focus—with more explicit examination of the mistakes entailed by too close or too distant a view—might, I suggest, do something to make them less rare.

I cannot myself see that Campbell himself was at all to blame here, or in any way invited this misunderstanding. Here is another reader who had the same trouble:

4.11. I am in general agreement with the writer's views on grammar, although I think that his argument may lead people to suppose that there are no definite laws in grammar. There are always definite laws, certainly dictated by fashion, which must be adhered to. This sentence 'Nothing is more evident, than that when there is no law, there is no transgression' is particularly misleading.

Here is one who is more widely misled:

> 4.12.* The author appears to deny the existence of grammar, 'I acknowledge myself . . . ignorant of this ideal grammar.' Of the English grammar—'whence has that grammar derived its laws.' And yet previously he has said that modes or fashions of speech become laws of the language, which it is the grammarian's job to tabulate. If, as one supposes, the grammarian is dealing with grammar, then the laws of the language are grammar.

He has, I am afraid, entirely failed to see Campbell's main point (and Campbell states it again and again!), which is to contrast two conceptions of grammar:

(1) As an external regulative prescription,
(2) As a digest of custom or usage;

and to claim authority for the second.

The task which was too much for this reader was to keep in his mind two different senses of 'Grammar.' And I took this passage chiefly because (in addition to being a useful introduction to some of the largest questions about language) it seemed a very representative example of an argument depending upon comparing several different senses of the same word—upon taking it successively in these different senses and seeing what happens. And that is the method of nearly all arguments in general (non-technical) discussions. Whenever we are debating two views of something, we have to pack the views up alternately into what will look like the same word (and what by ordinary tests will be considered the same word). Actually—for the purpose of analyzing the argument—it might often be better to treat $\left\{ \begin{matrix} \text{them} \\ \text{it} \end{matrix} \right\}$ as several words, and spell $\left\{ \begin{matrix} \text{them} \\ \text{it} \end{matrix} \right\}$ differently. And there are many controversies which will hardly be much advanced until we do this.

But before trying out something of this sort with Campbell's argument, let me show you a few more examples of this inability to take up two or more senses for 'one word' and consider them together and successively.

> 4.13. The author's argument is an attractive one and the reader who is open to conviction will surely agree with his main thesis; but *it is*

*not quite clear* whether he believes that grammar can be dispensed with or whether he means that the rules of grammar should be retained but that one should not necessarily conform to them. He says, just before the last paragraph, that 'where there is no law, there is no transgression.' Does he here imply that the laws of grammar ought to be abolished in order that the person writing an English sentence should not be hampered in his mode of self-expression?

It is, I think, very much our business to ask, What can this reader have meant by his opening sentence, 'The author's . . . thesis'? What 'argument,' what 'main thesis,' could it have been? He has failed to see that the point was not 'Shall we dispense with grammar?' but, 'What conception of grammar shall we use?' i.e. which among the different senses of *grammar* are we to employ? The mistake is typical of so much that occurs, undiscovered, in normal cursive reading that we may well invite the attention of curriculum builders to it. What is the worth of wide reading when practised so?

Another shows the same difficulty with a different instance. He has those unfortunate 'parallels' on the brain.

4.14. The first parallel is between 'minded' and 'understood,' i.e. if the justness of a complaint is not understood, it is not minded. I do not agree with the writer. If we may not understand the justness but we do mind the complaint and if once we mind the complaint, we cannot pass over without understanding the justness. And further we have rules of grammar = use of language = custom of speaking. I wonder if all this can be correct! Use and custom and rule are absolutely different things.

I am sorry that later on I shall seem to ally myself closely with this writer in his last remarks. It is, I think, more than a little important to recognize that 'use' and 'custom' and 'rule'—and 'correctness'—*can* be used to mean 'absolutely different things,' and I shall be arguing at some length in favour of so using them, and accusing the current tradition in teaching of missing great opportunities by not doing so. But here we are concerned with Campbell's argument and the reader's struggles to understand him. Whatever else Campbell may be doing, he is certainly sparing no pains to make clear that 'use' and 'custom' and 'rule' and 'law' *are* to mean just the same thing in his doctrine as to what grammar should be. If we are to understand what he is saying we must take him as using them so (unless we can catch him out as himself smuggling in other uses for them). It is no reply to him, and no objection to what he is saying, to smuggle them in ourselves, and then assert that *he* is making different things the same.

The writer is suffering from the commonest of all verbal diseases, the belief that words are just names for things distributed on the simple plan of one thing for one name. Of course, he does not *believe* this in the sense that if we asked him he would say it was so. He only acts (here at least) as though he thought so: but that is the important sense of believing. This sort of failure to take a point because of a private temporary attachment to other senses for the words than those the speaker is employing, is so excessively common and such an insidious obstacle to all communication (see e.g. 2.652) that I am in some danger of overstressing it in what follows. But current teaching technique is rotten with it; so is international and national politics, so is every serious subject, most of all the semi-technicalized subjects—economics, philosophy, criticism, social theory. Who has written a careful book on any of them without having privately to admit that all his reviewers have misread him? I trust then to be forgiven if I return frequently to dwell at wearisome length upon this conventionally neglected topic, the incursions of the other senses. I should maintain the usual decent silence about it if I did not think that remedies to reduce the loss in communication were devisable and even not difficult to apply.

Less conspicuous instances of this kind of misreading—where Campbell is not perhaps *so clearly* free from blame—occurred locally at several points. Contraction of attention probably explains them.

4.15.* The writer of the passage does not remark on the fact that both the speaking and the writing of a language may change considerably in a comparatively short time. Thus if the spoken English of the period of Chaucer be 'the sole original standard of conversation,' then we today are very wide of our mark. Also the same argument applies in regard to the writing of a language.

'Sole original standard.' 'Sole' and 'original' have been specialized here aside from the intention (I think, evident enough) of the rest of the passage. Campbell's 'sole' is a denial of other claims to authority and does not imply fixity necessarily; his 'fixed principles' in the line above (which may have influenced this reader) is merely his way of insisting that use—not necessarily permanently fixed use —is the standard. And his 'original' merely means 'as the source of the authority' not 'earlier in time' as some dozen or so took it:

> 4.151.* Then 'use . . . is the *sole* original standard.' But use varies from time to time and place to place. Which *different* uses should be permitted, and in which cases should a single use be insisted upon?

These, I agree, are very relevant questions to ask about Campbell's whole position, and he discusses them ably in later chapters. But he is not laying himself open to them in the sentence quoted. He is not talking about the singleness or multiplicity of his 'sole original standard' or about how it is to be determined, but only about the source of its authority.

The same writer says:

> Rev. Mr Campbell's attitude towards grammar is certainly the one which has been adopted in English. Usage is the supreme authority, and usage at times has tended towards bringing a greater regularity into English. His answer to 'whence has that Grammar derived its laws' is from general use. But later he says, 'Nothing is more evident than that where there is no law, there is no transgression.' He admits in the first instance that there *are* some laws, so it seems possible that he might have credited Swift with another interpretation —i.e. that English transgresses the laws that it makes. This might have been worth inquiring into as well.

It will have been noticed that all through this I am repeatedly trying to kill several birds with one stone—to illustrate different types of misreading, to apply the theory of interpretation, and to prepare for a discussion of the usage doctrine and other matters, logical as well as grammatical. The choice of the Campbell passage had more purposes than I have yet here explained and a minor one comes into prominence now. It is a merit of an exercise, which may strengthen its claim on the time-table, when it can be made to do many things at once, but without confusion. Here this one brings in a curious and instructive episode in the history of the language.

A number of the commentators were puzzled about the quotation from Swift (without necessarily recognizing him for Gulliver's Swift). They wondered whether Campbell was being fair to him, and some even felt convinced that he wasn't, and produced other accounts of what Dr Swift must have meant.

4.2.\* If grammar is a collection of language-fashions noted, collected, and, above all, methodised, it must be a sort of standard work of reference for all disputes as to the use of language. And once it has attained to this, it automatically becomes law, so that Campbell's point is defeated by his own argument.

Therefore Dr Swift's sentence is entirely in accord with the principle laid down by Campbell in the first paragraph and Campbell's sarcasm rather turns back on himself, while his supposings are entirely pointless, since it is perfectly obvious what Swift means.

Finally Campbell himself brings in a 'fixed principle' that the use of language is the only standard. This, therefore, being a fixed principle, makes a collection of the uses of language a collection of laws.

This also illustrates the inability to keep two senses for a word (here 'law') going at the same time, that was discussed above; and the influence of the combative spirit is very marked.

The next man saves Dr Swift by pulling him out on the other bank; and makes him a *defender* of some sort of grammatical licence.

4.21.\* Properly speaking, English is of all languages the least grammatical—and it has and continues often to have cases when a sentence grammatically incorrect is, nevertheless, good English. Dr Swift's statement seems to be very justified. A writer of some distinction . . .

A third combines these defences:

4.22.\* I entirely agree with the author's 'fixed principles' at the end of the passage, but I think he has misunderstood Dr Swift's remark. Although it is language in use which fundamentally makes the grammar, yet once the grammar has been formed, it is possible for language to offend against it, such as it is at the moment. In offending against grammar, grammar is changed.

And faith unfaithful kept him falsely true?

A fourth refuses to admit 'what every smatterer in philosophy will tell us.'

4.23.\* I agree that it is a disproportion to attach first importance to the rules of grammar as if they existed before the world began, but that is taking the word grammar plain, as it is not taken I think in 'our language in many instances offends against every part of grammar.'

Surely to be able to appreciate the real position of grammatical rules, in relation to the use of language it is necessary to see some natural connexion between 'the sounds of any language and the thing signified etc.' It seems reasonable to think that a realization of the first general feeling for a noise or word as expressive of an object, is the best way of using it rightly.

To know the career, the development of a word is to mark out more clearly the limits and reach of its significant path.

I return to this 'natural connexion' later; but we may notice, in passing, the curious circling movement of thought, dispelling in the first sentence what it is attracted to in the third. How frequently these 'winding, spiring, gyring treadmill' motions may be observed at all heights and depths in philosophy! But we must continue with Swift:

4.24.\* In the first paragraph the argument that grammar is a collection of general observations methodically digested and derived from the common use of language is clearly and logically worked out. Reason and common-sense incline one to agree that it is also probably correct.

But the author has been so zealous to prove his case that he has deliberately misunderstood Dr Swift, or if he has understood him, he has, by quibbling over his expression, refused to admit it. His three suppositions: that Dr Swift meant (a) an ideal grammar, (b) the grammar of a foreign language and (c) the grammar of the English language, are completely logical, delightfully tidy, and childishly naughty. The arguments against an ideal or Platonic grammar were doubtless as clear to Dr Swift as to himself: the second supposition is merely absurd, as he himself admits. Only in the third does he cease quibbling, and begin really to tackle Dr Swift's argument. Taking his own theory of grammar to be correct, the remarks he makes in connection with this third interpretation are just. But it seems doubtful whether Dr Swift meant that English was not susceptible to grammar. The interpretation given in last paragraph, that the best speakers and writers often offend against the laws of grammar, is the most fair inasmuch as of all those suggested it is the least wilful distortion of the words given. But surely what Dr Swift really meant was that there were almost as many exceptions in grammar as rules, and that therefore language frequently contradicts or offends against the rules it has itself made. A quibble of my own on the author is—does the custom in writing comprehend that in speaking—'and something more,' or does not custom in writing follow that in speech?

This is a really able piece of discussion. But it is high time to look to see 'what Dr Swift really meant.'

The complaint occurs in his *Proposal for Correcting, Improving, and Ascertaining the English Tongue,* in a letter to the most Honourable Robert Earl of Oxford and Mortimer, Lord High Treasurer of Great Britain, written in 1711. It is an attempt to procure the foundation of an English Academy, for the purpose, in part, as the tail paragraph shows, of distributing patronage, and contains a curious jumble of acute observations and absurd theories. Whether Swift was really as anxious about the language as he professes to be is doubtful. He supposes 'the period wherein the English tongue received most improvement . . . to commence with the beginning of Queen Elizabeth's reign, and to conclude with the great Rebellion in forty-two. . . . During the usurpation, such an infusion of enthusiastic jargon prevailed in every writing, as was not shaken off in many years after. To this succeeded that licentiousness which entered with the Restoration, and, from infecting our religion and morals, fell to corrupt our language.' Since then, the Court, 'the worst school in England for that accomplishment,' 'one or two more dunces of figure,' the poets, who 'although they could not be insensible how much our language was overstocked with monosyllables, yet, to save time and pains, introduced that barbarous custom of abbreviating words to fit them to the measure of their verses' and 'several young men at the universities, terribly possessed with a fear of pedantry' have brought things to such a pass that Swift 'must be so plain as to tell your lordship that if you will not take some care to settle our language and put it into a state of continuance, I cannot promise that your memory shall be preserved above a hundred years, farther than by imperfect tradition. . .. . If things go on at this rate, all I can promise your lordship is, that about two hundred years hence some painful compiler, who will be at the trouble of studying old language, may inform the world

. . . that Robert earl of Oxford, a very wise and excellent man, was made high treasurer and saved his country. . . . Thus much he may be able to pick out . . . but the rest of your character, which I or any other writer may now value ourselves by drawing . . . will probably be dropped, on account of the antiquated style and manner they are delivered in.'

Swift perhaps shows a deeper motive in elaborating this appeal: 'Besides, my Lord, as disinterested as you appear to the world, I am convinced that no man is more in the power of a prevailing favourite passion than yourself; I mean that desire of true and lasting honour.' 'What I have most at heart is, that method should be thought on for ascertaining and fixing our language for ever.' 'If it were once refined to a certain standard, perhaps there might be found out ways to fix it for ever, or at least till we are invaded and made a conquest by some other state; and even then our best writings might probably be preserved with care, and grow into esteem, and the authors have a chance for immortality.'

How seriously to take this, and whether Swift was thinking of himself, is not easy to make out. It makes a curious contrast to something a good young poet said to me recently. He wondered how much poetry a man would write who thought constantly that the human race has some millions of years at least ahead of it!

The passage that Campbell quotes from comes early in *The Proposal:* 'My lord, I do here, in the name of all the learned and polite persons of the nation, complain to your lordship, as first minister, that our language is extremely imperfect; that its daily improvements are by no means in proportion to its daily corruptions; that the pretenders to polish and refine it have chiefly multiplied abuses and absurdities; and that in many instances it offends against every part of grammar.'

Perhaps *all* of Campbell's malicious conjectures about 'the Doctor's notion of grammar, when he expressed himself in this manner' may have had some substance. Swift wrote at a time when many theories as to the norm of speech were mingling in the general consciousness to define themselves slowly and do battle through the century. A Platonic ideal language, the original Hebrew taught to Adam; man's first tongue arrived at in convention by agreement; references to the relations between words and things, to analogies with other languages, Latin above all; to Logic or Reason; to conceptions of simplicity, uniformity and 'the genius of the language,' whatever that may have been, as well as usage—any of these may have been, in varying proportions, among the ingredients of the notion. Moreover, like Pope, Swift was too desperate an ironist to be able to discard easily, in public utterances, a tone which makes it enticingly uncertain where he stood—especially in a matter he so much cared about. But certainly he would have added on to any usage doctrine considerations which would have taken its control out of the reach of shifting circumstance, and Campbell knew this when he attacked him.

However absurd some of the eighteenth century doctrines became, they did at least recognize the existence of a problem that the later views, represented by Campbell, lost sight of.

# *Chapter Thirteen:* What Thought About Language Should Not Be Like

*All hid, all hid; an old infant play.*
*Like a demi-god here sit I in the sky,*
*And wretched fools' secrets heedfully o'er-eye.*
*More sacks to the mill! O heavens! I have my wish.*

*Love's Labour's Lost*

Two hundred and twenty-five years after Swift's Memorandum, let me try to show what some current ideas about the regulation of the language are. If the specimens I bring out are boring, I can only say I am not choosing the dullest. But I have to illustrate the important truth that with a matter which might easily be made a vivifying and constantly enlightening interest, present-day teaching in England—the most expensive I believe in the world—has not succeeded even in hinting at the chief issues every sentence raises for everyone, or in stimulating any thoughts about language which would not be more to the point in a discussion of the proper cut of trousers.

> 4.3.* His theory is that Grammar does not consist in the drawing up of a series of laws as to how a language shall be spoken or written, but, in the methodizing of those rules which are established through use. He says in other words that grammarians are at the mercy of any popular but unworthy element which may come into the language. Surely, although a Grammarian cannot establish the laws, he can at least control over-exuberance of expression.

So a Cambridge tailor might keep a particular pair of plus fours from hanging quite to the ground. The writer has not profited much from making his précis of Campbell. How grammarians are to exercise such control or why they should be 'at the mercy of an unworthy element' he does not divulge. What 'unworthy' might mean, which would be the key to the whole discussion, he takes for granted.

4.31. The last sentence (from 'Only let us rest in these fixed principles . . . reversed') would seem to sum up the most sensible point of view towards grammarians. All rules and generalisations stand the chance of being successfully broken by men of genius. Rules based on what has been done in the past are useful to those of us who are not men of genius as controlling suggestions; but that alone must be the use of grammar.

Perhaps the word 'rule' has something to do with producing this blank and incurious state of mind. The next does not feel quite so far removed from the men of genius.

4.32. 'The custom of writing is the sole standard of style.' Blake was not completely wrong when he said: 'To generalise is to be an idiot,' the standard of style can be as much contained in speaking as in writing.

A typical irrelevant extension of the sense of 'style' to introduce a point Campbell is not in the least denying.

4.33.* The writer is right in declaring that Grammar is only an artificial code of laws made for the help of Society. What is in everyday use, that is correct. The Grammarian's business is to note and collect the different uses of language and form them into a code of laws. It would seem however as if the laws of writing should be stronger than those of speaking.

If that is all he can think about it, can we blame him for finding the subject uninspiring? Nor does the social contract much cheer things up!

4.34.* Once the 'rules' of grammar have been formulated by the method here suggested of collecting existing uses, they become not so much rules as a social contract, which, it has been agreed, will be kept as a regulation over changes in the general use of language. In time, fresh and almost imperceptible changes in general use will become formally accepted as a new part in this contract, but the contract established will always tend to restrain such changes.

Nor the cave-man:

4.35.* I definitely [Sense xi] agree with most of the statements made by this author: It seems quite obvious that grammar is a development which followed the development of language (as a means of communication). Cave-men etc. were probably quite capable of conveying some kind of meaning to each other and were most unlikely to have known much about such words as 'adjective'—'noun'—'tmesis,' etc. Grammar thus taken as the methodizing of language is not essential to communication: Bunyan could write a most intelligent book without much knowledge of 'Grammar' as such.

Nor the Académie française; nor, alas! The History of the English Language:

4.36.* It is most certainly true that the grammar of a language has not been layed down by the critics, but there is almost an exception to the rule, namely, in France where the Acadamie Francaise has the last say when there is any discussion over the proper gender of a word, or any other problems. The grammar of a language is built up by the speakers of it, and it is modified when that country is conquered by any other. Norman French taking the place of Anglo Saxon at Court, and the eventual modification and molding of both together.

Longer comments are no more encouraging:

4.37.* It is quite true to say that 'use, or the custom of speaking, is the sole original standard of conversation, as far as regards the expression' but all the same there must be some standard, or people would not know how to speak. Rules have been made from the best kinds of speech, and if these are susceptible of gradual modification, as the general character of the language changes, and are not regarded as rigid there is no harm done. The laws of grammar should not of course be regarded as outside the language, pre-ordained, and unalterable; they are more like chemical laws in that they are formulated from practical experience as to how the language works. But they are formulated from the way the language works best, and do set up a certain standard of correct writing and speaking, though this of course should be as wide as possible. A general consensus of opinion as to the best ways of expression govern the laws of grammar; but chaos would be attained if they were merely general observations on the way the language was used by any and every writer and speaker. Obviously this standard is only adopted for convenience and the general aesthetic good of the language and has no intrinsic authority in itself.

'Best,' 'harm,' 'best,' 'good,'—but esthetic only!—he wanders past the door but does not try to enter, does not even suspect that it is a door. Something equally prevents him from thinking twice about the 'standard' he mentions. How would it make people 'know how to speak'? When a bad ruler is on the Dragon Throne, according to Mencius, 'The black-haired people do not know where to put their hands and feet!' His glance at two kinds of law might have helped too but he does not let the chemistry analogy develop. He is too busy being 'as wide as possible' and 'attaining' chaos.

Other references to law went no further:

> 4.38.* The prolixity and tortuosity of the Common Law of the land has grown to so great a magnitude today, that it takes men of the most profound learning immense pains to understand it. Yet the average citizen is always presumed to have had a knowledge of the laws where he transgresses. So too the laws of the grammarians, were they to be comprehensive, would be equally prolix. But, on the other hand, as the tribunal of use is assuredly the supreme authority in the laws of language, so everyone has the opportunity and authority to make their own laws.

At this point he put in a flourish and wrote 'unfinished'—which was perhaps convenient for him. His escape from the analogy was taking him out of the frying-pan into the fire.

There is not much reason to hope that further teaching and discussion at the level of, or in terms of, such ideas as those used in 4.3 to 4.38 will bring their owners any profit, or lead to a closer contact with the realities of language.

What is needed is a fresh start with conceptions of a more adequate order. We cannot give such conceptions from without, through a discourse; we must find means to make them take place, develop, grow and come to birth in the mind, and that means can only be the mind's own experience of communication, of its own successes and failures. It is easy enough to explain that no grammarian can possibly control people's ways of talking (4.3); that genius, when successful, exploits powers in the instrument that others have neglected, powers not essentially different from those we all use (4.31); that there are many styles (4.32); that there are many kinds of writing as there are many kinds of speaking (4.33); that the restraint on change is failure, not any contract, even if more than one in a million were aware of its terms (4.34); that we all used nouns and verbs before we learnt the words 'noun' or 'verb' (4.35); that how to determine 'the best kinds of speech' is precisely the problem (4.37); or that a 'use' involves a conformity and is not a bit what anyone chooses to do (4.38)—easy enough to meet these and a thousand other such absurdities with more or less jejune commonplaces at much their own level. It is not so easy to say why this topic should ordinarily excite no better sort of discussion than this. Thought about language ought to be the most widely stimulating of all mental exercise. There is not much room to doubt that, as a rule, it is deadening in an extreme degree. How otherwise are we to explain the array of trivialities and gross blunders about the commonest facts of experience which the protocols of this experiment present to us? The writers are neither so ignorant nor so foolish as they seem; but 'language' has been mentioned and at once they forget things that ordinarily they would show themselves perfectly conversant with.

I linger over these unfortunate comments because there is a danger, if more time is given to the discussion of the theory of language, that it may be given to more of this sort of thing. I would be in favour of cutting the whole subject out rather than encourage these subnormal accompaniments of almost all general discussions of usage. They are hard to avoid so long as we keep to the accepted current notions of usage as governing 'correctness.' All the fructifying perceptions that should come from reflection on our experience with language are muffled and hidden from us by these confused notions. All the gains in 'that knowledge which re-appears as power' are prevented by them. And these are the reasons, in addition to the muddle they embody (which is vicious in itself), why, a little later, I give so much space to an attempt to sort out the senses of 'correct,' and to free the more important of them from their present entanglement with irrelevant considerations. For they should be, and in time must become, the guiding conceptions of the central all-connecting study of a modern education, the study of interpretation, or, if we prefer another word, of method:

'This act of the Mind, then, this leading thought, this "Keynote" of the harmony, this "subtile, cementing, subterraneous" power, borrow-ing a phrase from the nomenclature of legislation, we may not un-aptly call the INITIATIVE of all Method. It is manifest, that the wider the sphere of transition is, the more comprehensive and commanding must be the initiative: and if we would discover an *Universal Method,* by which every step in our progress through the whole circle of Art and Science should be directed, it is absolutely necessary that we should seek it in the very interior and central essence of the Human intellect.'                                COLERIDGE, *Essay on Method,* p. 3

To continue our tour of the battlefield, our walk through the wards, or, in a juster image, our comparison of some types of embryos, I will try now to illustrate some points at which the comments may give us hope for better things under happier conditions, points where reflections which might become illuminating seem to be beginning.

The allusions to laws (legal and chemical) of the last two writers mark such a point. If they developed we should be on our way to considering how language is and may be controlled. The references led nowhere, because thought about the different things we call 'laws' was too difficult for the writers. It is difficult. Everyone finds it so. I may quote from another place where I have written about these things.

'How varied and how curiously involved our ways of thinking about these matters may be is well shown by the following passage from an exceptionally precise critic:

When the laws of poetry are changed, the critic, of course, has to begin again; the judiciary must administer what the legislature enacts.

But is this what we mean when we speak of the laws of poetry? Do we not rather mean that poetry has laws, not such as a State has, but laws which are like those of nature?

Here is one of those distinctions which seem more obvious than they are. Human laws change, the laws of nature are unchanging and eternal. That is much less true than we think it, or true in a different sense from that in which we commonly take it. When we change a human law, a law of the State, what takes place is not properly a change of law, but a readjustment of the human mind and human behaviour to newly revealed conditions of the political and moral life, a new conception of law. The divorce laws, for example, do not change the law of marriage; they merely readjust our ideas about it. In just the same way Copernicus readjusted our ideas of the planetary system, he did not change the laws of astronomy.

H. W. GARROD, *Poetry and Life,* p. 153

One is tempted to ask what the law of marriage can be, if not a platonic myth of an exceptionally delusive kind? But I quote Mr. Garrod's paragraph not to quarrel with it, nor as an especially confused passage, but to show how much in need of increased refinement the writings even of very intelligent persons may be when they use these notions. And in our disordered world increased clarity as to these notions is very much needed.[1]

The separation of the multiple senses of Law and Order, Rule, Uniformity, Norm, Standard, Design and so on, is touched on further in the Logic Section. Here it will be enough to note that we can hardly expect a profitable discussion of 'usage,' 'rule,' or 'law' in language unless we are prepared to approach it through a recognition, and at least some clarification, of their worst ambiguities. Moreover the main profit of such a discussion would be in an improved command and use of these different ideas. None intervene more intimately in every variety of conduct, from the most superficial of our practical activities to the deepest moral decisions. What we are doing, what we can do, and how to do it, are questions that can be meditated only with their aid, and in the degree to which we are unnecessarily confused about them we are likely to be unnecessarily confused in our lives. Language, with the problem of how it is ruled, and in what sense of 'ruled,' is for innumerable reasons an unequalled occasion for studying these questions. They can be raised about it (any close study of it should automatically raise them) in all their varieties. And they can be presented for reflection in an immediately accessible concrete form as matters of observable linguistic fact—not as abstract philosophical speculations. The speculations require a preliminary labour of analysis—through which it would be ill advised to try to take our pupils until a later stage. But to make the problem of usage a living one (and with that to start the process of reflection upon most of the problems of law) by forcing attention on the questions 'Why is this sentence you have written not acceptable? How do the reasons for its failure differ from the reasons for the failure of this other sentence of yours?' and so on, is something we

---

[1] *Mencius on the Mind*, p. 121. The fourth chapter of this study of translation problems contains much that is supplementary to the discussions in this Section and the Logic Section, especially as to *Law, Order, Principle* and *Truth*. Compare also, *Basic Rules of Reason*.

can begin to do at a very early stage. And in most instances, the reasons will appear under questioning very plainly—if we do not prevent them by smothering the inquiry with some blanket theory from the start.

Instead of a general doctrine (of which the conventional 'correct usage' theory is, I believe, the worst) what we should offer as an aid to reflection is a sketch of some different possibilities corresponding to the different purposes (see p. 189 above) for which we may attempt to find laws of different kinds and apply them to the matter. My writers show these diff.rent backgrounds of supposed purpose fairly clearly:

4.4.* I do not agree with the author in his conclusion that the order of subordination, i.e. custom of speaking, custom of writing and finally grammar, ought never to be reversed. For customs of speaking and writing in human language have similar analogy with customs in human conduct. In order to regulate human conduct we derive from customs government and laws. But as soon as government and laws are established men must abide by laws though customs may change from time to time. Grammar, though it has its origin from customary use of the language, should be adhered to after it is recognised by the public. It is inevitable for an accidental breaking away from laws, but we must regard it as illegal. We must consider grammar first, otherwise writers might take too much liberty in their writing, on the pretext of customs, and, in a long run, our language would become unintelligible to us at all.

This evidently is a writer for whom English is not his native tongue. Naturally enough he is dominated by a conception of grammatical laws as a way of teaching a language to those who are not learning it in the nursery. Their purpose would be to secure a superficial uniformity (see p. 189, No. 1).

Here is a better reader than many, who sees the purpose of grammar as *description* (No. 2), separating this from explanation:

4.41. I completely agree with the writer about the function of the grammarian, who is regarded as a tabulator and recorder rather than as a lawgiver. He does not mention, however, the changes which take place in a language, and the consequent changing of 'grammar'; I think, however, from the way in which he speaks of the causes to which 'these modes or fashions owe their existence,' that he is aware of the process of change. The methodising of the grammarian, unlike that of the scientist, can never be final. The 'laws' of grammar can change, those of the universe (we hope) cannot.

The next one gives the grammarian a more ambitious intellectual task ( ? Nos. 3 and 8) and his own thoughts show much more lively possibilities of growth than any others we have seen so far:

4.42.* I agree with the author both in the building up of his position (that the fashion of language is the rough material on which grammar must if it will draw out its rules) and in its defense.

Use does determine the standard of speech and writing whether the grammarian likes it or not. The business of the grammarian is to understand why the usage is such as it is, and on those discoveries, to lay down a grammar that may be a flexible rule to future usage.

The three following show biological interests and thereby come nearer to some of the most important considerations that others overlooked:

4.43.* The writer's view of grammar seems to be correct. The primary function of language is communication and except for certain symbolic sciences, how this communication is to be achieved cannot be decided arbitrarily. One cannot really hold that our language sprang up, fully developed grammatically, any more than that it has reached a certain height and must be kept there by rigid adherence to a certain set of grammatical rules which were prevailing at any given moment in its history. Language is progressive, and it progresses not through any arbitrary legislation but by refinement in use. If you examine the history of a species you generally find that some limbs or organs which are now mere vestiges were at one time fully developed and necessary to the existence of the organism. The same phenomenon can be seen in the history of a language—many words have sprung up and been forgotten, while others survive as vestiges— archaic words, phrases, and grammatical rules. What the writer means then, is that Grammar is not static but dynamic and that to offend the rules of grammar means to offend the rules of grammar *at a given moment;* for the rules are always changing in some process of natural growth, keeping pace with or perhaps slightly behind the actual changes in the general usage of the language.

Common sense here ekes out knowledge about the development of languages and an optimistic view of evolution prevails.

4.44.* I think that form of·language is best which enhances effectiveness or lucidity. Use or custom will either strive for effective expression or (and this more often) lapse into the commonplace. There is no place for grammar for its own sake; it should be a means of determining which is the most effective or lucid manner of writing or of speaking. I think any grammatical 'law' which has outlived its usefulness will die by the process of natural selection. Likewise, the commonplace will die because it lacks effectiveness.

Optimism has triumphed still more and the purpose of grammar is now to be an aid towards perfection (cf. p. 190, No. 8).

4.45. Campbell leaves his statement vague, in not defining the 'custom of writing.' The 'custom of writing' has changed just as the custom of morals or thought have changed, but not always for the better. Here it is presupposed that what one might call the *current* custom of writing is the best possible and the most useful to the period which it serves. If Campbell intends this implication, it is a false one, for language degenerates just as (and many would say simultaneously with) morals and thought.

Therefore an appeal to the 'tribunal of use' is only justified when the current use of language is in a healthy condition: when it conveys a maximum of meaning in a minimum of words. At the present time no such appeal would be justified, for it is a time when the exceptions (in the form of experimenting by such men as Joyce and Hemingway) are healthier than the current 'custom of writing.'

Pessimism here has its turn, but good reasons why the criticism of language is important are not overlooked. In comparison with the last three, the writer. is perhaps rather using ready-made thoughts than thinking—as his explanation of 'a healthy condition' shows. But still they are thoughts about what language does; they are not like the effusions of my 4.3 group; they are worth discussing and are capable of development.

I add the next one with some hesitation. I seem to know where some of its doctrine came from:

4.46. This argument is admirably perspicuous for the time in which it was written; and I wholeheartedly agree with it, against the omnipresent Platonic fallacy, of archetypal models of linguistic usage. But the discussion ought to be pressed a little farther.

What is this tribunal of general usage? It is a thing very tenuous;

an abstraction, making a single standard of the usage of hundreds of millions of people, and of as many works as well; and in these, the fashions of speech change with the fleeting years; almost, in the case of the modern vernacular, each week. Grammar, in this sense, can only hope to lay out the broadest general lines of sentence structure, and trust the student to imbibe for himself the standards of 'good taste,' which is all that the great majority of grammatical dicta can foster, anyway. Beyond certain broad limits of intelligibility, the rules of grammar only add an aura of respectability and gentility to the spoken word. The fortunately grammarless Elizabethan proved how high a standard of speech and writing may be attained without formal rules of grammar. When these were set up, directing the shifting forms of the language into unalterable paths, the result was to cramp literature, and squeeze from it much of the individuality and freedom of its greatest period.

This is a negative observation: what grammar should not do. What it *should do* is to investigate the great tangle (indicated by Campbell in his sentence on the philosophers), arising from the fact that there *is* no direct connection between words and things; and, by making clear the tremendous significance of this in communication, serve as the salient front in an attack on the misconceptions, in all forms of communication, arising from ignorance of this elemental fact. The difference between these views, is that of grammar as a standard of 'good taste,' and etiquette; and grammar as an important foundation stone of the structure of sciences, literature, and all civilization.

The peculiarities of its expressions—the sad fate of the fosterlings in particular—will protect me from the supposition that *this* is quite what my recommendations aim at. I will however oppose to it a comment which properly belongs to the 4.3 group:

4.47. I agree with the author's view. What comes first, language or grammer? Naturally language. And grammer based entirely on the data given by language. Those who object to grammer being subordinate to language and its usage argue that once rules of grammer have been formulated then all language should conform to them. The answer is language came into existence first and rules followed it; and language is growing and ever changing so the rules have to follow language. If language is a growth and if rules tend to be static, rules will soon be out of date. So grammer cannot but have a subordinate position.

This reproduces, I think, faithfully, the reflections with which ordinary everyday current discussion, in the light of contemporary rhetoric and theory of language, is too often content. The fact that, with Campbell before him, he retains his own spelling for *grammar* should not prejudice us in judging the worth of the opinions he is expressing!

Here is another, equally representative of the muddled compromise, the havering, hazy acceptance of opposing views, the relegation to an unexamined background of the essential considerations, that are characteristic of contemporary thought on usage:

> 4.48. Professor Campbell's wide observation that Dr Swift's complaint was unjust because there is no universal archetype of grammar, and English cannot be expected to conform to the rules of other grammars, is sensible and just. But when he goes on to say that the use of speech itself is the sole standard of conversation, and in the same way the custom of writing is the sole standard of style, he is too free. The uses of language naturally change from time to time and rules of grammar alone give an absolute norm, a protection against too swift change—the tribunal of use is not enough.

And here, lest we should conclude in too gloomy a mood, is an example of careful and acute reading not lured from its task either by echoes of doctrine or by current commonplaces, but applying to the matter in hand an acute and resourceful awareness of some of the ways in which language may serve or mislead us:

> 4.49. Undoubtedly a just general argument. In the last paragraph however he pushes an important question out of the way in his second sentence. If the best speakers and writers *do* actually frequently offend against the general use of the language surely it is a matter that calls for enquiry, since theirs must be accepted as the best use and therefore as the court of appeal which he recognises as valid. 'The sole *original* standard' a little bothers me; is he wanting to make the standard fixed and permanent,—or is this a case where one needs to understand very delicately the particular shade of meaning which this variable word had at the moment when he wrote?

# *Chapter Fourteen:* Natural Connexions of Sound and Sense

*Visionary power*
*Attends the motions of the viewless winds,*
*Embodied in the mystery of words.*

*The Prelude*

'Languages were made not by rules or art, but by accident, and the common use of the people. And he that would speak them well has no other rule but that; nor anything to trust to but his memory, and the habit of speaking after the fashion learned from them that are allowed to speak properly, which, in other words, is only to speak by rote.' (Locke, *Of Education.*)

Like so much that Locke said, this is true if we limit it carefully; but, if we relax the limitations, it becomes false—and dangerously false because it borrows so much plausibility from the limited truth. It is true that languages were not made by rules, nor by *art,* in the sense of a conscious application of general principles. But none the less all languages grew and are maintained only by art, in the sense of a skilful adaptation of acquired means to new purposes. The new purposes may arise 'by accident,' but the shaping of language to them comes from skill and resource, and the resource is not mere memory or habit (unless we immensely extend and deepen the scope of these terms) but the understanding of what words will and will not do. Phonetically, and as regards a limited range of adjustments between words, we may, perhaps, 'speak by rote,' but we almost never, as intelligent beings, speak only by rote. Between what we have heard and what we say intervene our purpose and a process of fitting means to ends; and if we leave all this out we are leaving out all our chances of education. What was wrong with the dreariest exhibits of the last chapter was principally that the writers were speaking by rote.

In general the absence of anything which feels like a modern outlook or a live interest is the striking thing about this group of protocols—indirect witness that the subject has been allowed to lapse into a stagnant slough. A few however touched on contemporary matters:

> 4.5. A very big question. But there are general analogies—'the general use of our language' which do transcend and have authority against new formations, however widely adopted—e.g. few will deny that it is a pity that the word 'television' was ever coined, though now that it has been we have perforce to use it. And here perhaps the grammarians might have been consulted before it was formed.

His remark has a serviceable idea about analogies; but his example lets it down, for hybrids are, I understand, far too numerous in English for the complaint that they are contrary to the custom of the language to have weight by itself. Two others referred to the Radio:

> 4.51. The 'tribunal of use' is rather a complicated standard to which to refer as the supreme authority. The idea is undoubtedly good, but today it is less certain which is the authoritative mode of writing than in the eighteenth Century. B.B.C. pronunciation experiments, and influence of American films.

All relevant points.

> 4.52. The idea that the 'tribunal of use' is to be the ultimate authority on questions of grammar would put the B.B.C. in an awkward dilemma. Only a minority of Englishmen speak in the manner of B.B.C.

Little he knows! If he attended the B.B.C. Committee on Spoken English he would see soon enough how subservient we are to 'the tribunal of use.' That our business is 'to note, collect and methodise the modes and fashions' is *the* lesson the members of that Body most wish to show that they have not forgotten. Since Bridges' death, the reaction inside the B.B.C. Committee against attempting to use the unique powers of broadcasting to improve the language has been so strong that we may confidently expect that the tide will turn before very long. Why should not an instrument which has so fundamentally altered the conditions governing the control of language be recognized to possess powers of which great advantage might be taken. When that happens the B.B.C. will perhaps find itself in more than one dilemma. It will become a nodal point for intellectual statesmanship. Here is another reason for taking the critical theory of language more seriously. With the Radio as a link, the schools might soon be in a position to interfere on an enormous scale with the development of language.

A hankering to disbelieve what 'every smatterer in philosophy will tell us' moved a few:

> 4.6. Surely no one could disagree with the essence of the writer's argument—that the laws of grammar are merely derived from general use. Nowadays that would seem a 'self evident truth' and to continue to labour the point would in Johnson's words 'be unprofitably tedious.'
>
> The only criticism that seems necessary is that his opinion that 'there can be no natural connexion between the sounds of any language and the things signified' is manifestly untrue.

Campbell is quoting Aristotle and the point has, of course, been pivotal for theories of language ever since Plato—'to go no further,' as one of the protocol writers put it. The Greeks are often said to have identified the order of things with the order of their speech, through exclusive attention to one language. And, as Berkeley wrote,[1] 'There are some grounds to think that if there was one only invariable and universal language in the world, and that men were born with the faculty of speaking it, it would be the opinion of many, that the ideas in other men's minds were properly perceived by the ear, or had at least a necessary and inseparable tie with the sounds that were affixed to them. All which seems to arise,' he concludes, 'from a want of due application of our discerning faculty' and I think so too! Aristotle is certainly a weighty witness both in favour of the Greeks and against the 'natural connexion' between language and things, though Berkeley has his warning here too: 'When a schoolman tells me "Aristotle hath said it," all I conceive he means by it, is to dispose me to embrace his opinion with the deference and submission which custom hath annexed to that name. So close and immediate a connexion may custom establish betwixt the very word *Aristotle*, and the motions of assent and reverence in the minds of some men.' (Introduction, *The Principles of Human Knowledge*, XX.) None the less, Aristotle is right on the large answerable question here, as no one who is acquainted with two

---

[1] *A New Theory of Vision*, LXVI.

very different languages will doubt. The disputable point has always been whether there may not be some extremely far from obvious correspondence between recondite properties of the structure of language and the structure of things (e.g. between the noun-adjective division and the substance-attribute division or, more plausibly, between a completely definite (IV) statement and the fact which would make it true). But these are not the kind of question (I opine that they are *illegitimate,* the product of unnoticed ellipses; see below, Chapters XVII and XXII) that 4.6 is probably considering. If they were, there would be a pleasing freshness about his confident assertion, reminding us that the most dubious matters may seem patently evident before reflection has been focussed upon them. I think though he has merely mistaken the point and is just saying either that of course some things we say are sometimes true, or that some words are onomatopoeic.

> 4.61. In the sentence, 'One thing, indeed, every smatterer in philosophy will tell us, that there can be no natural connexion between the sounds of any language and the things signified, or between the modes of inflection and combination, and the relations they are intended to express.' It is not absolutely clear whether the writer himself agrees to this, although I think he does. And I am inclined to take the opposite view, that there is some natural instinctive connection, at least in primary words such as *ground, clear, jay.* Where things had a voice, that being imitated as with a cuckoo; where not, being named as nearly as possible to represent the sensations aroused by it.

This second dissenter is bringing up what is often loosely called onomatopoeia, or, nowadays, echoism, and this is worth some discussion—not because echoism establishes much of a natural connexion between words and sounds or things, but because the mode by which we probably come to think it does throws light on an important, often overlooked mode of operation of language in general. It can thus serve as an introduction to considerations which will be useful later. Onomatopoeia, moreover, is a curiosity that intrigues those who have otherwise no very lively interest in language and so can be used as a bait to attract their attention to something else which may take them in deeper.

There are, of course, an immense number of words that seem to illustrate their meaning more immediately than others; *glare, flash, flicker, flimmer, glimmer, glow,* and so on. As Bloomfield remarks, 'The explanation is a matter of grammatical structure . . . to the speaker it seems as if the sounds were especially suited to the meaning.'[1] The popular explanation—which 4.61 gives—is that these words were made up to be like their meanings. The grammatical explanation is only that there is a group of words which share an element of sound and also an element of meaning, and that it is other words parallel to it in this double fashion that make us feel that *bash* or *clash* is peculiarly expressive of its meaning. If this explanation is right, the popular view is turned back to front in an interesting fashion. Instead of a likeness between sound and sense being the cause of the existence of these groups of words, the existence of the group would be the cause of our feeling of likeness. The feeling thus generated might then add new words to the group, and so on. But 'root-forming morphemes,'[2] as these phonetic-semantic units are called, are not things to dogmatize about. As Bloomfield writes, 'The analysis of minute features, such as the root-forming morphemes, is bound to be uncertain and incomplete, because a phonetic similarity, such as, say, the [b-] in *box, beat, bang,* represents a linguistic form only when it is accompanied by a semantic similarity, and for this last, which belongs to the practical world, we have no standard of measurement' (p. 246). I would add—and this point is of quite subversive effect upon many types of word-counting—that 'semantic similarity' is dependent to a high degree on the verbal setting. Not only can it not be *measured,* but it cannot even be *estimated* fairly by taking words in isolation. Unless, of course, we confine 'semantic similarity' to just those similarities which we seem able to detect so— by the use, that is, of a very general or background setting—and no doubt this is the proper procedure for linguistic studies as opposed to critical interpretative studies which try to make a closer analysis. In special settings we shall find our words being backed up by unuttered words in countless ways. (See *The Philosophy of Rhetoric,* p. 64, for an example.) A theory which sets no strict limits to the ways in which a word in a passage may get its force from *other words,* not consciously thought of in connection with it, is useless

---

[1] L. Bloomfield, *Language,* English Edition, p. 156. I discuss this problem more fully from a literary point of view in *The Philosophy of Rhetoric,* Lecture III.

[2] Jespersen (*Analytic Syntax,* Chapter 29) draws needed attention to the disconcerting variations in the use of 'morpheme' in the writings of linguists.

mystagogy if these other words never come to be thought of; we should have no means then of knowing whether it was so or not. But sometimes they do come forward from the background in a peculiar fashion which shows that they were active already as controls upon the special meaning that the word has been taking. This is quite different from a course of 'free-association,' it feels different and its result is different. The other words confirm the meaning of the central word; they do not distract us from considering it.

These 'expressive words' are worth attention in teaching because they give us amusing cases of the dependence of one word, for its peculiar aptness, upon other words that back it up. But the lesson is spoilt if it is not generalized to offer an insight into the whole working of language, to show how words take meaning through their relations with other words. This is indeed so important a point that no occasion for stressing it in teaching should be missed.

But there is a further profit to be gained from studying these 'expressive' words. The summary implicit argument by which we come to think that they must have some sort of direct resemblance to the things they stand for can serve as a type specimen of innumerable illegitimate arguments which betray us in all branches of interpretation.

The argument I am thinking of goes somewhat like this: 'Why should all these similar words stand for similar things? There must be some reason. The same cause must be producing the same effect. The cause must be that the words were made up to match the things. They must therefore be *like* them in some way—and, what's more, which confirms the argument, we can see that they are!'

I am taking this as the sort of argument that may occur to anyone—especially if he is without, or doesn't recall at the moment, any knowledge of the history of language. I am *not* thinking of arguments which might have another order of plausibility to a philologist conjecturing about root-formations in the light of the elaborate and complex comparisons by which alone that dim and distant topic can be reached. Nor am I thinking of the arguments he might use in the equally complex task of estimating the factors governing the relative semantic and morphologic stabilities of words. These arguments have scores of premises and their force depends on the precision ('definite' IV) with which the premises are stated. My type argument has no precision about it anywhere; but it has a 'principle'

*—same effect ∴ same cause*—and this 'principle' makes it very well worth study.

It would not be rash, I think, to accuse this principle of having worked more mischief to mankind than any other that might be cited. It has a sense, of course, in which it is true,[1] and our lives minute by minute depend on its truth in this sense; and so does all science. But it has other senses too—not at all easy to distinguish from this true sense, unluckily—in which it is responsible for end-less baseless beliefs, superstitions, blunders, absurdities and futilely premature conclusions. The false senses of the principle—or if you prefer, misuses of it—occur implicitly in thought so incessantly that no general education deserves the name if it does not make some serious, deliberate and persistent attempt to protect us from them by developing, through practice, an increased ability to see when it can help and when it will only mislead us. And we have, in this argument about these 'expressive' words a subject matter ('copy' words) on which a common mistaken use of it can be conveniently demonstrated.

As we examine the argument it tends to elaborate itself in the direction of the philologist's possible arguments, but what we have to consider is its first form. We can cut the elaborations out best by remarking that it doesn't matter whether the conclusion—that the sounds are like the things—is true or not. All that matters is whether the argument is a good one. And, as perhaps always, the method of parallels—if it is warily used and severely controlled—is the best way of showing that it is a bad one. We may take first a case where a similar argument would be perfectly valid, footprints on the shore, say. *There* we understand the connection, which is extremely close, between the foot and its impression, the cause and the effect, as well as we can understand anything. And what we understand about it makes the argument safe. In fact, it collapses into what looks like simple observation, so that we may have to take some pains to show that a step of inference has been made. 'Why should all these similar marks have been left behind by similar things? . . . Because they were made by them—and the mode of making makes them like what made them.' All the conditions are clear here—that no sculptor has been faking them with his thumbs

[1] The needless ineptitude of our ordinary conduct with causal language is analyzed briefly, in Basic, in *Basic Rules of Reason*, pp. 67-78.

and so on. That is one extreme, the safe extreme, of the application of the *same effect ∴ same cause* principle. Now take an opposite extreme; a crude form of the Diffusion of Culture theory will do: 'Why should the Aztecs have had customs A.B.C. and the Ancient Egyptians have had customs α.β.γ.? . . . Because they imitated them, and now I am satisfied about that and look closer, lo! I can see that A and B and C *are* really like α and β and γ respectively!' Here the 'same cause' principle can be invoked in half a dozen different ways to support or to damage the argument. It supports it by alleging that the specific influence that makes A what it is must be the same specific influence that makes α what it is. It damages it by suggesting that A.B.C. and α.β.γ. may have arisen independently from similar social conditions. And this consideration —with our lack of clear precise understanding of how customs do arise—makes the argument, as it stands, and in parallel to the 'copy' word argument, weak to the point of helplessness. It can develop— as the 'copy' argument can, by analysis and precise comparison of thousands of partial parallels—but then it is no longer the same argument.

I sketch these arguments here because nothing in general education is so important as the ability to question ourselves, as we think, about how we are thinking. Inferences of this sort we live by; normally they flash through our heads—and may come out in speech —too rapidly and with too continuous a movement to be examined. It is well that they should when they are safe. But very few of those with which education need concern itself are safe; and for the perilous ones—those to which teaching can make a difference—the only known means of control is by slowing them down and by translating them into increasing explicitness (V), and with it, we hope, into increased definiteness (IV and IX), for reflection. Everyone knows how in the moment in which we are taking the step of inference (which movement is the life of thought) a hundred unformulated 'considerations'—premises, conditionals, provisos, differentiations, equivalences . . . —seem to be present, guarding, supporting, opening the way for, the step. Everyone knows too how hard it often is, once the step is taken, to keep the same 'considerations' still in control. The analysis of Locke's statement at the head of this Chapter is a fair example. Perhaps if we could sufficiently reproduce, in imagination, the thinker's actual process we should find no step of inference ever unjustified—if it is judged by reference only to what he was taking account of at that moment. But that is a rash speculation. Certainly many steps are utterly unjustified—judged with reference to what he *should* have taken account of for the purpose in hand. And no branch of intellectual discipline can possibly be more important to the teacher than those by which he can help his pupil to reconsider more reflectively the movements of thought, successful and unsuccessful, that have just been made. To repeat our thoughts more slowly and deliberately and freely (the *liberare librare* pun could tell the whole story) is the way to increased intelligence. To discover once that we have tricked ourselves, that we have mistaken two very different ideas one for the other, neglected an obvious qualification, or merged our conclusion in one of our assumptions, is to win power for the future—quite apart from whether we can or cannot describe later just what it was that we did wrong. This latter ability is another matter, calling for a different development of reflective control and, with most people, for a very specialized training. It may be valuable but is not so valuable as the capacity to think again, *better*.

Some allusions to premises in the above might mislead. Formal Logic, with its classifications of fallacies, was in part, a minor part, an attempt to assist this critical re-thinking—a not very successful attempt. The machinery was both too stiff and too crude. It transformed out of recognition what it handled (so does modern logistic) and translation into it was a distraction rather than a deliberation.

But this is for anon. I intended only to show how a relatively simple grammatical point about 'expressive' words can open into a lesson in method. It serves me also as an introduction to the more elaborate study of the process of re-thinking that a close examination of Campbell's argument, to which I now turn, will entail.

# *Chapter Fifteen:* The Doctrine of Usage

> *In those judgments where there occurs a misconception*
> *rooted in long habit it is not possible to bring the correc-*
> *tion within our grasp in the same degree as in those other*
> *cases where no such unavoidable illusion confuses our con-*
> *cepts. Hence this our emancipation of the reason from*
> *sophistical theories can hardly as yet have the clearness*
> *which alone produces perfect satisfaction.*
>
> KANT, *Prolegomena to any future metaphysic*

The first paragraph is the one that counts; the second is an 'offensive-defensive' excursion from it, and the third, except for a perhaps significant break (before 'Only') is a summary. I shall go through the first paragraph trying with each lock-word to indicate (as fairly as I know how) what I take Campbell to be doing. After that I shall stand back to consider what it amounts to in itself and in its consequences.

It would be convenient to have a notation to use in this sort of examination. The first occurrence of 'grammar' (line 1) is especially noteworthy. It is the use we must frequently make, at the beginning of a discussion, of words with challengeable and disputable senses—that is, of nearly all words but those for concrete things and acts. It is the use of a word prior to fixing any specific sense for it; a sort of reservation we make with it—without having settled yet, for the company or even necessarily for ourselves, who is going to be the passenger. Later, on re-reading, we know what meaning it is going to contain; but not yet. So far, for all we know, it is only equivalent to 'whatever people who use this word may possibly mean by it.' It is like 'the sublime' in Croce's most illuminating definition: 'The sublime is everything that is, has been, or shall be so called.' Its importance is that this non-committal use enables us to go on to enquire, without being hampered, into the different things that people may mean by it, or that our author may himself be meaning.

As such, this valuable use seems to deserve a technical name. I will introduce one provisionally in case it should prove to be convenient later, borrowing it from an illustrative instance. There is a very well-known story about an old woman who told her pastor that she 'found great support in that blessed word *Mesopotamia.*' No light has ever been thrown upon what she meant by the blessed word. It puts forward no view whatever as to the topography of the region between the two rivers and it is doubtful if it even refers to them. I propose now to call this use of a word, merely to create a gap-to-be-filled, the *Mesopotamian use*. It will be noticed though that the gap-to-be-filled here has still a distinctive character—a reservation, as it were, in a Tourist not a First Class coach. Here if Campbell had written 'logic,' or 'rhetoric,' or 'criticism,' his Mesopotamian uses of them would have invited different fillings, and one way of examining the passage is to replace 'grammar' throughout by these in turn.

This technicality is a device for drawing attention to the process by which, as we read on, the meanings we are already trying out, in some degree, for the words, hang in suspense, alternate, merge in, lapse—in a score of ways respond to (as they reciprocally prepare) the following meanings. Few words keep to a Mesopotamian use for more than a very brief moment, and we may have to make an effort to get back to it, when we need to. Some passenger, more or less definite (in several of the senses of 'definite'), almost at once occupies the berth; and we cannot too much realize how complex these dramas between rival tenants, all of whom hold tickets they believe to be valid, sometimes are. The Conductor goes by what the other passengers think, and they change their minds. As for the Engine Driver, well, the train only travels so far as the passengers agree about something! Thus two very different things may be called 'the argument.' One is this drama, the process of interpretation in action. The other is a resultant of it—what finally we take to be what the statements say, when we have settled, if we ever do, what that is—which then gives a definite (VI) meaning to each key-word. A key-word is one which thenceforward (unless the writer shifts it or the reader muddles) carries, packed up as part of its meaning, something that has been said with its aid in the passage.

In some writing, non-controversial technology, for example, only the outcome matters. In most interesting discussions, certainly in all these discussions about language, in criticism, psychology, logic, rhetoric and grammar, the other sort of argument, the drama over the berths, is the all important thing. With most of them we never settle finally just what has been said. When we think we have done so, a re-reading next month (if we have been mentally active in the interval) should teach us better! Here is one of the ways in which confusion between Senses IV, VI, VII and VIII of 'definite' leads to stupid misapprehensions of the value of such discussions. 'Didn't settle anything! Led to no conclusion!' is a frequent complaint. Sometimes it is reasonable, but more often perhaps it is imperceptive. To realize that a question has arisen and what it is, may be as positive a result as to answer another question. Answers, after all, breed questions, or should. And as to conclusions, thinking is living and that has its conclusion right enough. 'What is concluded,' asked Benjamin Paul Blood, 'that we should conclude anything about it?'

It may, I think, be reiterated that in these subjects, in thinking about how we think, our aim must be to perceive as distinctly as possible what we are doing rather than to arrive at any final-looking positive theories. As we do so a great number of theories that are too crude to sustain the examination and have only at a distance been supposed to apply, are discarded; and to be rid of them is a great gain. We may be left without any theory, but we are at least freed from the interferences of mishandled abstractions.

The next lock-word is 'law.' It must carry a sense in which it would be preposterous to imagine it regulating our speech. I touched above on the recognized multiplicity of our notions of law. Which comes in here? That of an 'ukase' imposed by an external authority. We are not very far from having to consider constitutional government, democracy, the will of the people and so on; Charles I seems to have slipped into the grammar berth and is being ousted. For what ousts him we have to consider 'fashion' and 'mode.' They may seem slighting words, but Campbell is meaning with them what 'manner,' 'sort,' 'way,' 'practice,' 'custom,' also mean; he is not over-insisting on their changefulness or on the possible triviality of the causes of their changes. As the protocols have shown, plenty of his readers would have liked him to insist more. 'A collection of general observations methodically digested' still keeps us, I think, in a legal atmosphere; a perspicuous record, rather than a scientific arrangement preparing for efforts at explanation, is in sight. But now we come to 'ascertained.' Campbell is using it in a sense that is now obsolete and this instance is later (1823) than any that the O.E.D. notes. It gives, 'to make (a thing) certain or definite: to decide, fix or limit; 1789'—with the quotation from Swift: 'Some effectual method for correcting, enlarging, and ascertaining our language.' Johnson gives Hooker: 'The divine law ascertaineth the truth,' and Locke: 'The quantity of silver in each piece is ascertained by the stamp.' Most of the protocol writers took it, I think, in the modern sense, 'find out for sure, discover,' but Campbell means 'establish as not open to doubt.' He is not (as the rest of his book proves) at all incurious or indifferent about 'to what causes originally these modes or fashions owe their existence.' He is only here setting these questions vigorously aside, as not, in his view, affecting their *authority,* which brings us back to 'laws' again. Its sense, in this last line but one of the paragraph, is now that other sense which challenged the sense, 'ukase,' of its first occurrence; and the perception of this difference is an obvious part of the drama of interpretation. And as the summary shows (and hundreds of places in the rest of the book) this other sort of law is not in the least *less* concerned to 'regulate our speech.' Transgression to be over-ruled is as much as ever being envisaged. This is no charter to individual licence which is being offered. But the regulation has a different sanction and in its details will presumably be different.

I have left out 'business'; it brings us back to 'grammar' and 'grammarian.' It is 'all that a man *qua* grammarian, i.e. as occupying himself with grammar, ought to do.' Anything further that he does, he will do in some other capacity. Whatever it is, it will not be grammar that he is doing, not grammar that he is studying therein. Whether with 'business' Campbell is going further than this and implying that nobody ought (in *any* capacity) to enquire into and work at the things which his first sentence sets aside as what 'some critics seem preposterously to imagine' to be grammar; or whether he is willing to allow them to do it under some other name, is, then, the question with which this first, and, as far as I can make it, non-controversial examination of the passage leaves us to contemplate.

I can restate it in the terms of his summary: it is whether *all*

*questions whatsoever* that people ought to ask about good and bad
in language are to be settled by appeal to use, or whether 'the
tribunal of use,' while having supreme authority in its own territory,
has only a restricted territory—that of 'grammar' in some sense
which will have to be carefully examined and precisely defined. In
brief, it is, after all Campbell has said with and about the word,
the question, 'How widely or narrowly is he inviting us to use it?'
And the difficulty in answering this is (and here I think I enter
the controversy) that Campbell—with others who write likewise—
is extremely confused on the point himself. 'Grammar,' in fact,
whether he is, as it seems, *defining* it or saying something with it,
is the scene each time of the struggle between rival claimants seeking to be what he is talking about; and it is because this is incessantly so in talk about grammar that I put a sketch in at page 189
of some different possible things that may be called 'grammar.'

This struggle is indeed where the main interest of the passage
comes from. It is much more complex than a first glance reveals
and its complexity conceals the trickeries that are taking place. With
each re-reading a different problem of mistaken identity, or illegitimate substitution, can come into the forefront. Thus, on a re-reading,
Campbell may appear in some danger himself, in what he says, of
here attempting 'to give law to the fashions which regulate our
speech,' *in the specific instance of the use of 'grammar.'* He seems
to be issuing an 'ukase' as to what it may properly be used to mean.
To guard him, if we can, from this, our attention goes off to the
different sorts of law, and meanwhile we fail to notice that if we
do take him as strictly limiting 'grammar' to 'a collection of observations methodically digested,' then no one would suppose that *that*
sort of grammar will give 'law,' in the offensive 'ukase' sense, to the
fashions. I remember a schoolboy's trick in which the boy held out
an apple, and said, 'I'll give you what's in my hand; would you
like it?' If the unwary one said, 'Yes!' round came the other hand
from out of sight with something less attractive in it. What is
happening here is not a lot more subtle, but we are distracted by
the other queer things that are going on.

The first 'grammar' alludes to something which is not again
referred to in the paragraph—a grammar which might be thought
able to issue ukases. Then in its place is put, with the second 'grammar' (and with the 'its' and 'it') quite another. And it is *this*

grammar, not the first, whose pretensions would be absurd if it issued ukases. Whether the first sort of grammar might do so Campbell doesn't discuss. He merely calls it a preposterous idea, but his only grounds, seemingly, are that something else—namely, his sort of grammar—couldn't do it and shouldn't try.

Compare: 'It is not the business of circles, as geometric figures, to quarrel with one another.' True, but irrelevant to the question whether literary circles don't fall out as part of their trade. *Or:* 'It is not the business of astronomers to predict human destinies.' Perfectly true, but still the claims of astrology are not disposed of merely by that. Or again: 'It is not the business of Ethics (as a general philosophic subject) to decide particular points of conduct; casuistry does that'—here there happens to be a technical term to remove the ambiguity. So too with 'It is not the business of physics to build bridges, engineering practice sees to that.'

Such parallels are probably the quickest means of exposing this kind of ambiguity, but analysis is more instructive. As Coleridge said, 'The shortest way gives me the *knowledge* best, but the longest makes me more *knowing*.' Continuing on the longest way, then, it is clearly open to any opponent of Campbell's doctrine—of whom I am one—to remark, 'In our sense of "grammar" it is very much our business, and therefore that of grammar, to inquire into, criticize, and give law to the fashions, for they are—even as you yourself show in following them—in an unnecessary and appalling confusion!' To which Campbell's reply might be, 'You can't do it. You'll make a fool of yourself if you try! It would be a bad business if you could!' and so on.

I have been perhaps at excessive pains to show that in the first sentence two senses of 'grammar' are in action. That, I think, is a convenient way of stating the situation. Alternatively we might try saying—as we often do say—that there is here only one sense of 'grammar'—a large, rather indefinite thing, 'a subject'—and that Campbell is putting one view of it and opposing another possible view of it. If so, what would this one sense (subject) be? What would grammar be? Something like, 'The only worthy, proper, right and useful way of studying language' and then perhaps the real issue would seem clearer. I contrast these two formulations in order to remark: (1) Whether we say that we have two *views* of 'grammar' taken in one and the same sense, or that we have two

*senses* is optional. It depends upon how we elect to use the word
'sense.' (2) The verbal disguises that result from mixing these ways
of presenting the situation are due to ellipses of language we cannot
avoid if we are not to be intolerably prolix and pedantic. The
remedy is not to try to avoid them but to learn to expect them. I
shall not avoid them in the obscurer but still more important con-
flicts between senses of 'grammar' in Campbell to which I now go
on. And so I approach what may rightly be called the great snare of
language.

The snare is the confusion between a *definition* and a *statement
that is not about the use of words.*

Suppose we were to ask Campbell what his warrant was for
'Grammar is no other than a collection of general observations etc.'
What could he reply?

Might he reply, 'Usage. That is how the word "grammar" *is* and
therefore *should* be used'? Let us see what the consequences would
be if he were careless enough to reply so. They are terrific. Here is
one: if it had happened that Campbell's opponents—using the word
in another sense than this—had got to work earlier and persuaded
all the writers of Campbell's day—as they very nearly did—to use
the word 'grammar' in their sense, then Campbell would have lost
his warrant. He would not have been able to state his view. Usage
having moved against him *at this point*—even though all the rest
had been as he thought it was—he would have been unable to say
what he has said here, 'Grammar is a collection etc.' Usage would
have ruled that out as a misuse of 'grammar'—as being not what it
means. He would, in fact, have been in just the position he seems
to be trying, in his first sentence, to put his opponents in—that he
may be alluding to with 'preposterously to imagine'—the position
of having no way of talking, of being prevented from saying what
they have to say; because the term 'grammar,' with which they try
to say it, doesn't mean what they try to make it mean but only
what in good usage it does mean. The assumption that 'grammar'
has only one sense: 'It is no other than . . .' is of course the key to
this. We may notice what a peculiar doctrine of prevenient providence would be required by Campbell if this were his reply.

But Campbell was certainly not taking his doctrine about usage
so seriously as this. Like Jespersen in his remarks about what 'may
properly be called a *thing,*' like so many writers on grammar, he

was, happily, forgetting his views about language while he was using it to utter them. He is free in practice from the restrictions of his doctrine. The way he puts his remark, 'It is no other . . .' shows, I think, that his own respect for and obedience to usage is, practically, very restricted. It is significant that all upholders of usage—who include almost all modern writers on the subject—are equally neglectful of this vital question, 'Just how far does its control go?' No usage man, I think, would explicitly and after reflection maintain that it governs *everything*. On the other hand I have not met any who clearly faced the consequences of admitting that its authority is limited. A fog, in fact, falls just at the points where the doctrine might tell us things we would like to know, for instance, whether Campbell intended his remark here as a definition or as a statement of fact.

This is the difficult and important question. On it depends whether we say, 'Quite so! Very well, go on, if you wish, with your grammar. We have other grammars we are interested in,' or whether we have to argue with him and show that his statement about grammar (in a further sense) is untrue. And it is because this is a situation so typical of all discussion that I am giving such an elaborate examination to it.

I very much want to avoid the appearance here of being a sort of rat-catcher. These logical analyses of the definition-statement imbroglio do commonly give that impression. We seem to be arranging that the victim shall have nowhere to run without—snap!— we have him. But that is chiefly the fault of the situation in which a man is saying, perhaps truly, about one thing, what he believes, and will have us believe, he is saying instead about quite another; and the exercise of seeing just how he succeeds in doing this without being found out, and thereby persuades everybody to assent to perniciously muddled doctrine, is so central a part of education that it may excuse some air of device and stratagem. The usage doctrine is so well established—barely half a dozen of my protocol writers, for instance, had any real qualms about it—that we must admit that its fallacies are cunningly hidden. If it is gravely wrong, as I believe it is (though I have not yet begun to argue directly against it), its defences must be difficult to penetrate, and Campbell's argument both historically and as a type of the expositions of the doctrine is among its chief defences.

His question looks like the introduction to a *statement*—not a definition. 'What,' he asks, 'is the grammar of any language?' Not 'How is "grammar" used?' or 'How shall we use "grammar"?' but 'What is grammar?' as though it were not a matter of deciding just what we are now going to talk about but of saying something, true or false, about something already picked out to be spoken about. But, if so, then 'grammar' must have some other sense than 'a collection of observations methodically digested,' or his answer lapses into a mere tautology, 'an x is an x'; and Campbell can be challenged as to what this other sense is.

On the other hand, there is the other possibility. 'It is no other than . . .' What are we to make of that? It may be but an emphatic mode of saying, 'Among other things it *is*,' but it certainly looks like a definition, as though he were telling us how he and we will be using the word henceforward.

Of the two forms, '—— is . . .'
and                              'By "——" I mean . . .'
the first may always be only a shortened and less pedantic-looking form of the second. If some linguist would collect and compare the different machineries that the languages of the world employ to mark this distinction he would be making an interesting contribution. For just here is the step at which discussion goes astray. How we take it has consequences, both in the immediate effects and the outcome, that are prodigious. Thus, if we read Campbell as giving us his definition of 'grammar,' we shall have nothing to quarrel with in all he goes on to say—except that, for safety's sake, we may insert, as a reminder after 'supreme authority' (four lines from the end in the middle of the emphatic summary), 'so far as grammar, as defined above, is concerned.' We shall agree with all he has said, accept it as outlining the general method of *descriptive grammar,* or as defending the descriptive survey of language from interferences by other inquiries with other purposes; but conclude that it was not difficult to say, since it followed obviously from his definition, and then go on to think, with other definitions of 'grammar,' about any other sorts of grammatical questions which interest us more. But if we do *not* take it as a definition (and it is hard to believe that Campbell took it so) then we must try to take it as a statement made by means of some other definition of 'grammar.'

And then we shall, I think, in the end be satisfied that it becomes, whatever definition we put, either trivial or unplausible. But Campbell—like other usage men—takes it to be both important and certain. How is this? Because, I suggest, he is having it both ways and using it, unwittingly, as a definition and as a statement at the same time.

There is nothing, alack! unusual about such a manoeuvre in argument. Logically it is fatal; rhetorically it is often triumphant. It is encouraged by the usage doctrine. For if we feel usage is looking after and regulating the 'significations' of words, we are inclined to feel less distinctly that we are giving a word its meaning (arranging by the setting how it shall be understood) and are more apt to assume that it comes to us with a normal and already settled meaning. Then, however arbitrary we may actually be, we tend to feel that usage backs up the meaning. Similarly the usage-indoctrinated reader tends to take it as backed up so, without looking to see just which of the countless usages is doing the backing. And *there* is the trap with these quasi-definitions. If usage does back it up thoroughly the thing turns into an empty tautology: 'a collection etc. is a collection etc.' But if usage does not back it up enough, then it is very doubtfully true. The peculiar half-way-between, looking both-ways, position gives it both its seeming truth and its seeming content, its plausibility and its air of saying something.

All this witnesses to a fundamental truth about language and we would argue better if we forgot it less. Argument is a peculiar, specialized use of language to which it has not yet accommodated itself. To put it more strictly, the logical use of words, with single constant senses that are the same for each recurrence, maintained unchanged through a series of sentence manipulations, is an extremely artificial sort of behaviour to which our minds do not lend themselves until after long and severe training. It is no more like our usual ways of talking than the goose-step is like our strolling gait. And the fluidity, the incessant delicate variation in the meaning of our words, which is a hindrance to explicit logical argument, is the virtue of language for our other purposes. This very irresolution between definition and statement, this way of making the best of both worlds, of eating our cake and yet having it, is a proper and normal source of power in ordinary discourse. It is a prime condition for the services language renders us. We shall never understand why so many logical arguments go astray, if we see this 'both and neither' trick, which ruins *them,* as a mere weakness. It is not. A method which is admirable and necessary for one set of purposes is getting in the way of another more specialized method suitable only for a different and more limited sort of purpose.

For narrative, description, comment, suasion, for all the normal forms of conversation in which we pass on from topic to topic and thought to thought without needing to concern ourselves critically with the *general* form of the relations between the things we are successively saying, it is an advantage that we should *not* try to isolate parts of the total meanings of our sentences as the proper meanings of their constituent words or phrases. Thought gets on (except for the purposes of explicit argument) excellently well without that. We apprehend, and respond to, far more interconnections in the discourse than anything but an intolerably prolix analysis (as I have been illustrating) can display. And there is no point in displaying them except in the unfortunately frequent instances where we are half-logicalizing our talk and professing in it a kind of rigour which it does not possess. Free discursive thinking, and its expression, are much more widely serviceable to us than the strict, explicit, checkable articulation of discrete, separately definable meanings.[1] What does us disservice is the case where something pretends to be the second but is not. Education should sharpen our sense of the difference between them but should not aim at training everyone in the arduous process of strict argument *in its application to complex and recalcitrant matters.* The relatively *simple* fields of the sciences are the place for that. It is no part of these proposals that we should force a practice of strict logical statement into subjects wherein that must inevitably be extremely difficult and for which ordinary freely expressed thought may be eminently successful without it. But we can clear away the half-baked imperfectible logic that at present clogs our minds without doing that.

There is a risk though—the protocols show that it is very present —that this sort of remark may be mistaken to imply that free discursive thinking is, in another sense, insusceptible to logic, or not logical. And this seems in practice a frustrating *malentendu* prevent-

[1] This describes a remote and ideal limit towards which logicalized utterance tends. I am not saying that any meanings could be completely such.

ing the self-examination of thought on occasions where it is all important. Discursive thought is *difficult* to put into strict articulated argument, because it is so complex, because it uses so many senses of its words, or word-substitutes, at once, in such a shifting variety of connections. But the connections are logical, all right, in the sense that they are of the same kinds—implication, operative likeness and difference, causal connection and so on—as those which appear one by one between the terms of a serial analysis. In this sense thought is logic and could, theoretically, be followed and stated—only, as a rule, there is too much happening for us to follow all of it at once. The prejudice against logic which so often makes people unfair to themselves, comes from the bad effects of incompletely logicalized *statements* which distort the thought they pretend to represent. It is this half-way thing by which, if we take it for what it is not, we are so constantly bullied or bully ourselves into absurdities which free thinking or common sense has no difficulty in avoiding.

The crucial point, the logicalizing step, comes when we distinguish between a definition and a statement, for with that we are attempting to isolate and fix for further use a single meaning for a word. This step is for language something as critical as the passage for matter from the fluid to the solid state—as many metaphors about 'crystallizing' thought and so on point out. Before it is taken, it is perhaps hardly fair to say that a sentence hangs in an undecided state between definition and statement, for the opposition between them only arises with the question, 'Which is it?' or the assumption that it is one or the other. Before that it is both and neither. And since most of our sentences are so, the difficulty we have in keeping sentences in professedly strict *arguments* from lapsing back is not surprising. For *argument,* the distinction must be enforced; it is the condition of argument's utility—which is in enabling us to pass by a series of sentences to a conclusion without having to re-examine every thought in the chain as we do so. Logic is a labelling, filing and manipulating system which lets us get the right letter to the right place without having to interview all the postmen.

The passage from ordinary discourse to argument cannot then be too carefully examined since it is there that most of our persistent distorting ideas are formed. Let me try to trace it schematically in yet another fashion.

In the first development from the Mesopotamian use, a word, A, has its immense field of possible meaning narrowed down by the influence of the other words it comes with: (ABC . . .) as they, reciprocally, have theirs narrowed down by interaction with it. Subject to the whole setting, of course—a remark which should occur here as a refrain between each two sentences of mine. As a result we have an utterance with an integral meaning, which we may symbolize in small italics:

*abc*

For this, the questions, 'Which parts of the meaning are carried by which words?' and 'Which would remain so and be stable in other settings?' have not yet arisen. Ask now, 'What does this utterance mean?' and with that we put it into *a new setting,* an extremely powerful one which may have violent effects:

> May I say that since I started this course I have found myself unable to understand English. Is this the effect of these lectures or am I merely realising the lack of understanding that previously existed? 'Except ye become as a little child ye shall not enter the Kingdom of Heaven!' i.e. except ye forget all your lectures on Practical Criticism ye shall not enjoy your reading.

Widespread sympathy will be felt with this reader. Both his explanations probably have something in them, but chiefly he has now been putting into this 'What *does* it mean?' setting many sentences which, quite rightly, never came into it before.

The mere blank out and disruptive effects of this new setting cease to be so troubling when the further steps that the question leads to become more familiar and habitual. These consist of trying out what we suppose will become the key-word in various other sentences with *their* other settings. (APQ . . .)(ARS . . .) and so on. The aim is to make what A is doing in ABC declare itself; and the process is guided by an attempt on the part of what looks like its separable meaning, *a* in *abc,* to acquire a distinctive form which will reappear, approximately the same, in *apq* . . . and in *ars* . . .

If it can do so without meanwhile making the total meanings of ABC, APQ, or ARS so unlike what they were before the comparative process began that we *have to* notice a change, then the aim is

attained, and we feel that we now understand A, or are clear about
what it means here.

Obviously I am simplifying things as much as possible. In any
doubtful case the range of parallels brought in will normally be
very much wider and more varied than I show. It will include
occurrences of A in all sorts of settings in which it has not at all
the same meaning as in ABC: in which its $a_1$ $a_2$ $a_3$ . . . refuse to
equate themselves with the $a$ of ABC. And, of course, the whole
process is usually extremely rapid and summary, is carried on *not*
with fully formed, uttered, and thought of words, but with word-
substitutes and image-borne context schemata. So if in one way I
risk over-simplifying, in another I risk making the process seem far
more explicit ('definite,' V and XI) than it need be. I am only
attempting a sketch: the prime point is that understanding here is
a process of parallelling, witting or unwitting, between different
suppositions (as the Schoolmen used to call them): which is the
familiar reason for the merits of translation as a mode of exercise
in it.

In all this we must bear in mind the enormously important circumstance that we separate our words as discrete entities in writing,
though we do not to the same degree in speech—except when arguing or when asking 'What does it mean?' Thanks to the writing
convention and the grammatical analysis which has made it systematic, we all ordinarily suppose that words have much more independence as units of sound than, in fact, they usually have. We go
on, similarly, to suppose that they have far more independence as
regards their meaning than is usual. In ordinary discourse the unit
is the *sentence;* and the process by which we break up its molecular
meaning into atom-like independent senses for single words is what
I am describing.

How much independent stable meaning we can give a word
varies with the type of discourse. In strict argument (to keep our
goal in view), for the purposes of *proof*—though *not,* of course, in
debate—our ideal is to give them complete independence. In a highly
criticized and developed science, mechanics, say, a very large proportion of them are independent, that is, technicalized. They have a
function which remains the same whatever the other words (in the
science) they are put with. If the sentence they are in means anything, their part in its meaning is the same.

As opposed to this, in most ordinary discourse the individual words have no *constant,* separable, definite (IV) meaning.[1] They co-operate with the other words to carry jointly a total meaning for the whole sentence. Change the sentence and they are no longer doing the same work. And in many sentences it is very difficult to decide just what they are doing, because other sentences in which they are doing just the same are not easily to be found. But, whether we can assign their separate duties to the words in them or not, we normally take sentences as wholes, give them an integral meaning without taking strict steps to trace down components in it as the contributions of separate words. Henry Sweet was putting this point in another way when he insisted that 'How do you do?' 'I can't help it!' 'Never mind!' are really on a level with single words like *salutation, inevitable, differentiation, differentiated.* In these last, though we could distribute components of their total meaning to different syllables, we don't have to do so to use them perfectly. And similarly, as every child shows, we can use a sentence perfectly without having to be able to make any analysis of it.

But for *argument* (though not for free intellection—the phrases 'loose thinking!' 'rigid demonstration!' 'hard and fast!' 'pin me down!' 'cut and dried!' . . . show the stages and the feelings of the struggle) the unity of the sentence must be resolved into separable constant units of meaning standing in unmistakable relations to one another. We have to find ways of segregating the parts of *abc* into (*a*) and (*b*) and (*c*). My symbolism of course does it for us; a better one would be a line

for which the question was just which parts of it were *a* and *b* and *c* respectively. What we have to find or fix is a sense for A which we can justifiably treat as the same in (*a*) *p q* as in (*a*) *b c*. And we start out normally under the important disability that we are not

---

[1] Even as sense (see pp. 197-9). *Omnium gatherum,* or composite photograph aggregates of possibilities are usual. A certain appearance of stability attaches to vaguenesses (—IV, —VI, —VIa). At the other extreme, no meaning is so definite (IV) that it may not have possible differentiations within it. We most easily think of meaning as though it were a stuff; but a better model for it is a system of variables. All our workaday notions about discrete things mislead us in analysis.

neutral in our readings of ABC and APQ. If we are inclined to agree with *abc* we shall have made (*a*) such a component meaning as helps to make *abc* acceptable. Similarly with the converse case.

An effort of the imagination is required in realizing how complex these processes may be that we so often perform with such amazing ease. If I add here, in passing, a more elaborate symbolism, it may be to some a hindrance rather than a help, but they can overlook it!

$$\left(\frac{a^1}{a^2 a^3 \ldots}\right)\left(\frac{b^1}{b^2 b^3 \ldots}\right)\left(\frac{c^1}{c^2 c^3 \ldots}\right)\left(\frac{a^p}{a^4 a^5 \ldots}\right)\left(\frac{p^p}{p^4 p^5 \ldots}\right)\left(\frac{q^p}{q^4 q^5 \ldots}\right)$$

In the original formation of *abc* there will have been an encouragement of $a^1 \ b^1 \ c^1$ and a discouragement of $a^2 \ a^3 \ldots b^2 \ b^3 \ldots c^2 \ c^3 \ldots$ in virtue of consiliences between $a^1 \ b^1$ and $c^1$ (in view of the whole setting) which exceed consiliences within any other set. But when we compare it with *apq* this distribution of consiliences is likely to be changed. To keep it steady and constant, while *abc* is being tried out with *apq,* is what is called the effort of thought. The difficulty, practically, is increased by the fact that as (*a*) goes over into *apq* there are likely to be changes not only in (*a*) but in *b* and *c*.

Compare Campbell's 'Grammar is a collection, etc.,' with J. S. Mill's 'Grammar is the beginning of the analysis of the thinking process,' or with Sweet's 'Grammar is a commentary on the facts of Language,' or with 'Grammar is that stuff I used to do at School,' or with 'Grammar is the study of the co-operations of words in their contexts.'

It is in this intricate situation that the division between definition and statement has to be effected. As we isolate an (*a*) there are two possibilities: (1) that (*a*) is a different sense from (*bc*) and (2) that (*a*) and (*bc*) are the same. This second is the dangerous, but, for argument, indispensable special case, where (*a*) takes all its sense from, and so duplicates (*bc*). Then (*a*) = (*bc*). That is definition. When we write it we sometimes put: 'A'BC, for clarity; or sometimes, still more warily: 'A' means what is meant by 'BC.' But usually we give no warning that the whole structure of the sentence has been thus specialized. We leave it to the reader (or ourselves later) to pick up from the other sentences what has happened. In speech, some stress on *is* may mark it; but this has other uses, may be merely emphatic or carry complex gestures having nothing to do with definition. So, too, with underlining and italics and quotation marks. Only the context can tell us, if anything can, that this identification of the meanings of a part of the sentence and of the rest of it has occurred.

The value of a definition depends upon its observance. We need not *notice* it explicitly, obedience is the important thing. I shall argue later in the Logic Section that definitions are essentially requests or commands, not statements. Statements 'that such and such a request has been made' may be derived from them and are easily mistaken for them (see p. 392 below). But that point is not important here. What matters here is the frequency, even at places of the utmost strategic consequence in all linguistic study (at these places perhaps most of all), of momentary identifications which are then dropped without the dropping being noticed. A sense of security, of 'all-rightness,' remains, though what it is sanctioning may be, in fact, all wrong. The feeling, 'That's, of course, so!' is instigated by a momentary identification: $a_1 = b_1 c_1$—'that's what we are talking about, just that'—and then $a$ in the following sentences fluctuates into $a_2$ $a_3$ . . . without our having the least suspicion that we are now talking about quite different things. Or if we do have doubts, the feeling, 'But that is what we mean by "——," just that!' is reinstated by recurring to the setting in which the identification is made; and we do not notice that in this recurrence we have shifted back *again* the roving $a$ $b$ $c$'s.

Thought struggles endlessly against these treacheries in all fields; but there are certain accursed, spell-ridden subjects in which they are especially deceiving. They are those in which the fluctuations of $a$ are duplicated or parallelled by the fluctuations of $b$ and $c$. Chief among them is the subject haunted by the Doctrine of Usage. Not only 'usage' itself—along with 'grammar'—but most of the terms by which either may be defined fluctuate together systematically. Among these are:—'correct,' 'good,' 'proper,' 'appropriate,' 'accurate,' 'exact,' 'precise,' 'expressive,' 'true,' 'real,' 'application'; and more will turn up under the pen point in any discussion of these things. All this makes a truly formidable matrix of misunderstandings. If we consider the central position of this subject, the importance of tackling it more thoroughly than has yet been attempted will not need urging.

# Chapter Sixteen: The Teaching of the Doctrine

*He told me that facts gave birth to, and were the absolute
ground of principles; to which I said, that unless he had
a principle of selection, he would not have taken notice of
those facts upon which he grounded his principle. You
must have a lantern in your hand to give light, otherwise
all the materials in the world are useless, for you cannot
find them; and if you could, you could not arrange them.
'But then,' said Mr——, 'that principle of selection came from
facts!'—'To be sure!' I replied; 'but there must have been
again an antecedent light to see those antecedent facts.
The relapse may be carried in imagination backwards for
ever,—but go back as far as you may, you cannot come to
a man without a previous aim or principle.'*

COLERIDGE, *Table Talk*, Sept. 21, 1830

In the discussion of many topics, the question should arise early:
On what scale, with what mesh, are the distinctions used being
made? Is a bird's-eye view or a microphotograph being taken? Are
the ideas in conflict of the same order and such as might serve the
same purpose? Or are they, perhaps, as different as *time* for a
farmer and for an astronomer; *speed* for an ant, an airman and a
planet; or *energy* for an electron and a lump of coal? Ideally, this
question should be settled before the controversy opens. Many needless quarrels would be avoided if it were; but the disparity in scale,
and the diversity of purpose which has produced it, are, as a rule,
revealed only in the last round of the fight. To make them evident
may be the sole useful outcome.

The reader may well have felt, throughout my dealings with
Campbell, that I was not discussing the view that he put forward;
that I was going over the canvas with a microscope and naturally
missing the perspective. In such a case interest shifts to a comparison
of the scales and the aims behind them. And, since to exercise the

faculty by which a man may disperse and dilate the view of his mind as well as contract it is a teacher's business, some pains in studying this general mode of misunderstanding further may be justified. The usage controversy can be made to yield insight into a type of interpretative situations. Only by so doing can its full instructive possibilities be realized.

I propose therefore to take up a modern exposition of the doctrine and treat it controversially as a means of contrasting the aims and resultant ideas which composed it with those that animate and implement the attack I make upon it. I hope thereby to illustrate a type of cross-purposed disputes. The type is that which arises when a traditional, macroscopic or distant treatment is challenged by the elaborated distinctions of a relatively microscopic analytic study. Another specimen would be the misunderstanding between technical psychology and common knowledge of human nature.

I take my text from the *Manual of Composition and Rhetoric* by J. H. Gardiner, G. L. Kittredge and S. L. Arnold, a book fairly representative of the main tradition in school and college teaching. The authority of Mr Kittredge's name is an additional reason for choosing it rather than another. No one, I hope, will suspect me of any failure to appreciate Mr Kittredge's great services to scholarship, in other branches, because I attack somewhat vigorously some of its paragraphs.

The Chapter on Words, from which my citations come, begins by denying, and rightly, that there is any 'essential connection, in the nature of things, between the word and the object it signifies.' Instead:

> It is only the general agreement of those who speak and write the language that gives to the particular combination of sounds its definite meaning, or to the particular combination of marks its power to represent the sounds.

The admitted necessity for broad and simple treatment which the authors had in view—and the difficulty of combining this with the avoidance of misleading suggestions—should be fairly taken into account. To combine them is, indeed, the chief teaching problem. But already a high price is being paid for simplicity with: 'gives to the particular combination of sounds its definite meaning.' Whether the authors intended it or not, the assumption is conveyed that a word essentially has 'its definite meaning' on all occasions. *Macroscopically,* if we let 'its definite meaning' cover a wide range of different meanings—choice between which may entail all the differences between good and bad reading and writing—the statement may be true. But general agreement only limits the range of a word's meanings (microscopically taken). And it does not always do that, or the language would not have grown as it has; we are continually forcing new meanings with new settings. Technicalities apart, general agreement rarely fixes *one* definite (VI) meaning for a word. The assumption that it does is a distorting factor in composition and interpretation alike, and no exercises in either can be fruitful while it reigns. The parallel between the way a word is given its meaning and the way a group of letters is given 'its power to represent the sounds' is especially likely to be misleading. There *is* a fixed usage in spelling—by which a given assemblage of letters usually spells one word. (But note *letter, spell,* and *word,* and *note,* here!) There is no such fixed usage determining that a given word can only have just one meaning. The two sign situations are different in principle, and the interpretation procedures are vitally different. If we were thinking not of printed or clearly written words but of hurried scribbles—where mere squiggles occur that have to be filled in as words by reference to the rest of what we make out of the script—the parallel would be much closer. So too if we were thinking of slurred talk, distant shouting or defective telephones. There we do have to interpret—so far as recognizing the sounds as these words and no others—somewhat as we interpret words to reach meanings. But with fully spelt words a 'one-and-only-one-reading' rule holds. The suggestion that a similar rule holds with meaning nips budding intelligence as frost will 'the new morsels of spring.' We make it if we parallel 'correctness' as regards spelling and 'correctness' as regards meanings.

> If, therefore, we are to use words in such a way as will convey to other people our own thoughts and feelings, we must conform to that general *usage* which settles the force and meaning of every word in the language.

By amending this to 'conform to those very general modes of employing the language which settle the forces and meanings of each word in its varying settings,' I can repeat my point. The authors may have meant something like this and then I would agree; but they go on to write of usage in ways which make it certain that—whatever their intention—the effect will be to *teach* a much narrower and a misleading doctrine.

> *Usage governs language.* There is no other standard. By *usage*, however, is meant the *practice of the best writers and speakers*, not merely the habits of the community in which we chance to live.

Sherlock Holmes, on a famous occasion, drew Watson's attention to 'the singular behaviour of the dog in the night time.' 'Singular behaviour, Holmes?' returned Watson. 'The dog did nothing in the night time!' '*That* was the singular behaviour!' remarked Holmes. Here the dog in the night time is the word 'best' in 'the *practice of the best writers.*' It signally fails to bark, also with the word 'good' in 'good usage' and 'good writers' all through these pages. And the way in which the 'allrightness' of what is going on is quietly guaranteed by this inconspicuous, overlooked word, which is nowhere taken up for further discussion, is indeed most significant. For it plainly appears, if we stop to consider what is being said, that 'the practice of the best writers' would be a fraudulently circular and self-swallowing standard if we had no measure, independent of usage, for *best*. Usage, by itself, will not tell us *which* the best writers or the good writers are. And if we slip 'best' into our definition of usage, without discussing it, as my three authors do here, then we are begging the very question we pretend we are dealing with.

That is the controversial retort. It shows, I think, that two very different questions are under discussion, and that 'standard' (like 'governs,' 'regulates,' 'controls,' and the rest) has two senses here: 1. A set of models of linguistic conduct (which will not mislead if we take it to represent a level of discrimination, coherence and efficiency we should aim at). 2. The criteria of that efficiency itself, the features which settle which the best writers are. I am not, of course, in making this distinction, for an instant denying that conformity has its important place. Since language is an instrument of communication, conformity (in a wide sense), and even, in certain limited respects, strict conformity, is among the many determinants of good use, taken here as successful or efficient use. 'Conformity' is evidently ambiguous. It may mean (1) mere simi-

larity to other utterances *taken as end-products:* the mere occurrence of a word or phrase as elsewhere. Or it may mean (2) similarity in the process by which the utterance comes into being. And
this is the only important sort of conformity here. For it guaran-
tees the only conformities of type (1) which matter—while avoiding 'the letter that killeth' and that manipulation of dead simulacra
which is beamed on by an eye looking for conformity of products.
In (2) we conform by following similar general laws as users of
English—not by employing, as discrete items, certain uses. (As a
child learns to run: he doesn't employ certain steps to do so;
when he can run, the steps are the outcome.) And these general
laws provide the standards which make some authors better than
others. The authors don't provide the standards, they exemplify
them. There are general laws not unlike those of dietetics behind
all better and worse in usage and only so far as an author exemplifies them is he good.

This zealous harnessing of the carts before the horses appears as
a rearguard antic in innumerable subjects. Compare 'engineering
practice' or 'proper treatment' in medicine. The engineering practice is not good because so many designers follow it. It is good,
when it is, because physics is behind it and it may always, with
a development of physics, be improved. So too 'proper medical
treatment' is not 'proper' because so many doctors give it; but for
reasons that ultimately have biologic laws behind them. Doubtless
in both fields—as certainly in language—there are many things
done because collective experience has shown them to be prudent
without anyone being able to show yet just why they are advisable. So current practice, current recommended treatment and current linguistic usage serve as convenient standards applicable even
when we cannot see why they should work. Their sanction is their
success in working, and that does not come from their currency but
from reasons which explain why they *are* current. Compare the in-
verse transposition in the argument about expressive words and
imitation in Chapter XIV.

All this is likely to occur more or less explicitly to any reflective
student. The statement *'Usage governs language.* There is no other
standard,' has, however, an air of authority; time rarely allows
such a doctrine to be examined; it takes its place among the many
that a clear receptive mind feels at first must be somehow wrong;

incessant repetition makes natural even what is incredible, and so an active preventative assumption is implanted at the very centre where it can do most harm.

The authors then give some assorted reasons for following usage:

> *Conformity to good usage* is not an arbitrary law . . . only by following it can we make sure that the reader will gather from our words the thoughts that we intend them to convey.

This is the efficiency principle, but when we introduce a new word, or specialize an old word with a definition, we are departing from usage for this very reason.

> Moreover disregard of good usage will expose us to the suspicion of illiteracy.

This is snob-appeal.

> Finally, English is what is called a *literary language*. It is not only *our* language that we speak; it is the language of Shakespeare and Milton . . . we should not use it unworthily.

They then, following Campbell and others, add the qualifications to usage; it must be

> of *our own time*. We cannot justify a violation of *modern usage* by quoting Shakespeare.

The problem raised by the two references to 'the language of Shakespeare and Milton' on the same page is not difficult to clear up, but it is the kind of thing that hurts the learner's mind, if it is not cleared up. (See 4.15 and 4.31.)

> One further caution is necessary. No writer, however eminent, is free from faults. . . . Besides, a great author may take liberties with his mother tongue which we cannot venture to imitate. The mere fact that a word or meaning occurs in one or two good writers is not enough to justify us in adopting it. The usage which we follow should be *general*, not peculiar.

My points here are: (1) 'Take liberties' is a viciously mystifying phrase. If the great author is justified we should see that his justification is in the special circumstances, and recognize that if we do otherwise that is because our purpose and circumstances are otherwise. (2) 'A word or meaning occurs': the all important thing is *how* it occurs. The writers very often may be the only people who happened to have just that to say. The externality of the fashion in which words are here supposed to be 'adopted'—like adopting somebody's fancy in hats—is what is misleading. (3) *'General, not peculiar'*: does this mean used by many or only by certain people; used for many different sorts of occasions, or only in very special settings; used so frequently that no one is surprised by it, or, though efficient, yet unusual enough to attract attention? These, and other contrasts, are relevant; and 'general' and 'peculiar' employed in this way blur them.

I now pass on to the authors' GENERAL PRINCIPLES OF CHOICE

> Within the limits of good usage, and in every case controlled by it, there are four great principles which should guide us in the choice of words,—*correctness, precision, appropriateness,* and *expressiveness.*

These four great general principles of choice, so far from operating only 'within the limits of good usage' and being 'in every case controlled by it' are, with some others, the principles which themselves determine what usages are good. If we understand them, the desirability of conformity is thereby explained, and we can only follow usage intelligently if we can see why it should be followed. Let us see how our authors expound them:

> *Correctness* is the most elementary of all requirements. The meanings of words are settled by *usage.* If we use a word incorrectly,—that is, in a sense which does not customarily belong to it,—our readers will miss our thought, or, at best, they must arrive at it by inference or guesswork.
>
> In the second place, we must fit our words as exactly and *precisely* as possible to the thoughts which we wish to express. We may write correctly enough and still, by neglecting *precision,* so blur or obscure our meaning by vague or ambiguous language as to leave the reader with a very indistinct impression of the thought that we wish to convey.
>
> In the third place our words must be *appropriate to the subject and occasion.* Otherwise, no matter how correct they are, or how precisely we fit them to our meaning, they will fail to produce the effect that we intend.

At the macroscopic common-sense level these remarks will seem harmless and obvious enough—until we try to gather from them notions of correctness, precision and appropriateness that might be helpful to some reader or writer in his management of words. We find then that the different principles are being presented with so little precision, and are so crossed with one another, that a reading which is not highly critical will result in a confirmed muddle only. In the second paragraph, 'We may write correctly enough . . . wish to convey' suggests that 'correctness,' as the authors are using it, has nothing *necessarily* to do with the efficiency of language; yet the argument they have just given for correctness is that without it 'our readers will miss our thought.' Again, 'the subject and occasion' are brought in as though relevant only to appropriateness. It is not hard to see what they are doing, if we *already* have a fairly clear view of the whole intricate business they are describing. But they are not writing for such readers. As an introduction, it fails through using accidental, non-essential, possible consequences as indications to *correctness* and *precision;* and for *appropriateness* only something so general that it must be assumed for the other principles already. They cannot suppose that either their correctness or their precision are attainable without reference to the subject and occasion. Once again, the controversial reply brings out the systematic ambiguity of the three lock words. Our sentences may be perfectly correct English and yet be unintelligible; precise and yet most confusing; or appropriate *because* slovenly and vague.

Finally, our words must be expressive. They may be correctly used, they may set forth our meaning precisely, they may be appropriate to the occasion; and yet, after all, they may be so dull and lifeless as to leave the reader uninterested and unmoved. If words are really to serve our purpose, they must express the color and vividness of our feelings about the subject that we are treating.

All true enough after obvious qualifications: and yet—what a needless and confusing overlap with *appropriateness!* If appropriate words 'produce the effect that we intend' won't they have 'expressed the color and vividness of our feelings'? They will, of course, if *that* was part of the effect we did intend. But we do not always intend this; and often, in letter writing, for example, must not let our feelings appear. Even in essay writing, the prescription that 'if words are really to serve our purpose, they must etc.,' is an arbitrary over-statement that will make the reader we most want to help go numb with inhibitions.

I am afraid that I shall seem niggling in these comments. But if by talking about these things we are to help anyone, we must deal honestly by them. In discussing the principles of the choice of words we must exemplify method ourselves. In showing the novice over the ship we must not make a hurrah's nest of the ropes, or he may conclude that we have nothing to teach him that is worth his attention.

In several places the authors show that by 'correctness' they *there* mean 'not mistaking one word for another, not committing Mrs Malaprop's error.'

> In studying the four great principles of choice, we observe that only the first involves the question of right and wrong . . . it is only in dealing with the first principle that we can keep our attention entirely on the single word. . . . Clearly, then, correctness stands on a different footing from the other three principles of choice.

We are incorrect when we put *sediment* for *sentiment,* as we are incorrect when we take another man's umbrella for our own, or ring the wrong number on the telephone. But with the 'right' and 'wrong' of telephone numbers, at least, no one is in danger of supposing that moral disapprobation comes in with the words. In this context we are not so clear of risk. Indeed it is not the least of the objections to this common way of talking that something very like guilt or suggestion of shameful illiteracy—is so readily implied in these cases. A suggestion any good teacher will do his best to avoid.

Strict malapropisms—where two words with distinct and separate ranges of uses are confused—are not of much importance, except as an indication that a vocabulary has been too rapidly extended or acquired by the casual processes that the usage doctrine, I fear, encourages. They are a symptom of an external interest in words, a disease best treated not by such warnings, but by encouraging a more intimate curiosity about them.

The other sort of 'incorrectness' (the authors' concept is more negative than positive) is use 'in a sense which does not customarily belong to it.' This covers indiscriminately a variety of ill-advised uses which differ immensely in the nature and the seriousness of the mistake made. The case where the other words in the setting show plainly what the novel sense must be is hardly a mistake at all. If the readers 'must arrive at it by inference' that will often do them no harm; it may even be a useful device for making them consider more closely what is being said. The opposite cases, in which the reader may be led to think the writer is saying something he did not intend, will be more or less serious according to the context. The between cases, where we detect that a writer is making some unfamiliar use of a word without being able to decide what it is, do at least sometimes reveal interesting features of his thought. From the writer's point of view to discover that one is specializing a word out of the normal range of its meanings is frequently a stimulating experience. Its value is destroyed if we are then summarily informed that we are talking incorrectly. Many of our most important words are always shifting their senses for us with the development of our thought.

The authors go on to contrast *specific terms* (bread, chair, awkward, quick, bark, jump, telephone) with *general terms* (science, intellect, revolution, literature, temperance, affectation, propriety).

> These differ from the specific words in being far less definitely limited in their application. Indeed the varieties of meaning that each of them covers are so great that every speaker may almost be said to use them in a somewhat different sense.

This would be a welcome expansion of thought if considerations as to settings were not still being so neglected. The example which follows shows the danger. 'Book' is declared to be specific, as opposed to 'literature,' which is general. But where 'book' *is* specific, that is thanks to a setting. Actually (in England certainly and I believe in America too) magazines and weeklies are called 'books' by a majority of speakers, and we all know plenty of specializations: 'It's a formidable volume, but not a *book!*' 'He has his mind full of his book,' 'Writing a book,' 'Printing a book,' 'Rearranging the books in the catalog.' All these are different senses of 'book.' We fail to confuse them because the settings are easy to take account of; not because the word in itself is specific. That explains why there is, as the authors say: 'no danger of our misunderstanding the word or misusing it.' They continue:

'Literature' on the contrary, is an elastic term. Its meaning varies with the person and the circumstances . . . (Of a list they insert) all are *books,* nobody can dispute that; (they have provided the setting!) but how many of them belong to *literature?* To this question a hundred different persons might give a hundred different answers.

Entirely so! But since this is an admirable example of one of the cases which give most trouble to inexperienced writers and readers—the case where value implications are being introduced, consciously or inadvertently, into a description—surely here, in a *Rhetoric,* some notice of it is called for? (See below, Chapter XXII, p. 366.) The authors treat it as though it parallelled with a mere case of multiplicity of objective classifications—What do we include among snails, among fish, among houses? Is a caravan a house? and does it become one when we take its wheels off? and so on. But it is not like these; it is like the problem of the range of 'beautiful.' They go on:

> Consider how men's opinions differ as to the *honesty* of a particular transaction, the *propriety* of this or that line of conduct, the *wit* or *wisdom* of some remark that they hear or read. Half our lives is spent in balancing and discussing the applicability of such general terms to specific acts or objects.

Indeed it is; and by all means let us really consider how men's opinions differ! But not by deliberately confusing at the outset differences of valuation, differences between the characters selected for contemplation in the objects, and differences of the meanings of the terms with which we compare them. Men's opinions of a particular transaction may differ while their use of *honesty* remains the same. They may agree, though their uses of *honesty* are different. The particular transaction is, for such judgments, as it is taken by the judge to be; it has countless aspects. To blur these problems into the relatively simple one of the range of the senses of *honesty* is the best possible way of defeating any approach except that of the most intelligent; and to present the whole muddle as though it were a contrast between *specific* and *general* terms, is a procedure which could hardly be improved upon if it were expressly designed to confuse.

Perhaps the most complete surrender to the usage doctrine and one of the most striking indications of its obstructive influence in the *Manual* comes in the NOTE which closes the discussion of correctness.

> The distinction between *specific* and *general* words should not be pushed too far. A word like *man* is specific as compared with *animal*, but general as compared with a proper noun like *Washington*. The ordinary rhetorical sense of *specific* and *general* is far less exact than the logical or philosophical use. In rhetoric, *specific* is almost synonymous with *concrete*, and *general* or *collective* often nearly coterminous with *abstract*. In like manner, we must not insist too strictly on the technical meanings of words drawn from the sciences. Such a word, as we have seen, often establishes itself in good usage in a new or more extended signification.

Yes, but *specific* and *general, concrete, abstract, collective* and other 'terms of art' are not borrowings from another subject, technicalities of a science. They are the very instruments of the comparative study of words. What could have been the Doctors' notion of Rhetoric when they expressed themselves in this manner? Whyever should we employ the 'ordinary rhetorical sense' which is 'far less exact' than the logical? Is it merely because so many writers on rhetoric have been lazy, ignorant and muddled, and by slovenly use have given *general* and *specific* a degraded sense? Must we therefore follow a *good usage* which defeats all the reasonable purposes we require the words for? It is as though they said, 'Don't push too hard on your scalpel, its edge will buckle, twist and divide agley. The ordinary dissecting scalpels we issue don't cut true; but that is right because it is the tradition to have them so in our school. There are fine reliable scalpels, of course, next door, but it's not the custom to use them in our operating theatres!' Actually they do say on the opposite page and on this very point of technical language, 'Here, as everywhere else, there is no standard but good usage.' How that poor little word 'good' has been gagged and muzzled!

Such procedures overlook all the most important distinctions in the subject—whether a fact is being stated or a value proposed, for example; or whether a multiplicity of different specializations, or generality comprising a varied extension, is the source of a possible misinterpretation. The last is a topic for the Logic Section—where *general* and *specific* need thorough discussion. The other should be a main branch of rhetoric—a comparison of the behaviour of *beautiful* and *blue* would illustrate it.[1] But neither can be reasonably treated while this typical lexical hocus pocus goes unchallenged. There is a vast physiology of the language uses waiting to be explored when the usage doctrine has been cleared out of the way. With it, our authors can only say:

> Obviously, then, there is ample opportunity for error in the use of general words, since it is so difficult to fix the bounds of their correct use.

There are no such bounds: they have variable powers instead which derive from the occasion.

> Such error may consist either in stretching their sense beyond what good usage has prescribed, or in limiting it too rigidly in accordance with some prejudice or pedantic whim.

There can be no prescription apart from a purpose and a pedantic whim is just an irrelevant purpose.

> Attention, clear thinking, and a knowledge of good literature, are requisite if we are to avoid the pitfalls that beset the use of general terms. Such terms are necessary in the expression of thought. *Inaccuracy in their employment, however, is fatal to perspicuity, and debilitating to the mind.*

It is worse than that, for it can prevent the growth of the mind. The most important of general terms are those with which we attempt to keep other words in order, and accuracy in their employment (as we saw with 'definite') is not submission to accepted practice.

But to all this my authors may reply, validly and effectively, 'We were not discussing that sort of thing. We were writing about the choice of words. You are mixing that matter with questions about the determination of thought.' That is true. The two positions differ in their conceptions of the relation of thought to language. The usage view goes best with the assumption that fully formed thought seeks words with which to utter itself, and that the attention and clear thinking which are requisite are concerned

---

[1] See *Practical Criticism*, Part III, Chapter III, and especially Appendix A, 3; and below, Chapter XXII.

with distinguishing which thought we have and with picking the right word for it. The attacking view holds that most thought forms itself in and through experiments with the language that is to utter it, and that a step between the choice of a word and the shaping of a thought is not easily marked—though this is not at all to say that they are the same. Minds may quite possibly differ in the degree to which either account of our dealings with words applies to them; everyone must decide for himself which best accords with what he does. But even those who most make up their minds before they seek for words, will best find them if they consider what this or that word will do rather than whether it conforms to usage.

Whenever we find a doctrine (or a sense for a word, when a word is a compacted doctrine) showing through centuries an extreme vitality in spite of what seem solid and obvious objections to it, it is well to ask, 'What other possible senses of the word (possible doctrines on the matter) may there be *from which* this objectionable sense or doctrine is an attempted escape?' Bad though it be, is it possibly a flight from and a defence against something still worse? If we ask this of the usage doctrine and of its sense of 'correct,' we get an answer at once. Its upholders are defending themselves against a far sillier and perhaps more disabling doctrine. The doctrine, namely, of the Divine Right of Names. That doctrine is that a meaning belongs to a word as a kingdom belongs to an absolute monarch, or as a soul belongs to a body (see Ben Jonson, p. 183 above). In the dawn of Western Grammatical study, in the first Alexandrian schools of grammar, the division had arisen, to be reflected, perhaps, in the controversy over interpretation between the analogists and the anomalists. There were those who held that words meant what they mean in virtue of mysterious analogies, amounting to a strict correspondence, between words and things, or words and meanings. And there were those who held that words took their meanings from the will of their users, and that there is no natural connection between sounds and senses. Now the analogy view, if we take account of its influence through Word Magic upon thought in general (see *The Meaning of Meaning*, Chapter II) is perhaps a deadlier mistake than the usage view.

And there can be little doubt that the strength of the usage view has come to it from resistance to the Divine Right Doctrines. The Chapter of the *Manual* I have been criticizing opened, it will be recalled, with the remark that 'There is no essential connection, in the nature of things, between the word and the object it signifies,' and Mr Kittredge, in his *Some Landmarks in the History of English Grammars,* writes as follows:

'Ben Jonson's posthumous "English Grammar" came out in 1640. The title page declares that it is "made . . . out of his observation of the English language now spoken and in use," and contains also a golden utterance of Quintilian calling *custom* "the surest mistress of speech" and making an apt comparison between current language and current coin. The lesson of this passage seems very hard to learn. Scholars have always consistently averred that good usage is the only conceivable criterion of good English, but most people still clamor for a heaven-sent "standard" to measure their words by.'

Just what scholars have consistently averred in this matter may be difficult to determine; but that a reaction to the popular clamour for a heaven-sent standard has been influential with them cannot be doubted. The usage doctrine comes forward as 'the only conceivable criterion' to replace these popular conceivings, as the only thing that will do the work that the soul-body, king-kingdom analogies were supposed to do: namely, *rule language.* As so often happens, however, when one form of government replaces another, changes of titles are more noticeable than changes in acts. The usage doctrine took over and perpetuated just those inadequacies that are the real ground for objecting to Rule by Divine Right. It retained the secret police, the mysterious, not-accountable type of control. What was wrong with a heaven-sent standard was not that it came from heaven but that it was unquestionable; and it is just this 'It is so and that's that!' imposition which we have to sweep out of the way. Custom is no criterion at all—unless it is the best custom—and we can tell which is the best custom, when we meet it or hit on it, only by using a standard with which custom has nothing *directly* to do, a standard that is not heaven-sent (unless γνῶθι σεαυτὸν be heaven-sent) but resides in us, as the active principle of communication, and is manifested in our developed skill with words.

This, it will be seen, is no charter of ungovernable liberties. Like other freedoms it requires submission to a government—but a more delicate as well as a stricter government that *can* control—as the old theory of correctness, could not. Instead of obeying imaginary correct uses and pinning our prospects to such clouds, we must, if we are to understand and be understood, respect the conditions of speech, respond to the contexts and so contrive them that they work for others as well as for ourselves.

Even as mere languages, no modern European language is so valuable a discipline to the intellect as those of Greece and Rome, on account of their regular and complicated structure. Consider for a moment what grammar is. It is the most elementary part of logic. It is the beginning of the analysis of the thinking process. The principles and rules of grammar are the means by which the forms of language are made to correspond with the universal forms of thought. The distinctions between the various parts of speech, between the cases of nouns, the moods and tenses of verbs, the functions of particles, are distinctions in thought, not merely in words. Single nouns and verbs express objects and events, many of which can be cognized by the senses: but the modes of putting nouns and verbs together, express the relations of objects and events, which can be cognized only by the intellect; and each different mode corresponds to a different relation. The structure of every sentence is a lesson in logic. The various rules of syntax oblige us to distinguish between the subject and predicate of a proposition; between the agent, the action, and the thing acted upon; to mark when an idea is intended to modify or qualify, or merely to unite with, some other idea; what assertions are categorical, what only conditional; whether the intention is to express similarity or contrast, to make a plurality of assertions conjunctively or disjunctively; what portions of a sentence, though grammatically complete within themselves, are mere members or subordinate parts of the assertion made by the entire sentence. Such things form the subject-matter of universal grammar; and the languages which teach it best are those which have the most definite rules, and which provide distinct forms for the greatest number of distinctions in thought, so that if we fail to attend precisely and accurately to any of these, we cannot avoid committing a solecism in language. In these qualities the classical languages have an incomparable superiority over every modern language, and over all languages, dead or living, which have a literature worth being generally studied.

J. S. MILL, *Inaugural Lecture at St Andrews*

# Chapter Seventeen: Grammar and Logic

> *Young men, young boys, beware of Schoolmasters,*
> *They will infect you, marre you, bleare your eyes:*
> *They seek to lay the curse of God on you,*
> *Namely confusion of languages,*
> *Wherewith those that the towre of Babel built*
> *Accursed were in the worldes infancie.*
> *Latin, it was the speech of Infidels.*
> *Logique, hath nought to say in a true cause.*
> *Philosophie is curiositie:*
> *And Socrates was therefore put to death,*
> *Only for he was a Philosopher:*
> *Abhore, contemne, despise, these damned snares.*
>
> NASH, *Summer's Last Will and Testament*

After all this I discussed the paragraph, from John Stuart Mill's astonishing three-hour *Inaugural Lecture* at St Andrews, reproduced on the opposite page. It would, I hoped, illustrate memorably the conception of Grammar against which the Usage Doctrine is a reaction. By discussing it I might also clear the view I wish to recommend from confusion with unacceptable views that at first sight seem like it, views that historically have often taken its place. I hoped, further, to use the passage to show again how much the merging of the different purposes of language study, which use the term 'grammar' in common, can be frustrating even with so acute a thinker as Mill. Moreover, some of its sentences offered opportunities for exhibiting general principles of interpretation, and the whole thing would serve as a transition from the problems of Grammar to those of Logic and be an occasion for warnings against a very common type of mistake about their relations.

I will begin with some details. The first sentence is an illustration of the control of the setting over interpretation. How do we know that Mill means that it is Greek and Latin which have a 'regular and complicated structure'? When I quoted the sentence, by itself, in *Basic in Teaching* the printer's reader (an intelligent and very careful man) queried 'regular'; should it not be 'irregular'? He may, of course, have been merely applying his own ideas about how regular Greek and Latin really are; but I think he was trying to guess at Mill's argument. How do we know what 'their' refers to? If we wrote 'their irregular and over-simple structure' the sentence would in several minor ways not mean the same, but most of Mill's main point would be preserved—only 'their' would have been switched over then to modern European languages, not to Greek and Latin. And equally it would be the context which told us how to read it. The pedants with whom we began this Part could doubtless complain of the sentence as faulty in form, and ask us to rewrite it:

> Even as mere languages, those of Greece and Rome, on account of their regular and complicated structure, are a better discipline to the intellect than any modern European language.

That would certainly throw less responsibility on the setting, but it would alter Mill's emphasis. With the setting he is not likely to be misread, for we know that Greek and Latin will be thought to be more regular and complicated than modern languages—whatever the facts in the matter, and the assumptions, as to the sorts of regularity and complication involved may be. Moreover, 'regular,' at least, in such an occurrence as this, seems a word of praise and so goes with 'valuable.' This joins with the setting to bar out the possibility that Mill (as others have sometimes thought) was thinking that the less regular a language the harder the task of learning it and therefore the better the discipline. There is an articulation between 'regular' and 'complicated,' which was lost by my rephrasing, 'their irregular and over-simple structure.' Mill's full point is 'though complicated yet regular.' And this articulation shows us that Mill is thinking of a certain sort of discipline which he expects from Greek and Latin.

This kind of analysis of the factors in interpretation can I believe usefully take the place of formal grammatical parsing. Parsing gave exercise in it incidentally, and had value as far as it did; but, in itself, it is an unnatural and distracting antic. This other sort of interpretative study follows closely the actual processes that take place in composition; parsing does not. No one asks, or should ask, himself in writing, 'What does this dependent phrase qualify?' We do all inquire, all the time we are writing, about the consiliences and the articulations of the meanings of the parts with one another; or, if we don't, we can very easily be made to.

All ordering of discourse derives from ordering of meanings. Those who are chiefly interested in the formal description of language, in *linguistic,* taken narrowly, tend to forget this. A distrust of meanings as 'things we cannot define'—which neglects the fact that in an obvious sense all use of language does nothing else— often appears nowadays in language-studies that take their assumptions uncritically from Behaviourism. A fear of complexities even greater than those of formal analysis drives some whose formal treatment goes much further in helpful directions than the school grammars have taken note of, to avoid explicit discussion of meanings where they can. I am thinking especially of Bloomfield here. Such work could help immensely in destroying the ridiculous philosophic blunderings of the school definitions and in putting the whole treatment of the analysis of language-uses on a better basis. It would be a pity if a misunderstanding about 'mentalistic' views of meaning prevented it from joining in the task of improving interpretation.

Mill goes on to tell us what sort of discipline Greek and Latin give us. He asks us to consider what grammar is, and his next two sentences look like statements. After the discussion of Campbell, we shall be nervous about accepting them as such. If we consider them as carefully as we should, we shall find ourselves asking, What can Mill be meaning here by 'grammar,' by 'logic,' by 'elementary' and by 'the analysis of the thinking process.' Our main guide in answering these questions is the rest of the paragraph. I need not insist that any profit whatever that study of his paragraph can yield will derive from an increased clarity as to the possible answers to these questions. They are not necessarily those that Mill would give.

(1) 'Grammar.' The rest of the paragraph shows that Mill means by this—'study of the distinctions between the parts of speech and study of the rules of syntax.' But what sort of study? A study in which the aims distinguished above as 1 and 4 (see p. 189) are miraculously combined. Mill is supposing that the traditional gram-

matical apparatus of the parts of speech and so on can be used, simultaneously and unchanged, as an instrument through which to examine the logical form of the thought the language is expressing. Countless others have supposed so too, but no one who succeeds in separating the two aims can fail to discover that they will not agree. The valid teaching purpose of the traditional account requires us to take, *as the same syntactically,* constructions which express thoughts of very *different* form. It is not true that the rules of syntax of any language correspond to the forms of thought in the way Mill pretends. The most obvious examples disprove it: 'I see a tiger' and 'I kick a tiger' are syntactically the same; the forms of the thoughts they express are extremely different. The sentences will follow one another through any *syntactic* manipulations we can give them: 'I am seeing a tiger.' 'A tiger is being seen by me' etc.; but if we start expanding one of them and giving it a more explicit statement, we find that the others will not translate the same way. They are not saying at all the same sort of thing. When I kick a tiger I do something to him, but not when I see him. The structure of every sentence is a lesson in logic, is it? It may be made into one, but the sentence does not give us one on its own account. We might get a final lesson in logic from the tiger, if we did not in practice know better than to trust sentence-forms this way. Good modern grammarians recognize this, of course, and have little mercy for the assumptions Mill is making. Jespersen, for example, writes:

> Relation of verb to subject and object. Here again some of the usual definitions do not hold water. The subject cannot be defined by means of such words as active and agent, for they do not cover such cases as 'He lost his father in the war' or 'he was surprised' or 'the garden swarms with bees' (otherwise expressed 'bees swarm in the garden'). Nor can the object be defined as the person or thing directly affected by the action, for in 'John loves Ann,' 'John sees the moon,' John is more directly affected than Ann or the moon. All this is a direct consequence of the many-sidedness of the relations that are found in human life and have to be expressed in human language.
>
> *The System of Grammar, 11*

If we needed support in accepting this, comparisons between languages would give it.

It is difficult to eradicate the belief that the forms in which we think are identical with the thought itself, and it is only linguistic science that enables us to see that many of the forms of grammar which we imagine necessary and universal are after all but accidental and restricted in use. The cases of Latin and Greek do not exist in the majority of languages; the Polynesian dialects have no true verbs; and the Eskimaux get on well enough without the 'parts of speech' that figure so largely in our own grammars. The distinction made by writers on logic between such words as 'redness' and 'red' is a distinction that would have been unintelligible to the Tasmanian; 'red' in fact, has no sense unless we supply 'colour,' and 'red colour' is really the same as 'redness.'

SAYCE, *Introduction to the Science of Language,* p. 328

But we need not go to vanished Tasmanians to learn how muddled Mill is about this. All our everyday experience with English depends upon our refusal to take syntax as Mill would have us take it. Syntax classifies the patterns in which we put our words together, not the forms in which we think. We use one word pattern with many different thought-forms; and, conversely, can put one thought form into many different word patterns.

> Socrates is wise
> Wisdom belongs to Socrates

are two different word patterns; the same form of thought might use either.

I shrink from labouring this point. ('It is laboured and therefore vague,' wrote one of my protocolists!) Everybody knows it perfectly well—until he begins to write about Grammar or Logic. More strictly, until he begins what is called 'analysis.' *Then* the danger of supposing that we are making 'the forms of language correspond with the forms of thought' becomes enormous, and persists in spite of the most arduous reflection. My example, 'Socrates is wise,' may remind us of the scope of the enticements which follow. Half the history of Western Philosophy turns upon supposing that 'Socrates' and 'wise,' since they behave differently in our word patterns, must have meanings of different orders, the one a particular, the other a universal. (See Part Three, Chapters XXI and XXII below.) The troubles, indeed, that Mill's mistake entails are so extensive and enduring that any efforts which might do anything to mitigate them, or reduce the probability of the mistake, would be justified.

(2) What does Mill here mean by 'logic'? His confusion between the forms of language and the forms of thought infects his use of 'logic' too. 'The distinctions between the various parts of speech . . .' and so on, that he is talking about, are, of course, sometimes used to mark distinctions of thought; but, often and rightly, are not. They do not mark them in themselves. By being a noun, not a verb, a word does not settle anything about what it stands for, or about the form of the thought which uses it. The pretence to the contrary that haunts traditional teaching is one of the greatest removable obstacles to intelligence. Our whole treatment of how words work is vitiated by it. As Bloomfield says:

> The school grammar tells us, for instance, that a noun is 'the name of a person, place, or thing. This definition presupposes more philosophical and scientific knowledge than the human race can command, and implies, further, that the form-classes of a language agree with the classifications that would be made by a philosopher or scientist. Is *fire,* for instance, a thing? For over a century physicists have believed it to be an action or process rather than a thing; under this view, the verb *burn* is more appropriate than the noun *fire.*
>
> *Language,* p. 266

He may be restricting the sense of *thing* a little arbitrarily here, as Jespersen did in the passage I cited early in this Part. But most school-grammars do so too, which justifies him and also explains Jespersen's odd observation. He goes on:

> Class-meanings, like all other meanings, elude the linguist's power of definition, and in general do not coincide with the meanings of strictly defined technical terms. To accept definitions of meaning, which at best are makeshifts, in place of an identification in formal terms, is to abandon scientific discourse.

This pours out the baby with the bath-water; calls for better bread than was ever baked from flour; closes the eye because vision is not complete. I do not think that a deeper inquiry into the conditions of 'scientific discourse,' or any other discourse, would let it pass. But the first point is obviously right and extremely important. Not so much, I would say, because to mix in crude class-meanings interferes with the establishment of 'identifications in formal terms,' however much that may be regretted, as because the translation of supposed class-meanings back into forms of thought is so disastrous. It produces a bastard logic which behaves with ordinary language as though the preparatory work on the structure of the thought that is to be manipulated had already been done. But ordinary language does not do this work. Mill, here, seems to be thinking that Latin could automatically guarantee the validity of the argument entrusted to it—as mathematics sometimes can. He has forgotten what ordinary language must be like when he writes, 'if we fail to attend precisely and accurately to any of these [distinctions in thought] we cannot avoid committing a solecism in language.' That is not true of any language that anyone has ever had the use of for ordinary affairs. No language ever has been, or ever, in all probability, will be, fitted with such vagary alarms! In all languages, sentences that are muddled in thought may be irreproachable in syntax, and, conversely, perfectly clear thought may be impossible syntax. We have only to write, 'The sky blues me,' as we write, 'The sun warms me,' to prove it. There is no difference in this between Latin and English or French. If Mill had tried to write his paragraph in Latin, would solecisms at every turn have revealed his inattention to the most important distinctions in the subject? 'Incomparable superiority,' whether as an English phrase or a Latin, rings no warning bell, for nobody takes it in the literal way that Mill's doctrine would require. His 'logic' here is just that miscegenation between language and thought which breeds most of our errors.

(3) But he says, 'The most elementary part of logic.' Could Mill turn on me with this qualification? Am I misrepresenting him? What does this 'elementary' mean? Perhaps, as in 'elementary' arithmetic, it means 'easy, suited to beginners.' Grammar has nearly always been supposed to be *that*. It might mean 'requiring only a slight study in order to be understood'; but the oldest hands at grammar do not pretend to have arrived there. It might mean, 'using only the simplest and most obvious logical distinctions'; but this sort of grammar uses and mixes the most complex and obscure of them. It might mean, 'at an early stage of development'; as in 'elementary organisms.' These distinctions that the grammatical forms seem to make may be this last, and Mill may be saying so.

(4) By calling grammar 'The beginning of the analysis of the thinking process' Mill may mean that (a) in the *individual's* reflection and/or (b) in the *history of the users of a language,* these distinctions represent first steps in the analysis of thought. If so, a very large question is raised. Possibly the comparative history of languages may have important things to tell us, after many days, about the early history of the development of thought. But thought, if we contrast this with grammatical theory, was never tied to linguistic categories. Its attempts to picture itself did not control it. But we have not to speculate further about that here; our business is with these grammatical forms as guides *in the individual's* first efforts to analyze the thinking process in himself, and, on that, it will be enough now to say that the sooner he dismisses these guides the better.

A further remark about 'analysis' may help to bring out the danger. There is a sense in which we are all, as owners of digestive systems, marvellously expert analytic organic chemists. So thought, in the practical handling of language, performs endless astonishing feats of analysis. But, as the laboratory chemist, until recently, would have made a very poor showing if he had to write out the chemical reactions which digestion effects, so the explicit analytic study of meanings lags sadly behind our skill. Traditional grammar has attempted to impose, on the working of language, some crude ('elementary'?) early theories. They do not apply, but in the absence of better information they have easily been made to seem applicable. Moreover the crude theories have great *philosophic* prestige, the result, so a cynic avers, of a very ancient bargain between grammar and logic to conceal one another's defects. Mill's doctrine here presents explicitly and theoretically what has been the practice, sometimes witting, often unwitting, of a majority of those who have thought about language ever since Plato's *Cratylus.* As being, for too many students of language, the only conceivable alternative to the Usage Doctrine, it is worth examining. But the right alternative is to discard both doctrines, study our skill more thoroughly and improve it by eliminating obstructions and providing more encouraging modes of exercise.

Mill is not alone in his conception of Latin and Greek as *the* logical languages—nor the last to be led astray by excessive veneration for the fashion in which he had happened to be taught himself. It will be only fair to append a passage from another distinguished teacher, who seems to be still more at sea about syntax.

> The position of the French and German people with regard to the mother tongue is very different educationally from the position of the English with regard to their mother tongue, for the simple reason that the English instinct for language is on the whole more slovenly, more slipshod, and less sensitive than in any other European country. English has divested itself of accidence, and has done the most that any language can to divest itself of syntax. Consequently, training in English is less effectual as an educational instrument than in French or German. The natural insensitiveness of the English mind to the graces and delicacies of language has been very largely redeemed and helped by the fidelity of the English to classical training. The greatness of our literature and poetry rests much on the fidelity of the English people to classical training in Latin and Greek, and it is an implement of education with which we can very little afford to dispense.
>
> DR RANDALL (Head Master of Charterhouse), *Journal of the Royal United Services Institution* for 1905, p. 655.

Comment is perhaps unnecessary: but 'divested itself of accidence' is hardly happy. If the writer is serious, he should not, for even a moment, be suggesting that accidence is like a dress. And the least acquaintance with the comparative study of languages—which, after all, is what he is talking about—would show that Chinese, for example, has very much less syntax than English. As for 'the natural insensitiveness of the English mind' and so on; that seems merely abuse. What sort of comparative observation could be supposed to attest it? If the Doctor's indignation is based on his own experience in the class-room, might it not equally be the teaching of English that is at fault? We may admit that we can very little afford to dispense with classical training if we do not develop English implements of education to take its place.

We have got to face the task of reconstructing our grammar because owing to the transformation which modern languages have undergone on the formal side, our grammatical categories no longer in any way correspond with the permanent logical categories, and now that formal distinctions are fast disappearing logical considerations are fast becoming all important in the analysis of our speech.

PROFESSOR ALLEN MAWER, 'The Problem of Grammar in the Light of Modern Linguistic Thought,' p. 12. *English Association Publications.*

With this (apart from 'no longer' perhaps) we are, and can feel that we are, in a new world.

But back to Mill. His sentence, 'The principles and rules of grammar are the means by which the forms of language are made to correspond with the universal forms of thought,' needs turning round to: 'The rules of grammar are the means by which grammarians have attempted to make the forms of thought correspond with the forms of language!' Modern philosophers, Wittgenstein and the Viennese School, the logical positivists, for example, taking a much deeper dive than Mill into the subject, are endeavouring with some success to reduce logic to the fundamental grammar of a perfect language. They too would say that the laws of thought are the rules of language, though they would not mean by this at all what Mill meant here.

'Rule,' of course, is the word most profitable to study. We have glanced above (pp. 229-232) at some of its ambiguities and noted the importance, for every branch of teaching, of clearing our ideas about rules as far as possible. The sense in which the laws of thought, the right working of intelligence, may profitably be regarded as the rules of an ideal language can be approached from all the main everyday uses of 'rule.' These are:

(1) A prescription or command issued by an authority. Extend this by admitting that we are all under the command of existence.

(2) An agreement, such as anyone joining a Club makes, to abide by certain understandings as to what shall and shall not be done. Joining the company of speakers of English, we will speak so. Extending it, joining the company of the sane, we will think so, and have our advantage in so doing.

(3) An observed uniformity, an empirical law of events, what is seen to happen—a segment of the operation of (1) as apprehended by us.

Taken superficially these seem very different and are the positions from which the traditional philosophies—Rationalism, Pragmatism and Empiricism—have battled with one another. Taken more deeply, it becomes very difficult to distinguish between them, especially if we do not forget, in considering them, to *ask* (we shall not answer it, for they are the attempted answers) how we come to consider them, what we are doing, or what is being done in us, when we consider. Taken so, we approach a sense for 'rule' which includes them all [1] and is that in which the necessities (as distinguished from the accidents) of language and the necessities of thought seem to be the same.

But this is a long way from Mill's paragraph, though not so far from some pages in his *Logic*. I put it in here because a feeling that there may be, in a deep sense, a real identity between the forms of thought and the forms of language, lends plausibility to a doctrine of correspondence between them that no modern grammarian has the least difficulty in utterly demolishing. The identity, though, would have to do with the grammar of an imaginary language which no one has ever written or talked. Some mathematical notations approximate to it. But the correspondence Mill is talking about has to do with the different tricks of different extant languages. It has to do with 'mine square tables is brown,' not with 'my round table is square.' The first breaks the Club Rules, the second may break the fundamental grammar which may be thought to be identical for language and for logic.

'Rules,' in addition to being a word of the shiftiest philosophic duplicity, has minor treacheries. Here is Mill on rules again, also from that hastily composed Inaugural Lecture.

> But in great things as well as in small, examples and models are not sufficient: we want rules as well. Familiarity with the correct use of a language in conversation and writing does not make rules of grammar unnecessary; nor does the amplest knowledge of the sciences of reasoning and experiment dispense with rules of logic. We may have heard correct reasonings and seen skilful experiments all our lives—we shall not learn by mere imitation to do the like, unless we pay careful attention to how it is done.

The last sentence has much to commend it; but 'pay careful attention to how it is done.' Is *that* what most things which school-

[1] Some further speculations along these lines will be found in the Appendix at pp. 407-11. *See also* the Motto to the Third Landing Stage.

masters call 'rules' make us do? On the contrary, the commonest function of a rule is to save us this trouble, it tells us what to do, not how or why to do it. And thus, as the history of grammar and logic in the schools displays *ad nauseam,* rules are the enemy of understanding. Learning the rules is the fatal course, if we do not, by some other means, also learn to look behind them to the reasons which make them useful.

# The Third Landing Stage

> *Everything, that is, implies everything else. But in judge-*
> *ment you fail to include the condition on which your idea*
> *is true of the Real. And you also fail to include the con-*
> *dition on which your judgement itself, as a fact, exists.*
> *And these two disabilities in the end are one.*
>
> F. H. BRADLEY, *Essays on Truth and Reality*

As all teachers know, the *actual* difficulty of a passage or exercise is extremely hard to estimate in any reliable fashion. 'Difficult?'
For whom, in what ways, for what causes, under what conditions
of time, of inducement, of preparation, and in comparison with
what? Still harder is the *appropriate* difficulty to estimate. Whether
lingering is profitable depends on what is being lingered over, and
that is harder to know than we sometimes suppose. Even instruc-
tors in physical exercises are often uncertain whether it would be
better, looking ahead, to polish easy tasks or open the first clumsy
essayals of new ones? And their problem is easier in that they can
see more clearly what is happening. Behind the frowns and sighs
of our pupils may be a real travail of spirit, or merely the boredom of blind routine, or, very likely, irrelevant gestures. Nor do
the scripts that result separate themselves, except here and there.
The absurd and muddled rigmarole may be much nearer the student's problem (at the stage it has reached in him) than the good
sensible second-class product which has come easily to its author.
And we are always guessing whether the problem ('and the use
of theorems,' said Hobbes, 'is for the construction of problems') is
behind a pupil or still ahead of him on his secret private course.

We know this well. The morals that I find in the discussions
of this Grammar Section are, first: that old one again, that the
pupil must herein be his own adviser. He can see, as we cannot,
where his doubts come from and where his efforts are aimed. But
sometimes we can help him in this, by helping him to see how
many more alternative modes of reasonable understanding are open
to him.

So the second moral is that very few tasks we can offer are actually, as they will work out in the minds of the class, nearly so

simple as we will suppose them to be—after even our best efforts to make them unambiguous. And, if the task is worth setting (except as a routine check-up), those will not be the worst minds which surprise us by 'entirely missing its point,' or rather by finding lines to follow that we did not suspect were there. When this happens we have two regions to cultivate, where the new line leads and the region from which it led off. If thought about Grammar—about the interactions of words—can teach us teachers anything, it should be to be tolerant and patient and sympathetic about such vagaries; to recognize them as inevitable, and as much part of our own interpretative practice (with its only slightly altered problems) as of the ways of a normal child.

Misunderstanding, then—unless it springs from persistent special causes and so should be a medical matter—is no crime. If it is not actually to be *welcomed,* it is at least *an opportunity for teaching* which, in the absence of overt misunderstanding, will not so certainly be occurring. And the same comprehension by the teacher that the ways of reasonable misunderstanding, as of understanding, are many, will not only make him charitable to his pupils but charitable to himself and to his own efforts in teaching. It is not the most orderly and uncriticizable exposition that throws the most light as a rule. When the class marches in step with its teacher and arrives without break of rank at the destination, members of it may for a while be able to repeat *that march* by themselves; but they will hardly have a general grasp of the terrain. It is the traveller's *judgment,* always and *only,* that we have to train. All else is means and occasion merely.

Lastly, since we cannot, with any good exercise, tell which decisions between rival ways are bringing in what further ramifying, *but then's* and *if so's* that never will be expressed except by the outcome; and since the outcome—except in the sciences—is no certain test of the merits of the internal dramas (p. 248) of interpretation which have led to it; and since the self-control (p. 16) these internal dramas require and develop is our concern and not any outcomes except as they are a part of the dramas; we shall not be afraid of exercises that take time, that may even seem to ask for the rest of life, or for eternity, to settle them. Factual manipulations and indoctrination so hold the field today; so many teachers submit to the flattering expectation that they have the answer and will produce it when they think fit, that the opposite view may safely be urged. It is, then, not our business to teach conclusions, but to help in the framing of questions; that is to say, in the choice of definitions—which is the central problem of Logic.

## Part Three: LOGIC

*That it may be of itself clear and perspicuous to all men;
as indeed it is, saving to such, as reading the long discourses made upon this subject by the writers of* metaphysics *(which they believe to be some egregious learning) think they understand not, when they do.*

HOBBES, *Computation or Logic*

# Chapter Eighteen: The Interpretation of IS

> *It is the more striking that the common-sense world with its things, classes, and laws, should consist of phenomena, that it has all been felt and lived, growing for us with our growing grasp, and that no belief is imported that is not an expectation of which sense can give proof. For animals this world is free from reflection and language; and, in spite of both taints, ours can be seen in quite the same practical character. Common sense is not so guilty as its language appears to say. It stands a poor examination on the meaning of simple words like thing, is, has, I, act. But it learns them not as definitions but as physical signs; it knows nothing of them but their applications; and so their implication is felt as merely a mutual analogy among the instances. When it says 'this thing has an odour,' there need be nothing vague, let alone an error. When it says 'a stone broke the window,' there need be no confusion till it is cross-examined; it is saved from confusion, as well as from error, by its ignorance.*
>
> SIR WILLIAM MITCHELL, *The Place of Minds*

This Part is, for a number of reasons, more tentative than the others. The ground it explores seems, at first sight, less promising as an exercise field for relatively unambitious teaching—Milton's complaint that the Universities presented to 'unlearned novices, at their first coming, the most intellective abstracts of Logic and Metaphysics' returns warningly to the mind. I have to present things that are hardly distinguishable from these, and all will depend upon how it is done. Can they be presented in a way that is tolerable to the pupils—not as mere 'intellective abstracts,' but as urgent, necessary, unavoidable, and fruitful questions? That is the teachers' problem. I need, I think, spend little time insisting that they are such. These questions are no recondite things to be left to sheltered academic experts. They concern the warp and woof of all our thinking. Without some practical mastery of them thought goes astray every hour. But thought is not the same thing as deliberate reflection; it commonly succeeds *in practice* with problems which baffle it at once when they are explicitly set for reflection. 'Should we not then,' someone will ask, 'be content to let thought, in practice, be as logical as it can; and not bother our pupils with these abstruse puzzles which they—and more eminent logicians—are quite unable to settle?' The answer is that they will bother *themselves*, the more hopeful of them, in any case. A point must come, in all education, and often comes early, at which these matters are forced into prominence *in and through* the other things we are endeavouring to teach. And we could teach these other things much better if we could find good ways of making the logical troubles less perplexing. The difficulty of finding good ways will not be underestimated. Neglect of the subject, all but universal in modern teaching, witnesses to it. I hope to show that this neglect is unjustified, and I believe it to be most unfortunate. Some of the difficulty would vanish if the subject became more familiar. It will be soon enough to be sure that Logic is unsuitable in school-use when it has been tried out by modern-minded teachers. But the worst part of the difficulty would remain. It needs a preliminary word here.

Because they are so central and so universal, these problems of the forms of thought have been worked at, *technically*, with good *and bad* techniques, more than any other problems. Inquiry into them has been, in a sense, over-developed; the ground has been dug and mined until the workings in it are a danger to all who come near. The labours of generations of logicians have added maze upon maze to a terrain initially labyrinthine enough. Thus the questions that automatically occur may easily be lost, if we take expert guidance upon them, in a new set of worse questions about the answers we are offered. No one who spends much time on Logic refrains from comparing it to a cave—to one of those awesome intricate pot-holes of the limestone country, or to the grim gorges that some mountain torrents cut—so deep that it seems impossible for the stream of thought falling down out of sight in the depths to find its way into daylight again. The image not unfaithfully suggests some of the dangers that the introduction of novices to Logic must incur. With these problems we cannot help

feeling that we are losing sight of the outer world of common experience, that dark vacuities surround us, that there is nothing under
our feet and nothing to grasp but obsolete tackle, left dangling by
former explorers, from Aristotle to Jevons, men in any case long-
dead and probably ill-advised. These feelings are inevitable when
thought turns to consider itself, and no discussion of logical problems can avoid them. The remedy is to recognize this peculiar
vacuousness and blindness of the subject as essential to it, and as,
indeed, a source of the values of the study. In some Swiss gorges,
engineers have hung a convenient hand-railed track through the
more spectacular gulfs. It is no part of a teacher's duty to do that
for Logic; our aim is not to attract tourists but to train thinkers.
We want to make nothing in this subject easy—except the genuine
exploration of it by minds that are relying upon their own enterprise.

We can however save them some of the embarrassment that comes
from the excessive provision of duplicatory and reciprocally en-
tangling tackle. Above all we must try to see that they get at the
problems before they get at the traditional answers. Most logic-
teaching has failed in the past because the students have had to learn
a doctrine before they realized, in their own experience, how interesting and important the questions were that the doctrine was trying to explain. I shall, therefore, be studying here the presentation
of only a few typical logical problems, and the presentation rather
than the problems themselves or their treatment. This will explain,
I hope, some things which would seem odd about my treatment if
I were writing for logicians. It cuts rather drastically through some,
and ignores others, of the traditional expected formulations and
distinctions. But I am convinced that the growing mind can take
up these problems much more directly than it has been encouraged
to do. The technical apparatus should only be brought in later—
and then frankly as mere bits of apparatus bringing their own
problems, as interesting to the student as the uses he will try to make
of them. So the physicist must understand his apparatus *physically*
if he is to use it; when he does not, it becomes the object of his
research. Here, in the elements of Logic, more than in any other
study, what we must avoid is the incantation. The Terms of this Art
work no wonders. 'Open, Barley!' 'Open, Oats!' 'Open, Beans!—
Open, Rye!—Millet! Chickpea! Maize! Buckwheat! Rice! Vetch!'

There is not even one 'Open, Sesame!' to be remembered. That was another cave and in another story. Yet have I seen the ghost of more than one wretched Kassim lying in the mouth of this in six parts.

I began my experiments with the word 'is'—putting the following set of sentences before my audience and the appended request:

## EXERCISE FIVE

(1) Barkis is willin(g).
(2) The Emperor is captured.
(3) A bacillus is a vegetable.
(4) To obey is better than sacrifice.
(5) To doubt is to think.
(6) She's a duck!

Please distinguish between the uses of 'is' in the above, and say which, if any, of the sentences you take to be true by definition. Write, if you can, a parallel set of sentences between which the same distinctions may be made.[1]

By way of encouragement and to forestall despair I gave a little preparatory homily somewhat as follows: I mentioned our astonishing practical command over the complexities of language and our relatively limited theoretical understanding of how it works. Alluding to the analogy I had been using about the skill of our digestive system and our lack of skill, until recently, as chemists (see page 288), I remarked that the parallel was hardly fair, and that a better one would be with our practical ability as cooks, say in contriving suitable sauces, compared with our inability to explain the physiological principles of taste they depend on. I pointed out that we do all use the word 'is' with incredible adroitness, but that our theoretical understanding of *how we do so* lags far behind. And that in inviting them to test how far they could theoretically explain and describe differences in their uses of 'is' I was not suggesting that we do not all, in practice, succeed pretty well in coping with its tricks. The experiment, I said, would not reveal anything new or startling or disconcerting. Still less would it suggest that we should change the ways in which we ordinarily use 'is.' On the other hand, it might draw attention to some risks we run of misunderstanding one another through the trickiness of the word; and it might shake our bad habit of treating most things we read or hear as though *of course* we knew what they meant and, conversely, of writing as though no one but a fool could possibly mistake our meaning.

[1] This request, as the outcome showed, was excessively ambiguous—both as to 'uses' and as to 'true by definition.'

I put in all this here in case any part of it may help to explain some of the strange things that happened in the next half-hour. They need a great deal of explaining and might easily be conjectured about on the scale of Exercise Two. I believe that a full analysis and discussion of a similar experiment might be extremely valuable. It should be more carefully prepared and followed up by interviews with the writers, perhaps, to bring out more clearly whether they really thought at all as they wrote. A large proportion were too baffled by the novelty of the task, or too distracted by uncertainty as to what it was, to be held responsible. They did not collect their wits enough to consider what could reasonably be being asked, and wandered every way in pursuit of random reflections. These protocols chiefly point towards the improvements that would be desirable in further inquiries, but some of them also show well enough what a need there is for more inquiry and what interesting things it would have to look into.

I will illustrate both aspects briefly. But before the mystery men begin, let us have a comment from an intelligible writer to serve as a norm:

5.1.* (1) Not true by definition. Parallel case: This dog is friendly. It means Barkis is possessed by or possesses a certain characteristic.

(2) This means the Emperor *is now* captured. Cf. The war is over, The meal is finished etc.

(3) Definition. (I know nothing about this but should assume, if I read it, that I was being given a definition.) Cf. Iron is a metal, Fear is an instinct (perhaps it isn't; but if I read this I assume it is a psychologist's definition).

(4) Nothing to do with definition—'is' here relates obedience to sacrifice in a certain way, 'better than.' Cf. 'To be weak is miserable.'

(5) This looks like definition. It might mean 'In the ensuing passage I intend to mean by doubting, thinking.' It might mean to be a general definition—Doubt and think are interchangeable—to doubt is always to think [which it clearly isn't], to think is always to doubt [unfortunately equally untrue]. The sentence seems to me to be really an expression of an attitude of mind towards doubt.

(Cf. Donne's 'Who stands inquiring right' etc. (Satire III) or Tennyson, *In Memoriam*.)

(6) This is clearly not definition! The duck has become through some language history unknown to me a symbol which we recognise as standing for 'charming' or the like.

This is the kind of comment I was expecting. What I got was more often like this:

5.11.* In all these sentences it is perfectly clear what is meant, owing as has been said to the way in which after years of use we are able to interpret the meaning of the word 'is.'

The word 'is,' if one wished to be pedantic, has probably no proper use with anything which is not animate. As ~~the~~ a part of ~~the word the to~~ verb to be *is* implies living or being, all being is in essence presumably confined to living things. Therefore to say that 'the table is . . .' is probably incorrect, although it is habitual.

In the sentences 'is' performs many duties. In (1) it is equivalent to (is in a state of). Barkis is in a state of willingness—as it were. (2) It is equivalent to *has been* and carries some of that sense. (3) ~~This is probably the most correct (in academic use)~~ use of is. A ~~curious~~ use of is, ~~not~~ with the same meaning as equivalent to. Bacillus may be a vegetable. But ~~And~~ a vegetable is a bacillus. (6) Not an equivalent. A duck is not necessarily a she.

I hope that this 'correctness' talk is not the effect of my struggles to analyze Campbell—and Gardiner, Kittredge and Arnold—before the class! I had been giving them the gist of Part Two at some length, and I would feel a little dashed if I thought this writer had been listening to me all those hours. But the audience changed somewhat between the Lent and Easter Terms, and I like to think that this man was a new-comer. I have left in all his corrections to show that some of his oddest ideas were not first thoughts. They may be compared with some of the exhibits in the pedantry-shy which opens Part Two.

He was not alone in feeling that if is is used in various ways, all but one of them should somehow be wrong:

5.12.* In Nos. 1 and 2 'is' is used in the same manner except that one is followed by the present participle and the other the past. It is quite a correct use of 'is' as an auxiliary.

No. 3 is a statement of fact and is also correct.

Nos. 4 and 5 are proverbial uses of 'is' and it is here that 'is' does not come under the proper definition of the word.

No. 6. A slang expression—and does not come under the definition of the word. A human being cannot be a duck!

He is one of several who took 'true by definition' not as applying to the sentences as wholes but to some supposed true or 'correct' use of IS:

5.13.* (1) By definition 'is' would seem to refer to a state of present being. To say, therefore, that 'Barkis is willin'' presents no difficulty, for that sentence conveys the simple sense that Barkis, for whatever reasons, is disposed in such a frame of mind that he will be responsive. The only function of 'is' is to link the adjective to the noun.

(2) If one attempted to translate this sentence the fact would emerge that 'is' has here a double sense. The Emperor is in a state of being and therefore 'is'; captured may be looked upon as an adjective describing his state of being. Yet 'captus est' would mean 'is having been captured,' so that the function of 'is' either becomes enlarged to include some of the past tense of the verb; or is relegated to the smaller category of the previous example.

(3) Assuming that a bacillus may justly be called a vegetable, which I, in botanical and zoological ignorance, am inclined to doubt, the function of 'is' appears to consist in identifying one class of objects with another, in whose larger scope the laws of the universe have placed it. 'Is' breaks down the differentiation between the two classes of objects, but only in so far as one might later suppose that any particular bacillus was not a vegetable.

(4) This dogmatic utterance lays down the law that by a particular standard of moral values, obedience is superior to sacrifice. For the didactic purpose of the phrase a positive and definite form has been adopted, snatched by force from its true meaning of a state of being.

Any stick will do to beat a dog with; and perhaps 'the true meaning' of IS, in the last remark, is being merely turned to the service of a prejudice which several obscurely felt against sentence (4)—that 'dogmatic utterance.'

5.131. To obey $\left\{ \begin{array}{l} \text{is better than} \\ \text{has less benefit than} \end{array} \right\}$ sacrifice.

Freud, or Adler, would enjoy this *lapsus calami!*

5.132. Sentence (4) is the most baffling. 'Is' here has a smaller number of possible meanings than 'is' in (5), where it might possibly mean 'entails,' 'implies,' 'includes,' etc., as well as 'is the same process as.' In (4) 'is' is used vaguely, as a piece of stuffing, to give the sentence orthodox shape.

Quite why (4) is not entitled to use the word ɪs, and why ɪs should be thought vaguer here than elsewhere are points that might well have repaid a little delicate questioning. The separation of 'entails,' 'implies,' 'includes' etc. from 'is the same process as' is also interesting. Differences in the uses made of these terms are among the chief matters an elementary Logic course could clear up.

A large number seem just unable to separate ɪs for contemplation; they load it with the meaning of the whole sentence or with functions which the other words perform:

5.2.* (1) 'ɪs' stands for the state-of-being-willing. Barkis admits to being equal to an indefinitely protracted state-of-being-willing, i.e. the state-of-being-willing is what he wishes his name to stand for for the present.

'ɪs' = Barkis

(2) 'ɪs' = has been

Neither 'is' nor 'has been' are true by definition.

(3) 'ɪs' used instead of =

Not entirely true by definition, a vegetable must mean one vegetable among the whole class of vegetables before it is true.

(4) The act of obeying is better than the act of sacrificing. 'ɪs' = an act.

This is not, I think, what it seems; but just the effect of attempting an unwonted sort of abstraction.

5.21.* (1) Barkis *is* willin'.—Used to signify 'is in a state of'

(2) The emperor *is* captured—'has undergone a certain experience'

(3) A bacillus *is* a vegetable—'Belongs to a certain $\begin{cases} \text{species} \\ \text{class} \end{cases}$ of things' [which has been defined]

(4) To obey *is* better than sacrifice—'Accords with accepted standards [of behaviour]'

(5) To doubt *is* to think—'Produces as a necessary consequence'

(6) She'*s* a duck!

Some struggled in much the same way at greater length and what is happening is easier to follow:

5.22.* (1) Defines by attribution a mental state of a particular person. The situation is particular, and the statement entirely acceptable in so autonymous and arbitrary a thing as a novel.

(2) 'is' has a descriptive force here. It *describes* an alteration of external factors. It is true in the sense that it is unambiguous and possible. In so far as it is a report it is subject to further confirmation or modification.

                                                     particular
(3) ~~This is a highly generalized~~ Here *one* ~~kind of~~ being is attributed to a *kind* of being. It is untrue ~~of~~ by definition.

(4) This might be called the judicial use of 'is' whereby a superior quality is attributed to *one,* of two considered complex dispositions of will ~~reason~~ and impulse. It is a highly general statement possible to make only in a highly particular set of circumstances. ~~It~~ As such it cannot be true or untrue by definition. The situation itself would dictate several criteria for truth, pragmatic or absolute.

                                         assert
(5) The use of 'is' here is to ~~attribute~~ one particular set of mental operations to as comprehending the whole. It is untrue by definition for the powers free to make this categorical assertion are not agnostic. To doubt is to doubt. There are of course certain suppressed mental operations in the statement which when explicit, define and qualify until a certain kind of assent is possible. In so fundamental a statement about consciousness 'is' is important as attributing a certain underlying quality to both doubt and thought—i.e. being.

(6) Here 'is' attributes not so much a definite quality to a person as inhering in them. It is a social judgement. It describes the effect of one person on another—perhaps in a very special situation— almost empathy.

The writer steps over, with the word 'attributes,' what he intends to be talking about; and then finds himself discussing other differences between the sentences. The others will have seemed naïve; this one's difficulties at least are not due to unfamiliarity with or fear of philosophic verbiage. 'Categorical,' 'pragmatic,' 'empathy'! I wonder what he made of the books or talk from which he learnt them. This is the use of language that a good course in Logic would NOT tend to promote.

At this point let me put in two ordinary normal sets of comments —otherwise I shall feel too like 'Our Sam' in the story. His mother, it will be remembered, was watching them march past and cried, 'Look! They are all out of step except Our Sam!'

    5.23.* (1) This 'is' means in context, 'has the emotional state of being . . .'

(2) In its context, this 'is' means 'has the physical state of being . . .'—But in both cases, this sort of explanation necessitates a just as involved use of 'has,' and 'being'—In each case, the 'is' may more simply be considered as a copulative between two phrases or words, which are somehow related.

(3) This statement is true by definition (if my meagre biology does not play me false). The 'is' is that of classification; a member is shown to be included in a larger class.

(4) This statement, owing to the ambiguity of terms, *might* be true by definition, depending upon which senses are given to 'duty' and 'sacrifice.'—Since the last example involves rigidly defined scientific terms this ambiguity does not there arise.

The only way this 'is' can be interpreted, it seems, is to consider 'is better than' as a unit, which connotes a certain relation between 'obeying' and 'sacrificing,' in the mind of the speaker.

(5) This statement, by the usual psychological interpretation of the two words is true by definition.

If so, again, the 'is' is that of inclusion in a 'class'; those facts denoted by the state of 'doubting,' are included in the larger class of facts denoted by 'thinking.'

(6) The exclamation mark leads me to expect that this, too, is true by definition: 'duck,' in a colloquial use, connoting almost anything complimentary the speaker wishes.

The 'is' may be interpreted as 'attributive': *she* having the *qualities* denoted by *duck*.

5.24.* 1. is—simple connection between person and attributed quality—*now* understood.

2. denotes state of the Emperor. *now* understood.

3. *can be proved to belong to the class of* (vegetables)

4. is—positive affirmation—*is,* in the face of those who behave as if it were not so.

5. (The action of doubting) *leads to, causes, necessarily implies* (the action of thinking).

6. ostensibly 'belongs to the class of' and in certain contexts could be taken literally as parallel to 3 in some respects.

In other contexts—as an emotive statement—she has the qualities which for people using my slang vocabulary are denoted by the word 'duck.'

I'm still not sure that I understand what 'true by definition' means —but I think it could apply only to 3, to 6 in certain contexts (if you could take her out of the pond and see that she had all the necessary parts of a duck), and—if you interpreted *is* in 5 in a different way from mine, possibly there.

*Presentness*—is *now*—only implied in 1 and 2.

To return to the mystery men:

5.25.* (i) *'Barkis is willing'*—This use of 'is' shows that it cannot convey sense by itself—the sentence is only half complete. In the context of course the meaning is clear, but as an isolated remark it is not; the 'is' does not explain 'willin(g)'—willing to do what? or what is B willing about? or does 'willing' express a feature of B's character? 'Is' is not a 'self-contained-sense' word. Not true by definition.

(ii) *'The Emperor is captured'*—The 'is' again depends upon the word it described (?), namely 'captured,' and since 'captured' contains its own meaning the 'is' becomes unconsciously joined to it, so that it is no longer 'is' but 'iscaptured';—it is simply the auxiliary showing that the capture has taken place and it is elided into 'captured.' True by definition.

(iii) *'A bacillus is a vegetable'*—this is the use of 'is' which most gives it an existence as a word in itself. It is a connection; 'bacillus' and 'vegetable' are related to each other by it. On this use of 'is' all other words depend, it expresses existence (as, in another person of the verb, Jehovah is called 'I am,' with the same significance of the word 'is' or 'am.'

(iv) *'To obey is better than to think.'*

Any, all, and none of the sentences were declared with some confidence to be 'true by definition.' Sentence (2) was especially a favourite for this distinction, I suppose, because whether he was captured or not was felt to be the sort of thing that somebody could be 'definitely' certain about. These protocols confirmed a suspicion I had been long entertaining that any attempts I might make to discuss definition would have to start by assuming a very much blanker background than, for example, Part Two above assumes. But 'blank' is a misdescription. The background is not merely blank; it is not open to us to fill in as we will. It is actively hostile, I believe, to thought about definition. The word excites a peculiar resistance, rather like the word 'obey' in Sentence (4). Suspicions arise that 'catches' are being planned, that liberty is being stolen, that somebody is going to be made to seem stupid, unfairly and by mere cunning. In the more docile a confused stupor takes their place, similar to, but even more disabling than, the clouding of the faculties that follows the word 'grammar.' The feeling that one will be expected to follow and remember something that one has not 'seen' or 'taken in,' is paralyzing to us all. Any discussion, then, of definition must be very wary, must expect to be often a failure, and should begin by attempting to win a much more positive interest in the topic than is usual. Otherwise the outcome will be the despair voiced under (4) by 5.25 above.

It would be useful to know whether those who picked out (3) as the only sentence which would naturally be taken as true by definition were mostly science students, familiar with that sort of classification and its uses. We would also wish to know what science they had studied. Biologists, chemists and mathematicians develop different attitudes towards definition because the characteristic definitions of these sciences are of different types. The biologist is more familiar with reclassifications, for example, and uses a definition as a provisional instrument; the chemist thinks of components in a structure; the mathematician, since he relies on definitions more than anyone else, wobbles between an extreme freedom and an extreme dependence on them. We may agree that one of the chief benefits of some scientific training is that it forces the student to recognize, in his own subject, the difference between statements that are true by definition and those that are not. But we may doubt whether, by itself, it helps him very much with the same distinction in general non-technical matters. We all know eminent scientists who, when they talk politics or morals, mix, quite as badly as any of us, the sentences which are true because the words are being so used that they must be, with the sentences that may not be true, and need inquiry. A more general ability to distinguish between these cases, or at least to keep on the lookout for the distinction, would be a main aim of a course on Logic. But, *above all,* in pursuing this aim, we must beware of haste. Fluid thought can change meanings in a flash; but solid logicalized argument, using discrete meanings, preferably fixed and constant for its chief words, has lost this happy freedom. It may take a long time to dismantle one definition and erect another. We often think we have changed them when we have not. Moreover the initial process of freezing solid meanings out of a flux often needs hours when discourse only gives it seconds. I am inclined to think that 'the definition horrors' are largely due to this. We expect *not* to understand the moment people start giving us their definitions or attacking other people's. We have been forced too often to try to follow these movements in the fluid state; and the required adjustments can only be made when ideas 'stay put' in the solid.

Let me review, a little further, what was said about Sentence (3). A number, quite properly, did not know whether a bacillus is a vegetable or not. But that did not prevent 5.1, 5.21 or 5.23, from recognizing the sentence as of that sort. 5.24, with his 'can be proved to belong to the class of' is with them; his 'proof' would be a comparison of the characters of bacilli with those defining the class of vegetables. 5.13 tangles himself up with his word 'identifying' but perhaps breaks his way out again. 5.2 more thoroughly merges the notion of inclusion in a larger class with that of identity. What 5.22 is doing I decline to say.

The other protocols supply scores of varied confusions about (3):

> 5.3. (3) 'is' is used in its purest sense, i.e. as a simple equivalent between two things to express their identity.

Others pointed out the obvious objection to this:

> 5.31. 'is' is used to attach a small thing to a group or family of things. It does not identify the Bacillus with the vegetable, because otherwise every vegetable would be a Bacillus. It merely adds the Bacillus to a long list of vegetables.

The 'small thing' is the sub-class, not the minute bacillus; and I expect he has some reasonable notion of how the 'long list' is made in the back of his mind.

'Equivalent' and 'equals' were used in very free and unconventional fashion, and gave much trouble:

> 5.32.* Two uses of 'is' seem quite obvious; one of them is that of replacing other words while the other is that of serving as an 'equals' sign. 'The Emperor is captured' means 'The Emperor has been captured.' As for the equals sign, I should say that a proper illustration of this would be Mussolini is Il Duce or Il Duce is Mussolini. I doubt if any one of the examples presented fits in this category. 'To doubt is to think' can be reversed and the product of such an operation, to think is to doubt, although possibly a true statement, does not have the same implications as the other, nor would it be the product of the same reasoning.

It seems to me that 'is' can serve as various other algebraic signs as well as equals. For example, the sign > (meaning is greater than) means 'is' with a comparative adjective. 'To obey is better than to sacrifice' fits in this category.

Another use of is is that of serving as 'resembles.' When we say 'She is a duck,' we imply a metaphorical use.

This is useful thinking of a kind which, if continued, *via* 'The King of England is the owner of Buckingham palace,' 'A three-angled figure is a three-sided figure,' 'Henry is Ford,' and so on,[1] would take him to a happy clarity. The opening suggestion about is replacing other words is particularly promising. The next writer would be harder to help and is in more need of it:

5.33.* '*Is*' The first use of 'is,' descriptive.
The second use of 'is' verbal (implies 'has been')
The third use of 'is,' as identically $=$
The fourth use of 'is' within a phrase that might be written as one word isbetterthan—comparative
The fifth use of 'is' (mistaken) as identically equal ? (allied to 3).
The sixth use of 'is'—as identically equal (allied to 3)

Of these the third use is the one that can be least quarrelled with. It approaches the mathematical sign $\equiv$ . Even so it must be understood that a vegetable is not used in the sense of one of the many different kinds of vegetable, i.e. as cauliflowers—but as a single one of a certain variety. It would therefore be just as possible to say 'bacilli are a vegetable.'

The fifth use carries this point to a further stage. The identically equals sign cannot possibly be placed here, for if to doubt does involve a process of thought, it certainly does not involve the whole process which 'to think' here implies. And yet the objection is only the same as that raised against (3)—so if 3 is allowed to stand 5, should be.

A large amount of proof would be necessary for 6. The use is 'identically equals' but it has to rely on the hearer's idea of duck—used in this sense.

The itch to quarrel with is goes well with the false confidence about 'the mathematical sign $\equiv$' of equivalence. I can't believe he meant that 'A bacillus' should mean 'a single one' rather than 'any bacillus.' And why may we not say, 'Cauliflowers are a vegetable'?

---

[1] See the discussion of descriptions and names below, pages 328-33.

Probably these remarks are just fumblings towards 5.31's point, fumblings which have lost it in quite different considerations. He crosses yet more threads in trying to deal with (5) and (6). We could hardly have a better example to show how perniciously the minor matters of variants in grammatical formulation can interfere with the perception of the important thing—the logical form of the thought expressed. I shall be coming back to these difficulties in Chapter XXIII when I discuss what may be called the Principle of Equivalence in Grammatical Formulation.

Some, when dragging in 'equals,' were careful to explain that they did not mean it! I give whole protocols whenever other fascinating problems occur in them:

> 5.34.* True by definition are (2), (3) and possibly (4). (2) is true because 'is,' an auxiliary to a transitive passive verb, is a mere device to change the emphasis of thought. (3) is true because 'is' means 'equals' in the sense of a part being included in the whole.
>
> (1) is not true by def. because an opinion is all that is stated; hence 'Barkis is a man,' etc., but 'Barkis seems to me to be willing,' or 'I think Barkis's mood is such that he may be urged to . . . etc.' A proper authority for Barkis's willingness is lacking; so 'is' has not the axiomatic truth of definition that it has in (3).
>
> (4) is possibly true by definition; difficulty here is closeness of bond between 'is' and 'better than.' 'is' means more than 'is' in (4); it means not only 'is,' but more, 'is better than.'
>
> (5) is not true by definition; like (1) it merely uses 'is' to express an opinion and not a self-evident fact. Logically, it might eventually be proved that (5) is true, in fact the syllogism I think would prove so, but as it stands, (5) is opinion.
>
> (6) is an ellipsis, is not true by definition, although true *enough* for practical purposes in discussion. 'She's a lady' would be true use of 'is,' 'She's a duck' means she is in one or more ways agreeable, etc., and the trouble arises not from 'is' but from the more or less colloquial use of 'duck.'

The second sentence gives much too good a recipe for truth; grammar is again interfering. The absorptive 'better than' again, the puzzles of 'opinion' and 'self-evident fact,' the mysterious powers of the syllogism, the imagined 'discussion' of (6) and the 'true use of "is"' in 'She's a lady' are noteworthy.

5.35. In (3) 'is' is an equals sign that only works one way. Its expanded meaning might be 'comes under the general heading of.' 'Is' in (6) is, in one context, a sign of equivalence. In one context, this sentence seems to me the only sentence true by definition.

This 'equals sign' is horribly like Mussolini's adherence to the Covenant. What a way to handle the fundamental machinery of intellectual order!

5.36. (5) Here 'is' has a rather difference sense—a less 'direct' meaning. To doubt is not the same as to think. In (4) 'is' does not mean equal to, but it belongs to the class of 'equal to' meanings. To obey is not only equal to sacrifice it is *better*, but that may be called a 'degree' of 'equal to.' (5) carries its meaning by saying at first to doubt = to think but this is complex for actually not even the *exact* opposite is meant. A certain amount of doubting is contained in thinking i.e. as a stimulus to thought but 'doubt' cannot in *any sense* be used as a substitute for 'think.'

(6) She is *not* a duck. Dare I say that this is a metaphor? Rather similar to (5). (5) being a metaphor connecting 2 'abstract' things, 'doubting' and 'thinking' and (6) between 'She' a *person* and a 'duck' a *bird*.

I suppose I must take some responsibility for the 'metaphor' fog here. But, if how 'equals' works here is so dubious a matter, I can hardly feel aggrieved that my attempts to expound a theory of metaphor sometimes met with little success. In the next, some very giddy changes are worked with the senses of 'particular' and 'general'; 'converse,' as usual, misleads; and 'equal' does its worst:

5.37.* The use of the word 'is' in sentence 3 is the direct converse of its use in sentence 1. Of all the things that Barkis might be said to be, the statement directs our attention only to the fact that he 'is willin',' the word 'is' leads the reader from a general idea to a particular circumstance. In sentence 3 this process is reversed, and the particular idea of the bacillus is placed among the ideas bounded by the word vegetable. In sentence 2 'is' is a substitute for 'has been.' In sentence 5 'is' is used to place one idea within another idea, as in sentence 3: but sentence 3 cannot be reversed: 'A vegetable is a bacillus,' whereas it is possible to say 'to think is to doubt' with as strong an appearance of truth as 'to doubt is to think.' The meanings of the words 'doubt' and 'think' are assumed to be equal, and therefore transferable and able to substitute for each other: but in sentence 3 there is no such assumption of equality between 'bacillus' and 'vegetable.'

If sentence 4 ran 'to obey is to sacrifice' the use of the word 'is' would be as in sentence 3. A difference is introduced by the words 'better than' and it is there that the difference must be sought, the change that takes place in the word 'is' cannot be discussed separately.

The manoeuvre in the middle of this protocol is worth special attention. It shows how easily the experimental manipulations which logic must give exercise in and on which it partly depends, may increase stupidity at first, not remove it. The writer notes that (3) cannot be reversed and that (5) can. So far good. But he does not notice (unless, of course, his 'are assumed to be' means 'I here will assume') that, though 'To doubt is to think' and 'To think is to doubt' may both be true, this need not be in virtue of any formal equivalence, and is no proof of it unless we have means of knowing that 'doubt' and 'think' retain the same senses. He has either set aside or blurred out the common reading 'If you think, then, as a consequence, you will doubt.' (Compare 'If you breathe in, you will then breathe out.') And I cannot help thinking that he is rather blurring this than setting it aside, together with the interpretations that occurred to 5.36.

After this we can appreciate the simple confidence of the next at its right value:

5.38.* (1) Here 'is' denotes the state of mind of Barkis. It almost means 'exists.' 'Barkis exists in a willing state of mind,' giving a sense of continuity.

(2) Here 'is' hardly means 'is' at all but something far more like 'has been.' The Emperor has been captured, and, so far as is known, he is still under captivity.

(3) This one and nos (4) and (5) are very similar. They are plain statements with no tricks in them, the only difference being that in (3) 'is' links two nouns, in (4) a noun and a verb-noun, and in (5) two verb-nouns.

(6) This also would be a plain statement if it weren't for the metaphor. It can be taken for granted that 'she' is not a duck. Therefore 'is' is lying and it is difficult to determine its exact function, but it appears to do very much the same work as the 'is' in number (3).

True by definition are numbers (4) and (5), particularly (5), and perhaps also number (6) according to who and what 'she' is.

Nothing could better show where Grammar, as it has been taught, stops and Logic begins.

Comparing the results of manipulating sentences is the analytic *method* of Logic. Here is a healthy effort:

> 5.39. In 1, 2, 4 and 6 the reversal of the subject and complement does not alter the meaning as it does in 3 & 5. There is therefore a fundamental difference between these two sorts of uses. This (on second thought) does not get us far, for only in 3, 5 and 6 can the symbol = be substituted for 'is' and in 3 and 5 it cannot be used with mathematical precision. A bacillus is contained in the classification of things called vegetables and there is a feeling that there is the same sort of meaning of 'is' in 5 though different words are needed to express it.
>
> From the vast multitude of *elements* of meaning that can be expressed by 'is' in different contexts compounds of these elements are chosen in each particular context. The compounds vary in composition, and in the 6 sentences differ in varying degree. But there can be seen elements of meaning common to more than one of them, and different common elements are used in the following sets.

$$\begin{array}{lccc} \alpha & 1 & & 6 \\ \beta & 3 & 4 & 5 \\ \gamma & 1 & 2 & \end{array}$$

> This latter method seems the only possible way of finding elemental meaning, and if I had time, I might find it possible to continue to classify the sentences as above until every element in the compound meaning would be indexed.

Let us now try to see how far, with time, he might have continued along these lines.

# Chapter Nineteen: Some Senses of IS

> *A mighty maze, and all without a plan.*
> *A mighty maze! But not without a plan.*[1]

Pope's hesitation certainly would have been in place with the uses of IS. Any attempt to sketch their plan (if there is one) suffers from having to use IS itself in the plan, or, at the cost of painful grammatical contortions, to use words—'has,' 'does,' 'existence,' 'ascribes,' 'attributes,' 'connects,' 'relates' and so on—which themselves reproduce, in their own multiplicity and with their own variants, portions of the maze. Yet no one who looks beyond his momentary embarrassments will blame IS for its changeableness, its adaptiveness, its occasional obstinacy or its trick of suddenly sometimes disowning all responsibility. It is the servant, the all-but inexhaustibly resourceful servant, of a number of masters who by no means coincide in their demands. If language in general does not work well enough there are still cases in which it works too well. But the very difficulties that IS creates in meeting all demands are among its best contributions to civilization. We have only to compare the work it does and the way it sometimes goes on strike, with the behaviour of the agents which take over some of the same functions in other languages, to appreciate IS more justly. Here, for example, is Mr Arthur Waley's account of the doings of *yeh,* in ancient Chinese. (*The Way and its Power,* p. 63.)

> In all languages it is the smallest and most innocent-looking words which have given rise to the most trouble. A large number of the tangles in which European thinkers have involved themselves have been due to the fact that the verb 'to be' means a great many different things. The fact that Chinese lacks anything exactly correspond-

[1] Mr Empson's remarks (*Seven Types of Ambiguity,* 259) that a maze *is* only a maze by having a plan, etc., are to the point here: we learn or impose the plan in varying degrees.

ing to the verb 'to be' might at first sight seem to put Chinese logicians at an initial advantage. But this is far from being the case. Chinese assertions take the form 'commence begin indeed,' i.e. 'To commence is to begin.' And this pattern of words, attended upon by the harmless-looking particle *yeh*, 'indeed,'. has caused by its reticence far more trouble than any Western copulative by its assertiveness. Some of the things that this simple pattern can express are as follows: (1) Identity, as in the example given above; (2) that A is a member of a larger class, B. For example 'Boat wooden-thing indeed,' i.e. 'boats are made of wood'; (3) that A has a quality B. For example 'Tail long indeed,' i.e. 'its tail is long.' [1] If words have a fixed connection with realities, the Chinese argued, *yeh* ('indeed') ought always to mean the same thing. If for example it implies identity, one ought to be able to travel hundreds of leagues on any 'wooden-thing'; but in point of fact one can only travel on a boat.

There is a case for saying that IS—and its opposite numbers in the other Western Languages, together with the verb-forms and verb-functions which IS in English can replace—deserves a main part of the credit for the peculiar intellectual development of the West. It has drawn and held attention to a set of problems that the still more versatile 'empty words' of Chinese may have managed to prevent from becoming too notorious as scandals.

How to begin giving some account of the uses of IS, which might be helpful—to the protocol writers, say—will be admitted to be a delicate problem. Evidently, misunderstanding must be expected in this subject. But if everyone, writers and readers alike, could be made to expect these misunderstandings a little more frankly, and with a little more comprehension of the reasons why they must be expected, that, by itself, would be a substantial gain. Here, as with my other sets of protocols, there were moments when I felt that the best possible thing I could do would be simply to have the whole collection of comments reproduced, to give every member of the audience a complete set, and get them to spend the rest of the time

[1] Mr Waley adds in a footnote, 'This is in reality only a special case of (2); for the category of "long things" is a large class, embracing such tails as happen to be long. But the Chinese regarded "qualities" in rather a different light, looking upon them as "something added to" the thing in question.' So, I may add, do a large proportion of a Cambridge audience and eminent Western logicians are not exempt and have at times thought of some qualities in this way. It may be doubted if there is any 'reality' to be appealed to here. See pp. 324-7.

studying the discrepancies between their neighbours. So most Examiners, I fancy, must have felt that if they could commandeer the examinees and force each one of them to go through the toil of perusing and marking the scripts, that in itself would be a more educative thing for them than anything else they have undergone in all their years of schooling.

This may seem too simple a recommendation to be made seriously. But in all seriousness I would urge that something of the sort would be well worth trying. A collection of protocols is not an unmanageable thing—when the class is less than 100. And with sets of protocols such as these, to give a selection to each member of the audience and invite the preparation of a report upon them, would be a good way to begin to teach Logic, for it would mobilize, as nothing else could, native interests, and that immense already acquired aptitude in such things, to which, after all, we must ceaselessly appeal. We can only work with and from what is there already. It is at once the handicap and privilege of the Logician that he employs in his exposition the very processes of distinguishing and analyzing that his discourse is intended to dissect. So before attempting to clarify the uses of is before my audience, I would have preferred to give them first as big a display of the protocols as appears in the foregoing chapter. But to read out such things is impossible. To expect anyone to be able to reflect in any useful way upon them *as heard* would be to forget the most elementary things about interpretation. It may, in passing, be remarked that countless ventures in lecturing founder upon this obvious reef. The ear cannot replace the eye—certainly not for a modern audience unaccustomed to listening. I thought when I taught in Peking that some of my Chinese audiences had an advantage here, but I really know very little about what was happening in their heads. In general, the efforts that lecturers and audiences in the humanities make to study by the ear what can only be studied by the eye are ridiculous and pitiable. They are as wasteful with poetry as with Logic. No one can think intelligently about a poem if he has only heard it once, or if he is expected to be somehow able to remember it sufficiently on the mere mention of its name. So too with every effort to improve our conduct of language. We sometimes need not look very far to see why general courses on Literature, for example, are not profitable.

I began with a Short List on the blackboard of the main jobs (a safer word here than *functions*) that is may be required to do. Usually it will be doing several of them at once.

1. Assertion: it can assert something
2. Existence: it can assert the existence of something
3. Naming: it can bestow a name
4. Connection: it can connect
5. Identity: it can identify
6. Modification: it can modify
7. Belief: it can indicate and invite believing
8. Presentness: it can assert contemporaneity

In trying to explain these, it is well to admit frankly the troubles likely to arise through our use of is (or some equally versatile substitute) *in the explanations.* We might cut these troubles out, if we could find specimen sentences in which is occurred with only one job at a time. But we cannot. Sometimes a special setting may cut them down to two or three and some are often taken over by other words in the sentence; but against this must be set off the fact that there are a large number of minor jobs that is can do (emphasis, correction, ironic overtones: 'Lo and behold,' 'Though you may not think so,' 'after all,' etc.) which often come in to be combined with a selection of the above. What is is doing is never independent of the setting, nor can we settle it by summary inspection. So, in a detached sentence, such as those offered for comment in the last chapter, the best we can do is to suggest, in order of probability, some of the things that is might in varying settings be doing.

Since we cannot, for reasons which soon become obvious, find pure uses, we must do the next best thing: find uses in which as few jobs are being done at once as possible, and thus proceed from the moderately simple to the more complex. The list begins at least by following this plan. The simplest use of is is a combination of (1) and (2): an assertion of existence—'I am' or 'it is.'

It is difficult, and perhaps impossible, to say less than these say. Which says least is a problem which—though they do not put it so—splits modern philosophers into camps; but we need not be troubled with that here. is in 'It is,' AM in 'I am,' say something, that is, *assert;* and what they say is that something *exists,* namely it or I.

So far we seem on safe ground. But it is extremely important to realize how little we have said so far. A chief trouble in Logic is that we nearly always suppose that much more is being said. If we suppose so, everything goes wrong. I have known scores of earnest students who never realized how little Logic said and therefore never understood why it could be so confident. Here, for example, both *assert* (*say*) and *exist* must be drastically pruned down to the bare minimum or we will have said too much. This drastic elimination of extras is so contrary to our ordinary procedures with language that we easily relapse into complexity.

(1) ASSERTION

Take *assert* (or *say*) first. When a man asserts something we ordinarily take him to be believing it, or at least pretending to believe it. We take him to be saying it is *so,* whatever *it* is, or, at least, to be professing to think it is so. We may add in too some suggestion of vigour, as in 'an assertive person,' 'busy asserting all sorts of things,' 'a remarkable assertion,' and these often carry implications that what is asserted is *not* necessarily so, etc. All these things must be left out if we are to get to the minimum sense in which IS asserts; though all these and many more can be added in to be carried by IS in special contexts and with special intonations and so on. In this simplest sense of *assert,* in which IS in 'It is' asserts, nobody's belief is implied. The assertion just puts the proposition forward. Believe it or not, as you like; but before you can do either you have to have it to believe or not and IS gives it you so.

But you may say, 'No! The proposition can stand by itself, without IS to assert it—witness single word sentences such as "Fire!" or "Rain!" ' The reply is, Yes, of course, but *that standing* is the assertion I am talking about; that coming forward, or being put forward for contemplation—that *pro*position—is the assertion carried peculiarly by IS, and in sentences not containing IS by the verb component; to say that IS carries assertion is not to deny that in special cases other words may not carry it in place of IS.

The danger of such explanations as these is that they go on too long; the reason for a distinction is lost in the pains taken to make it. The reason here for clearing out all but a minimum sense of 'assert' is to keep the formal relations of sentences to one another free from confusion with anyone's attitudes of accepting, believing, doubting, questioning or disbelieving them. That is why Logic makes such play with the technical term 'proposition.' But that term, as we shall see later, is a potent bewilderer: it is better, though, than 'judgment' and 'belief,' which are frequent substitutes for it in Logic. I recommend 'assertion'—with the explanation I have sketched—as the key-term because it happens that its etymology provides a convenient mnemonic which will keep its minimum sense in mind. [f.L. *assert-, asserere,* to put one's hand on the head of a slave, either to set him free or claim him,' says the O.E.D.]

### (2) EXISTENCE

Now let us consider 'exist.' To get at the sense in which 'It is' asserts that It exists, we have to turn out time and place from *exist,* as well as all assumptions about the status, or mode of being, of the things said to exist—that they are private experiences or public objects, for example, products of perception or of fancy, illusory or real, substances or qualities, abstractions or concretes and so on. Events have times and places, and we are commonly much interested in their times and places, but we talk about things which are not events—the number five, red, inches, laws and the word 'not.' Whatever account we give of these miscellaneous other things (see Chapters XXI and XXII) we certainly talk about them, and rightly, as though they were nowhere and nowhen. So *exist,* in the minimum sense, discards place and date, and all prescriptions as to status. 'It is,' in this minimum sense, merely puts It forward, lays a hand on It as 'being what it is' regardless of its here or there, its then or now, or any other allegation as to its mode of being. (See pp. 329-333, below.)

These minima are uncomfortable things to handle, the mind holds so little with them that they seem to merge into one another and then fade into a common nothingness. The reason is that to think of them is to use such universal contexts. We only keep one notion distinct from another in virtue of differences in the contexts which support them; and these supreme abstractions, the minimal senses of is, have all things and all experiences as their contexts. So it is not surprising if *exist* and *assert* seem to come to the same thing—that is, virtually nothing. But they are different: talk about 'nothing' drops *exist.* The point to insist upon is that these all but vanishments do not show that thought has failed with them but that it has *succeeded*—as has been frequently remarked by the best logicians.[1] The advantage of making this movement of thought, in itself, is nil. It is useful only in dealing with the more complex uses of is that we now go on to. We can only see clearly what they *add*, if we have seen, for a moment, what they add *to*. Resistance to these manoeuvres easily takes the form 'Isn't this simply not so?'—but the right question would be 'What is this being set up so for?' (See pp. 370-373.)

### (3) NAMING

'Who is he?' 'He is Barkis.' Naming, fortunately, can be taken here as an obvious and easy matter, though if we do not separate it from the other jobs of is, or extend it to cover some of them, we land ourselves in endless trouble. To give a thing a name says nothing whatever about the thing *except that that is its name*. Names here, then, are 'proper' names, Barkis, Tom, Fido, *Paradise Lost* and the rest—not to be confused with other descriptive (i.e. connection) words. (But see pp. 338-341 below.) 'This is *Paradise Lost*' and 'This is Milton's poem' will here make different uses of is, if the first merely names the thing and the second tells us something about it. We may, of course, know things already about *Paradise Lost*—for example, what the second sentence says—but we are not told them when the thing is just given its name. 'This is Barkis' is short for 'This is named Barkis.'

### (4) CONNECTION

How is, by connecting *words* together, tells us that *things* are connected may be explained in a variety of ways. None of them should profess to be more than a device for helping the mind to think about what it is doing. None of them can claim to state what really happens, for each has to assume in its statement the very thing it pretends to be describing. But, naturally enough, logicians

---

[1] 'To speak, indeed, of "pure, unrelated Being," and at the same time admit that there is none such, means the same as to speak, not of the existent (which it is still necessary somehow to make good as *"existing"*), but of the non-existent,—something which this view considers possible, but which we consider a mere abstraction that has absolutely no direct significance with reference to actuality.' Lotze, *Outlines of Metaphysic*, § 14. It is comforting to note that Lotze began his course with the remark: 'The two simplest of the conceptions here employed, that of a "Thing" and that of its "Being," however lucid they appear at first, on closer consideration grow always more and more obscure.'

can rarely be bothered to remember this; they may feel that they would stick fast at the start if they did. So too much of traditional logic has been a wrangle about the rival claims of the various ways —not as being more or less helpful to thought, but as being true or false accounts of what 'in reality' is the case.

(a) If we like, that is, if we find it helpful, we can take any word or phrase as covering a certain field of things. (This is 'reading propositions in extension' as the books say.) Then is, as connecting, puts the field of one word inside the field of another: puts the field of the Barkis things (there happens to be only one of them) into the field of willing things.

(b) If we like, instead, we can take our words as being handles to properties. (It is honester to be frankly metaphorical in our talk here. To do so is not popularization: it is only avoiding technicalities in a subject where unsuccessful attempts to technicalize are the main obstacle.) These properties (qualities, attributes, characters, etc.) we shall have to think about later (Chapter XXI). Here, any specimen will do to work with, say 'willingness.' If it helps, we can think of is in 'Barkis is willin'' as attaching the property 'willingness' to Barkis. To be a little more elaborate: 'Barkis is willing' can be read, 'The thing named Barkis has the property of being willing'; *being named Barkis* is one property and *being willing* is another and is puts them both on to the same thing.

(c) If we like, we can take a third way of explaining what is does here. We can take it as a mark of relation. (But that is the sort of empty sentence which stumps all but the logician who writes it!) To try again, it may help to think of Barkis as linked by 'willing' to what he wills. But what is it? The sentence does not tell us, though the David Copperfield setting does.

No matter; let us write 'Barkis is loving Peggotty.' Then the connecting job of is seems to have been taken over by 'loving Peggotty.' That phrase by itself connects whatever it applies to (here Barkis) with Peggotty. But is then still seems to have to apply 'loving Peggotty' to Barkis. So the connecting job may seem to be done twice over, by 'loving' and by is. But there is no catch, and neither account is mistaken, or less 'the right account' than the other. Prejudices one way or the other, though, die very hard because these alternatives may be useful for different purposes.

In this third way, is is taken as noting a relation between Barkis and something else, and we then can give various accounts of the something else—make it Peggotty, or 'being willing' or 'being in love with Peggotty' or 'loving Peggotty.' These, if we were sorting *language* forms, or analyzing mental processes, or doing lexicography or several sorts of grammar, might have to be treated as very different, but for this relational explanation of the *connecting* is, their differences do not matter. is just notes a relation between various things, and to make plain how specific the relation is and what the things are, is a job left to the rest of the sentence and the setting.

The three ways of explaining is can be pictured; and usually picturing them makes what we are doing much clearer. It drops the misleading threads of the verbiage. It also helps to prevent us from supposing that we are settling something in our choice of way; or doing more than can be done. In picturing we are frankly 'as it were'-ing. In the strictest would-be-technical writing we are doing no more.

     **(a)**                **(b)**                **(c)**

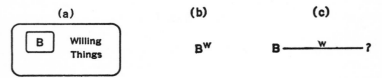

(a) The B things (here Barkis only) *are in* the Willing Things
(b) The B things (       "       ) *have* willingness
(c) The B things (       "       ) *will* whatever it is
    i.e. are related in such or such a way to whatever it is.

The classes, fields, or *extensions* way (a) gives little trouble and often clears up tangled topics like magic. But there are other tangles that (a) does not help with, for which (b) and (c) are useful. I shall be touching on two groups of them later: the Projection Group (compare 'A is beautiful,' 'A is pleasing,' 'A is solid,' 'A is sweet') and the Organic Group (Does the mind change with what it thinks of? Do relations modify their terms? See p. 339, below.). Here I want only to note that these different ways of discussing the use of is, as connecting things, are all useful and not rivals or exclusive of one another. Let us take them, provisionally at least, as machinery, as modes of considering how is (that machine which they too use) does its work. is connects, we say; and whether we say it does so by putting things with others in a class, or by attaching characters (which other things may also have) to things, or by relating things to things, is no matter to quarrel about. We can profit by our supernumerary resources in description, if we do not let the *embarras des richesses* hold us up before we start.

## (5) IDENTITY

An old puzzle, said to have been started by Antisthenes the Cynic in the 4th century B.C. (who got a bad name for it, perhaps undeservedly, for he may merely have been sketching out this paragraph for us) haunts this use of is. If A is B, in this sense, then A and B become not two but one and so cannot be said to be the same. By mixing up this sense of is with others, drastic general consequences can be made to seem plausible, including the impossibility of discourse. These amusing but unprofitable tricks can be exposed by noticing that 'A is B' may be written ' "A" means what "B" means,' or ' "A" and "B" are names or descriptions of the same thing.' Whenever we say that one thing is another, or that one set of things is another, i.e. is identically the same with it, we are, for Logic, talking about the names or descriptions which apply to one thing (or one set of things). I put in the reservation, 'for Logic,' not because in some other study this can be otherwise, and different things somehow mysteriously be one another, but because the pretence that they can is so often *rhetorically* successful. Exercises in the shift from the thing (whatever it is) to the words we are using as name or description of it, the shift we make when we write in or cross out inverted commas (in one of their uses) could be developed into an extremely valuable mode of teaching.[1] The shift needs practice, and I do not see why we should disdain to play games with it in school. The bearing of the question 'Am I talking about my words and their uses or about things?' on the Definition Problem is direct; and I fancy that one way in which the resistances I spoke of in the last chapter, the Definition Horrors, might most easily be broken down or smoothed out would be by systematic exercise in this shift—exercises which need never mention Definition. After all, most people would have a heavy resistance against mental arithmetic, if they had never been given any systematic exercise in add-

[1] Some simple suggestions for beginning teaching in this matter (for pupils of 13) will be found in Mr Roy Meldrum's *An English Technique*, pp. 246-251.

ing or multiplication. The word-thing shift is a far easier operation than subtraction; but that does not keep us from going dizzy or from making absurd mistakes with it. This ıs of identity (No. 5) is a matrix for any number of exercises in the shift, from 'Henry is Ford,' at one end of the scale of complexity, to 'Love is God' at the other.

I have used the phrase 'name or description of a thing.' I had better say a little here about 'descriptions,' though a proper discussion of them should come much later in a course on Logic. We need to clear up first a fairly large number of other problems, and for lack of this, the theory of descriptions has been made by modern logicians an extremely fearsome subject.

We describe things by connecting them, through general words, with other things. A descriptive word or phrase—whether definite, *my right hand*, or indefinite, *some readers*—can be regarded as a compacter notation for a sentence with a connecting ıs in it. ('X is my right hand and,' 'XYZ . . . are readers and'). To write them out looks very artificial and deceptive until we consider how we use them in sentences. 'My hand holds a pen,' expands to 'X is my hand and X (the same X) holds a pen.' But in doing this we have to be careful not to put an ıs of belief, or an ıs of presentness or other specification, in as well, without making sure that they are safe. For example, 'The roc picked up Sinbad' can only be expanded to 'X is a roc and X picked up Sinbad' provided it is clear that no one is invited to believe there was historically a bird, the roc, which did such things. Formal Logicians want to study pure forms of thought regardless of what is put in the form. They therefore write their sentences with symbols in place of words. Thus: $(x) : \varphi x > \psi x$ is their way of writing 'All that is $\varphi$ is $\psi$.' It reads 'for all values of $x$, $x$ is a $\varphi$ implies $x$ is a $\psi$.' Obviously, we might deny that the roc swallowed Sinbad on many different grounds: for example, on the ground that there was never such a bird, or such a man as Sinbad; or on the ground that he didn't *swallow* Sinbad. So modern mathematical logicians have had to devise very ingenious formulations to make statements containing descriptive phrases safe for manipulation and to keep themselves from saying more than they want to.

To explain how they do it would take a longer chapter than this, and the account usually needs a year's familiarity with it before it becomes intelligible. The devices can be picked up as a rote-technique quickly by persons of mathematical ability or training, but to understand anything about the philosophical assumptions made in the modern logical doctrine of *propositions* and their *constituents,* which may include *particulars;* or to see where any modern formal logician is drawing his lines between the sentence, its general form, the proposition it expresses, its meaning and, let us say, *Charles the First* himself—who commonly is presented as a typical particular that gets into some proposition we may happen to be denying—all this is a very long business. The logician usually becomes so accustomed to these assumptions that they no longer seem to him in the least odd. But to an outsider—that is to all our possible pupils—they are likely to seem utterly unintelligible. It is a pity that this survival of an extreme philosophic Realism in modern logic, a Realism which has been in our time more widely and firmly removed than ever before from all other studies, and which is now yielding ground rapidly in the mathematical field from which modern Logic derived, should prevent what is still taught, say, at Cambridge or Harvard (and recently at last in Oxford, the home of lost causes!) from being of much use to us here. The barrier is philosophic. To note it regretfully is not to imply any under-estimation of the logical achievements which in spite of it have made this century already very eminent in the history of Logic. For the teacher, the trouble is that these modes of formulation presuppose certain habits of analysis and to break these down in an adept's mind is a formidable undertaking.

A short view of the struggles of this school with ıs when they tackle it without their symbols may help to show that I am not exaggerating its hydra-like proclivities. I take this from Dr Stebbing's *A Modern Introduction to Logic,* pp. 159-160. It will be observed to illustrate the discussion of ASSERTION and EXISTENCE above, as well as the strangely humble dependence of this school upon the Doctrine of Usage.

'Nevertheless, a certain difficulty may remain as to how it is that we can *think of* that which in no sense is. It is this difficulty that has tempted many philosophers into holding that there are "different modes of being," so that *men* exist, or have being, in one sense, and *ghosts* have being in *another* sense, for which the word "subsists" is sometimes used. Mr Russell, who has now shown us how to avoid these difficulties, at one time himself maintained that "whatever A may be, it certainly is." '[1]

'That whatever can be thought of must *in some sense be* seems plausible at first sight. Professor Moore has formulated a possible argument in favour of this view in order, it seems, to bring out clearly the errors involved. He suggests that it might be argued:

' "A thing cannot have a property unless it is there to have it, and, since unicorns . . . *do* have the property of being thought of, there certainly must be such things. When I think of a unicorn, what I am thinking of is certainly not nothing; if it were nothing, then, when I think of a griffin, I should also be thinking of nothing and there would be no difference between thinking of a griffin and thinking of a unicorn. But there certainly is a difference; and what can the difference be except that in the one case what I am thinking of is a unicorn, and in the other a griffin? And if the unicorn is what I am thinking of, then there certainly must *be* a unicorn, in spite of the fact that unicorns are unreal. In other words, though in one sense of the words there certainly *are* no unicorns— that sense, namely, in which to assert that there are would be equivalent to asserting that unicorns are real—yet there must be some other sense in which there *are* such things; since, if there were not, we could not think of them." '[2]

'This passage states clearly the view that there *must* be *some* sense of "there are" in which it would be true to say "There are unicorns," and *another* sense in which it would be true to say "There are no unicorns." The second statement is equivalent to "Unicorns are unreal," so that this other sense of "are" would have to be such that we could say that *being unreal* (or *being real*) is a property which could belong to something in the same sort of way as the property of *being yellow* can. We have already seen this not to be the case. As Professor Moore points out, "unreal" does not stand for any conception at all. We use the *expression* "are unreal" to express the *denial of existence*, not to assert a *special mode of existence*. In an analogous manner we use the expression "are real" to assert an *affirmation of existence*. With this affirmation of existence we shall be con-

[1] *Principles of Mathematics*, p. 449.
[2] *Philosophical Studies*, p. 215.

cerned in a moment. We must first consider what is involved in our *thinking* of unicorns.

'Professor Moore contrasts three pairs of propositions, viz.: (a) Unicorns are thought of; Lions are hunted; (b) I am thinking of a unicorn; I am hunting a lion; (c) Unicorns are objects of thought; Lions are objects of the chase. The second proposition in each pair could not be true unless there *were* lions; but, Professor Moore urges, "it is obvious enough to common sense that the same is by no means true of the *first* proposition in each pair, in spite of the fact that their grammatical expression shows no trace of the difference." ' [1]

An attempt to thread this maze would be a very advanced exercise. I insert it partly for Professor Moore's lovely supple prose, partly to suggest how technical habituation may make it difficult even for very able people to notice or remember many things ordinary folk are in no danger of overlooking. Have no alchemists hunted for the Elixir? And if you are looking for a man who will lend you a thousand pounds must there be such a man? The outsider's frequent reaction to such pages is: 'What, do you mean to say they haven't settled long ago which senses of IS, PROPERTY, REAL, STAND FOR, and CONCEPTION they are using? I should have thought they would have had to. They are the tools for the work. You must be mistaken. They must know how they shift and have done something about it.' He turns a few pages and comes to, say, this:

'Socrates and Aristotle are of the same logical type, because *Aristotle* can be substituted for *Socrates* in any significant proposition about *Socrates* and the result will not be nonsense, though it may be false. But I cannot significantly substitute a *number* for a *unicorn*. I can say "I fed a unicorn," but not "I fed a number." To see that this is so it is sufficient to know what "number" and "unicorn" respectively *mean*; we do not further need to know whether there *are* any unicorns. The point is that no one can use "There are unicorns" with the sense of "are" appropriate to "numbers" or "relations." Hence, there is no justification for saying that unicorns *subsist*. If there *were* any unicorns, they would be individual objects of precisely the same type as *horses*.[2] Now, it is clear that it does not fol-

---

[1] *Philosophical Studies*, p. 215.

[2] How 'horse' or how 'unicorn' is to be read is *assumed* to be understood ('no one can use etc')—but that is the problem the discussion requires us to solve. All these troubles in fact derive from naïve notions about 'usage.' And no attempts are made to connect the 'unicorn' senses with such things as rainbows, objects seen in mirrors,

low from *I am thinking of a unicorn* that there is an individual object with regard to which it can be said "*This* is a unicorn"; hence, we can think of unicorns although there are none.'

Then, seeing that they are still asking language to do for them what they should be doing for language, he closes the book with a feeling that mother-wit after all provides him already with a better technique.

The problem of how to talk about unicorns even if there are none is troublesome only when we add in a *belief* IS, or a *now* IS or some specification as to a mode of being, to the *assertion* IS; that is, when we take ourselves to be saying more than anyone who talks about unicorns ever says. Or, when we confuse tales or pictures with the imaginary things they are of, or these last with things we might ride on, or hunt outside a story. We all manage to keep these different familiar sorts of things in fairly good order with very simple devices. The logician's way of doing so is very complex. Roughly, he takes a remark about a unicorn as being really about 'The property of being a unicorn.' This he thinks is safe, on the ground that 'even if there were no unicorns there would still be the property of being a unicorn—though, it applies to nothing.' Thereby he aspires to formulations which escape saying that anything is a unicorn, and so cannot lead even the most distraught logician to suppose that because we can talk of a thing it therefore must 'exist'[1] to be talked of. But did anyone who was not stuck fast in an injudiciously technicalized set of words ever suppose anything of the sort? In interpreting ordinary fluid language with full settings there is no need for these ingenious devices. And, if we want to argue, a simpler plan, which will deal with such possible troubles and with many more, is to anatomize the uses of IS in the fashion which I am sketching here. It will be noticed that 'is' and 'exists' in the passages I have been quoting have much more than my ASSERT and

represented in drawings, told of in stories, dreamed of, hoped for and so on, which are in varying aspects parallel. The unicorn case is taken as the type and argued about without being compared carefully with its more *and less* similar analogues. Such comparison is however the only safe and useful method of enquiry.

[1] Inverted commas here to mark that 'exists' is taken as meaning *something more* than 'can be talked of' (the IS of ASSERTION and mere EXISTENCE). What the *something more* might be, which varies greatly from case to case, would be the profitable thing to inquire about.

EXIST senses. Belief certainly and some special mode of existence, and presentness probably, come in too. The riddles that Phoenixes must exist if we can deny that they do, or that there must be a King of France if we can deny that he has a beard—to solve which Russell invented the theory of descriptions—can be solved equally well by discriminating better between our uses of IS. And to do so is much more useful in the ordinary conduct of language. But I am not, in this, denying that *for the calculus purpose of formal logic* Russell's formulation is a valuable device.

All this is an excursion or anticipation which should not, I think, properly come at this early stage in a course on Logic; though, for some, the 'Phoenixes exist' riddle—like the paradoxes of the Theory of Types—is, I have found, a popular diversion, and, perhaps, even a useful enticement into Logic. Let me finish off more briefly the rest of my short list of IS jobs.

### (6) MODIFICATION

This might perhaps equally well be taken as a special case of (4) Connection. It sometimes stands, though, in a rather important sort of opposition to other connection uses. The typical case is when something is broken. When I merely move a bit of chalk, take it in my hand or lay it on the desk, we get a series of sentences describing its adventures. 'It is on the desk, up in the air,' and so on. But when I break it, the case is different, 'It is broken.' When I gradually spread it on the board, still more so, 'It is spread out as a dusty film.' Am I, in saying so, making a different use of IS? In the first series of sentences I am putting one thing, the bit of chalk, into various relations with other things, the desk, my hand, and so on. In the second series, I seem to be no longer talking about one thing. I seem to be saying that it has become, or is becoming, another. We can, if we like, as I have said above, include this under (4) by saying that what before had the character of being one piece now has another character, of being several pieces. But, still, this seems to miss something important and peculiar to uses of IS in describing changes—not in a thing's relations to other things but in the relations of its parts to one another. And as remarks recording and communicating this sort of change (change of nature, of constitution, of being) are evidently extremely important to us all, there seems enough reason to mark this off as another sense of IS. Moreover, remarks about these changes are often extremely tricky and give rise to different interpretations that have immense practical consequences. Most questions about growth bring the difficulty up. Am I the man I was yesterday? Is the child only father of the man, or is the man still the child? So do political questions: What has happened to the Germany that was Goethe's in the Germany that follows Hitler? Is Mazzini's Italy Mussolini's? All this has, of course, to do with the process of thing-making, by which we receive, or frame for ourselves, the objects we claim to be saying something about. But with the statements in which internal changes in these 'things' are being discussed goes a peculiar use of is (and of the is component of any verb which takes its place). And that is what this separate listing of an is of modification proposes to call attention to. I think it would justify itself by heightening that 'sense of position' on which intelligent discourse depends.

### (7) BELIEF

On this is component much might be said. The less, perhaps, we introduce about it in an elementary study of logic the better. The deeper problems here may be left to ripen for later years. But if they are to ripen a clear separation *early* of the is of mere assertion, the is that merely presents the meaning of a sentence for contemplation, from the is that announces the speaker's, and claims the listener's, adhesion to what is stated in the sentence, is very desirable. Without it, we can neither develop 'the sunshine comparative power' (p. 12) nor go on to meditate the differences between the kinds of adhesion appropriate to different purposes. Every teacher knows the pupil who is too busy believing or disbelieving to pay any serious attention to what it is he is so honouring or contemning; and that other equally frequent pupil who can take no interest whatever in subjects which offer no food for private fanaticism. I do not suppose that a course on Logic can do much for the extreme cases, but a recognition that belief expressions are no necessary part of exposition, and acceptances no necessary part of understanding might, I think, ease the strain, or elicit response, in much work which is over- or under-belief'd at present, owing to the supposal that every assertion is an utterance of and an invitation to belief. I am not, of course, in this touching the problem of the liar!

## (8) PRESENTNESS

This is the only is job that is not puzzling, except in the special case of relativity physics in which events which are neither before nor after a given event may surprise us by being not contemporaneous with it but just elsewhere. In ordinary language everyone understands contemporaneity and the simple transferences—the historic present and so on—from it.

The above attempts too much in too compact a form for the opening of an introductory course in Logic. On the other hand, a worse mistake would be to attempt too little, since to be intelligible, here, is to be hard. All the central problems of thought depend upon one another, lead into and out of one another and, with luck, illumine one another. So the shape that may be given to any *exposition* of a fairly wide range of them, may vary immensely without the problems themselves or the treatment they receive being much changed. The order in which they are taken makes great differences, and only experiment can show which order would be best.

However, if this chapter seems needlessly pernicketty, if it splits hairs in one paragraph and is too all-inclusive in the next, if it is alternately inarticulate and diffuse, trite and obscure, these defects should be judged with reference to some of the stresses in what follows. Though a modern Logic would discard and discourage metaphors from building (Who can *understand* the *foundations* of anything? How tell the top from the bottom of an explanation?) preferring a general 'astronomic' metaphor by which how any problem behaves is a reflection of how all other problems are behaving, yet in exposition, if not in thought, we have to prepare for what follows. And here the peculiar would-be-infinite rigour of Logic has to be remembered. Perfect, impeccable consistency is something the boldest logicians can hardly aspire to—for long. Those who have been most interested in language have seen that a logical treatment of language cannot dream even of *high* consistency. To expect beyond a certain point that words will behave with regularity (even after we have allowed each of them a large variety of senses) is to pay for illusory order with blindness to the facts. For words, following the thoughts they convey, vary their behaviour with their company, and, as no one is ever thinking of everything at once, or ever of one thing at a time only, words have no absolute ways. The value of a piece in a position in chess varies with the positions of all the other pieces. But chess is a small and simple system compared to language; and as we further logicalize (that is try to provide for consistency in) the central operative parts of language, up jumps the order of interconnectedness that would have to be respected. It very quickly jumps right out of sight or reach. So, a prudent and sagacious Logic uses a language *inside* the language and cares about the uses of only a few important words and about only a few of their senses. Then ordinary language-users complain that Logic is not helpful and condemn it as scholastic, out of touch with modern needs, and academic.

A more venturesome, faith-ridden Logic—such as is sketched here—risks over-cultivating the meanings of too many words. It multiplies its distinctions to a point where their interaction becomes too complex for any man's watching or control. Meanwhile it tends to say—against the prudent who weed and are exclusive— that words have more senses than we can find them in, and that ordinary unwatched thinking is really in much better order than we could admit, unless we allowed for these unmarked multiple shifts. If we knew what he was *thinking,* then what he said would not seem so silly, is its shy and tender-minded creed.

There is, we will agree, only one Logic; but we may cultivate different parts of its field. Logical cultivation imposes the peculiar task of remembering what we have done, and observing our own ordinances. The most general ordinances are not our own; we are not free to vary *them,* for all order would vanish if we did. But under them we have freedom to vary our arrangements and try experiments. If we can make our pupils realize this, Logic changes for them from a tyrannic mystery into an enticing game. The parallel with games like Bridge and Chess is close and instructive— up to the point when we forget that the ultimate rules of Logic rule us too and that we are part of its game. As in Bridge, say, there are certain rules which constitute the game, and, under them, a choice of plans that we can make and change, so in Logic. If I decide to try it *so,* then, remembering that, I must do *so.* But

Logic, when it uses ordinary language, is playing almost blindfold. The first part of its training is to increase our power to remember what we have done, and what we want to do; which comes down to remembering which of their possible senses we are giving to our words and why.

# *Chapter Twenty:* 'True by Definition'

> *In general, it is safe to suppose that, whenever any prob-*
> *lem proves intractable, it either needs definition or else*
> *bears either several senses, or a metaphorical sense, or it is*
> *not far removed from first principles; or else the reason is*
> *that we have yet to discover in the first place just this—*
> *in which of the aforesaid directions the source of the dif-*
> *ficulty lies.* ARISTOTLE, *Topica*

If we now look through the sentences I offered in the experiment, with some such list of is jobs at our elbow, the practical advantages of discriminating between them become prominent. We
have, of course, in each case, to supply, by recollection or invention, a setting; and by changing the supplied setting we can change
the use of is. This in itself can be no slight lesson in interpretation.

### (1) BARKIS IS WILLIN'

Few recalled the David Copperfield setting in any detail, and
those who recognized it vaguely may have suffered from the fact
that 'his being willing' was the only thing they did remember
about Barkis. So, a feeling that 'Barkis' was less a name than a
substitute for 'a man who is willing' may have helped some to
decide that (1) was true by definition—but I doubt if that happened often, and I have no clear case of it. The same trouble
would arise with other literary references, 'Poor Tom's a-cold' for
example. His 'being a-cold' might seem to be implied by 'his being
Poor Tom' in a way that 'his being plump' would not be implied
by 'his being Napoleon' in 'Napoleon is plump.'

But taking 'Barkis,' with most, as a pure name with no descriptive component beyond 'being the name of someone,' is it not interesting that many thought it true by definition? It is easy to
show why, on any recommendable view of definition, it could not
be. Barkis is his name, was his name before he became willing,

would be his name, if, later, he became unwilling. His 'being *named* Barkis' settles nothing about his willingness; and in considering whether he is willing or not we are not asking anything about whether he is named Barkis. The is of connection just puts him in the class of willing things (there might have been no one else in it, of course, if Peggotty had been very unlucky: but a class can have only one member, or no member). Alternatively (p. 326), it attaches the quality willingness to him, or it links him to what he is willing, as we please. However we describe it, what is does in no way makes his being willing a part or a consequence of his being Barkis, and so the sentence is *not* true by definition.

Has the last sentence, I wonder, given any reader *a turn?* There is a way of reading it in which it seems openly false as well as one in which it is undeniably true, and the wobble between these readings is the heart-beat of many uses of is. It accounts, I fancy, for very much of the difficulty of thinking clearly about definitions. Here is the turn. Are we not saying with 'Barkis is willing' (or was not Barkis saying) that the Barkis who is willing is a changed man from the Barkis who once was not willing? This brings in the is of modification and Barkis might be compared to my piece of chalk which is broken.

The sentence may very well be taken to be saying this, and taking it so was possibly a reason why some thought it true by definition. They felt that a Barkis who is willing couldn't be the Barkis he is unless he was willing, that his willingness was part of his Barkisdom and so his Barkisdom implied or included his willingness. All that is so, but it does not give us any good reason for saying that the sentence is true by definition, and to see why it does not, and also why it is thought to give one, is important.

I can reproduce the misleading ambiguity conveniently with the word 'meaning.' Whether a sentence is true by definition or not depends upon the meanings of the parts which are separated by is or some equivalent. And here willingness is *not* part of, nor does it derive from, the meaning of 'Barkis.' If we question this, we are using a different sense of 'meaning' from the one used in the last sentence when that sentence is certainly true. Which these two senses of 'meaning' are, and how they differ, can, I think, be sufficiently clearly shown without much trouble and with that the imbroglio is temporarily cleared up. It returns, though, and has to be cleared up again and again.

To avoid a lot of notation tricks and parenthetic explanations, I introduce a picture: this, 𝖄, is Barkis, the complete actual man with all his characteristics, including his willingness, his handkerchief, his morality, what you will, and the rest of him. And 'Barkis' is his name. If now I say

　　　　　　　　'Barkis' means 𝖄
and　　　　　　　'Barkis' means 'the man named "Barkis"'

I shall sometimes be saying the same thing with them, sometimes not. For the phrase 'the man named Barkis' may slip over to mean 𝖄; or it may stay doing no more than I here want it to do— that is, pointing to a man in respect only of his having that name. But this phrase, and all possible phrases, will slip too—to mean 𝖄—if we let it.

This shift (which is a normal and invaluable fluctuation of innumerable words) can be followed more easily with a word like 'song.' Suppose so and so sings that song, and suppose we agree that that song is tuneful. Does it follow that what so and so sings, i.e. his singing, is tuneful? By no means, as, were I so and so, would soon be proved. Here we don't have any trouble in seeing that 'What I sing' and 'my singing' are to be distinguished, or how to distinguish them. We do have recurrent and terrifying trouble in distinguishing between 'what it means' and 'its meaning.'[1] The reason is that with 'song' we are free to concentrate upon one ambiguity; with 'meaning' a hundred others in the background are distracting us.

This may seem an odd way in which to expound an old distinction—between the properties in virtue of which a word or name is applied (no properties in the case of the pure proper name) and the properties in fact possessed by the things to which it is applied. But it attempts to start from the actual puzzles, and the shifts causing them, for which that distinction and the whole technical apparatus of denotation, connotation, comprehension, essence, attribute, accident etc., have been contrived as remedies. These

[1] In such uses as those I am making here, of course. For innumerable purposes there is no need to bother about the fluctuations of either phrase.

remedies are perhaps more dangerous than the disease if the patient does not first realize what they are for. Frequent analysis of actual occurrences of such shifts is the way to make Logic useful. The technical apparatus may be brought in later, but not without warnings that its use is exposed to similar troubles, and that it will make confusion worse confounded unless we are able to watch for them.

The 'catch' here with 'what it means' and 'its meaning'—with ⅄ and 'the man named Barkis'—is not, of course, merely a case of 'language tripping us up'—though it makes a good point against Mill's simple view that in learning Grammar we are learning Logic. It is a case of gross confusion of *thought* that enshrines and protects itself in language, and mere changes of terms will not avoid it. Heaven knows how much thinking has lost its way here. Most of the situations in which we use words of the 'meaning' group give occasion for it. I will take only obvious examples where the slip or shift is easily followed and therefore not dangerous: you may desire something which will in fact destroy you; you don't therefore desire your destruction; and yet you do! You may know someone who is in fact a murderer; you don't therefore know a murderer; and yet you do! Similarly—but this *is* dangerous—we may mean by 'Barkis' someone who in fact is willing; we don't therefore mean by 'Barkis' a willing man.

No one can reasonably be expected to study Logic unless he realizes that he needs it. Here is a confident student:

> At first I attended my lectures assiduously and faithfully; but the philosophy would by no means enlighten me. In the logic, it seemed strange to me that I had to tear asunder, isolate, and, as it were, destroy those operations of the mind which I had performed with the greatest ease from my youth upwards, and this in order to see into the right use of them. Of the world and of God, I thought I knew about as much as the Professor himself!

'Performed with the greatest ease from my youth upward'? Well, this is Goethe, on his Leipzig Lectures, and perhaps *he* may have done so. His was not an ordinary youth. But most minds do not perform their operations of strict reasoning with any ease, and those do best who are most discerningly aware of the dangers. To know them better is the way to escape being frightened by them.

## (2) THE EMPEROR IS CAPTURED

This is an easier sentence than (1) since the IS connects without modifying. We can, of course, imagine if we please, that the Emperor was heartbroken by his capture, that he never smiled again, and was an utterly changed man and so on. But none of this is said by the sentence. So we escape some of the reasons which perhaps made some take (1) as true by definition. None the less, more still took (2) so—a fact I am too curious about to speculate on without better evidence. 'The Emperor' is a description, not *a name* like Barkis, which makes it clearer that, however we read it, it is *not,* and does not contain, a description, of *something being captured.* We could invent a context to make it true by definition, imagine a tribe which chose its Emperor by a ritual of capture, so that no one could be Emperor without being captured, but *that* was not how people came to think (2) was true by definition. And it is obvious that, when they said it was, they meant by this phrase something quite different from anything relevant here. For example, perhaps that it looked like 'a matter of fact' and that to say that something is 'a matter of fact' is sometimes a way of saying that it is true!

## (3) A BACILLUS IS A VEGETABLE

This, too, is an easy sentence, if, as we are entitled to, we take 'bacillus' and 'vegetable' as being words with settled satisfactory definitions in biology. There may be problems about these definitions, but they are biology's business, not ours. We can accept the sentence as true by definition without having to know exactly what the definitions of 'vegetable' and 'bacillus' are which make it so. In fact we should have had to have done not a little work on minute organisms to get at them. So, recognizing that a sentence is true by definition is not necessarily seeing in detail how it is so. A main purpose of definitions is to guarantee sentences without our having to go into just what they say.

There are two main, equally reasonable, ways to read (3). Either as a statement about the things named bacilli saying that they are vegetable organisms; or as a statement about the use of the word 'bacillus' saying that it is to be used only for certain organisms which are vegetable. In this second reading it is, itself, a definition, or rather a part of one; the rest would go on to say more about the organisms the word could stand for, separating them off from other vegetables. Read so, to say it was true by definition would be a way of saying that this definition was an agreed one. But most people, I think, would read it in the first way— as telling us about the things, not the word; and then, 'true by definition' would mean that while we were using the words with these definitions no bacillus would be found which was not vegetable, because the definitions had been so arranged that this must be so. A non-vegetable organism would not be counted a bacillus.

### (4) TO OBEY IS BETTER THAN SACRIFICE

Nobody identified this as Samuel's utterance, though I suspect a feeling that it was Biblical had something to do with its unpopularity as a sentiment. The word 'obey' also has an important place in the marriage service. However, those, at least, who wrote, ' "is" is a forceful way, an exaggerated way, of saying "in the opinion of the speaker may quite possibly be," ' and '(4) is a speculation in which "is" suggests the attitude of the writer but little more,' were free to invent their settings. If any had remembered that Samuel was speaking to Saul from the Lord, they might have had a good reason to take it as true by definition. For 'to obey (the will of God)' might well be, by definition, 'the best possible course of action' and 'sacrifice,' here, might be short for 'sacrifice when sacrifice is not the will of God'; and then the sentence would be true by definition. As they read it, forgetting Samuel, it is just a statement with a plain connecting is in the forefront and a strong belief is in the background. It is parallel to

This line ———— is longer than this line ——

which is a statement not true by definition but true in fact, since the lines just have lengths but are not given them by definition. What may have worried some is the fact that 'line' and 'longer' have definitions and we can only set about verifying the statement by respecting these definitions. But the statement is quite different in form from

A three-inch line is longer than a two-inch line

which would be true by definition. How different they are we can see at once, because nobody will try to verify this last statement.

The trouble that so many took to pack is somehow into is-better-than may be partly explained by what I wrote about the class, quality and relation interpretations of the connecting is. This is a case when to think of is as relating one thing to another, as better-than it, is rather easier than to think of is as putting obedience into a class of things better than sacrifice, or as attaching a quality, better-than-sacrifice, to it.

### (5) TO DOUBT IS TO THINK

This, since we are so free to shift the imaginary settings, is the most puzzling sentence of my six. The protocols showed in how many ways it could be interpreted. We can make it true by definition by taking thinking as a genus of which doubting is a species; or, non-technically, by calling everything that happens in the mind 'thinking,' when doubting would be of course included. But there are plenty of other ways of taking them: 'Only think, man, and you can't doubt it!' 'Truths no thinking man can doubt,' 'Doubt is the enemy of thinking,' 'The purpose of thinking is to remove doubt.' We could contrast Descartes with Blake:

> What I can't doubt that I must think

with

> If the Sun & Moon should doubt
> They'd immediately Go out.

It is an interesting witness to the mind's subtlety in the interpretation of fluid discourse—making a sad contrast to its clumsy blundering with solid or logical argument—that we manage all these shifts without difficulty. When we are oppressed with unmanageable complexity it is comforting to admire ourselves in the fields of our success. There is no advantage in logicalizing this field—except of course for psychology. So too with:

### (6) SHE'S A DUCK

Some, of course, kept it to ornithology and played Ducks and Drakes over the mill pond. Taken as a fervid compliment, it certainly does not, though many said so, accuse the person it is said about of being at all like a duck, of having a bill and paddles for example. The metaphor, whatever its semantic history may have been, probably works in most minds through our attitudes to pets —'tender and amused liking' as one writer said.

In this we have left the appropriate field for logical cultivation. However this sentence works, we would surely be more than ordinarily confident—if we said it to someone—that it would be saying for us just what we wanted to say. And the person of whom it was said would feel so too. In this it is a type of the language which works best and may fitly close this discussion of an experiment in which we have seen language struggling with tasks it cannot manage so happily.

# Chapter Twenty-one: Logical Machinery and Empty Words

> *As the manes of the departed heroes which Aeneas saw in the infernal regions, were so constituted as effectually to elude the embrace of every living wight; in like manner the abstract qualities are so subtle as often to elude the apprehension of the most attentive mind.*
>
> CAMPBELL, *The Philosophy of Rhetoric*

In discussing senses of IS I have allowed more than a little which would have no proper place in an *elementary* Logic course to intrude; and thus illustrated the worst risk in the venture. You cannot defend a subject against philosophy without turning philosopher, any more than you can put down violence without using force. In this chapter the risk is greater. The way to meet it is to acknowledge it, study it and limit it. What I am noting down here are, at best, only the materials of a possible teaching subject. What should be considered *early* is still entwined with what should be considered *late,* if at all. But the separation must proceed by steps and any step here is better than none.

The protocols of Part One showed that current teaching leaves the use of words like 'concrete,' 'abstract,' 'general,'[1] 'particular,' 'definite,' 'vague,' in a state of confusion which makes them active adverse influences upon thinking. Can anything be done, by exercises and exposition, to clarify their use? A very great deal can be done, I believe; but, in attempting to do it, we have to take note of the sources of the confusions and that leads us inevitably into philosophical questions which are hardly elementary. Moreover the best and clearest instances for study occur in the writings of logicians, whose thought has developed some of the mistakes, which are embryonic or implicit in current practice, into open and

---

[1] See too Chapter XVI, p. 275.

sometimes glaring absurdity. But these instances, being in semi-technicalized language, are hardly suitable for a course which is endeavouring only to help the conduct of ordinary everyday thinking, and therefore does not aim at (should, in fact, do its best to avoid) producing logicians.

What follows, in these three chapters, is a sketch of a highly simplified exposition of some of the more important uses of the chief terms we may employ in analyzing meanings. It is interrupted from time to time by defensive excursions illustrating how they should *not* be employed and trying to say why. To decide just where the negative excursion ceases to be helpful in the understanding of the positive and recommended uses calls for the uttermost of the teacher's tact, since what helps him will not necessarily help others.

Let us begin with a list of the words which are our chief machinery for distinguishing, in analysis, between

(1) What we are talking of
(2) What we are saying about it

| | |
|---|---|
| Subject | Predicate |
| Substance | Attribute |
| Entity | Property |
| Particular | Quality |
| Thing | Relation-ship |
| Being | Character-istic |
| Class | Universal |
| | Essence |

All these words (except 'thing') have been introduced to help us in separating the 'its' we are talking about from the 'whats' we are saying about them. Most of them still carry, for some users, implications from the philosophic purposes and systems for and with which they were introduced. Some ('subject,' 'predicate,' 'attribute') have grammatical specializations. About most of them, if we may judge, say, by *The Times Literary Supplement,* there will ordinarily be some doubt as to just how they are being used. We have to look critically at the whole article or review—and, as a rule, beyond the immediate setting—to decide whether they are being used technically (according to the philosophy the writer was taught when an undergraduate), or in a broad and popular way, quite at random, for merely decorative purposes, or to make the sentence look as though something carefully considered were being said. It would be easy to collect passages to show that all these words are frequently employed in such a way that it would not matter a jot if others out of the same column were put instead—and this in settings where, if the scale of the inquiry were more microscopic, a change would make important differences.

When serious and close attention to what is being said is not invited, such free indifferent usage is no occasion for complaint. But in most places where these words should be used we should be able to attend closely with profit, for an anatomizing or explanation should be in progress. And, apart from mere loose use, discrepancies between the implications brought in with these terms by writers of different training give much avoidable trouble. No one with an eye on actualities would recommend *uniformity* as a cure, or would try to prescribe fixed uses. That is not the remedy, for the training that puts the different implications into the words is going on, and must go on, in numerous *independent* centres, and it is not susceptible of regimentation. Moreover, uniformity would be disastrous, if it were possible. To take two current examples. Until recently Oxford-trained men and Cambridge-trained men hardly ever understood one another on any abstract topic—because their key explanatory words turned in different locks.[1] More recently something of the same sort seems to be dividing those who have absorbed Whitehead's influence directly or indirectly, from those who have not, and the same was true of Dewey's influence. The point is not merely that people with different general outlooks are out of touch. The differences are more detailed and specific; the modes of framing questions differ and the explanatory words work in ways which to the uninitiated are misleading.

The remedy is not regimentation into uniformity, but a lively awareness of the other things that may be being said. 'How are we to get that?' someone will ask, 'Is everyone to go and work diligently at all the intellectual centres, and read all the books with an intelligent eye? Splendid! But is this a practicable proposal for general education?' The answer is that none of the special

[1] A fuller account of these differences, with examples, will be found in my *Mencius on the Mind*, pp. 94-99; and I may perhaps refer the reader to Chapter IV in that book for a discussion of topics closely germane to those touched on here.

uses that may mislead are really unfamiliar to anyone. In learning ordinary English, even in gaining a very modest competence in it, we become acquainted with *all* the forms of thought. But the acquaintance is commonly fleeting and distant. What a regional philosophic tradition does is to concentrate attention upon some of the forms to the neglect of others; and make them seem the only possible forms. But meanwhile every mind is using (outside philosophy) all the forms in the common routine of existence. Using them, but *not* meditating them, that is the point. The task of education is—not to teach everyone all the philosophies but—to turn the attention more equally upon all the forms used in the everyday articulation of non-specialist thinking.

We could do this, I believe, by a direct study of these words and their uses, without allowing this study to wander far into the dangerous debatable lands of the philosophies. If we cannot yet do it, that may be mainly because we have not tried to.

The first division of the two columns into 'its' and 'whats'—things talked about and things said of them—breaks down. It has broken down in the last sentence with my shift of 'things.' We break it down whenever we talk about 'whats'; and this has given rise, in the technical discussions, to a thick growth of very subtle, perplexing and embarrassing questions. From these we must make a careful selection. Many of them are bred by miscegenation of Grammar and Logic, and these we can, at least in part, eliminate. Among those left are the questions from which, through familiarization, meditation exercises, analysis and exposition, we could effect, I believe, a considerable enlargement of intelligence.

I will begin with an example which will show how a traditional approach to the abstract-concrete divisions brings in things that need to be eliminated.

The distinction between concrete and abstract names, as ordinarily recognised, may be most briefly expressed by saying that a *concrete* name is the name of a *thing*, whilst an *abstract* name is the name of an attribute. The question, however, at once arises as to what is meant by a *thing* as distinguished from an *attribute;* and the only answer to be given is that by a thing we mean whatever is regarded as possessing attributes. It would appear, therefore, that our definitions may be made more explicit by saying that a *concrete* name is the name of anything which is regarded as possessing attributes, i.e.

as a subject of attributes; while an *abstract* name is the name of any-thing which is regarded as an attribute of something else, i.e. as an attribute of subjects.[1]

The writer then points out that though, if we are comparing 'triangle' and 'triangularity,' 'man' and 'humanity' and so on,

> there will never be any difficulty in determining which is concrete and which is abstract in relation to one another, yet the application of our definitions is by no means always easy when we consider names in themselves and not in this definite relation to other names. We shall find indeed that . . . the division of names into abstract and concrete is not an exclusive one in the sense that every name can once and for all be assigned exclusively to one or the other of the two categories.
>
> We are at any rate driven to this, if we once admit that attributes may themselves be the subjects of attributes, and it is difficult to see how this admission can be avoided. If, for example, we say that 'un-punctuality is irritating,' we ascribe the attribute of being irritating to unpunctuality, which is itself an attribute. Unpunctuality, there-fore, although primarily an abstract name, can be used in such a way that it is, according to our definition, concrete.
>
> Similarly when we consider that an attribute may appear in dif-ferent forms or in different degrees, we must regard it as something which can itself be modified by the addition of a further attribute; as, for example, when we distinguish physical courage from moral cour-age, or the whiteness of snow from the whiteness of smoke, or when we observe that the beauty of a diamond differs in its characteristics from the beauty of a landscape.

This leads him

> to give up for logical purposes the distinction between concrete and abstract names, and to substitute for it a distinction between the concrete and the abstract *use* of names. A name is then used in a concrete sense when the thing called by the name is contemplated as a subject of attributes, and in an abstract sense when the thing called by the name is contemplated as an attribute of subjects. . . . It may be added that as logicians we have very little to do with the abstract use of names.

Not forgetting that Logic has been described as the art of mis-understanding whenever you can, let us look at this closely and

[1] J. N. Keynes, *Formal Logic,* p. 16.

critically. What has happened in it? The main change might seem to be the substitution of 'contemplated as' for 'regarded as' in the definitions! But this would be niggling; for the writer certainly supposed himself to be making a more important change and to be correcting, in the light of the admission that we say 'unpunctuality is irritating,' some serious inconvenience in the former definitions. What was this correction? Let us see more of his reasons for making it. The first definitions gave as a result,

> that while some names are concrete and never anything but concrete, names which are primarily formed as abstracts and continue to be used as such are apt also to be used as concretes, that is to say, they are names of attributes which can themselves be regarded as possessing attributes. They are abstract names when viewed in one relation, concrete when viewed in another. It must be admitted that this result is paradoxical. As yielding a division of names that is non-exclusive, it is also unscientific.

This is a harsh description of the result, but it need not frighten us. That is how 'names,' as the writer is using the term here, do behave; and in substituting 'uses of names' for 'names' as what are to be 'abstract' and 'concrete,' he is recognizing that the word 'name' in this connection needs much more careful handling than we usually give it. It is a correction in our definition of 'a name' that he is making. In the first definitions names were regarded as things with meanings apart from their use, and it is this assumption, not 'the result,' which is paradoxical and unscientific. But to write 'use of names' for 'names' for a page or two, will not put things right. We must clearly and persistently realize that a name apart from our uses of it is nothing but a shape on paper or an agitation of the air. One would suppose that nobody could forget this, least of all a writer discussing distinctions between the uses of names, yet we all do endlessly forget it; passages which show a similar oblivion could be found in a score of deservedly esteemed logicians. With such things in view, we need not wonder that Logic has not done for the study of interpretation all that we may hope that it can do.

My quarrel then with this passage is primarily that it is disablingly unreflective in the conception of names which it displays. True it corrects the error in some degree; but insufficiently, for it

treats a fundamental and always stultifying misconception—that of
the Divine Right of Names—as a mere difficulty to be avoided by
an *ad hoc* subtlety. I have further bones to pick with it however.
The next one is that it mixes the grammatical forms of speech with
the logical structure of propositions. In 'unpunctuality is irritating,'
'unpunctuality' is *grammatically* the subject and 'irritating' grammatically the attribute. But we can put the same proposition [1] into
other speech forms—'irritation is caused by unpunctuality,' or 'We
are irritated when something happens before or after the time we
expect it,' and then we get new grammatical subjects and attributes.
Similarly, in 'snow is white' and 'white is the colour of snow'
*grammatically* the attribute of the first becomes the subject of the
second, and yet there is at least one proposition which they may
indifferently express. It is both a besetting vice of Logic and an inexhaustible subject of complaint by logicians that we mistake the
forms of speech for the forms of thought, and yet elementary Logic
does little or nothing but encourage it by the way it talks about
terms and by the choice of its examples.

Thirdly, 'an attribute may appear in different forms . . . we
must regard it as something which can itself be modified by the
addition of a further attribute' and so on. May it? and Must we?
Why? Because language, in our Indo-European syntaxes, behaves
so? But these are the very questions which Logic has to enquire
into! And answers to them are here being docilely accepted from
language as though language had some unquestionable authority
to teach us them. How do we settle that an attribute which appears in many forms is one attribute? Why do we take it as one
sometimes and at other times as many? Is it because we happen
to have one name for it (them) or can stretch 'white' to cover
snow and smoke? Or because it suits our purposes to do so? It is
the business of Logic to study these sorting operations which language can be made to record. By studying them it can free us
from endless mistakes between sortings made for, and useful
for, different purposes. But it will never do so while it takes its
lessons from language in this unwary fashion. It is by this sort
of subservience that most of the idle problems of the speculative

---

[1] When it is the same proposition and when not is, of course, the important thing,
practically, to decide. It is just because this mixing of Grammar with Logic hides and
blurs the grounds for such decisions that I am objecting to it.

subjects are perpetuated. For example, the beauty of a diamond, the beauty of a landscape, the beauty of a hot gammon![1] A library of wastepaper esthetics has been written by people who tried to observe how they differed in their characteristics instead of reformulating the questions. (See p. 367.)

Lastly: 'As logicians we have very little to do with the abstract use of names.' This means that logicians read the terms in propositions as 'subjects of attributes' and it cuts their logic down to that examination. It leaves out, as something they have not to do with, a great part of the conduct of their own discussions, and so can summarize my complaint. They *have* had far too 'little to do with the abstract use of names'; seeing that they are making that use themselves half their time. They have been too much occupied with the technical developments *within* the subject to spare enough attention for the presuppositions of their work.

I must come back now to my two columns of verbal machinery and try to suggest something more helpful that can be done about them. Three things can, I think, be done. (1) We can give reasons which will prevent certain obstructive and inappropriate questions being raised about these words. (2) We can supply a kind of natural-history classification of their varied uses in ordinary speech and thought. (3) We can show how confusion between these creates innumerable bogus and unanswerable questions and prevents important answerable questions from being raised or pursued.

The obstructive and inappropriate questions may be put in the form 'What *is* a thing, an attribute, a subject etc.?' If we ask such questions and persist, we land ourselves in the toils in which thinkers from Plato and Aristotle onwards can be observed to struggle. They may have gained something for the world from it all; our pupils will not, and what was gained is now attainable otherwise. Perhaps few will persistently ask such questions, but still they will feel, if we direct their attention, as we must, to such words, that there *ought* to be answers forthcoming. They will feel that in default of respectable answers, the whole thing is airy and vague. So there is a very considerable advantage in showing that the lack of answers to these questions is no defect, that there

---

[1] See *The Waste Land,* line 166.

cannot be answers and that why there are no answers can be reasonably explained. This then is a first step, not very important in
itself, but removing a frequent obstacle to intelligent interest.

I must now show more clearly just what questions these are. Suppose someone asks, 'What is an apple?' Our answer might be, 'It
is a fruit that grows on a tree.' To which he might reply, 'I was
not asking you where it grew; I was asking you what it is.' We try
again, 'It is a refreshing fruit.' He replies, 'I was not asking you
what it was like or what it did; I was asking you what it is.'
Suppose we say, 'It is an assemblage of cells, a system of molecules,
atoms etc.' He can always reply, 'I was not asking you what I
should see if I took a microscope to it or what chemical hypothesis
would explain what would happen to it if we did certain things
to it etc. I was asking you, quite simply, what it is?' In this way,
he has us beaten from the start. We can only dispose of him by
saying that his question is illegitimate, and that, if we define a
question as something that theoretically can have an answer, his
demand is not a question. It is only supposed to be one by having
the same verbal form as some things which are questions and so,
theoretically, can be answered.

We can put anything we like in place of 'apple' here and if our
questioner will not accept as an answer, either a statement about
causes or effects, or a statement grouping it with other things that
are like and unlike it, or a statement about its parts and their
relations to one another, or a statement about its place as a part in
some larger whole, but insists on being told *what it is* in some
other sense than these, then we have to leave him unsatisfied. Or
rather, the only way to satisfy him is to show him that he is not
asking something that can possibly be answered, that he is mistaken as to what he wants, that he is seeking perhaps some rest
of mind in the wrong fashion. It is interesting to consider how
much embryonic philosophizing of an unprofitable kind would
be prevented by a recognition of the emptiness of this question.

This aberrant use of is with what, since the question is equally
empty whether we ask about the self, an apple, the universe or
the number 2, is *not* the one in which to ask 'What is a thing, a
subject, an attribute etc.?' is illegitimate and fruitless, though it
often comes in to complicate this other seeming-question. I have
discussed it first to get it out of the way. The more troublesome

question about an attribute, an essence, a substance, an entity, a relation and so on, is one we *can* legitimately ask with most other words. We can ask, 'What is a man?' for example, and get all the useful sorts of answers which our enquirer above rejected in the case of the apple. And even for the Universe we get some of them —though no one will tell us what it is like or of what whole it is a part.

'What is a man?' may be taken as asking a variety of questions, which can be written otherwise:

What things are we calling men? or What are we putting inside the sort 'man'? What set of properties (attributes etc.) is peculiar and common to men? i.e. What have men in common that no other things have? To what other sorts (e.g. animals) do these things belong? How do these things behave? What are the parts of one of these things?

But these questions, if for 'a man' we put 'a particular,' 'a property,' 'a substance,' 'a thing,' and so on, no longer make sense, and cannot be answered; and therefore are not questions, if by a question we mean something that can be answered. Of course, we can say, as Dr. Keynes did above, 'By a thing we mean whatever is regarded as possessing attributes' and 'by an attribute we mean whatever a thing possesses.' We could continue, for a short while, ringing the changes on our small collection of bells; but that is not a way of providing information *about anything but the formal relations between bits of this machinery.* And we can say of them all that they are machinery, or a 'dodge' (as Jowett called Logic) for helping us to talk about the forms of thought. But of a 'form' we have then to say that it is another dodge for the same purpose. And if we do this we see that we are talking *about* the practical uses of the words 'form,' 'property,' and so on, not talking *with* the words about something else, as we were in the case of 'a man' and might do if instead of 'a man' we put anything—except a bit of logical machinery.

There are many ways of explaining this peculiar emptiness of logical machinery, but it is not hard to see that they could not do the work we require from them if they did say anything. They must not say anything, for they are our means for analyzing other things that have been said. They are dissecting instruments and their virtue is to divide without separating and without adding or distorting. Any comparison with other words will show why they are empty: to say what things we are calling 'men,' for example, we take a sort, things-to-be-called-men, M, and then create another sort *in another way,* say, rational-animals, R-A, or featherless-bipeds, F-B, such that

All the things in M are in R-A (or F-B) and
All the things in R-A (or F-B) are in M.

That is, the sorts are coincident. But to say what things, T, we are calling 'things' in a similar fashion is impossible. How are we to create another sort, X, *in another way,* such that

All the things that are in T are in X and
All the things that are in X are in T?

We cannot, with the inclusive sense of 'thing'; because to create a sort is to separate what is in it from what is not in it. Hence the convenience of using a circle ◯ to represent a sort. In this sense of 'thing' there is nothing outside. If we throw everything we have (i.e. that there is) into a bag, we cannot be said to have done any *sorting!*

All we can do with 'thing' is to find another word, such as 'being' or 'entity,' and say

All things called 'things' can be called 'entities' and
All things called 'entities' can be called 'things.'

But that plainly is not what we did with 'Man' and 'Rational Animal.' 'Man,' 'Rational Animal' and 'Featherless Biped' did separate what is from what is not a Man, a Rational Animal or a Featherless Biped. They could be used in statements about something else than uses of words. The sorts they control link up with, or exclude, other sorts and so are useful to us in ordering knowledge. But 'thing,' 'entity,' 'property,' 'attribute,' 'substance,' 'relation' do not create such sorts and do not link up with or exclude all other sorts in a similar fashion. They can be made to link up with, and exclude, *one another,* in an analogous way, as we shall see, and that is a main part of their service. They could not be used as an abstract schema of everything unless we could make them do this. But they are not names for things in the fashion in which other words are names for things; and no question we can ask with other names can be legitimately asked with them.

To ask 'What is a particular?', 'What is a substance?', 'What is a property?' as though we were asking, 'What is a man?', is like asking, 'What is the universe inside?', or, 'What is space in?', or, 'Could time stop and go backwards?' These likewise are forms of words which only seem to have a sense through illegitimate analogy: for 'universe' and 'space' and 'time' are also bits of logical machinery. We can ask 'What is the earth inside?' or 'Can a train stop and go backwards?' But we cannot ask 'What properties has a property?' or 'What sort of thing is a thing?' And 'sort' and 'link' (as I have been using them through this discussion) are logical machinery belonging with the rest, unquestionable because assumed in the framework of every question.

'Sort' along with 'kind' is popular English for the technical logical term 'class,' and Logic has devised a number of ingenious paradoxes about the use of classes which illustrate the more general point. One of these has proved in many classrooms a favourite and unfailing stimulant to interest. Try to think of all classes. That is a class, seemingly—the class of all classes. What will it contain? Will it contain the class of 'all classes' among the rest? And can it reasonably be thought both to contain itself and to be contained by itself? Try to escape from this by a declaration that no legitimate class can be a member of itself. Legitimate classes are those which are not members of themselves. Then that declaration has created the class of all classes that are not members of themselves. Now, suppose we ask, of *this class,* 'Is it a member of itself?' what happens? We are in a fix either way. If we say it *is,* damning it, then it becomes all right, *not* a member of itself; but if we say it *isn't* a member of itself, hoping to save it, then it becomes a member of the class of all classes that are not members of themselves, that is to say, alack, an indubitable member of itself. There is no way out, except to agree that either to affirm or deny that a class can be a member of itself is nonsense.

What this ingenious riddle shows about 'class'—namely that we should not ask of a class anything that we can ask of a member of it—is true *mutatis mutandis* of 'property,' 'relation,' 'substance,' and 'thing.' To have a property is not a property; a relation is not related to what it relates; substances have no substance, and thing-dom is not a thing. Whenever we think of logical machinery as though it were of the same kind as what it handles we are thinking nonsense through bad analogy. So to ask about any of these words any questions which we rightly ask about other words, is, in Dodgson's parable, looking at the grin without the cat.

Instead then of asking 'What is a property, a particular, a universal?' and so on, we must ask another question, namely: 'What use to us are these terms?' A full answer would be a complete course in the classification, ordering and articulation of thought, and to give it would be the second of the things we could try to do (see p. 353); but I can only sketch and illustrate a few leading uses in the next chapter.

# Chapter Twenty-two: Logical Machinery: Some Uses

> *He that knows names do not always stand for ideas, will spare himself the labour of looking for ideas, where there are none to be had. It were therefore to be wished that everyone would use his utmost endeavours, to obtain a clear view of the ideas he would consider, separating them from all that dress and encumbrance of words which so much contribute to blind the judgment and divide the attention. In vain do we extend our view into the heavens, and pry into the entrails of the earth; in vain do we consult the writings of learned men, and trace the dark footsteps of antiquity; we need only draw the curtain of words, to behold the fairest tree of knowledge, whose fruit is excellent, and within the reach of our hand.*
>
> BERKELEY, *A Treatise concerning the Principles of Human Knowledge*

All thought is sorting. We never think of a mere 'it'; we always must make a 'what' of it in thinking. Similarly we never contemplate a mere 'what'; we always must take it as the 'what' of 'its.' This, which in technical language is the inherence of universals in particulars and of particulars in universals, has been central doctrine since Aristotle, offering, through the mistaken analogies glanced at of the last chapter, plenty of chances for misunderstanding. What it says fundamentally is that the terms in the two columns on p. 347 (and any substitutes we give them) are relative to one another. We never have to do with a thing apart from its attributes or with attributes apart from things which have or haven't them. Language by its ellipses will often make us think it is otherwise; but if we expand our language we find that we are always referring to things and referring to them in some distinguishable way.

359

Let me now attempt a summary descriptive classification of a selection of the words in my two columns. It does not pretend to indicate current usage faithfully; that is so shifting and free that a whole book would be required to display it. My notes are no more than a hint as to an obvious form of exercise that could, I believe, be made both attractive and instructive. In settling some words to fixed uses for my purpose in the rest of the chapter, I am being arbitrary. That does no harm if it focusses attention on their uses. We have nothing to teach here; all we have to do is devise good ways of directing attention, so that our pupils may take note easily of what they know already.

What we have to avoid is the suggestion that each of these words has only one proper use, and that if we use it otherwise we shall be wrong. That suggestion leads to mere despair. As a specimen of the wrong way of explaining their uses, here are some extracts from a worthy work on *English Synonyms* by George Crabb, 1826:

> *Quality* signifies such a thing as really is; *property* signifies belonging to a thing as an essential ingredient; *attribute* signifies the things bestowed on or assigned to another. The *quality* is that which is inherent in the object and co-existent; 'Humility and patience, industry and temperance, are very often the good qualities of a poor man.' ADDISON. The *property* is that which belongs to it for the time being; 'No man can have sunk so far into stupidity, as not to consider the *properties* of the ground on which he walks, of the plants on which he feeds, or of the animals that delight his ear.' JOHNSON. The *attribute* is the *quality* which is assigned to any object;
>
> > Man o'er a wider field extends his views,
> > God through the wonder of his works pursues,
> > Exploring thence his *attributes* and laws,
> > Adores, loves, imitates, th' Eternal Cause.
> >
> >                                        JENYNS.
>
> We cannot alter the quality of a thing without altering the whole thing; but we may give or take away *properties* from bodies at pleasure, without entirely destroying their identity; and we may ascribe attributes at discretion.

It will be noticed that the author's various declarations disagree sadly: can we take away at pleasure essential ingredients? that his distinctions do not distinguish, and that his quotations fail to support him; but the important point is his pretence to possess some mysterious warrant to arrest these words if they do not behave as he would have them. Actually he is trying to give them, *in general,* what are specialized uses taken out of various different philosophic traditions. If we can avoid doing this, avoid, above all, adopting the legislative attitude in our turn, then, I think, a very important use in teaching might be made of such examples from the Synonym Books. It would be worth while to experiment with them; to give sets of words that occur frequently (perhaps easier words than these, say, *Beautiful, fine, handsome, pretty,* as well as, say, *Cause, condition, conduce, contribute*) with some attempts such as the above to discriminate them; and to see what a class could do with them at leisure and with some weeks perhaps in which to collect and study examples. I can think of no more fruitful way of show- ing them how words really take their meanings from their settings.

Not forgetting this, let me in my turn attempt a classification of these words.

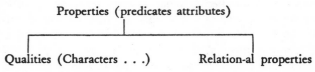

*Properties,* as the table suggests, I take as a general term includ- ing Qualities and Relational attributes. Perhaps through the modicum of life left in its metaphor, *property* seems to resist the specializations that *predicate* and *attribute* undergo. *Predicate,* hav- ing a main use in grammar for the part of the sentence containing what is stated about the subject, keeps the fact that something is being said in mind; it may carry suggestions that something is being seriously maintained, but is not necessarily so; like *property* it includes both Qualities and Relational properties. *Attribute,* too, covers both; but has often a strong suggestion that what is thought or said to be so is not so, or may not be (from 'attributed to Shakespeare,' and so on) and sometimes an equally strong 'of course' gesture ('to bear a club is an attribute of Hercules; being Hercules, he has his club, of course'). This can go further to sug- gest that a thing's attributes are what make it what it is, that is, are among its defining properties. *Predicate,* I fancy, keeps clear of this. But *character* and still more *characteristic* do not; both sug- gest 'really belonging,' not accidental to a thing but essential and inhering, *part* of or manifesting its *nature*—to bring in two more words that are sometimes only bits of logical machinery, and may be used as freely and loosely as any of them.

*Quality* I am technicalizing by putting it where I do in the table as a sub-division of properties over against relational properties. Actually it wanders with the rest and can be used for an unmistakable relational property ('Autolycus in his quality of a picker up of unconsidered trifles'). It has an important specialization in suggesting value, 'good quality.' *Character* shares this. Both are often words of praise; *characteristic* on the other hand has sometimes a derogatory smack. These gestures are worth noting because undoubtedly the complex ironies these words have been used to carry have been among the factors preventing any development of rigid logical uses. They have had, from the point of view of the conversationalist and the literary man, more important work to do.

For our purposes here, though, the contrast between *qualities* and *relational properties* is what matters most. A quality is the simplest form of property. But this, for the reasons discussed in the last chapter, is a way of putting it which is likely to mislead. As the simplest form of property, we ought, we may think, to be able to give examples. *Red, cold, painful* may occur to us as names of qualities. If we look into what we mean by them, however, doubts will arise. Do they, after all, stand for qualities or for relational properties? But this again is not the best way of putting the question. Not *what they stand for* but *how we take them* is what we have to inquire into.

Consider 'Diogenes is wise.' We can take it as attaching a predicate (attribute, quality, character, characteristic or universal) to Diogenes. All these words may in some settings be interchangeable indifferently, but in others a change may make an important difference. But before discussing that, it will clear things to consider 'Diogenes' a little. What does it do? With this, we take a glance at some of the words in my left-hand column. We can take it as doing various things and some of these will give us different propositions.

(1) We can take it as a mere name, that is, as 'the thing called Diogenes'—regardless of which thing it is except as having that name. It might be a dog, for example, and I have known a tortoise of that name.

(2) We can take it as more than a mere name, as carrying with

it a further description, say, 'the Greek philosopher who lived in a tub.' That is, we are sorting differently as we use it; we are taking the 'it' we are talking about as being a 'what' in further respects. It is no longer just 'what has that name,' but also 'what was a Greek philosopher who lived in a tub.'

(3) We may (on either (1) or (2)) take what we are talking about to be the whole life of the thing (the man, Diogenes, say, for simplicity) or some limited period in his life (when he came out of his tub for example) or more narrowly still, some single instant of his existence, some one of his acts, not his acts in general. And, with that, one of the main uses of 'particular' comes in to mark whether it is some particular act that is wise, or whatever Diogenes does (among such of his doings as can be wise).

This instance is almost as simple a one as I could choose; but, even in the simplest cases, there is room for such alternatives, between which we must decide, with the help of the setting. The fact that the examples we can hardly help using in these discussions are without settings has had an unfortunate effect throughout Logic. We have to compensate for it by frequently reminding ourselves that sentences never occur in actual speech without some guiding setting, shadowy or full, suggestive or decisive.

Here the setting consists only of 'is wise'—little enough, but still something,—and what we take ourselves to be *talking about* with 'Diogenes' is governed in part and varies with what we take ourselves to be *saying about it* with 'is wise.' What *are* we saying with 'is wise'? Grammar suggests, and logicians have too often been ready to follow it blindly, that 'wise' names a simple predicate. That is, all 'is wise' does is to attach a quality 'being wise' to Diogenes. A diagram of the proposition would then be $D^w$. Or, to use other machinery, that we are putting Diogenes in the class of 'wise things,' when the picture would be

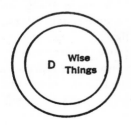

and wise things would be things having a quality, W. That may be a sufficient account for some purposes, but if we go on asking what we mean by 'wise' it is clear we may mean something much more complicated than this account takes note of: e.g. 'Diogenes is wise' = 'Diogenes sometimes (or always) does what, under the circumstances, is the wise thing,' and then, pursuing the question, 'What is the wise thing?' we may get, say, 'The thing which will lead, in all reasonable expectation to the best result.' And then, if we ask about 'best' in its turn, we shall get a definition out of some ethical doctrine. In this way the simplicity of $D^W$ as a picture of what we are saying becomes inappropriate. We shall need more complex machinery to exhibit the form of the proposition expressed by 'Diogenes is wise.' Something more like this for example:

'Some of the acts of Diogenes, occurring, as they do, in certain relations to other things (events, say, happening before, during and after his acts) cause (short for a very complex set of relations between the acts and other things) events which are the best (which, let us say, means are such that they will lead to all concerned being as happy as is possible).' A picture of this would be unendurably complicated but an outline of it would be something like this:

| Things being thus and thus | D ⋮ his acts | Cause | Events which make | A B C etc. | happier than if D's acts had been otherwise. |
|---|---|---|---|---|---|

This is a long way from the seeming-simplicity of $D^W$. But there is no doubt that anyone who on an ordinary occasion said, of a man he knew, 'He's wise' or of one of his acts, 'That was wise,' would be saying something of this order of complexity, and would, for most purposes of discourse, be using the word 'wise' as a short handy expression for a proposition whose form would be more like my picture than like $D^W$. Just what form he would take his proposition to have (or we, in listening to him, would take it as having) would depend upon the purpose and occasion. But only if we were talking to tots in the nursery would we give it a $D^W$ simplicity! For all ordinary purposes it will be pretty complex, as we can see from the remarks it normally calls forth; for example, 'I don't know about that. He seems to be forgetting what nationalism is like.' Here 'having taken account of the relevant factors' has been included in the form of 'is wise.'

The point I am making is the one discussed in Chapter XVII—that the forms of propositions do not tally with the verbal forms of their expressions. It is an extremely obvious point, but, like other obvious points, is incessantly overlooked, and overlooking it is the source of much stupidity. As Mill wrote, 'Were we to search among men's recorded thoughts for the choicest manifestations of human imbecility and prejudice, our specimens would mostly be taken from their opinions of the opinions of one another.' And this comes about chiefly through giving inappropriate logical forms to what they are saying.

The degree to which we illegitimately derive our opinions of other men's opinions directly from the verbal forms of their expressions can hardly be over-stressed. But before discussing some mistakes it leads us into I must say more about our choices of variable forms of proposition for sentences that remain verbally constant.

It may be thought that this variability only occurs with such words as 'wise'—that the trouble is that this word stands for a peculiarly nebulous, shifting and unstable notion. Let us take 'white' instead, and say 'Chalk is white.' This looks much more certainly a proposition of the form, $Ch.^W$, in which a quality, white, is just attached to a substance, chalk. These colour adjectives are in fact the favourite examples used in illustrating the simplest types of propositions. And for most purposes such an analysis is sufficient, but only because the conditions under which we say that chalk is white are so conveniently constant. We can pack them all up (normal lighting and eyesight, no colouring matter added, and so on) into a conditional clause which we need not express because everyone will suppose them assumed. But go outside the routine of ordinary settings in any direction, start talking physics or physiology or psychology, and 'Chalk is white' has to be given a much more complex form. It becomes a relational proposition with a large number of different terms, among others the condition of the visual system. Have a bad enough attack of jaundice (or take a dose of santonin) and white chalk will turn into yellow chalk. This, you will say, is a catch. I have shifted my sense of 'chalk' from the substance, chalk, to what I see when I look at it, i.e., the appearance of it to me. If I have, that brings out my point here, that even so seemingly simple and reliable a sentence as 'Chalk is white' or 'I see yellow chalk' can express propositions which must be given highly complex forms if they are to be understood sufficiently for even a mild discussion to be possible. Everybody perhaps will grant this. But the fact that so much of the practical daily routine of language keeps within spheres for which the governing conditions (as with buying and selling coloured chalks) remain so constant that they can be assumed unmentioned, misleads us. We think that what we are saying is much simpler than it is. All that is true is that we can *safely take it as simple*. The constancy of the conditions keeps the complexities from worrying us.

Compare, now, 'loud,' 'long,' 'sweet,' 'warm,' 'hard,' 'heavy.' We take all such words for most purposes as standing for qualities; but everyone is familiar with the situations in which we have to give this up and take them as making a covert comparison. Whether it is loud then depends on the rest of the hubbub and so on. So, too, but more frequently and obviously, with 'pleasant,' 'boring,' 'exciting,' 'wonderful.' They are often used as though it was safe to take them as qualities, but we all know that what pleases one does not please another; and their grammar here gives a hint that they name complex properties.

We have an interest often, in addition to our inclination to simplicity, in taking such words as standing for qualities. To say 'It's boring!' is not the same in its effects as to say 'It bores me.' The first suggests that all right-minded people would be bored by it too, that its power to bore is inherent in it as part of its very nature. The second is humbler and opens the gate a little wider to speculations about the causes of the boredom.

These everyday problems in the choice of logical forms swell suddenly into what seem formidable and profound philosophical affairs when we come to the use of 'beautiful,' 'good,' and 'true,' but are not changed. The disputes which have raged over them make us suppose that whether Beauty is a quality inherent in things, or a capacity for arousing certain effects in beholders (and equally disturbing problems for 'good' and 'truth') is a momentous question to be settled. But 'Is Beauty a Quality?' (Or, 'Is Beauty Objective?' which may sometimes mean the same) is a question very likely to be vitiated by the vacuities I discussed in the last chapter. To say it is a quality is to say *nothing*—except that, for certain purposes, to take it so would be a sufficient analysis of a proposition about beautiful things. It would be in 'She was only a beautiful Princess,' for example. But in 'Beauty resides in the eye of the beholder,' it would not.

I do not know whether it is more saddening or encouraging to reflect upon the enormous labour of thought which has been devoted to these topics; devoted so often in vain because the thinkers failed to observe that they dealt with similar problems all the time successfully in their conduct of other words. There is no 'general problem' of Beauty, or of the Good or of Truth, any more than there is a general problem of Funniness, of the Clean, or of the Straight; of Oddness, of Health or of the Exact. There are a million specific problems about beautiful, good and true things, in the many senses of these words, instead. But this is only a provoking way of saying that some problems which men have set themselves under these titles are products of the mistaken analogies which make us treat qualities, properties, universals, essences and so forth as though they were not logical machinery. How this happens both in these august topics and in humbler everyday matters is for the next chapter to discuss. Here I want only to insist that every sentence we reflect upon brings up questions about the choice of a logical form for it, and that *that* can never be settled apart from its purposes and occasions. Thus, in a very different sense from Mill's, every sentence can be made a lesson in logic; and the best sentences for that purpose are not those of philosophy but those of everyday life, for with them we are all, at times, consummate practical logicians. To control our skills a little more constantly is all we need.

So far I have been discussing the uses we make of this logical machinery in the background of every sentence, in settling what form we give to the proposition. But there are more explicit uses and abuses, and failures to notice the logical form of the proposition appropriate to the purpose beset whole subjects. Consider the logical forms appropriate in discussing for different purposes what we so easily call 'a poem.' We have a choice of many different types of object here. Among them are:

(1) Some one person's reading of certain marks on paper, his experience, let us say, as he reads them. As such, it has a date, lasts two minutes and, to turn to Column One, is an individual or a particular, that is, *unique,* as all occurrences are. And, as such, it is excessively hard to talk about with any certainty that we are not talking instead about what we remember of it, which may be very different and is of another type. For memories recur and recur, but the poem (in sense 1) does not. What memory holds of it is certain similarities between recurrent 'rememberings' which call themselves 'rememberings of it' and, as the psychology of evidence shows very disturbingly, what we think we remember grows and changes strangely with frequent rememberings. Thus already we have two poems: (1) the vanished particular occurrent, (2) a memory of it which is a recurrent product of various efforts to recall it. This is not a particular in the strict sense; it is something we can have more or less the same again and again. It is a class of similar rememberings and therefore a thing of a different logical form. (3) Now suppose we re-read the lines and study them. So we arrive, perhaps, at 'an understanding of the poem.' By this let us mean, for simplicity, some fairly settled interpretation which we expect will be our interpretation of it in the future—whenever we read it while alert, and unless we improve or deteriorate as readers, or unless someone points out something new about it. (4) Now suppose a number of people read the lines and agree 'in admiring the poem,' as we say. What are they admiring? Each is admiring a poem of type 3 let us suppose. In all probability, however, some of them will only have got as far as 2. So 'the poem,' which they all admire, cannot be what we will pretend it is, if we have not thought about the problem. It is not a single thing, however much we talk as though it were a single thing *there* publicly before us all to be directly examined. Instead it is a class of things (interpretations of different people and of the same people at different times), which we replace, for social reasons, by a fictitious single object.

In having this status, or being of this type, it is not at all peculiar. Tables and chairs have the same status and are of the same type. But the conditions under which we perceive chairs are fortunately much more constant than those under which we interpret poems. Otherwise we would all die young of broken backs. Thus in literary gossip we would, if we ventured more often to go into details about our interpretations, find ourselves patently talking about differing poems. But talk about poems may have all sorts of purposes behind it: social, suasive, literary, comparative, analytic, scientific. . . . Behind the words, 'literary criticism,' we will find at least as many different studies with diverse aims as was the case with 'Grammar' (see p. 189). And here too these aims get in one another's way. The parallel deserves to be worked out in detail. Meanwhile confusion between these aims is the chief source of controversies about general critical theory. While it reigns no one can expect his opinions to receive what will seem to him fair treatment. Undoubtedly, it would be healthy for literary studies, if the different logical forms of 'Shakespeare wrote a good poem,' appropriate for different purposes, were more widely recognized.

It will be noticed here again that the pretence that the appropriate logical form is $S \rightarrow P^G$ is much more *persuasive* than, say,

$$S \rightarrow \text{words which} \begin{cases} \text{interpreted by A give } a \\ \text{ " " B give } b \\ \text{ " " C give } c \\ \text{ " " " give " } \end{cases} \begin{array}{l} \text{and } a \text{ (mine) ex-} \\ \text{cites, under} \\ \text{heaven knows what} \\ \text{conditions, in } me, \\ \text{enthusiasm} \end{array}$$

$S \rightarrow P^G$ is more apt to make people think they agree. In this it is useful. The same inducement that we noticed with 'objective beauty' is at work. But for other purposes a fuller analysis is more useful. This need not lead anyone to abandon the customary modes of writing and talking about poems. I am not suggesting that anyone should adopt the ridiculous plan of trying to make his conversation, or his Essay, accord verbally to what he takes to be the logical form of his propositions. (See Chapter IX, page 152, *re* definite, V, ideas.) He would soon become unbearable if he did. This disclaimer would be out of place if readers were not so fond of supposing that this *is* the recommendation. I have been complaining that we too often derive logical form, mistakenly, from syntax. The remedy is certainly not in pretending to reverse the process and to derive our syntax from logical form. We cannot do it, and would deceive ourselves if we tried. What we can do is to separate them more clearly; write in one way and think in another, which I believe is what the best writers do. And their readers must follow the thought, not the words. As Berkeley wrote, 'They advise well, that we attend to the ideas signified, and draw off our attention from the words which signify them.'

But Logic is an exception. In examining logical problems we have to try to make our analyses accord with or indicate form more fully *when we can*. For, on the forms of propositions their relations to one another depend, and we can only contemplate forms persistently when they are expressed. But because the forms of most propositions of ordinary discourse are too complex to be represented with any precision, Logic confines itself to studying a few simple forms out of which by combination the more complex forms are built up. This gives an artificial air to its treatment which is depressing, unless the student understands why it must be so. The examples that logicians discuss are usually *not* instances of what they profess to be discussing—unless we agree to treat them as such, that is in a fashion quite unlike that in which we treat them in ordinary speech. For example, a logician will say [1] that

(1) *Mussolini is mortal*
(2) *Voltaire is witty*
(3) *Havelock Ellis is old*

express propositions of the same form. The moment we look into them and ask 'What do "mortal," "witty" and "old" mean?' we see that this is flagrantly not so. *In an ordinary setting,*

(1) 'is mortal' = 'will die sometime'
(2) 'is witty' = 'makes remarks which cause, in certain people, a peculiar pleasure, and in others a peculiar annoyance'
(3) 'is old' = 'has lived through many years'

And with these expansions the seemingly similar adjectives stand for very different logical forms. But that was not what the logician was interested in. His point was that if we took these adjectives *as standing for qualities,* and thus took the three prepositions as

[1] Cf., e.g. Dr Stebbing's *A Modern Introduction to Logic*, p. 51. I have discussed this question from another angle in *Basic in Teaching, East and West*, p. 9.

having the forms $M^M$, $V^W$, and $E^O$, they would have the same form. And, if we did so, undoubtedly, they would. There is thus a very important 'Let's pretend' condition governing the logician's choice of examples. They are chosen, *not as examples,* from current speech, of certain forms, but as *illustrating* them, if we agree to accept certain conventions. And these forms we must not expect to meet with in ordinary discourse any more than we expect to meet with geometrically straight lines or perfect circles in our ordinary commerce with things. And the parallel may be carried further. The fact that nothing in experience is straight does not make geometry useless. Similarly Logic's concern with simple forms does not make Logic useless; the simplicity is the condition under which logical analysis can be conducted with rigour. But an explanation of this point would prevent much misunderstanding.

Similarly, Logic commonly takes a proper name, such as 'Socrates' as naming a particular. When we learn what Logic means by 'a particular,' we see at once that 'Socrates,' as we commonly use such a name, does not stand for a particular, but for a class. It stands equally for Socrates-at-that-moment and for Socrates-at-the-next-moment and so on. The virtue of a name is that it does so. It is only useful if we can go on using it for different occurrences of Socrates. But a particular does not recur. It is something on the model of our old friend, a point (or a point-event)—something unique and single which we invent (as we invent points) for purposes of analysis. As such, it cannot be *named* in the fashion in which we name other types of objects, for these other types of objects are classes or series of particulars, or universals.

This brings up a more troublesome matter. Logic invents for purposes of analysis, objects which it calls, in opposition to particulars, 'universals'—that is, whats. A universal (other names for it are 'predicate,' 'attribute,' 'property'—including qualities and relational properties) is, for Logic, an instrument in analysis which, if we do not see what Logic is doing with it (and too many logicians also do not see this) will rightly seem to us very queer. I remember spending some of the leisure of youth disputing with certain logicians about their doctrine that 'even if there were no things at all, there would still be the property (universal) of being 107 in number.' It would, they agreed, belong then to nothing at all, but still would be a universal. The dispute was idle; each thought the other was being wilfully perverse. We were forgetting Aristotle and taking these universals, and the word 'is,' too seriously.

The point, however, is worth some attention, since no beginner in Logic, at present, can avoid some struggles with it. Current doctrine in Logic invites misunderstanding, many logicians are themselves ensnared, and one of the most important of logical distinctions is commonly expounded in a fashion which makes a distracting miscomprehension all but inevitable for a while. This is the distinction between what are known in Logic as the *connotation* and *denotation* of terms. Both words have a long and varied non-technical usage. Mill, I believe, technicalized them for Modern Logic; at least the references given usually do not go further than him. In non-technical use, the connotation of a word or phrase is what it suggests—often something extraneous and quite inessential. 'Pinks,' for example, may make one think of summer gardens and the sea-side, things not at all necessarily involved in something's being a pink. That may be the connotation of the word, for someone on a given occasion—what it suggests to him. And, similarly denotation, in free usage, is often no more than a name or description applicable to a thing. But technically the two words mark distinctions, which, if we can avoid the misconceptions which much current teaching imports, are extremely useful in any discussion of definition and in any attempt to explain the differences between the necessary, or essential, and the accidental, or contingent, characters (or properties) of things. These distinctions are a main part of the machinery with which we handle the link-up of words with things (see Chapter XXIII, pp. 385-389), and the shifts I was illustrating in Chapter XIX, pp. 338-341. These matters are so important for the conduct of thought that even the most elementary logic course must treat of them. The danger, as the history of the subject proves, is that we are thereby so likely to introduce metaphysical suggestions that are much more a hindrance than a help. In itself, a grasp of the distinction between an accidental and an essential property is as easy to acquire as it is useful. In practice, in choosing an apple for example, we have all mastered it perfectly. But in the process of reflection and analysis the student is likely to develop a conception of properties which will do him nothing but harm.

The *connotation* of a name, let us say, is the set of properties that anything must have if the name is to apply to it; the properties implied by the name. The *denotation* of a name is just the things the name applies to; the things which have these properties which entitle them to be called by the name.

Try this distinction out with the words for which it was introduced, class names like *cat, pint, triangle,* and no difficulty arises. It is obviously useful in cleaning up several sorts of ambiguities in 'What the word means,' 'The meaning of the word,' 'What I mean by it' etc. It helps us to separate (1) *All* the properties possessed in common by all the members of a class (or the comprehension), and (2) The properties we happen to think of as possessed by all the members (subjective intension), from (3) the connotation proper, those properties on account of which anything is put in the class and called by the name; and to separate all these from the things, the members of the class. These are great services. On the other hand, if we try making the distinction with other kinds of words, the perils that were discussed in Chapter XXI crowd upon us *and others with them.* In what follows I shall keep to these others, though Chapter XXI is also being illustrated here.

A chief trouble comes with abstract names. Dr Keynes writes, 'An abstract name *denotes* the qualities which are *connoted* by the corresponding concrete name.' *Redness* denotes what *red* connotes. This looks neat and right and seems to say something useful, until we try to see just what has been said. Then we notice that we may be introducing a very rash piece of metaphysics with the universal that *redness* denotes, or shifting the sense of 'denotes,' or both. The metaphysics appear very plainly in such an account as Jevons gives:

> Abstract terms are strongly distinguished from general terms by possessing only one kind of meaning; for as they denote qualities there is nothing which they can in addition imply (connote). The adjective 'red' is the name of red objects, but it implies the possession by them of the quality *redness;* but this latter term has one single meaning—the quality alone. Thus it arises that abstract terms are incapable of number or plurality. Red objects are numerically distinct each from each, and there is a multitude of such objects; but *redness* is a single existence which runs through all these objects, and is the same in one as it is in another. (*The Principles of Science,* p. 33.)

The artificiality of this account and its arbitrariness are very evident. But, and this is perhaps the most important point for the teacher, the account is by no means put forward, nor are such accounts usually taken, as either arbitrary or artificial. It is the orthodox view of the grammar books (so far as they have one) as well as of Logic, and readers all but inevitably get the impression (so far as they get hold of anything at all) that it is an account of some very fundamental facts about language and how it works, not a tricky set of suggested definitions to be used only for certain purposes of analysis. Of course, I am not complaining that the account is artificial. The burden of Chapter XXI was that any account of this machinery must be artificial, since the machinery itself is. The complaint is that such accounts pretend to be about something other, and more, than our devices for displaying differences of meaning. They pretend to be about the structures of meanings in some 'absolute' sense of structure. Thus, at the heart of our whole system of distinctions for comparing our meanings we have, in traditional teaching, a gross case of that very confusion between statement and definition which we have seen, at so many points above (especially in Chapters XV and XXI) to be most frustrating. And it occurs just where thought is most needed; that is, on the 'how' of all our distinctions. It imposes upon what is in any case a hard enough matter a dense unnecessary mystery. 'Abstract' and 'concrete' are words that cannot be easy to handle. Their *useful* senses are too mixed and too shifting for that; but there is no necessity to make them more obscure still by giving a first place, in this fashion, to a sense for 'abstract' which is *not* useful, which is a strayed piece of metaphysics unintelligible *out of its supporting system,* and which is therefore a prime source of the fear of bewilderment that haunts this subject. It is vitally important that we should make the differences, and the peculiar powers, of abstract and concrete thinking as clear as we can to our pupils. But we cannot hope to give them any insight if we encourage this traditional confusion. On the other hand, we cannot ignore it. Our pupils will have received it already, and language prompts it with a thousand suggestions a day. The only thing to do is to take some vigorous statement, such as this from Jevons, invite close attention to it, and expose it boldly. We shall find, that such an examination gives, at the same time, a useful exercise in several other matters: among them, in that manoeuvring with inverted commas (see Chapter XIX, p. 327) for which a perfected curriculum would willingly find abundance of time.

First as to the metaphysics: 'redness is a single existence which runs through all these objects, and is the same in one as it is in another.' Or, as Dr Keynes wrote, summarizing this view, 'An attribute considered purely as such and apart from its concrete manifestations is one and indivisible.' That is a familiar kind of Platonism and delightful, and much more, *in its proper place,* which is not here in the theory of words. So I should be brief, and say dogmatically that any philosophic doctrine such as this is something to be considered in the light of everything we can consider (The Ideas are, in origin, *religion* and belong there), not something to be smuggled, as a light assumption, into our account of how language works. If we smuggle it in, we will naturally then find that language supports it. It is probably not true that Plato, as some have said, derived his doctrine of Ideas from the behaviour of language; but, in any case, the behaviour of language can be made to support all conceivable views as to the nature of the universe. Assumptions about language are necessarily chief determining factors in all brands of metaphysics; that very fact should make us wary in basing our linguistic theories on any metaphysical doctrine. And we should be still more distrustful of any attempt to draw philosophic conclusions from what we suppose, or profess to observe, about the ways of words. If we keep the Doctrine of Ideas for elsewhere, and refrain from treating 'redness' and *redness* as more than analytic devices for comparing red things, we will be better placed to make observations about what words do. And it is these observations which are helpful. Anti-metaphysical (or, more specifically, anti-Realist) bias here is simply a protest against a method which needlessly obscures these observations.

One of them is that, in Jevons, 'denotes' shifts its sense importantly between '"Man" denotes *men*' and '"Redness" denotes *redness.*' For men are only denoted by 'man' through possessing the properties which 'man' connotes. 'Denotes' and 'connotes' in this sense are correlative and co-operative words. But with 'redness,' according to Jevons, this is not so. And we shall find this a case in which metaphysics, if taken seriously, interferes with Logic.

The reader may have felt that Jevons was niggardly, if not harsh, in the passage I quoted. Why should not poor 'redness' have its connotation? Why should there be 'nothing which it can in addition imply'? As *denoting* a quality, why should not 'redness' connote such properties as *redness* must have in order to be properly called 'redness'? For example, being a colour, being extended, being the colour opposite to greenness? Why should he not treat 'redness' as we treat 'man'? The answer is that to do so would expose the artificiality of the whole business too much. There is nothing formally to prevent our doing so to any length we think worth while.

A diagram will perhaps help:

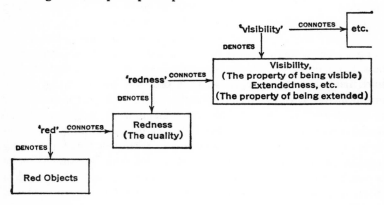

We could go further and say that 'visibility' connotes being perceptible; and 'perceptibility' connotes being apprehensible. If we want to carry on further still, we shall have to invent some new words, but there is nothing *formally* to preclude us from introducing, for contemplation, abstractions of any degree of remoteness from red objects that we please.

And for the view of logical machinery that is recommended here, there is no objection to doing so, since these terms are merely instruments of formal analysis. And there are clear advantages. The distinction between connotation and denotation has often been described as the *pons asinorum* of Logic. If we preserve the symmetry of their applications by keeping the metaphysics out, the distinction becomes very obvious. When we talk of pickled walnuts no one has any difficulty in distinguishing between the walnuts that are pickled and the pickling they have gone through. The denotation-connotation distinction, if handled by itself, is no harder to grasp than that.

This abstraction scale runs parallel with a more familiar scale of generality, which we can picture simply with an enclosure series.

This scale of higher and higher generality is the one we commonly use, and the more elaborate-looking abstraction series is derived from it. Generality (or inclusiveness) is the handier comparing device, because while there need be no doubt that 'to be visible' is a wider notion than 'to be red' (since we know many visible things which are not red, but no red things which are not visible) there may well be doubt whether visibility is more abstract than redness. In fact there must be doubt until we have settled just what we mean by 'abstract' and in what sense one abstract thing can be more abstract than another.

The reason why accounts of abstract terms, such as Jevons', stop short so arbitrarily may now be evident. Give an abstract term an inch of connotation and it takes an ell! Jevons, of course, is well aware of this danger. Having said, in my quotation, that 'abstract terms are incapable of number or plurality,' he adds:

> It is true that we may speak of *rednesses* meaning different kinds or tints of redness, just as we may speak of *colours* meaning different kinds of colours. But in distinguishing kinds, degrees, or other differences, we render the terms so far concrete. In that they are merely red there is but a single nature in red objects.

The cloven hoof shows most in the last sentence. That is how the realm of thought is peopled with the natures that most lead men astray. That is the magical trick by which the Bushman finds a single malefic nature in all the objects in connection with which death has occurred. It is a queer part of the Principles of Science that there should thus be 'but a single nature' in blood, sunsets and rags, and all that is 'merely red.'[1] But more to the immediate point here is the manoeuvre in the preceding sentence. If, in distinguishing kinds, 'we render the terms so far concrete,' it is in quite another sense of 'concrete' (and 'abstract') from that in use in his opening sentence. For 'bright-redness' and 'dull-redness' are every bit as abstract (in his first sense of 'abstract' as being the name of a quality, not of an object) as 'redness.' By distinguishing degrees of an abstract quality, we do not make the words we use, or our meanings, less abstract in this sense. There is a confusion here, which appeared above in my citations from Dr Keynes; and if we wonder whether, after all, these abstruse-seeming topics *are* of any importance for general education, the answer is that while such confusions lurk in the teaching of them, we can hardly expect them to be of much benefit.

My point is that these topics are only abstruse because unnecessarily and remediably confused. And I give this avoidable confusion a high place among the factors which prevent that self-examination and self-control of thought on which improvement in general intelligence depends. Anyone who asks himself what he is doing in abstract thought and how to do it better must encounter these difficulties at present; and we make no attempt to help him with them. We cannot, unless we can first clear them up, in some degree, ourselves. I do not pretend that this account clears them up; but it attempts to show that they can be cleared up, in some degree, and that here is one way in which education might become less wasteful in its technique. The struggles of the protocol writers with 'concrete' and 'abstract' over the case of Love and the Motor Car will remind us that these problems cannot profitably be dealt with by dodging them.

In much of the above I have been following Sweet, whose dashing paper, 'Words, Logic, and Grammar' (1876), marked the beginning of a new epoch for linguistic studies. His discussion will state one of the main confusions clearly for us:

> An instructive instance of the dependence of logic on the accidents of language is afforded by the distinction it makes between such

---

[1] I am not quarrelling, of course, with the view that red things share a common property, but with a misleading mode of formulating that view.

words as 'white' and 'whiteness.' 'Whiteness' is correctly described as an 'abstract' name, as signifying an attribute without reference to the things that possess the attribute. 'White,' however, is held to be connotative: it denotes particular objects and connotes the attribute 'whiteness.' How a word can be said to denote an object which is entirely unknown until the name of that object is joined to it, was always a matter of bewildering astonishment to me, when I first began to study logic, and probably has been to many others as well. The truth is, of course, that 'white' is as much an abstract name as 'whiteness' is, the two being absolutely identical in meaning. I consider, further, that all attribute-words are denotative and connotative, they denote an attribute and connote attributes of that attribute. (p. 19)

Unluckily he now shifts the sense of 'connote' inadvertently, impeding his exposition but providing a useful exercise in these distinctions. He continues:

Thus the word 'colour' is the name of an attribute, but it also connotes all the various kinds of colour, red, blue etc.; 'bright' connotes various degrees of brightness, and so on.

This, I think, is a slip, not an intentional change of 'connotes.' 'Colour' is the name of a general attribute and 'red,' 'blue,' etc. are names of relatively specific determinations of colour, but 'colour' does not connote them any more than 'animal' connotes being a pig, a donkey, etc. Reds, blues, etc. may be denoted by 'colour' and their specific attributes *being red, being blue,* etc. are included in *being coloured* as the members of a class are included in a class, but they are not, except in a changèd sense of 'connote,' connoted by the name of *being coloured,* i.e. 'colour.' Similarly any brightness will have some degree, but the various degrees of brightness are not connoted by 'brightness.'

However, on page 18, Sweet states the source of the main confusion about abstractness admirably.

Such a sentence as 'Whiteness is an attribute of snow' has identically the same meaning as 'snow is white,' and 'white snow,' and the change of 'white' into 'whiteness' is a purely formal device to enable us to place an attribute-word as the subject of a proposition.

This takes us back to Dr Keynes and his 'unpunctuality is irritating.' (p. 350) His 'abstract use' and 'concrete use' of names derives from the grammatical distinction. Whether a word is put as a subject or as an attribute in a sentence has nothing to do with whether, in another and a more important sense, what we are thinking of is thought of abstractly or concretely. This more important sense is best explained by means of an instance.

Suppose we are thinking of a bit of chalk. We can think of it as a white, light, smooth, smeary, small, fragile, rigid thing, here, now, in the hand. It has its own peculiar shape; it is going to be used in a certain way; it has a history behind it, was made by a certain process out of stuff which may have been dug out of a certain pit and once was laid down on the bed of an ancient ocean. The more completely we take note of it, and of everything that has to do with it, the more *concretely* (in this sense) we will be thinking of it.

Instead we may, for convenience and according to our purpose, set aside some of these innumerable possible aspects of it. If we only care for it as something to use on a blackboard, we think of it as just a bit of chalk. If we are chemically interested in it we think of it as calcium carbonate. Or, going a step further, we can think of it as a solid, or finally as just a thing. These may (in the sense) be said to be progressively more *abstract* ways of thinking of it. We have left out more and more of its distinctive properties.

There are clearly innumerable ways of abstracting. For example, we can think of this bit of chalk as being yellow, as being coloured, as being visible, as being able to be perceived by the senses, as being able to be thought of. This is another way of leaving out its distinctive properties. It will be noticed that these two ways of abstracting seem to end at the same point, the point at which we are merely thinking of it as a something—as a mere *it* with hardly any *what* about it, at which point it is barely distinguishable from a nothing. This is the most highly abstract sort of thinking and it is evident that so far from being difficult, highly abstract thinking is extremely easy. What is difficult is to keep *distinctions between abstractions* in order. And our logical machinery is intended to help us in this and has its only justification by so doing. Unhappily, instead of helping it usually hinders.

It is perhaps important to insist at this point that abstract thinking is not a highly specialized sophisticated intellectual feat. In all our thought we are abstracting to some degree, and the simplest organism when its behaviour is selective is abstracting. As William James said, 'A polyp if it ever thought "Hallo thingemabob again!" would thereby be a conceptual thinker.' English philosophy throughout its best century was distracted into fruitless argument by a blunder about this. And I could have taken my examples not from recent text-books of Logic but from Locke and Berkeley. It was supposed that the mind began with concretes and then performed a peculiar operation which resulted in abstract ideas. But the mind is primordially abstractive; of whatever it handles, it takes some aspects and omits others, and the distinct things (Sense One of 'definite') it thinks of are from the beginning themselves products of abstraction. Thus we are naturally skilful beyond description in abstracting. What we are not sufficiently skilful in, as this chapter has tried to show, and has doubtless also inadvertently shown, is in reflecting on how we abstract.

# *Chapter Twenty-three:* The Essential and the Accidental, and the Freedom in Definition

> Man, proud man,
> *Drest in a little brief authority,*
> *Most ignorant of what he's most assur'd,*
> *His glassy essence, like an angry ape,*
> *Plays such fantastic tricks before high heaven*
> *As make the angels weep; who, with our spleens,*
> *Would all themselves laugh mortal.*
>
> Measure for Measure

The reason for cultivating reflection upon the process of abstracting—and with this I return to the point touched on when I began to discuss connotation and denotation (p. 372 in the last chapter)—is that only so can we improve discrimination between what is essential and what is accidental in a matter.

The flounderings of the protocols show how frequently people do not know what they are talking about: in this sense, that they cannot separate *the properties which determine the thing they are talking about* from other properties which may or may not belong to it *without* its being thereby any less itself. They wobble in a fatal indecision as to which exactly of the things they happen to know *about* a thing they will include *in* it, and constantly use accidents, or inessential properties, as defining 'its very nature.' The process, then, of clearing up their views must be that of giving them increased power to form new and better arranged *things* to think about. Or, rather, of making them recognize that what they mean by a word is within their own control—not given them inexorably by the language. And that in their choices here they create the things they are talking about.[1]

---

[1] For example, every sentence here may be confidently misread by those who wish to. 'Create'? We do not create anything ever! 'Its very nature'? As though things possessed natures of their own! 'Not know what they are talking about'? Who does ever? And so on.

Exercises with this intent are easy to frame. Most controversies supply them. Best of all, perhaps, as I have suggested above, are selections of protocols illustrating other people's conceptions of a common topic. Sets of sentences following familiar *ambiguity paradigms* (See Appendix) may be useful and need less preparation. And translations into or from Basic force these decisions ceaselessly into attention. But what matters most in all such exercises is that the learner should be made to watch the consequences of his decisions, and see that what a word means (that is, here, what the *thing* is that he is talking about) depends upon the purpose in hand. It is no use expounding to him the difference between accidental, or contingent, and necessary, or essential, properties unless he sees that what is essential for one purpose is inessential for another and why. Thus many favourite ways of illustrating the difference do little good. If, as logicians have lately been fond of doing, we take our examples out of the exact sciences, or from those parts of them for which the problems of definition have been finally settled, we are likely to create an unhelpful impression that the task turns on *knowing* the answer, not on *finding* it. Thus, if we explain that 'being a plane curve,' 'having its radii equal,' and 'having the angle in the segment subtending a diameter a right angle,' are *essential* properties of a circle; but 'having a diameter 3 inches long' is an *accident,* we will be illustrating the difference but may hide the reason. It suggests that circles *are* so; not that for the purposes of the geometer circles have been made so. And this often imports a notion of 'correct meanings'—valid enough and for good reasons in the sciences—which is not valid and merely obstructive outside them. It is better to take some word like *man* or *beautiful* or *poetry* in place of *circle,* and try what happens with say,

> Human nature never changes
> Man is a creature of infinite variety

There is no 'correct meaning' for man or human in such sentences. The task of interpreting them is that of finding out which meanings work best for which purposes. In other words, of trying various choices among properties which may be taken as essential to the meaning of *man* and seeing what happens with them.

*Man* is, in one way, better for such purposes than *beauty* or *poetry.* For it is not quite so likely as with other words that we will suppose that there is something which man *really is,* and that we could know what this is and thereby settle the question of his changeableness. But people do very frequently behave as though there were something which beauty *really is,* and another thing which poetry *really is,* and that doubts about questions using the words *beauty* and *poetry* are due to our ignorance about these things and not about our use of the words. I will not dilate upon the mischiefs which these absurd supposals cause. I have written about them elsewhere, especially in *Basic Rules of Reason,* and could write again for they are an inexhaustible theme.

This has brought me to the last main point I can discuss in this summary sketch of a course in Logic, namely the freedom of definition. I have said something at several places above about the peculiar paralysis which the mention of definitions and, still more, the discussion of them induces. It can be prevented, I believe, by stressing the purposive aspect of definitions. We want to do something and a definition is a means to doing it. If we want certain results, then we must use certain meanings (or definitions). But no definition has any authority apart from a purpose, or to bar us from other purposes. And yet they endlessly do so. Who can doubt that we are often deprived of very useful thoughts merely because the words which might express them are being temporarily pre-empted by other meanings? Or that a development is often frustrated merely because we are sticking to a former definition of no service to the new purpose?

The limitation of thought to successive moments, its discursive character, we can bear:

> The troubles of our proud and angry dust
> Are from eternity and shall not fail.
> Bear them we can, and, if we can, we must.

But that our thought, which is clear and in order one moment, should, in the next, be twisted, clouded, closed, merely because we are insufficiently supple in changing the meanings of our words, is harder to bear; for it is, in a large measure, unnecessary and remediable. Logic usually stresses the other aspect—the excessive ambiguity of words—but their excessive rigidity and obstinate attachments to inappropriate meanings should be at least equally noticed. It makes a happier starting point for a discussion.

Subject only to our purpose—which, I need hardly say, *includes communication*—we are free to define our words as we please. This, of course, applies also to the word 'definition'; and I am availing myself of this freedom here. A first consequence is that there will be many different things which, for different purposes, will equally properly be called definitions. Logicians, who tend to neglect explicit discussion of purposes, usually attempt to restrict the word severely, and economize in their explanations. But a fairly full explanation is the only way to disperse the atmosphere of mystery, if not of hanky panky, which hangs over the topic.

The main varieties of definition have been touched upon already in discussing denotation and connotation. A statement of the connotation of a word is what is usually meant in Logic by a definition. I pass by the familiar troubles that afflict the question; 'Does such a definition define a *word,* its *sense* or a *sort of things?*' noting only what an opportunity for exercises in the use of inverted commas it affords. Let us consider definitions by denotation, or exemplificatory definition.

I defined in this way the most important sense of 'abstract' above, and in Chapter IX the most important sense of 'definite' (Sense IV). As we all know, such a method is very often by far the most convenient and the clearest way of showing how a word is to be used. The most effective definition of a finger (or of 'finger') is 'This and this and anything like them!' Similarly an epic may often most conveniently be *'Paradise Lost, The Odyssey* and such.' 'And such' is, of course, the difficulty: 'anything like them' in what respects? It may be excessively hard to say. In the limiting case there may be no relevant similarities whatever between our examples. Then we shall be deceiving ourselves, persuading ourselves that we are talking about a kind of things when there is no such kind. This happens probably more often than we would care to believe. Fairly often the only similarity is just that we call them alike—as Croce suggested in his definition of the Sublime (p. 247 above, Chapter XV).

But, none the less, we do succeed frequently in using these exemplificatory, extensive, denotative definitions with great advantage, in spite of being unable at the moment, or perhaps ever, to *say* what are the common properties which make what we are talking about into a kind. Of course, they are a kind in so far as we call them by the same name; but they need to be a kind in another way, and this other way is, we hope, the ground for our calling them by a common name.

It is a fundamental truth that we can sort things rightly without knowing how we sort them. If we could not do this, we could never know anything. From our earliest, our behaviour is all sorting. William James' polyp with its 'thingemabob again!' was sorting. We may pick out things as alike in relevant respects without necessarily being able to say (or even think) anything about the respects in which they are alike. Between merely *recognizing* things and being able, in reflection, to discern the respect of likeness there is an immense gap in development. Most human beings grow across.it at some points. Chimpanzees may perhaps cross it here and there; the lower animals probably never do. But even the most reflective humans cross it, hitherto, at relatively few points. Those who pretend that there is little further scope for human development are being unimaginative. We might indeed describe general education as the process of advancing this development at the nodal points. And one of the nodal points is certainly this question of our use of the word 'definition.'

Some logicians object to the process of giving examples being called 'definition,' and the objection will make the problem clearer. Dr Stebbing, for example, writes:

> It may, however, be doubted whether the giving of typical examples can be rightly regarded as a process of defining. . . . After being given the examples a man would then know more or less how to apply the word, but it seems doubtful whether he would know what the word (say, 'sonnet') expresses. Definition is only one of the means through which we come to understand words. We must be careful not to use 'definition' so widely that it comes to stand for any process enabling us to learn the application of names. These processes are so different that to call them by the same name leads to confusion. (*Op. cit.* p. 422.)

The first sentence, with its 'doubted' and its 'rightly,' seems to me to suggest that we are supposed to be inquiring here into facts about *something other than our uses of the word* instead of discussing a policy. If so, it illustrates my freedom of definition point.

The suggestion would be that, *if we knew more,* we could some-how settle the question whether giving typical examples is a process of defining or not, one way or the other. But we already know here all we need to know. This is not a question of fact like whether the tallest man in Cambridge has a g in his name; it is a ques-tion of policy, namely, whether, if we call this process 'definition,' we shall mislead ourselves and other people. And to *that* question the answer is, I think, that it depends on the explanations we give, and on our and their conceptions of the uses of words *in general.*

The rest of the passage is about this large question of policy. I must insist how large it is, otherwise there is some risk of the question seeming petty and 'merely verbal.' What is at stake is not just whether this one word 'definition' is to be used widely or narrowly, in one technical use or in many varying uses, but our whole conduct with words in assigning to them their meanings. Are we to control them by fixing, and remembering, single tech-nical meanings or by familiarizing ourselves with the paradigms of their fluctuations in different settings? That is the really important question.

I grant, of course, and at once, that for technical purposes the logician can restrict the word 'definition' in any way he chooses. And if the 'we' at the head of Dr Stebbing's penultimate sentence stands for 'we Logicians,' I have no complaint. Let them be as careful as they like, if they let us see what they are doing. But this 'we' is not so unambiguous. On the opposite page we find 'what is ordinarily meant by "definition"' is the object of the chase and not just a technicality; and Dr Stebbing introduces the prob-lem by considering 'under what circumstances in ordinary discourse we should need to ask for a definition.' So the caution seems to be addressed to users of the language in general, and it is this general legislation that I am concerned to challenge as being strategically calamitous. But as the situation is **highly** complex, the strategy is complex too.

The technical sense of 'definition' **which** Miss Stebbing recom-mends is described as follows:

> Two expressions are used, so related that the one is equivalent to the other. Definition always involves two expressions: the expression

(which may be a single word) to be defined, and the defining expression (which must contain more than one word).

The last qualification seems wilful and would be inconvenient for the Esquimaux or any other user of one-word sentences; moreover, may we not define 'incomputable' with 'incalculable' as well as with 'not able to be calculated'?

But this is trifling. The important points concern the words 'expression' and 'equivalent.' An expression, for the logician, is a word or group of words (or a mathematical or logical symbol); and the two expressions are equivalent if whatever we say with one can be said with the other. But 'say' is, as we know (along with 'expresses,' see Chapter VIII, pp. 135 ff. above), a trickily ambiguous word, and we shall do well to keep our eye on this. However, the logician's purposes are such that many things that are very troublesome to the literary man and the student of interpretation need not often bother him. The important point for him should be, how is he to prevent his definitions (in this sense) from remaining merely a circular system of more or less complex equivalent symbols? In other words, how is he to get them to apply to anything? For if, when we define a word, we merely supply an equivalent group of words for it, then the question 'What is this word's sense here?' just gets bandied about through the vocabulary and is not answered until and unless we apply some other mode of definition in answering it. The question is rarely if ever, 'What other words could I use instead?' *That* question this restricted kind of definition does answer. It is, 'What sort of thing does this word stand for?' or 'What should I understand by this word' or 'What should I be saying (expressing, etc.) with it?' and these questions the account of definition I have been considering does *not* meet, though it professes to do so. We can see this by challenging it to define 'say' or 'express' or 'understand.' It can then take either of two courses. It can ring some changes with further words that may take their place; or it may reply that these words are *indefinables*. The first course does not meet the demand but only shifts its incidence. The second brings me to the point I have been approaching; which is that the 'equivalent expression' mode of definition (*the* logical mode) only does the work that both the logician and the general public require definitions to do when, at very many points, it links up with modes of defining of *another sort*. Unless verbal expressions are equivalent at certain points with *other things than words*, definition remains merely a system of verbal manipulations unable to answer the reasonable and necessary demands, of many distinct kinds, which 'in ordinary discourse' we make when we ask for 'what is ordinarily meant by a "definition."' And it is because an understanding (we *all* understand—until we discuss the subject) of how verbal definition links up with other modes of definition is supremely important in the conduct of thought and language that I described the logical strategy in the matter as calamitous.

What we have to do is to extend the senses both of 'equivalent' and of 'expression' and then Dr Stebbing's process of definition becomes a special case of a more general process. We can also then take account of the articulation of words and meanings with life and action in a fashion which Logic too often neglects to do. But not all logicians leave that problem out; W. E. Johnson, for example, included it by recognizing what he called *ostensive* definition, that is, 'the act of indicating, presenting or introducing the object to which the name is to apply.' In brief by pointing to it, with our finger or with a glance. That is the fundamental mode of definition, as we all know if we are beginning to learn a language. The word thereby becomes equivalent *to the pointing*. We should be rather careful here not to suppose that the word on this view is said to be an equivalent for *the thing pointed to*. Dr Stebbing, for example, makes this mistake and refutes the view by writing, 'The process of pointing (whether metaphorically or otherwise) to the referend (her term for "what is signified"; here, what is pointed to) is not a process of defining since the referend is not another expression equivalent to the defined expression.' The referend is not, of course; but the pointing to it is. The word and the act are, with respect to the setting and purpose, *equivalent expressions*. This extends 'expression' to include any act whatever that may be found (in a given setting) a useful way of indicating the sense of a word. If we want to show what 'smirk' means, and have some voluntary control over our features, we do not try to give a verbal definition; we give an ostensive definition! This extension of 'expression' also establishes that wide and varied articulation between language and life that Logic sometimes leaves in such mystery. Indeed, if language were not being incessantly con-

trolled by extra-linguistic, non-verbal, definitions, and if words were
not constantly equivalent to acts, it would soon lose all touch with
anything, and simultaneously we would all lose intellectual touch
with one another.

Extending 'expression' so, we are forced to recognize that 'equivalent' thereby acquires a variable range of senses. The strictest sense,
which Logic aspires to use, makes two expressions equivalent where
the one does *everything,* and no otherwise, that the other does. But
this (as our discussion of translation in Chapter VIII showed) is a
limit not in actuality ever attained. But with respect to some restricted purpose (for Logic, plain sense) one expression may on
occasion be a perfect substitute [1] for another. Thus, as with translation—it is the same problem—we should recognize that definition
is always *partial.* If we disregard all but a restricted purpose (or
limited mode of communication, as Logic commonly does) we can
overlook this and set ourselves very rigorous standards of precision.
But a general theory of interpretation, which takes strict logical
statement as only one mode of discourse, will remember our inevitable partiality, and point out that no expression whatever is
entirely and in all respects equivalent to any other.

There is then nothing lost but everything to be gained by using
different sorts of definitions for different purposes, or giving the
word 'definition' various senses, provided we know and can make
clear if need be to others what we are doing. That making clear
will be itself a process of defining, of showing how we are proceeding. To put the matter in these terms is, I believe, a good way of
dissipating the obstructive mystery about definition that is so daunt-
ing. Another is to invite the view that a definition is itself an invitation, a request, or, on occasion, an imperative; but *not* a statement.
It is difficult in practice, so strong are normal writing habits, not to
*urge* that this *IS so.* There is a temptation here to *insist* that definitions, properly regarded, are not statements, not true or false therefore, but only wise or foolish, prudent or imprudent, more like a

---

[1] Dr Stebbing (*op. cit.* p. 423) regrets that 'Mr Johnson has been led to the
extraordinary view that definition is *nothing but substitution.*' She says, 'In defining
we do not *substitute* one expression for another. We use *two* expressions related as
we have explained. It is true that since the expressions are equivalent it is permissible
to substitute one for the other on any occasion of its use. But the definition is not a
*statement* that the one *can* be substituted for the other.' Johnson said that a definition
was a substitution, not that it was a statement about it.

resolve to eat six dozen oysters than a record of fact. But if we adopt this plan, then clearly we have no business to insist or make statements about it: we are offering a definition (of 'definition') and if a definition is a request it should be expressed accordingly in the appropriate mood, which is not the indicative but the optative. So I should not say 'A definition is a request' but 'Come! let us understand by "a definition" an invitation to regard a certain word as meaning so and so. Will you be so good as to accept?'

This is the principle of Freedom in Definition and, evidently, like other freedoms it increases our responsibilities. I would add a subprinciple, or special assistant, namely, the Equivalence in Grammatical Formulation—which may lighten them. To propose a defining choice *in one grammatical form only* is always dangerous. The classical examples have been 'What is Truth?' and 'What is Beauty?' These suggest that our job is to catch an already determined universal.[1] Let us agree instead that:

> What sorts of things are beautiful?
> When are what beautiful?
> Beautiful things are which things?
> How is 'beautiful' used here?
> With which logical form would it be convenient here to take 'x is beautiful'?

and so on . . . are all proper alternative formulations for the definition question we are asking. If we do so, we are much better placed to avoid mistaking logical machinery for what it handles.

A choice of a grammatical form very often seems to impose the use of a logical form. As I have urged repeatedly in Chapters XVII, XXI and XXII, this misleads us; a given sentence may, and often must, be read with varying logical forms. This principle, that we are free to use different grammatical forms in definitions as logically equivalent, states the complementary case and is a further defence against the tyranny (which feels like support) of logical machineries —against the restrictions we suffer if we forget that they are devices with no authority which does not derive from their services to us in analysis and comparison. They are modes of apprehension (mental

---

[1] We may recognize universals to be logical machines and thus harmless and yet note the distortions that metaphysical beliefs in them induce. In this they are like ghosts—to be feared though not believed in.

forceps), not things we grasp; but, forgetting this, we take them to be the very things themselves we aspire to talk about. 'Things themselves'! It is a notorious phrase and may make me seem here to be overlooking the limitations of thought. My point is only that what we think of is not to be regarded as necessarily having the logical form we find convenient in handling it. But still we can handle it only with some form of thought, with some logical instrument, though we can vary these—very much as we vary a word without changing our meaning. Logical machines are not themselves words; but they behave like language; so our handling of them reproduces the alternatives of the verbal situation.

In all this I am using my freedom of definition, offering an invitation to try how a view serves.

Of course, every such invitation can be parallelled by a statement 'that it has been offered'—as here—and so this proposal is not as drastic as it may seem. Yet the indicative mood is nowadays frequently a tyrannous usurper and—to continue in the optative—may we not think it would be a big mistake to identify the *invitation* with the *statement* that it has been offered? The advantage of regarding a definition as a request is that this clears up the question why it is neither true nor false. Bertrand Russell pointed this out in the Introduction to *Principia Mathematica*: 'A definition is not true or false, being the expression of a volition, not of a proposition.' I do not know whether he was consciously echoing Aristotle's remark in the *De Interpretatione*: 'Every sentence is not a proposition; only such are propositions as have in them either truth or falsity. Thus a prayer is a sentence, but is neither true nor false.' But Dr Stebbing is misreading him when she comments: 'This statement is certainly false. If a definition expresses a volition, it must be of the form "I am going to use 'X' to express what 'Y' expresses." This is a proposition which will be true if the speaker does so use "X," false if he does not.' Quite so, as to the last point; but a volition and a prediction are, alas! not the same. 'Expresses' is a terribly deceitful word, if it catches Dr Stebbing out so. For who will not agree that a definition, if it does express *a volition,* should be of the form, *'Let* "X" express what "Y" expresses'—as the mathematicians have it?

This is a rear-guard skirmish. None the less such things suggest exercises in interpretation that would open a new sort of approach to many old questions. And the considerations that decide them have a bearing beyond Logic, or even beyond Grammar: they go to the heart of Rhetoric and Poetics, and concern the deepest divisions of the language functions. Perhaps Ethics and Religion, like Logic, should be written in the optative; make no statements but express volitions. Perhaps they *are* so written (in an ellipsis which can be mistaken for the indicative) and perhaps they are read so by those who best know their way about. The difference between these moods is often no more than an intonation. If so, the sometimes crude antithesis between Emotive and Scientific utterance would be translatable into happier terms. There would, of course, as with Logic, be always a possible derivative statement describing and distinguishing between the choices that were being made. But that would merely *represent* what was done by the utterance; it would not be the utterance. If we recognized more frankly that *how* any word whatsoever is used is a matter of choice, of invitation and consent, not of regimentation, conformity and compulsion, should we not *then* better understand how artificial are the imagined discrete senses of our words, how dependent they are on the meaning we give to the sentence. The more optative our view of definition, the more humane Logic becomes. On this view we can do as we please and the more we take any sentence as an invitation or request, to be considered on its merits—rather than as a mere statement, like a blow, to be suffered or repelled—the more we civilize communications. The thresholds of the moods are within our control, though as we change them, we are changed with them. And they shift perceptibly from generation to generation. What the mid-19th century parent thought was a mild appeal, we are apt to look upon as a bit of emotional bullying. So, all through the scale, the modes of utterance vary. Our meanings, not only in content but in modality, are in flux. Until recently, however, it would have been supposed that at least the indicative mood stood put! We are beginning to know better:

> What one in the rout
> Of the fire-born moods
> Has fallen away?

Nowadays, very evidently in Science, the indicative rests on an optative basis and is indicative (over widening fields) only within optative constancies. 'Let us think so, and go on still further thinking so, while we see what happens,' that is what we have to compare today, have we not? with 'It is so.' Admitting this, though *overt* syntax denies it in every sentence, we see that an optative, or invitational, Logic requires a more subtle and versatile, a better sustained and a more sensitively ordered art of interpretation. Otherwise our choice is only between crudity and chaos. An exploring writer not only uses more varied words than the ordinary man but he uses most of them in *many more ways*. He has to offer a far wider range of invitations to interpret, though never so many as Shakespeare was prepared to extend to *his* audience. Shakespeare's extreme freedom of definition has triumphed because he combined with it an unparallelled virtuosity in Grammar and, when he needed it, a supreme rhetorical tact. But let us remember how far we have come from the cradle, and then even Shakespeare will not seem too far above the generality of mankind to serve as an ideal of the command of life in language.

# The Final Landing Stage

> *We can by no means require of the pure practical reason to be subordinated to the speculative, and thus to reverse the order; since every interest is at last practical, and even that of the speculative reason is but conditional, and is complete only in its practical use.*　　　KANT

From this vantage point we may look back to observe the incessant interaction and interdependence of Rhetoric, Grammar and Logic, and the strategic importance of keeping their problems in mind together. The Optative view of Definition (which is the central problem of Logic) makes the creation of the-things-to-be-thought-of, that is, the demarcation of Sense from the other language functions (which is the central problem of Rhetoric), a matter of our choice—subject, however, always to the exigencies of communication, that is, the provision of sufficiently stable inter-verbal action (which is the central problem of Grammar). By Definition things arise. If Berkeley had said of the objects of thought that TO BE was, for *them,* TO BE THOUGHT OF, few would have hesitated to agree; and yet this is not far from what he was most concerned to say. If we choose, wittingly or unwittingly, to think as the passions rather than the reason—the most inclusive integrating action—would have it (thus forcing on Rhetoric its degraded sense), or to speak without regard to the extant articulations of the senses of the words in the language (the dehumanizing disintegration of Grammar), we thereby become incapable of human companionship, that is, insane. The two departures often go together; but not always, alas! There are several spell-binding maniacs among the great personages of the world today. But, in general, the loss of reason entails the loss of efficient speech. Perhaps, if we can take a long enough view, that may be true too of the ruling madmen, their speech may destroy them; but meanwhile it is only too effective upon the correlative madmen who are subservient to it. However that may be, it is still certain—

> That this pragmatical, preposterous pig of a world,
> its farrow that so solid seem,
> Must vanish on the instant did the mind but change
> its theme [1]

We can, moreover, almost daily notice that it changes. 'The eye altering, alters all,' and the eye—the intellectual organ that, in defining, determines the limits of things—is always altering, for worse there, for better here, we hope. But no one eye, no one creative outlook, settles anything. Like the words in a sentence, we are meaningless unless we take our senses from one another. The individual, alone, is nothing; though the whole takes its value from the individuals within it. Society thus has a Grammar—the co-operation of its members. This breaks down easily unless the instruments of co-operation, the languages of its members, serve and grow with it. And the sciences, the operative Logic through which alone modern societies live, have equally to be preserved—from the distortions and the taints of disloyal desires. The physical sciences are comparatively free from this danger. The social sciences are much exposed to it, and among them the linguistic studies, the practice and theory of the teaching of literature, for example. Rhetoric guards from these contaminations both Logic, and the deeper integrations of myth which speak for reason. It contains religion, as Logic contains science, and Grammar contains communication, and has the largest scope of the three. For in Rhetoric's care is that unity or, as Coleridge would have written, coadunation of the mind which is, whatever the deviations, the aim behind and before our strivings—an increasing organic interinanimation of meanings, the biologic growth of the mind in the individual and in a social inheritance maintaining the human advance.

---

[1] W. B. Yeats, on 'God appointed Berkeley that proved all things a dream.' 'Blood and the Moon,' *The Winding Stair*, p. 12.

# *Appendix:* Some Suggestions Towards Class-room Exercises

> *For one instance of mere* logomachy (*i.e. unnecessary re-finement of distinction*) *I could bring 10 instances of logodaedaly, or verbal legerdemain, which have perilously confirmed prejudices and withstood the advancement of truth. . . .*
>
> *For one useless subtlety in our elder divines and moralists, I will produce 10 sophisms of equivocation in the writings of our modern preceptors; and for one error resulting from excess of distinguishing the indifferent, I could show ten mischievous delusions from the habit of confounding the diverse.*          COLERIDGE, *Aids to Reflection*

I put together here, in very tentative form, some Notes on a few types of exercise that might be modified by trial into means of implementing the policies suggested in the text. As I treat them, they are evidently of University, rather than of School or College order, though a good teacher would manage to scale the best of them down to near the Kindergarten level.

I will begin with those 'parallels' which caused so much headache when the comments on Campbell (see Chapter XII) were being collected. I gave this problem to my audience: [1]

Please frame parallel sentences to the following, indicating whether your parallel supports, or does not support, the argument that the author in your view intended to urge.

1. Let those who look upon style as unworthy of much attention, ask themselves how many, in proportion to men of genius, have excelled in it?

2. The teaching of a foreign language can as little replace the teaching of the mother tongue as a finger can replace the use of the hand.

[1] The instruction was very badly phrased.

3. Meaning is an arrow which reaches its mark when least encumbered with feathers.

The last two were exercises in the interpretation and judgment of argumentative metaphor. The first seems simpler; it was an outcome from an experiment with a passage of Landor (from *Opinions of Caesar, Cromwell, Milton, and Buonaparte;* see Mr H. Read's *English Prose Style*, p. 171) that I had earlier put before my class for comment. I have not used their comments. They were too bewildering. The passage from Landor was too difficult. All that the comments would have shown is that a majority of the audience were quite unable to interpret such prose, or form a defensible opinion as to what it says or as to its merits. This second experiment with a detached sentence from it (the audience being already very familiar with the context) was also disappointing. The closer parallels offered ranged from 'Let those who look on penmanship as unworthy . . .' to 'Let those who look on virtue . . .' but the further task of comparison was so confusedly handled that I must conclude that the exercise was unsuitable. A few pointed out that 'those who look upon style' so are the last people in the world to be influenced towards a more *favourable* view of style by such a request. But, in general, the problems raised by the sentence were too intricate to be discussed without taking more time (with my voluntary audience) than the upshot seemed likely to warrant.

The second sentence is from Sir Philip Hartog's *The Writing of English*. On the whole, my audience did succeed in displaying it as a comparison which will bear very little study.

The third sentence is from Mr Herbert Read's *English Prose Style*, p. 16; it gave rise to a large number of interesting comments. I append later the full context from which it comes.

The adventures of this sentence in the minds it went through were remarkably various; and illustrate the processes of interpretating metaphor very clearly. I will give some analysis first:

The sentence contains a double metaphor. Meaning, before it is compared to an arrow, is already conceived as something *expressed*, something *shot out in language*. (Though the degree of adequation of course differs greatly from mind to mind.) The expression or missile-vehicle is so familiar that we may hardly recognize that it is a metaphor. When we consider it we may find that we are giving more attention than it can support, and are in danger of asking it to do more than, in free common use, it is attempting to do. Common sense with it, as with Sir William Mitchell's 'a stone broke the window' (see Motto to Chapter XVIII) is saved from error by its ignorance; and it would be silly to quarrel with so handy and unpretentious a stopgap in language—unless someone takes it more seriously. The missile-vehicle is so familiar that it does not need comparison with an arrow (the second vehicle) to support it. In fact it is so ready to a mind thinking about meanings that *it* supports the arrow-vehicle, rather than the other way about. Very few of my commentators refused to let it do so, rejected the first latent vehicle (shot out = expressed) and therefore complained of the second vehicle (the arrow) as inappropriate.

App. 1.1. Meaning is *the mark*: the sound made by the mouth, or the sign made by the pen, is the arrow.

What the arrow-vehicle did for the others was to offer a specification of the latent missile-vehicle. And whether it was acceptable or not to them—the feathers question—turned partly on a struggle between the general and specific vehicles as to which should control how the other was taken.

Everybody knew—quite apart from the arrow's appropriateness—what Mr Read meant. They knew this in virtue of the general missile metaphor + 'encumbered.' 'Meaning is a missile which reaches its mark when least encumbered with extras.' Obviously, in general we can only ask whether an author has written as he should if we know somehow what he is trying to say. The readers knew this here. And two sets of considerations controlled the way their decision as to the appropriateness of the phrasing went. Thoughts about meaning (the tenor) and about the behaviour of arrows with and without feathers (the specific vehicle). Thus a large number of objections with very different sources were possible.

The main problem I thought I was setting them was this: To contrive other sentences either about meaning, or about something else, which would raise similar questions as to whether the comparison was apt or not. A number took it so:

App. 1.2. Meaning is an airship that reaches its base when not encumbered with a rudder.

App. 1.21. . . . a bicycle which will travel most swiftly and directly when relieved of the weight of handle-bars.

App. 1.22. . . . a mousetrap that works best when least encumbered with a spring.

App. 1.23. . . . a bird which reaches its mark when least encumbered with wings.

App. 1.24. . . . a swimmer who gets furthest when least weighed down with clothes.

App. 1.25. . . . a poison which works best when least diluted with water.

The first four, I think, were intended to show up an absurdity in Mr Read's sentence. Whether they are fair or not depends on how we read 'least encumbered.' If we take this to suggest that any feathers at all are an encumbrance, then evidently the sentence disregards the behaviour of arrows. I have tried it out on some eminent literary men (in as unprejudicial fashion as I could contrive) and they have usually asserted strongly that *that* is the suggestion they receive and that therefore the sentence is unhappy.

On the other hand, it may be taken only as saying that *any excess* of feathers would impair efficiency and that only the excess would be an encumbrance. Reading it so, several (rightly) said the comparison was apt and clear.

App. 1.3. Yes! But the metaphor is not all embracing. The epigram is more effective than pages of wooliness; but it is possible to 'reach the mark' by a cumulative process—building up an edifice or wearing down the reader or what not. But a sound and effective metaphor so far as it goes.

App. 1.31. Meaning is like a letter which gets there when concisely and clearly directed.

It will be noticed what a wealth of queer problems most of these parallel sentences raise in their turn. A letter arrives by the same post even if its address is redundant!

App. 1.4. Meaning is a machine gun which kills most men with fewest bullets.

Does it? Or is the writer attacking Mr Read's sentence? I doubt it.

App. 1.41. Meaning is a motor-car which reaches its destination when least encumbered with petrol.

This *is* an attack, but it has shifted the point too far to be fair. Motor cars rather haunted the protocols:

App. 1.42. Meaning is a car which is more likely to break the world land speed record if it is stream-lined.

This is either in support of Mr Read, or an 'improvement' on him; but the mark to be reached has faded out of the problem.

App. 1.43. Meaning is like a man with a purpose who accomplishes his end the less scruples that he has.

The inadequate feathering of the thought here seems well parallelled by the verbal deficiencies.

With the next a throw back to the tenor has brought up a different problem:

App. 1.44. Meaning is a picture most easily appreciated when enclosed in a simple frame.

This, in its turn, would require just as much care in interpretation as Mr Read's metaphor. So too with:

App. 1.45. Meaning as a pill is most efficacious when uncoated with jam.

But what a pill will *do* is to be distinguished from how readily it will *be taken!*

App. 1.46. The simpler the gown the more likely it is to be well cut.

I am told that this is unfortunately not so; it is only more necessary that it should be!

But the most interesting comments were those which showed how a difficulty in fitting the arrow-vehicle to the tenor—of finding as close a resemblance between them as was desired—broke down the underlying shot out = expressed vehicle:

App. 1.5. The parallel does not hold good, because 'meaning' is an infinitely complex and difficult matter whereas the shape of an arrow is constant. The abstract word is narrowed down to something only true of the concrete.

This would prevent us from ever talking simply about anything if we pressed it. (See 'Definite,' Sense V, Chapter IX.) The 'concrete' versus 'abstract' troubles that arose over Love and the Motorcar (Chapter III) are back in action. A half-way house to this:

> App. 1.51. Carries an unfortunate suggestion that meaning is a simple straightforward thing, whereas it may be very complex and inevitably encumbered with feathers.

Why so few took up the question, 'Just what do the feathers on an arrow do?' is difficult to explain. Many were, I believe, just ignorant, and being unfamiliar with arrows, thought that feathers are a decoration only. Others simply overlooked their function. Others still, like the last, were, I fancy, distracted by other considerations.

A few held that, since the sentence used a metaphor, things might pass which would *not* do in a simile; that 'meaning is like an arrow' would have been wrong, but that with a metaphor we are asked to imagine a special kind of arrow exempt from the necessities of real arrows and able to fly straight without the aid of feathers. I do not think that this distinction will save the situation. But it is true perhaps that we are more likely to challenge a bad simile than a bad metaphor, and current teaching, I am afraid, encourages the assumption that metaphors are somehow not to be looked into. The merit of such exercises as this would be to reverse this tendency.

I append Mr Read's account of the difference between simile and metaphor—as an example of the sort of teaching which is not very helpful:

> Simile and Metaphor differ only in degree of stylistic refinement. The Simile, in which a comparison is made directly between two objects, belongs to an earlier stage of linguistic expression: it is the deliberate elaboration of a correspondence, often pursued for its own sake. But a Metaphor is the swift illumination of an equivalence. Two images, or an idea and an image, stand equal and opposite; clash together and respond significantly, surprising the reader with a sudden light.
> This light may either illumine or decorate the sentence in which it is found; and perhaps we may divide all metaphors into the *illuminative* and the *decorative*. By doing so we can make more distinct the limited relevance of metaphor to prose writing; for while both kinds

are appropriate to poetry, only the illuminative metaphor will be found appropriate in pure prose style. (*English Prose Style,* p. 28. This passage introduces the translation discussed in Chapters V-IX above.)

I do not think I am being perverse in finding something amiss in every sentence of this. 'Degree of stylistic refinement': what is that here? 'Deliberate elaboration': sometimes, perhaps, but by no means always. The usual trouble about 'images' (see pp. 34-37 above). 'Equal and opposite': both words are very questionable, and they must be questioned if we are to advance at all in the theory and practice of metaphor. 'Clash together'?—my decorator recently declined to paint a bell-push white for me. He said, 'I don't think white would clash well, Sir, with the wallpaper!' We may perhaps ask whether the metaphors in Mr Read's account are themselves *illuminative* or *decorative.* It is a way of discovering that the division does very little to help us.

I append further the paragraphs in *English Prose Style,* pp. 15-16, from which the sentence we have been examining comes, as an example of the kind of discussion of the choice of words which a study of interpretation should question:

Man is no doubt an abstraction, built up of many particular events and acts of perception; but there is a limitation in this very abstraction; a vague but ready image is present in the mind, ready to be particularized by some concrete epithet. To say *a man* is merely to conjure up our own private idea of the typical man, perhaps a man in a black coat, striped trousers and a bowler hat, or perhaps the ideal athlete of Greek sculpture, or anything between these two extremes. To add an epithet implying an abstract quality like goodness scarcely makes any difference to our image; and this is the simple reason why such epithets are to be suspected of redundancy. To add a numerical epithet like *many* either multiplies the image in its indefiniteness, or creates another indefinite image of quantity, that is, *many men* is equivalent to *a crowd.* But to add an epithet of *quality* is to progress from the abstract and therefore vague entity of *substance* to the definite entity of a *sense perception.* And since this is a progress from vagueness to vividness, it suggests that clear definition is an elementary need in prose style. But not all substantives are vague; and of epithets, not all that are appropriate are necessary. Indeed, we shall consider epithets under these two heads: namely, their Necessity and their Appropriateness.

A loose orotundity leads to the insertion of unnecessary attributes. It might seem to a novice that to introduce as many words as have a bearing on the subject must necessarily enlighten it. But meaning is an arrow that reaches its mark when least encumbered with feathers. *A man crossed the street* is a definite statement, vivid enough. To say *a man in black crossed the busy street* is to lose a certain immediateness of effect; for unless the context of the statement requires a man 'in black' and a 'busy' street, definitely for the furtherance of the narrative, then the understanding is merely delayed by the necessity of affixing these attributes to the general terms; for men are often enough in black, and streets busy. To say *a man in scarlet crossed the deserted street* is indeed to add to the vividness of the phrase; but these exceptional epithets, 'scarlet' and 'deserted,' would never be used unless demanded by the context.

We may notice the misleading remarks about images; the confusion in 'abstract and therefore vague'; the queer play with *definite, definition* and *definitely;* and the consequences of comparing with one of the assertions,

'Many men have gone mad in solitary confinement.'

I have no wish to suggest that Mr Read's conceptions of language are in any way exceptional. On the contrary, the case for such exercises in school as I am suggesting comes wholly from the prevalence in all quarters of first thoughts on these matters. A considerable step might be taken merely by putting such accounts before our pupils and inviting them to mark (with signals borrowed from the railway perhaps, ⋀ and ⌐ ) the words and phrases that they think, after a careful reading, may be safely treated as suggesting 'Line open!' or 'Line closed!' Whether we would succeed finally in eliciting their doubts clearly (which amounts to settling them in most cases) may be doubted. But if we manage merely to cause them to attend sufficiently to feel the stir of a question, we shall have done a great deal. To give such discourses on language without a warning and without opportunity and stimulus to examine and dissect them with care is a ruinous procedure. It blunts all the edges of thought.

Other exercises with the same modest aim—to excite a heightened, more leisurely and reflective attention to verbal differences—seem easily devisable. I illustrated them in the text, with 'concrete' and 'abstract' (Chapters III and XXII), with 'expresses' (Chapter VIII), with 'definite' (Chapter IX), with 'ungently' (Chapter V) and with a sample synonym exercise (Chapter XXII). And the comments on the protocols were raw material for hundreds more. Indeed almost anything general that anyone says may be made into a useful exercise if taken from the right angle.

Any sentence which enshrines a general problem, the simpler and more general the better, with a sufficient but not too complete setting, will serve. We have only to vary its wording:

> These conceptions of language are in no way extraordinary
> Such ideas about language are not at all unusual
> These opinions about speech are not in the least peculiar

and invite our pupils to indicate any differences they detect between what is said. Their comments will then guide the discussion if the sentences are judiciously chosen. These examples above may combine too many variations and draw distinctions that are perhaps too fine. We may find that though our pupils can *perceive* differences between them they are unable to describe them. To avoid this difficulty we may perhaps borrow from the technique adopted in some psychological experiments [1] and invite the class to *match* the variants against a supplied list of sentences. Thus, sentences containing the key-words, 'composed,' 'consists,' 'constituted,' 'formed,' may be matched against some such set of sentences as these:

> A pile of sand is made up of the grains of sand in it.
> A sentence is made up of words.
> A plant is made up of cells.
> An hour is made up of minutes.
> A nation is made up of individuals.

The task might be to match with these, say:

> A sonnet consists of fourteen lines.
> A mind is an assemblage of experiences.
> A cloud is composed of minute drops of water.
> A yard contains three feet.

[1] Notably, for our purposes here, in Dr Thouless' experiments on 'Phenomenal Regression to the Real Object,' *British Journal of Psychology*, XXI, 4 and XX, 1, 3. These are experiments that show how factors of setting enter into the judgments of the apparent size, shape and distance of objects. They can be illuminating as regards parallel problems in the interpretation of words and may, indeed, be used as a means of reinforcing with a new, accessible, and amusing subject-matter the lesson of the dependence of interpretation upon setting.

And the class might be asked to suggest briefly the reasons of their choice, or if they cannot decide, to note any considerations that seem to them to bear upon the decision.

Only experiment would show how far such methods of introducing important general problems—here the different kinds of unity—*as mere exercises in verbal discussion* could be taken. But, as all the main key-ideas, and indeed the ground plans of all the philosophies, are already implicit in everyday language and are handled there with astonishing skill by us all, *provided we do not ask explicit questions about them,* I do not doubt that this is the way to go to work to improve still further our skills.

Other games with such words as 'agreement,' 'meaning,' 'cause,' and 'reason' readily suggest themselves. Some materials for them as to 'agreement' may be found in *Basic Rules of Reason.* As to 'meaning,' a bundle of sentences such as

> Do you mean beautiful or pretty?
> Do you mean John or James?
> Black clouds mean rain.
> He means well.
> He means mischief.
> That word means nothing at all.

to be compared, say with

> Do you mean 100 yards or 100 meters?
> Do you mean manslaughter or murder?
> Bad dreams mean a guilty conscience.
> That means war.

would, if we were not too ambitious, be a good exercise ground on which perceptions we are all possessed of already but do not keep in good *reflective* order may be at least made a little more controllable. That an improved reflective command here gives a *general* benefit I have no doubt. I had intended as part of my experimental course to prepare and try out some more precise experiments upon the uses of 'meaning.' But time, and the elaborations of a similar experiment on 'reason,' prevented this. What happened with 'reason' confirms my feeling that something useful could be made not only out of 'meaning' but also out of 'knowledge,' 'beautiful' and 'true.' For materials see *Mencius on the Mind,* Chapter IV. As the 'meaning' exercise stands above some preparation would be required before it could be tested.

My experiment with 'reason' took this form. I gave to my audience:

'Why do we believe that 2 + 2 = 4?'
If you find that that answers itself too easily, then take the most important word in the answer and ask, 'Just what does —— mean here?'

The answers I got were as varied as I could have desired. All the main philosophic doctrines on the problem appeared among them, usually with no sign that the writer took them for philosophical theories, or was remembering an opinion rather than framing one for himself. I shall not give much of the protocols here in detail— rich though they were in minor points of interest. I can summarize the main positions without citation; it will be easier so to sketch clearly the kind of discussion which may profitably be developed, and the morals that may be drawn.

The main views offered may be grouped under five headings:

(1) Something happens in the head—as a consequence the belief occurs.

(2) Experience has taught us that it is so; i.e. associations have been formed through which the ideas of 2, +, and 4 have become progressively welded together so that now the connection is irresistible; and the reason for the belief is this association or close connection.

(3) The reason is that I see it must be so and cannot be otherwise. Two cannot be two and four be four without 2 + 2 being 4; and that is a better reason than anything else I could appeal to in support of my belief.

(4) We were told so authoritatively when young.

(5) We believe it because to do so works well.

Having indicated by citations the general division of the answers under these five heads, I began by pointing out that we should not hastily say that there were thus five different answers to 'the same question.' It was more likely that they were answers to five different questions, and so naturally different. And that, in any case, to put it so gave us a more hopeful start in going on to consider which of them were good answers than if we assumed right away that we must choose between them. They were (it was) the same question in the sense that the same words were used in asking it (them). But whether any more than this was the same would have to be shown.

I then widened the moral by saying that in this respect the question is a central typical model for innumerable other disputable matters over which muddles are always being made; and that, more immediately, it was a model on and with which to study a muddle which may be expected whenever anyone is giving *reasons* for beliefs, alleging *grounds* for convictions, *proofs* of assertions, or *causes* of views and so on. Knowing the Marxist tendency of a section of the audience, I cautiously suggested here that the problem had a bearing on the theory of the Economic Determination of History and the derivation of individual attitudes from the class bias. Similarly, for possible psychoanalysts, and followers of Mr Eliot, in the audience, mentions of rationalization and of tradition seemed to be in place. The discussion, I continued, was not intended to throw light on the multiplication table or on the foundations of arithmetic so much as on what is likely to happen generally when we deal in reasons and connect remarks by 'because,' 'for,' 'since,' and such.

I then tried, by directing attention to each statement in turn, to make the differences between the questions they answered more clearly apparent, pointing out, meanwhile, that the ordinary way of showing that two questions are different, *namely by stating them in different terms,* is not very satisfactory here. We could try by saying that the first doctrine states something about the physiological antecedents or concomitants of the belief; that the second talks about the psychological causes of it, that the third declares the immediate ground or justification of it as a valid belief, that the fourth alleges a fact in the history of the belief, and the fifth dilates on its consequences. All these are distinct enough and unlikely, so formulated, to be confused; but the task is not to distinguish *them* so much as to distinguish, *with the original formulation, 'I believe it because . . .'* the varied interpretations that are being taken up *there.* In ordinary talk all these different things may be said with words like 'cause,' 'reason,' 'ground.' We may regret it, but it is so; and we shall not protect ourselves from misunderstanding (of or by ourselves or others) by pinning down different meanings for these words and trying to hold the words to them. We have, instead, to

trust ourselves to distinguish their possible meanings, one from another, even though we (or others) are using the same words and
phrases for them all. And we can do this.

This incidentally discourages much crude theory, which is currently preached, about language being identical with thought.

The next step is to consider whether these answers, when we
realize what questions they answer, conflict with one another. They
certainly have been supposed by many to be in violent opposition.
The camp-followers of the philosophers, if not the generals, have
endlessly scrapped over the question, 'Which is right?' But, if each
keeps to its own business, there seems nothing to object to in any
of them. They don't *then* seem to conflict more than, say, 'The
Baby is called Peter,' 'He is very beautiful,' and 'He is digesting his
last meal,' conflict.

And yet a large proportion of thorough and careful students of
these and allied subjects have held that a choice between them is
necessary, and have been led, at points, into violent battles about
'The right answer.' Why should this be so?

To suggest that it is because they can be stated in similar words
and so be made to seem rival answers to one question, would be
far too simple an explanation. The *grounds, causes, reasons* (I am
using all three words here in many senses) of the dispute go much
deeper and concern the ways in which the accounts fit in with the
much more comprehensive accounts, not just of such beliefs
(whether they are a priori, a posteriori, intuitive, analytic, synthetic,
empirical, pragmatic or what not) but of *everything,* the accounts
of the world which different thinkers have found most acceptable.

The philosophic topic—at least, if handled as the philosophies have
handled it and in such-like' terms—has no place in the schoolroom.
What is useful to the growing mind can be taken from what the
protocols themselves provide in terms of everyday speech. But, in a
few sentences, the bearing of the deep differences of philosophic
positions on ordinary non-technical thinking, and their consequences
for ordinary discussions, can be indicated. We cannot ignore these
differences; they reveal themselves in the interpretations of the
simplest every-day remarks—as the protocols show. We ought not
to try to go into them *technically* as part of general education; but
we can and should note, and enforce attention to, this much about
them. That, since not only 'cause,' 'grounds,' 'reasons,' but almost

all the general connecting words of the language show this versatility and can be using profoundly different assumptions and presuppositions (and thus can systematically offer, sentence by sentence, paragraph by paragraph, book by book, similar opportunities of treating one question as though it were another); it is an elementary part of intelligent behaviour in dissenting from or assenting to anything, to be on the lookout for evidence of the fundamental presuppositions. And we can perhaps go further, and suggest that this very versatility of language—being so systematic and extensive that holders of the most different philosophic positions can yet say almost everything in parallel forms—supplies an initial case for supposing that the different persistent philosophic outlooks (Materialism, Idealism, Empiricism, Rationalism, Pragmatism, Realism, Conceptualism, Nominalism, etc., etc.) are not necessarily so opposed as their professors commonly deem them to be. Though throughout in such speculations, we must bear in mind how different their appeal is to different moods which set as temperaments and are maintained as faiths.

The literary or plain man—not committed to any of them, or capable, for lack of a specialist's training in technical speech, of consistently maintaining any of them—uses them *all* in ordinary fluid discourse, freely changing from one to another as suits his purpose. They are, when elaborated into philosophic systems, only interpretations of our common courses of thought. We should not let any interpretation tyrannize here over the processes which it claims to interpret. To do so is to forget where its sanctions ultimately are to be found.

Thus the plain or literary man will do well to use all the philosophies—so far as he apprehends them—*positively* whenever he can, but not *negatively*. He must not let them bar him out from views to which his own thinking, if it is genuinely reflective, leads him. How many of the *best* minds prevent themselves from fairly understanding things most needful to them, and understood well enough by inferior minds, merely because they are trying to use some philosophy excogitated for other purposes.

The chief use of some knowledge of philosophy is this; that without it, even in the most seemingly simple and obvious matters, we shall endlessly be supposing other people to be saying things they neither intended to say nor said. Philosophic theories (in the large non-technical sense I have here in mind) are intellectual organs—

very like eyes. We think with them, not only when we are overtly talking philosophy, but equally whenever we are apprehending, trying to 'account for' or 'explain' anything. A philosophy, in this sense, is no more and no less than the mode of the contexts we are using (see Chapter II). Our meanings—that is, here, the things we think of, and the ways in which we combine and connect them—are to our philosophies as light is to the eye or hardness to the hand, or sound to the ear, or warmth to the skin. And as the ear does not hear light nor the eye see sound, so a man using one philosophy apprehends with it things, or meanings, that are not apprehensible with another. More often than we suppose, what we call differences *of opinions* are differences *of views;* the speculative organs that apprehend them are different, though often they will use the same words.

This moralizing is easily illustrated from the accounts of 'Why we believe that $2 + 2 = 4$?' They arose from looking at this seemingly simple question through different speculative instruments. When we survey them and compare them we are likely to do so again through different speculative organs; and, if we could not use several of them freely (but, in fact, unless we have been trained out of common sense, which is partly an ability to translate, we can), we should misread them. So the question 'Do these accounts of the reasons conflict?' carried much too simple assumptions about the philosophic organs by which we perceive them. Of theories, at least, what Berkeley said of all things is patently true—they exist only as they are perceived; and as Blake said, 'The eye altering, alters all.' As we change our perceiving organs these accounts sometimes conflict and sometimes do not. What we have then most to look out for is sudden unheralded changes in the modes of context, the speculative instruments, used. To follow them is the art of reading. It is these shifts, constantly necessary as they are to any non-technical writer's purpose, which make fair criticism so difficult and most polemical writing and controversy so profitless.

*None the less,* within the scope of any one speculative organ, there is, of course, good and bad perception. The protocols admirably illustrated this; and they showed too the systematic, cyclic ambiguities which have often been described as the gyres or spirals of thought. The same words, even within the scope of the same type of theory, may stand for views of very different merit. Thus answer Number Four—the most popular type of answer: that we believe it because we have been told so—was sometimes silly and sometimes sensible. Some made it merely 'nurse's ascertion' [1] and left it at that. One put this into verse:

> App. 2.1. You are old, said the nurse, 'tis time you knew
> That four is the product of twice times two,
> And later to dour enquiring expound
> 'Twas nurse's ascertion and therefore 'tis sound.
>                                          Q. E. D.

But obviously that does not go far enough. We were told in the nursery 'that the Moon is made of green cheese,' but we still don't believe it. Some of those who alleged authority as the source of the belief, showed too a kind of hankering to disbelieve—feeling it perhaps as an annoying sort of apron string. A few of them went further still into silliness and voiced surges of romantic rebellion against the multiplication table. Others seemed to think they might see one morning in the paper that someone had proved that $2 + 2 = 5$—a consequence, I suppose, of the debilitating influence of Relativity Popularization. Others, who stressed tradition, seemed to feel $2 + 2 = 4$ was a cultural treasure which might need defending!

> App. 2.2. The problem here offered—why does $2 + 2 = 4$—is one which has repeatedly occurred ever since the first day of my kindergarten education. The answer, 4, was many times the goal of endless hours of intellectual toil, a goal which, once attained, marked the end of an epoch in my life. It is the basis of modern religion and modern sanity, and if this cornerstone of modern thought, this bulwark of civilization were swept away, the world would be cast into a state of blind and panic-stricken chaos.
>
> We believe that $2 + 2 = 4$ because we believe in the existence of reason.

Against this let me put:

> App. 2.21. '$2 + 2 = 4$' (are *identically* equal to) would be the extreme form of this mathematical *claim*—and '$2 + 2 = 4$' in common speech *does* claim that identity; a geometrical figure being produced to reinforce the arithmetic 'definition.' But we could of course

---

[1] Influenced by *'ascertain,* to establish,' see Chapter XV.

build up a whole new mathematics on $2 + 2 = 5$ surely without destabilising anything in ourselves.

The *mythology* would be an equally *useful* one—emotionally of course NOW it would be addedly satisfying as a departure from *habit*. But 'Why do we bother to make "claims" for the Nature of things in this patronisingly fatherly way?' is the next question to ask—Some 'mythologies' are apparently more 'useful' (in particular *contexts,* at least: e.g. the medical in a railway accident, etc.) though their 'usefulness' *except* as life-preservers may be questioned: we want greater psycho-physical health, and will get it somehow—'$2 + 2 = 4$' sometimes 'helps' us—and then we say we 'believe' it—But we should admit it is often use*less*.

A scorn-filled rebel, truly! How he would hate my saying that he does need a little help towards this greater psycho-physical *health!* The more desperate sceptical ventures merit some pedagogic attention as well as illustrate the gyres of thought. Doubt has its depths and shallows like belief, and it is important to disconcert those who enjoy doubting without realizing in some degree how far their doubt would take them.

The better authoritarians added such phrases as 'and have never had any occasion to doubt it' to their, 'We were told so,' or said, 'We were taught to use the symbols in such a way that it is true.' Many straddles between different accounts occurred. The last is not far from views of Groups Five and Two. Some in Group Two distinguished between habit (or association) as causing us to use the symbols as we do, and habit as the reason for the belief. Very crude association theories were frequent. Here is a gloomy protocol:

App. 2.3. I think we believe that $2 + 2 = 4$ because we are taught so from our childhood. If formerly in order to go to Liverpool from London one had to go via C as there was no direct train, an old man would not believe that the new direct route A → B would be nearer because he had all his life looked at the journey from A to B through C. Experience only confirms our prejudices, what we learn in our childhood. Hence we go on believing that $2 + 2 = 4$ and not 5 even if we are shown that it is $= 5$.

Character is the result of suppressed impulses and moulded into one channel. Character stands for something definite, otherwise there is no character, 4 stands for what we have been taught, our character, the resultant of all our inhibitions and the lack of them.

On a crude enough association theory it should be impossible to learn anything new after one had heard or experienced the contrary often enough. But, of course, we all know that it is not so. The possible gyres of thought may however be observed here again. There are habits of thought that we are not able to change even when the desirability of changing them has been made plain. The gyres perplex the doctrine of associationism especially; it is easy to refute simple associationism and not very hard now to improve it to the limit of Bradley's or Koffka's ranges of attack. But is it then still associationism?

Pragmatism, too, was maintained foolishly *and* wisely:

App. 2.4. We believe because it is more convenient for us to do so, and man is naturally lazy. 'Convenient' = what will cause us least effort or discomfort.

That might be a good enough account of why we hold some beliefs, for example, that our handwriting is sufficiently legible! but it is no sort of adequate reason here. I cite it because, although pragmatic reasons for beliefs ('that they work well') can be very good ones, and sometimes are by far the best and most fundamental reasons that can be given, they can easily be cheapened and parodied in this fashion to become very superficial and easy to refute. If we are going to appeal to the work that a belief does as its justification, then we must really look into the sort of work it does for us and compare this with what rival beliefs (if there are any) would do. The important thing of course is to realize on what different planes different beliefs are, as regards their pragmatic sanctions.

Group Three ('that I see it is so') displayed the gyres too. The 'lower rounders' hung themselves up by exaggerating *vision,* mere optical vision through the eye, not allowing 'see' to take its metaphorical extensions. 'Because I can actually *see* the material relations.' 'The belief is dependent on the honesty of the visual sense.' The reply is of course that blind men can count! Even without touch or motor sensations we could count sounds. Another writer, taking a speculative dive, and echoing Locke, said, 'If we had had no senses we could never have known it. 'But if we had had no senses, could we ever have known anything? To give *this* as *the reason* of the belief would be like giving, 'Because we are alive!'

This may seem frivolous, but it brings up a vital point in all explanation, which is, Where does it stop? How much should an explanation include? How do we pick the relevant explanation out of all the rest which is implicated as the indispensable background of conditions. There is no useful *general* answer. Practice, reflection on particular cases, and the liberal arts teach us; and nothing is more important than this for all forms of intelligent behaviour.

One last incidental point arose often and a discussion of it might look back to the 'consists of' exercise on unity above. It is 'What is one thing?' and was provoked here usually by that troublesome object, a drop of quicksilver. Add 2 drops of mercury to 2 other drops and the result is not 4 drops but one big one! A surprising number were too content with this observation to look for the answer, which is, of course, that $2 + 2 = 4$ applies to units and to things only as far as they are units. And a unit is a logical machine, something we use in counting. Units need not be similar (except as being taken as units). Many assumed and some actually insisted that units must be exactly the same in all respects. But a whistle and a bang and a smell and a pain may be added together to make a group of four. ('Longinus' e.g. enumerated five sources of sublimity: 1. great conceptions, 2. passion, 3. figures, 4. choice of words, 5. spirited composition; but left out pen, ink and paper or he could have made them eight!)

This exercise seemed to me capable of becoming a really useful tool. Its initial simplicity allows deeper and deeper questions to develop naturally out of the first thoughts. With a well-managed circulation of a selection from the protocols, I believe a class could in a few hours be given an insight into some extremely important matters involving every aspect of their practical conduct as well as their abstractive intellectual range. I have evidence that the interest taken in it was exceptionally keen, and that the questions raised were felt to be important *and* manageable. It might do something to encourage a speculative curiosity about types of reasons, in time to protect the learner from the destructive efforts to doctrinize him that he is likely to suffer from all but the better teachers of philosophic subjects later on. And it might help him to recall that these processes of speculation—which, if treated in the wrong ways, yield elementary logic, methodology, epistemology, psychology, and metaphysics, in sets of more and more distractingly abstracted, will-o'-the-wisp jargons—are still the springs of thought and that a 'knowledge-how' of them is the whole secret of intelligence. If this danger is remembered the exercise can be followed up by rather more complex studies which rely upon the same groups of perceptions; for example the following pages on the same topic by Sir William Mitchell might be offered, as an admittedly tough, and perhaps uncrackable, morsel for interpretation. If we frankly admit that perhaps no one but the author (and perhaps he only at his best) is fully able to understand them, there will be advantage in the very difficulty. The process of slowly recognizing what has appeared already in the protocols will increase confidence, and the residuum is too deep in its implications, however simple its language, for failure there to feel humiliating or frightening to anyone.

What are the causes of my belief that twice two makes four? Four answers have been given, of which three are good.

The physical cause has to be imagined. We have to suppose that portions of brain-tissue have already taken a disposition or pattern whose reaction gives my belief. The pattern has to be copied from what I feel, and is therefore diagrammatic at best. Room for it is found by following the growth of my sense of number from its beginning in perceptions, whose cortical areas are known. But there is no temptation to press the pattern on the room, any more than to press a colour, or a second, or anger, on their places. Two is a small number, but the sense of it is no easier to place than the sense of twenty; twice two is difficult, for there is no observer. Worst of all, the calculating machine has to substitute causes for reasons, which alone command my belief. What I feel would therefore be very hard to copy. Next, is the pattern to be histological, chemical, or electrical? And, in all, the same piece of tissue has to serve two masters; there is the belief which is its product, and there is its own cause from outside. Suppose we knew the physical means by which number makes itself known, why do they give knowledge at all, and why not of themselves but of number? These questions are too hopeless not to be in error. But rather than surrender a likeness we may think there is a secret one, the cortical cause being merely phenomenon. That calls for cause number two.

Since there is nothing in nature out of which feeling can come, and yet feeling comes by physical causes, is there not a secret cause of which the physical are phenomena? It would be the real cause by which number makes itself known through cause number one. Such causes were first introduced for the ordinary work of nature, but there, having been left with nothing to do, the concurrent causer of causes has become superfluous. Physical causes are no longer completed by such a means. They are completed by their system, or by a more general system, never by a cause from which nothing can be calculated. There is no reason for dealing otherwise with the cause of knowing number, and we strike this one from the list.

By the third cause my belief that twice two makes four is product of my past experience; and the force of the belief is product of an association of ideas, or their more intimate welding, that has grown from strength to strength, and made the belief inevitable. By the fourth cause, on the contrary, my belief is due to my knowing arithmetic, and its force to nothing but arithmetic. So far the two are quite separate causes, and conflict. They cannot be reconciled by saying that the third is a cause of which my belief is effect, while the fourth is only a ground, of which my belief is a consequence. For the ground is cause when it is known.

It does not enter like an autocrat, tyrannising over the power of old associations and empirical beliefs, as reason was thought to do; it rules by persuading. But so do they. The fourth cause enters as early as the factors of the third, when the factors persuade. It is their unity, their function, their final cause, the end to their means. An idea is born knowing; its function is born with it, and it develops into a body of knowledge at the object's behest.

This language about a final cause, and about an object as cause, to say nothing of its behest, makes the fourth cause appear metaphorical, and ask to be dissolved into means. But it is the very character of minds, which makes them higher forms of life, that their reaction is to objects. Their degrading consists in reducing them to organised energies, mental or physical, which a stimulus discharges. Their actual decadence is a falling to that. My belief may answer from the theory of numbers, or from instances, or from the 'indissoluble association' of the multiplication table. These mean three grades of mind, and, though the higher among them grow from the lower, the lower do not become the higher, but become tools. If the three came to blows, it is the meanest that would prove universal; I might babble the table though unconscious. But the strength of my belief is not from the strong association either in instances or in words. They are both

superseded, without any effort, when I happen to know better. There ·
is nothing indeterminate about the final cause, which is the object.
I am still bound to believe; but it is arithmetic, not habit, that has
cost me my liberty to think that twice two makes five.

*The Place of Minds*

That would be a luxury task however for an exceptionally good
and leisurely class. So too would be this:

Compare the uses of *surface* in:
'Familiarity with scientific experiment at least does the useful service
of inspiring a wholesome scepticism about the conclusions which the
mere surface of experience suggests.' MILL, *Inaugural Lecture*

and, 'The sensible world is the surface of nature; it consists of phenomena, and therefore answers all its own questions. The deep questions that seek a better grasp accept the surface, and their answers have
to be verified by it.' SIR WILLIAM MITCHELL, *The Place of Minds*

More needed are simpler exercises which must not, however, be
therefore 'merely verbal,' as they say; catches, that is, without a
*general* problem in them. Puzzles are useless unless they turn on
language tricks that recur and can be seen to be likely to cause
trouble. Here is a famous conundrum which turns on an extremely
simple ambiguity of the words 'round' and 'opposite.' I have tried
it out, and feel some confidence that it is neither too hard to be
practicable nor yet too obvious to be diverting.

Some years ago, being with a camping party in the mountains, I
returned from a solitary ramble to find everyone engaged in a ferocious
metaphysical dispute. The corpus of the dispute was a squirrel—a live
squirrel supposed to be clinging to one side of a tree-trunk; while
over against the tree's opposite side a human being was imagined to
stand. This human being tries to get sight of the squirrel by moving
rapidly round the tree, but no matter how fast he goes, the squirrel
moves as fast in the opposite direction and always keeps the tree
between himself and the man, so that never a glimpse of him is
caught. The resultant metaphysical problem now is this: Does the
man go round the squirrel, or not? He goes round the tree, sure
enough, and the squirrel is on the tree; but does he go round the
squirrel? In the unlimited leisure of the wilderness discussion had
been worn threadbare. Everyone had taken sides, and was obstinate;
and the numbers on both sides were even. Each side, when I appeared,

therefore appealed to me to make it a majority. Mindful of the scholastic adage that whenever you meet a contradiction you must make a distinction, I immediately sought and found one, as follows.

WILLIAM JAMES, *Pragmatism*

Can you state, unambiguously, a distinction which solves the problem and shows clearly what each side was maintaining?

All sorts of things happen when this question is asked, and by pooling the results for study a great deal can be taught about how and how not to think. I will only give one specimen comment—by a Scholarship Candidate of 18:

App. 3.1. The writer clearly states that the man and the squirrel each go round the tree in opposite directions. Let us suppose that the man goes round in a clockwise direction. The squirrel therefore goes round the tree in an anti-clockwise direction. Consequently at two points, the man must pass the squirrel, assuming that the squirrel's speed is not greatly in advance of the man's. We must say therefore that the man was inobservant enough to miss the squirrel when he passed it.

It seems possible to carry out William James' intention here and make the passage not only an example of the varying interpretations of a word, but also a type of, and introduction to, the sources of controversy in general. Thus some two such statements as the following—in which to decide whether they disagree *or not* is a matter of nice discernment—make a good sequel.

The proper stimulus of the will, namely, some variety of pleasure and pain, is needed to give the impetus. . . . Without an antecedent of pleasurable or painful feeling—actual or ideal, primary or derivative—the will cannot be stimulated. Through all the disguises that wrap up what we call motives, something of one or other of these grand conditions can be detected.                                                  BAIN

It has been proved beyond all controversy that even the passions commonly esteemed selfish carry the Mind beyond self directly to the object; that though the satisfaction of these passions gives us enjoyment, yet the prospect of this enjoyment is not the cause of the passions, but, on the contrary, the passion is antecedent to the enjoyment, and without the former the latter could never possibly exist.          HUME

It may be wise to insist that both passages are about matters with which we are all as familiar as ever Bain or Hume were, and that it should not be beyond anyone's interpretative power to decide what each means, or at least what the alternative possibilities in each case are. *Then* whether they do or do not conflict and, at what points, settles itself. To make all this out takes some time, and few can do it in their heads as few can compare maps there. But with paper to blacken and opportunity to experiment,

> And time yet for a hundred indecisions
> And for a hundred visions and revisions . . .
> For decisions and revisions which a minute will reverse,

these give good practice in distinguishing just what is being said from what is just not being said. And these provisos are required for all exercises whose aim is to teach us how to think. 'Time,' Bergson once wisely said, 'is resistance; the resistance against everything happening at once!'—which would come perhaps to the same thing as nothing happening at all; nothing worth *while*.